Genealogical
Pragmatism

Genealogical Pragmatism

Philosophy, Experience, and Community

John J. Stuhr

State University of New York Press

Published by
State University of New York Press, Albany

For information, address State University of New York Press,
State University Plaza, Albany, N.Y., 12246

Production by Diane Ganeles
Marketing by Hannah J. Hazen

Library of Congress Cataloging-in-Publication Data
Stuhr, John J.
    Genealogical pragmatism : philosophy, experience, and community /
John J. Stuhr.
        p.   cm.
    Includes bibliographical references and index.
    ISBN 0-7914-3557-1 (hardcover : alk. paper). — ISBN 0-7914-3558-X
(pbk. : alk. paper)
    1. Pragmatism   I. Title.
B832.S78   1997   97-1948
144'.3—dc21   CIP

10 9 8 7 6 5 4 3 2 1

For Jennifer and Robert

I am a child, I last a while
You can't conceive of the pleasure in my smile

—Neil Young

There may be always a time of innocence.
There is never a place. Or if there is not time,
If it is not a thing of time, nor of place,

Existing in the idea of it, alone,
In the sense against calamity, it is not
Less real. For the oldest and coldest philosopher,

There is or may be a time of innocence
As pure principle. Its nature is its end,
That it should be, and yet not be, a thing

That pinches the pity of the pitiful man,
Like a book at evening beautiful but untrue,
Like a book on rising beautiful and true.

—Wallace Stevens

Good things change and vanish not only with changes in the
environing medium but with changes in ourselves.

—John Dewey

Contents

III. Community

Preface

Can a book have a preface? Can it, unlike life and thought, begin before its start? And, is its start really a beginning? Isn't it always a rebeginning, a redirection, a reconstruction?

Pragmatism is a reconstruction. It reconstructs philosophy, experience, and community. This reconstruction is piecemeal, multiperspectival, uncertain, and always unfinished. This book seeks to analyze and advance this reconstruction.

As reconstruction, pragmatism's intellectual orientation is intrinsically critical and its subject-matter is irreducibly moral. As criticism, pragmatism faces forward and identifies itself as the future of philosophy. It is instrumental: a criticism of the present on behalf of possibilities for the future inherent in the present; an inquiry into today in the service of more enduring and extensive values tomorrow. At the same time, as criticism, pragmatism also faces backward and presents itself as the history of the future of philosophy. It is genealogical: a history of the present on behalf of future possibilities that are not inherent or imagined in this present; a detection of the past and its effects in a struggle against today's supposedly more enduring and extensive values.

As criticism both instrumental and genealogical, pragmatism must also face the present, and face itself in the present's possibilities and limitations, creations and deformations, empowerments and subjugations. It is only through this process that pragmatism becomes fully instrumental—intelligence directed at the problems of men and women rather than the problems of philosophers—and genuinely genealogical—a destabilization of the present rather than the chewing of historic cud long ago reduced to woody fiber. In the phrase of John Dewey, this sort of pragmatism is an "intellectual disrobing"—a critical inspection at times of some of the intellectual habits that clothe us as members of a particular culture at a particular time and particular place.

This activity constitutes a major break from most traditional philosophy and from business as usual in contemporary philosophy. Pragmatism does not even attempt to solve the problems of these philosophies. Instead, studying both their ends and the means by which they have cloaked these ends in their self-proclaimed problems, methods, and systems, it localizes and abandons these philosophies. This is revolutionary, but nothing brand-new: Dewey called it a return to the Socratic view of philosophy as moral search for wisdom to guide life.

Except in name, perhaps, this pragmatic view of philosophy may not appeal to many persons. It is not likely to become the philosophy of persons characterized by Emerson as meek young scholars growing up in libraries. It is unlikely to satisfy the individuals labeled by William James as sick-souls with fundamentalist demands, other-worldly longings, and absolutist temperaments. Nor is it likely to attract the professional philosophers whom Dewey identified as skilled technicians of the merely abstract and the purely formal, defeatists without the courage to recover a philosophy or theory relevant to actual life or practice. Finally, it will find few customers today among the culture industry's theory producers and consumers who demand something more entertaining, more shocking or confrontational, and less demanding in day-to-day practice.

As a result, pragmatism may not turn out to be the philosophy, or even the professional philosophy, of the future, as James once predicted. However, as Dewey often pointed out, while it is crucial that this pragmatic reconstruction of philosophy, experience, and community—itself just one aspect of a much-needed larger reconstruction of social practices, institutions, and associations—supplies the future work of intelligence, it is not important from the standpoint of culture that it do so in the name of philosophy. Of course, as Dewey added, it may be vital to the self-esteem and popular respect of philosophers that this work be undertaken in the name of philosophy. When philosophers fail to address in the name of philosophy the reconstruction of philosophy, experience, and community, their failure does not render their work or their culture post-philosophical. Instead, their efforts simply ensure that philosophies and their cultures remain pre-pragmatic. Today we do not live after pragmatism; with imagination, however, we may live before it.

In any event, imagination by itself is not enough. Intellect and will are required also. The pragmatic reconstruction of philosophy, experience, and community must be understood, extended, and acted on. In part, this requires a grasp of its relations to other philosophies and larger cultural arrangements in, and through, which philosophies operate. Accordingly, the five chapters that form the first part of this book begin to address this complex of issues. In "The Humanities, Inc.," I examine the spread of a business culture and corporate mentality in America, the increasing interpenetration of business, government, and education, and the impact of these developments on the self-understanding, mission, and critical possibilities in philosophy and the humanities. I argue that the available critical responses to these developments are few and inadequate, and that philosophy increasingly confronts a postcritical containment within universities and a wider system of corporate/university/government knowledge production. In this situation, philosophy substantially has produced its own trivialization and contributed to its own marginalization. In "Do American Philosophers Exist?: Visions of American Philosophy and Culture," I contrast this development to the public mission and pragmatic self-understanding of philosophy present in classical American philosophy. This philosophical tradition, I suggest, provides a basis for rethinking philosophy, its vision and its stance toward different and opposed visions, and its institutional place in the academy. In "Re-Visioning Philosophy and the Organization of Knowledges," I explore these possibilities and outline broad intellectual and institutional changes that their realization would require. Above all, this re-visioned philosophy would be centrally a pragmatic philosophy. In "Pragmatism versus Fundamentalism," I set forth the outline of this philosophy, and identify its pragmatic character in terms of its irreducible commitments to practice, purpose, and pluralism—a pluralism with concrete implications for teaching, research, and educational administration. The genealogical character and critical aims of this pragmatism share much with many philosophies often classified (and often undertheorized) as postmodern. In "The Idols of the Twilight: Pragmatism and Postmodernism," I interpret and assess some of their differences and similarities, always attempting to sound pragmatism's strengths and weaknesses in the twilight of other, once-dominant intellectual traditions and in the ever more total eclipse of criticism. (This chapter, with chapters 9, 13, and 15, occupies a central position in my view of genealogical pragmatism.)

Pragmatism's future as effective criticism is tied to its capacity to reconstruct experience. In the five chapters of the second part of the book, I turn to this issue. Above all, pragmatism is a reconstructive theory of experience. Because this theory is radical and novel, it often has been misunderstood and neglected by both its friends and enemies, old and new. Today its recovery requires an analysis of these mistakes—mistakes that are common both to idealist dreams of language, narrative, and self, and to naturalist dreams of matter and independent reality. Thus, in "Rorty as Elvis: Dewey's Reconstruction of Metaphysics," I critically contrast Richard Rorty's linguistic "neopragmatism" with Dewey's experiential pragmatism. In "Experience and the Adoration of Matter: Santayana's Unnatural Naturalism," I carefully distinguish this pragmatism from George Santayana's naturalism, realism, and materialism (as well as from all versions of nonnaturalism, antirealism, and idealism). Finally, in "Socrates and Radical Empiricism," I demonstrate how this radically empiricist and relational account of experience allows pragmatists to reply successfully to a familiar line of Socratic questioning by identifying and rejecting its metaphysical assumptions. This view of experience, moreover, goes hand in hand with a pragmatic account of inquiry and makes possible an experiential ethics. This ethics is a temporal ethics, and it requires courage. In "Chronophobia," I trace the ways in which fear of time undercuts this courage through its demand for epistemological, metaphysical and, above all, moral order. Philosophies that make this demand fail to take time seriously. In "Taking Time Seriously," I develop a pragmatic, experiential account of time and a pragmatic, temporal account of experience, and outline some of its moral and political implications.

The politics of a genealogical pragmatism is a politics of community, and its reconstruction of experience is one with its reconstruction of community. In the book's third part, I evaluate and extend pragmatism's reconstructive account of community in three ways: (1) by examining the successes and tracing the failures of this account as it is set forth in the work of Peirce, James, Royce, Santayana, Dewey, and Mead; (2) by critically comparing its view of individualism to different views in other philosophical traditions such as personalism, naturalism, and postmodernism; and, (3) by linking this account of community to contemporary political issues and proposals, and to actual economic and educational conditions that are prerequisites for the existence of community. Thus, in "Theory, Practice, and Community in Peirce's Normative Science," I investigate, criticize, and rework the practical implications for community of Peirce's account of the normative sciences of logic, ethics, and aesthetics. In "Bodies, Selves, and Individuals: Personalism and Pragmatism," I contrast personalist and pragmatist accounts of persons, demonstrating the reciprocal relationship in pragmatism between the development of individuality and community. I extend this analysis in "Education and the Cultural Frontier: Community, Identity, and Difference" through a critical interpretation of Royce's account of the Great Community, an articulation of an alternative account of community that stresses difference rather than identity among individuals, and an analysis of the role of education in the creation of this community. Some of the conditions upon which the creation of this sort of community depends are economic conditions. In "Community, Economic Growth, and Family Income: It's the Community, Stupid!," I present economic data in order to demonstrate the increasing erosion of these conditions in America. In turn, I argue that the pragmatic notion of community makes possible a moral critique of these conditions and justifies a moral demand for sweeping change. The possibility of just this sort of change lies at the heart of pragmatism's meliorism. In the final chapter, "Persons, Pluralism, and Death: Toward a Disillusioned Pragmatism," I analyze this meliorism and uncover its presuppositions about the nature of the individual, the capacity of the individual to live strenuously on behalf of goals and values that are not merely individual, and the moral significance of death. It is this critical recognition of unreconstructed personal death that must render pragmatism's reconstructive account of community disillusioned: In community there may be salvation, but there surely will be death. As disillusioned reconstruction, pragmatism is a genealogical philosophy, a philosophy dedicated to children.

Acknowledgments

Grateful acknowledgement is made to the following publishers and individuals for permission to reprint selections from the following copyrighted publications:

Richard Brautigan, "The Memoirs of Jesse James" and "We Stopped at Perfect Days," *Rommel Drives Deep into Egypt* (New York: Dell, 1970). © (1970) by Richard Brautigan. Used by permission.

Jackson Browne, *For A Dancer* and *For America*, words and music. © (1974 and 1986) by Swallow Turn Music (ASCAP). Used by permission of Warner Bros. All Rights Reserved. Warner Bros. Publications U. S. Inc.

John Dewey, *The Collected Works of John Dewey: Middle Works, 1899–1924*, Vol. 9 (Carbondale, Ill.: Southern Illinois University Press, 1980). © (1980) by Southern Illinois University Press. Used by permission of Southern Illinois University Press.

John Dewey, *The Collected Works of John Dewey: Later Works, 1925–1953*, Vol. 1 (Carbondale, Ill.: Southern Illinois University Press, 1981). © (1981) by Southern Illinois University Press. Used by permission of Southern Illinois University Press.

John Dewey, *The Collected Works of John Dewey: Later Works, 1925–1953*, Vols. 2, 4, 5 (Carbondale, Ill.: Southern Illinois University Press, 1984). © (1984) by The Board of Trustees, Southern Illinois University. Used by permission of Southern Illinois University Press.

Allen Ginsberg, *Howl and Other Poems* (San Francisco: City Lights Books, 1956). © (1956) by Allen Ginsberg. Reprinted by permission of HarperCollins Publishers.

I

Philosophy

1

The Humanities, Inc.

Reason, Persuasion, and the Business Mind

Many philosophers today proclaim that the philosophy of the future—by which they usually mean just their own views at present—must be radically different from the philosophies of the past. Like many other scholars in the humanities, these philosophers have become impatient with much philosophy itself. They now make their livings, ironically, by professing over and over that we should stop doing philosophy, by offering us therapies for philosophy and the urge to philosophize, and by articulating alternatives to most or all existing philosophy. For example, Richard Rorty, one of the best known and most influential of these writers, urges us to complete a "rejection of metaphilosophical scientism." He explains: "That is, we should let the debate between those who see contemporary democratic societies as hopeless and those who see them as our only hope, be conducted in terms of the actual problems now being faced by those societies. . . . it would be well for us to debate political topics explicitly, rather than using Aesopian philosophical language."[1]

What follows from this advice? What are its implications? For his part, Rorty foresees a "post-Philosophical" future. From this perspective, he thinks, we may recognize at last that theoretical reflection is not likely to help us and that twentieth century theory (whether Marxism, analytical philosophy, or postmodernism) has not clarified actual problems or developed conceptual instruments superior to those made available to us by American pragmatists such as James and Dewey at the beginning of this century. This enables us, Rorty continues, to grasp that we are just where our grandfathers and grandmothers suspected we were: in the midst of a struggle for power between

---

1. Richard Rorty, "Philosophy as Science, as Metaphor, and as Politics," *Essays on Heidegger and Others: Philosophical Papers*, vol. 2 (Cambridge and New York: Cambridge University Press, 1991), p. 25.

those who possess it and those who are suffering from it, terrorized by it, want it, and, I might add, for the most part do not have the luxury of theorizing about it. We would see, Rorty concludes, that the familiar vocabulary of social democratic politics probably does not require today any further sophistication, at least by philosophers.

This conclusion is both mistaken and dangerous. As he frequently does, Rorty here has drawn the wrong conclusions from his own analysis. Rorty's sound advice to debate political topics explicitly does not imply that concerned philosophical theorists should cease and desist, becoming, in his own terms, content post-philosophical "ironists" or "postmodern bourgeois liberals." Instead, Rorty's advice implies—indeed contains—a new set of marching orders that should transform theory in philosophy and across the humanities. The theory and the vocabulary of social democratic politics—here Rorty is simply mistaken, I think—*does* require further sophistication and a more fully self-critical, self-reflexive, self-aware character.

This transformation is necessary and timely because today the vocabulary of social democratic politics really is being stripped of its critical power—and stripped of its power in a manner not apparent to our grandfathers and grandmothers. Philosophers today face no more important problem.

I want to develop this claim—that the vocabulary of democratic politics is being stripped of its critical power—by means of three initial observations. I find all three observations terribly disturbing. The first comes from Rorty, again. Calling himself a pragmatist and berating philosophers who still cling to foundational, absolutist, realist, or scientistic notions of truth, Rorty succinctly states that "for us [pragmatists] 'rational' merely means 'persuasive,' 'irrational' can only mean 'invoking force.'"[2] To hold a rational view, as pragmatists realize, according to Rorty, is simply to hold a view that is persuasive.

The second observation comes from the well-known post-structuralist French philosopher Michel Foucault. Responding to an interviewer who suggested that his genealogical studies of systems of discourses and webs of power undermined rationality—and even the possibility of rationality—in human history, Foucault replied that no particular, given form of rationality constitutes reason and, thus, that no transformation from one form of rationality to another constitutes a collapse of reason or the end of reason. Because different "forms of rationality are created endlessly," Foucault concluded

2. Richard Rorty, "Cosmopolitanism without Emancipation: A Response to Jean-Franois Lyotard," *Objectivity, Relativism, and Truth: Philosophical Papers*, vol. 1 (Cambridge and New York: Cambridge University Press, 1991), p. 220.

that "there is no sense at all to the proposition that reason is a long narrative which is now finished, and that another narrative is under way."[3]

The third and final observation comes from the American pragmatist John Dewey. In *Individualism: Old and New*, Dewey criticized outdated but still commonplace notions of individualism in America. Seeking to develop an alternative and attempting to identify roadblocks to the realization of this alternative,[4] Dewey set forth a scathing, radical critique of American thought and life. Because of its significance for present purposes, I quote at length a passage from this work:

> The significant thing is that the loyalties which once held individuals, which gave them support, direction, and unity of outlook on life, have well-nigh disappeared. . . . Some persons hold that a genuine mental counterpart of the outward social scheme is actually forming. Our prevailing mentality, our "ideology," is said to be that of the "business mind" which has become so deplorably pervasive. Are not the prevailing standards of value those derived from pecuniary success and economic prosperity? Were the answer unqualifiedly in the affirmative, we should have to admit that our outer civilization is attaining an inner culture which corresponds to it, however much we might disesteem the quality of that culture. The objection that such a condition is impossible, since man cannot live by bread, by material prosperity alone, is tempting, but may be said to beg the question. The conclusive answer is that the business mind is not itself unified. It is divided within itself and must remain so as long as the results of industry as the determining force in life are corporate and collective while its animating motives and compensations are so unmitigatedly private. A unified mind, even of the business type, can come into being only when conscious intent and consummation are in harmony with consequences actually effected. This statement expresses conditions so psychologically assured that it may be termed a law of mental integrity.[5]

Let me outline an initial response to these three observations. First, in reply to Rorty, it simply is *not* the case that rationality "just means persuasion"—even for pragmatists. To think otherwise is to empty pragmatism of its concern with intelligence and inquiry. Rorty does just this, trading pragmatic inquiry into experience for a pseudo-pragmatic redescription of language. In doing this, Rorty is simply continuing a linguistic turn that he took

---

3. Michel Foucault, "Critical Theory/Intellectual History," *Politics, Philosophy, Culture: Interviews and Other Writings, 1977–1984*, ed. Lawrence D. Kritzman (New York: Routledge, Chapman & Hall, 1988 [1983]), p. 35.
4. See the discussion of economics, communication, and education in chapter 13.
5. John Dewey, *Individualism: Old and New*, *John Dewey: The Later Works, 1925–1953*, vol. 5 (Carbondale, Ill.; Southern Illinois University Press, 1984 [1930]), pp. 66, 67, 69. Hereafter abbreviated "*I:O&N*; *LW* 5." in this chapter.

years before his self-identification as a pragmatist. It is, moreover, a linguistic turn from which he has yet to return. No matter how liberal or bourgeois or pluralistic one's intent, to identify rationality with persuasion is to reduce criticism and philosophy to marketing and advertising. It is to exchange love of wisdom for the business mind. Neither genuine individuality nor genuine democracy is possible in this context.

Second, as Foucault noted, new forms of rationality surely do arise and old forms surely do disappear. Today, at least outside the academy, rationality increasingly is understood as, practiced as, and identified with, persuasion. To the extent that this is so, the "business mind" apparently is becoming, or has become, largely unified. In theory, careful, detailed genealogy may trace and fragment this unity and its subjects. In this work, pragmatists may locate the "cash-value" of a great deal of Foucault's work. In practice, such genealogy will have a critical value only to the extent to which it is not marginalized, contained, or absorbed by the "business mind." In this event, any post-structuralist politics of discourse becomes little more than a distracting and trivial discourse of politics.

Third, despite his questionable appeal to a so-called law of mental integrity, Dewey did not insist that the business mind could not in principle become unified. Instead, he simply thought there was evidence that it was not unified—as a matter of fact. Since Dewey's time, I think this evidence has shifted. On Dewey's terms, this means that conscious intent is now largely in harmony with consequence effected. It means, moreover, that collective forces in our culture have been harmonized with private motives and results. Both seem to be the case. In fact, the business mind seems to have become unified to such a high degree that it does seem over and over again to contain criticism directed at it. As the critical theorists Horkheimer and Adorno observed in analyzing the "culture industry," marketing has triumphed over thinking, evidenced by the fact that even though we see through the claims of advertising, still we feel compelled to buy its products.[6] Today, to be is to be in business; to be is to have—and, ideally, to have more and more.

What If They Gave a War and Nobody Came

The expansion of the business mind and the constriction of criticism may be seen more sharply by focusing more narrowly on higher education and connections between higher education and democracy. There is good

---

6. Max Horkheimer and Theodor Adorno, *Dialectic of Enlightenment* (New York: Continuum Publishing, 1982 [1944]), p. 167.

reason for this. Depressingly, the business mind today has expanded into, and reaches throughout, education—including higher education, the humanities, and philosophy. The consequences of this for democracy are large and terrible, as Dewey insightfully noted:

> If our public-school system merely turns out efficient industrial fodder and citizenship fodder in a state controlled by pecuniary industry, as other schools in other nations have turned out efficient cannon fodder, it is not helping to solve the problem of building up a distinctive American culture; it is only aggravating the problem. That which prevents the schools from doing their educational work freely is precisely the pressure—for the most part indirect, to be sure—of domination by the money-motif of our economic regime. . . . Such an education is at best extremely one-sided; it operates to create the specialized "business mind," and this, in turn, is manifested in leisure as well as in business itself. The one-sidedness is accentuated because of the tragic irrelevancy of prior schooling to the controlling realities of social life. There is little preparation to induce either hardy resistance, discriminating criticism, or the vision and desire to direct economic forces in new channels. (*I:O&N*; *LW* 5:102–3)

Where there is little vision or desire, moreover, there is little will or capacity to change. Instead, in higher education today, the humanities have become a battleground. Like most battlegrounds, this one is littered with uniformed casualties and innocent bystanders, spent shells and disappointing duds, sophisticated weapons and expensive delivery systems, oaths of allegiance and chains of command, and the public hopes and private ambitions of academic glory seekers.

These brave philosophers, historians, literary theorists, artists, and other humanist foot soldiers are fighting divisive skirmishes on several fronts. These battles—today's so-called culture wars—are now familiar.[7] They include:

---

7. There is a vast literature on this cluster of issues. The following are some of the best or most influential book-length contributions. James Davison Hunter, *Culture Wars: The Struggle to Define America* (New York: Basic Books, 1990); Paul Lauter, *Canons and Contexts* (New York: Oxford University Press, 1991); D. Gless and B. H. Smith, *The Politics of Liberal Education* (Durham, N.C.: Duke University Press, 1992); Martin Anderson, *Imposters in the Temple* (New York: Simon and Schuster, 1992); Michael H. Mitias, *Moral Education and the Liberal Arts* (Westport, Conn.: Greenwood Press, 1992); Paul Bové, *In the Wake of Theory* (Hanover, N.H.: Wesleyan University Press and University Presses of New England, 1992); S. Greenblatt and G. Gunn, *Redrawing the Boundaries* (New York: Modern Languages Association of America, 1992); George H. Douglas, *Education without Impact* (New York: Birch Lane Press, 1992); Barry Schwartz, *Educating for Civic Responsibility in a Multicultural World* (Swarthmore, Penn.: Swarthmore College, 1993); Charles Taylor, *Multiculturalism: Examining the Politics of Recognition*, ed. Amy Gutmann (Princeton, N.J: Princeton University Press, 1994); E. Messer-Davidow, D. Shumway, and D. Sylvan, *Knowledges: Historical and Critical Studies in Disciplinarity*

disputes that pit advocates of a new multicultural curriculum against defenders of a traditional Western canon; related bitter battles over "political correctness," institutional orthodoxy (both liberal and conservative), and intellectual openness; ongoing infighting about teaching, teaching loads, incentives and rewards for teaching excellence, and the relation of teaching to research; charges and countercharges about the educational significance and practical value of humanities research, and the energies and resources devoted to it; and deep disagreements about intellectual agendas and educational missions—from scholars who pursue business as usual to those who announce "the end of philosophy," "the end of art," "the end of history," "the end of literature," even the "end of theory," and, in short, the end of the humanities as now understood and practiced.

Intellectual controversies are reflections of conflicts within vital social organizations and movements for change, and so it is a sign of openness and health that education is marked by theoretical disagreements and practical differences. Our present intellectual controversies, and the values and assumptions that underlie them, surely merit careful attention and informed action. They merit all available, relevant insights drawn from literature, history, philosophy, the arts—in short, the best that the humanities can provide.

However, today's culture wars rarely evidence anything close to the best that the humanities have to offer. Instead, humanists today engage in very little open discussion, shared inquiry, sweeping imagination, constructive criticism, or joint action and policy-making. Instead, debates among professional humanists are marked by remarkably low levels of trust, respect, and fair play, and by disastrously high levels of suspicion, polarization, and distorted communication. Indeed, humanists now often seem more interested in making converts than in making inquiries. And, whatever the place of "difference" in humanistic theory, humanists rarely value it in practice.

What Good Are the Humanities?

If these bitter disputes had no implications beyond the ivory tower, they would not matter much. In fact, however, they have far-reaching off-campus consequences, at least in combination with the steady flow of well-publicized

---

(Charlottesville: University Press of Virginia, 1993); Peter T. Marsh, *Contesting the Boundaries of Liberal and Professional Education* (Syracuse: Syracuse University Press, 1988); Abraham Edel, *Interpreting Education* (Buffalo: Prometheus Books, 1989); John Arthur and Amy Shapiro, eds., *Campus Wars: Multiculturalism and the Politics of Difference* (Boulder, Colo.: Westview Press, 1995); M. N. S. Sellers, ed., *An Ethical Education: Community and Morality in the Multicultural University* (Oxford: Berg Publishers, 1994).

scandals that now seem commonplace—the linguist who faked research data, the humanities dean who plagiarized, the football player who graduated but cannot read, the philosophy department head who appointed his wife to the faculty and sexually harassed his female students, the sophomores who could not locate the United States on a world map or determine the century in which World War I took place, the historian who destroyed documents sought by other scholars, the professor spotted in France sipping wine throughout sabbatical, the endowed professor of religious studies who always flew first-class, the big-name literary theorists lured to new positions by six-figure salaries and tiny teaching loads, and on and on.

In this context, the nasty, shrill disputes among humanists have eroded significantly public confidence in higher education in general and education in the humanities in particular. At best, humanists seem unable to put into practice what they put into theory. At worst, humanistic theory seems silly and indefensible.

As a result, humanities scholars have a lot to prove to taxpayers, administrators, foundations, prospective donors, students, and even their colleagues. This point is absolutely critical because education in the humanities is sold in America in a what economists call a market with asymmetric information—a "trust market." Taxpayers, legislators, administrators, and students support education in the humanities not because they are experts in the humanities or know in advance what the humanities will do for them, but because they trust the humanities deliver value even though they are not exactly sure how. As is the case in any trust market (such as medicine or law), when trust in education in the humanities is low—as it is now—support for this sort of education will be correspondingly low—as it is now.

It doesn't have to be this way. Humanists need to go public and spread their message; in an advertising culture, humanists must deliver their critical message. Although they have not done so, there is no reason to think they cannot do better. As John Dewey noted:

> I do not hold, I think, an exaggerated opinion of the influence that is wielded by so-called "intellectuals"—philosophers, professional and otherwise, critics, writers and professional persons in general having interests beyond their immediate callings. But their present position is not a measure of their possibilities. For they are now intellectually dispersed and divided. . . . This internal dissolution is necessarily accompanied by a weak social efficacy. The chaos is due, more than to anything else, to mental withdrawal, to the failure to face the realities of industrialized society. Whether the ultimate influence of the distinctively intellectual or reflective groups is to be great or small, an initial move is theirs. (*I:O&N*; *LW* 5:107)

Overly absorbed by intramural squabbles and struggles to the death (or at least tenure and promotion), professional humanists have obscured the commitments historically central to the practice and aims of the humanities. These commitments, essential for the public trust and public support of the humanities, are sustained by the following three-part realization: *Education in the humanities is essential for the realization of basic professional, personal, and social values.*

First, as study after study documents, the humanities provide remarkably practical preparation for a successful career or profession. In an increasingly competitive, dynamic, international marketplace in which yesterday's training is obsolete tomorrow, there is a premium on the skills that the humanities develop—communication, reasoning, analysis, and imagination. From the standpoint of a career, investment in the humanities pays an exceptionally high rate of return.

This is especially important because the majority of college and university students today report that they don't care much about developing a meaningful philosophy of life. Instead, they say they are in school for financial success and social status. They want a "good job" and they feel an unexamined life definitely may be worth living—worth it all the way to the bank. They feel the humanities are not very practical or useful for this. Of course, there is something pathetic about having to respond to this concern. After all, this is an age of white-collar criminals and rogue politicians, a time of covert military operations and overt personal consumption, an era of cancerous cultural illiteracy. We have big business, big science, big technology, and big weapons, but also lots and lots of very small people. As a result, it is tempting simply to register the moral bankruptcy of much of this concern—and its striking inability to distinguish education from training, and a profession from a series of jobs. But today humanists cannot afford the luxury of this sort of response.

Instead, they must stress that the humanities in fact do provide practical preparation for a successful career. Consider the information that emerges from recent studies: Undergraduate humanities majors outscore most all of their fellow students on graduate and professional school admissions tests; students with degrees in the humanities secure employment and financial compensation at rates similar to or higher than students with degrees in other fields; and, employment opportunities for humanists (and liberal arts students more generally) appear to be improving further. Employers do realize, then, that today's workplace requires workers who can critically and imaginatively respond to rapid change and new realities.[8]

Second, and much more importantly, the humanities provide crucial preparation for life—human development, in addition to human employment.

---

8. See the discussion of family income and education levels in chapter 14.

What the humanities do, in other words, is humanize. While the humanities disciplines include sophisticated skills of analysis, interpretation, and communication, and vast amounts of information and knowledge (some of which is written into notebooks each term by students seeking the "right answers" to a future exam), this is not their core. Instead, the core of the humanities is the power to illuminate and enlarge our understanding of who we are, increase our choices of who we meaningfully might become, and expand our abilities to attain the goals we choose. Our most fundamental individual decisions, repeated day after day (though seldom consciously), concern what sort of life to lead and what sort of person to become.[9] The humanities—the study of languages and literatures, philosophies, histories, and religions, for example—offer a wealth of wisdom for this choosing. This wisdom and these skills are readily available; unfortunately, in humanities education today, at least, supply-side theory is not working. In sharp contrast to the situation in the sciences, technology, and the professions, the products of the humanities—self-understanding, illuminating interpretation, imaginative perception of alternatives, clarity and wisdom about values, rationality in choice, and the unwillingness to be deceived or manipulated—are little sought for by the majority of people. As a result, few lives today are self-chosen, and few decisions are free expressions of personal life. In this context, the humanities offer significant possibilities for much needed change.

Third, the humanities provide wisdom and skills vital not only for the improvement of individual life, but also for the enrichment of culture, the realization of societal ideals, and the creation of community. Democracy is intrinsically and inextricably connected to education in the humanities because self-government requires citizens who can act with self-awareness and understanding of others, face the future with imagination and vision, and participate effectively in the cultural practices and institutions that affect their lives. Effective citizenship and public discourse are simply impossible without large doses of humanistic education. The humanities can provide interpretive skills needed to utilize successfully immense amounts of information and data, imaginative capacities needed to deal effectively with ambiguity, multiplicity, and diversity, and reasoning abilities needed to identify and resist dogma, slogans, rhetoric, prejudice, propaganda, and otherwise hidden and obvious agendas marketed incessantly. In the United States, a legitimate or justified government long has been understood, at least in theory, as a government that embodies the will of its people—as self-government. Self-government, however, requires selves—individuals who understand themselves and their situation, creatively choose from among alternatives, and

---

9. See the discussion of this issue in the context of personal death in chapter 15.

realize such choice in active participation in community life.[10] Humanistic education is the development of these abilities—it is self-development. Self-government requires this self-development. To the extent that effective humanistic education is lacking, then, individuals fail to become fully human selves, governments and other institutions fail to operate in a fully democratic manner, and societies fail to be genuine communities. To the extent that education in the humanities is absorbed or contained by science, technology, and business, these possibilities for individuality and community vanish. And although public support for the humanities may not absolutely guarantee anything, it does clearly demonstrate the will to act on the moral and intellectual requirements of a country conceived in liberty.

The Education Business

This points to the biggest challenge now facing the humanities, although humanities faculty seem not to realize it. So far, at least, they just don't get it. Perhaps they don't want to get it. As John Dewey observed:

> It is indeed foolish to assume that an industrial civilization will somehow automatically, from its own inner impetus, produce a new culture. But it is a lazy abdication of responsibility which assumes that a genuine culture can be achieved except first by an active and alert intellectual recognition of the realities of an industrial age, and then by planning to use them in behalf of a significantly human life. To charge that those who urge intellectual acknowledgment or acceptance as the first necessary step stop at this point, and thus end with an optimistic rationalization of the present as if it were final, is a misconstruction that indicates a desire to shirk responsibility for undertaking the task of reconstruction and direction. Or else it waits upon a miracle to beget the culture which is desired by all serious minds. (*I:O&N*; *LW* 5:110)

While philosophers and other professional humanists busy themselves with bitter intramural battles, the real, decisive cultural war is being fought—and lost—on another front. Just as the family farm largely has been replaced by Agri-business, the liberal arts (and especially the humanities) largely have been replaced by *Edu-business*. In earlier times, education in the humanities was controlled by religion or family or the State. Today it is controlled, directly or indirectly, by business.

To understand Edu-business, it is crucial to grasp three points. First, private business is taking over more and more the public role of traditional higher education. Education, that is, has become increasingly business-based.

---

10. See the discussions of self, individuality, and community in chapters 12 and 13.

Corporations in America now spend vast sums to train and educate their employees—more than $40 billion annually and perhaps as much as all of America's four-year colleges and universities combined. They educate huge numbers of students—at least 8 million annually and, again, perhaps as many as all American four-year colleges and universities. These students participate in seminars, institutes, and in-house educational programs. In addition to instruction at the workplace, they receive education at corporate campuses—facilities, often resembling traditional college campuses, designed specifically for employee education. These corporate colleges increasingly grant their own degrees, and these degree programs increasingly are being recognized by the same associations that accredit traditional colleges and universities. An early, influential example of this corporate college is the National Technological University. NTU beams instruction by satellite to corporate classrooms around the country. This noncampus corporate university has served and been supported by IBM, Digital Equipment, Hewlett-Packard, RCA, Control Data, NCR, and many other major companies. In short, as *Corporate Classrooms*, a 1985 study funded by the Carnegie Foundation for the Advancement of Teaching, observes, traditional schools, colleges, and universities no longer have a monopoly on education: "New corporate institutions are operating on the same academic turf, and new technologies have the power to bypass the classroom and the campus. . . . The danger is that, in a bid for survival, higher education will imitate its rivals, that careerism will dominate the campus as colleges pursue the marketplace goals of corporate education."[11]

---

11. Nell P. Eurich, *Corporate Classrooms*, with a foreword by Ernest L. Boyer (Princeton, N.J.: The Carnegie Foundation for the Advancement of Teaching, 1985), p. xiv. Here too there is a large literature of books, including the following: Sande Cohen, *Academia and the Luster of Capital* (Minneapolis: University of Minnesota Press, 1993); Mark R. Schwehn, *Exiles from Eden: Religion and the Academic Vocation in America* (New York: Oxford University Press, 1993); Herbert I. Schiller, *Culture Inc.: The Corporate Takeover of Public Expression* (New York: Oxford University Press, 1989); William H. Berquist, *The Four Cultures of the Academy* (San Francisco: Jossey-Bass Publishers, 1992); Thomas Bender, *Intellect and Public Life* (Baltimore: Johns Hopkins University Press, 1993); Zygmunt Bauman, *Legislators and Interpreters* (New York: Polity Press, 1987); Alexander W. Astin, *Academic Gamesmanship* (New York: Praeger Press, 1976); Robert Birnbaum, *How Colleges Work: The Cybernetics of Academic Organization and Leadership* (San Francisco: Jossey-Bass Publishers, 1988); F. Rourke and G. Brooks, *The Managerial Revolution in Higher Education* (Baltimore: Johns Hopkins University Press, 1966); Burton J. Bledstein, *The Culture of Professionalism* (New York: W. W. Norton, 1976); Joseph J. Kockelmans, *Interdisciplinarity and Higher Education* (University Park, Penn.: Pennsylvania State University Press, 1979); Arthur Levine, *Higher Learning in America, 1980–2000* (Baltimore: Johns Hopkins University Press, 1993); W. Neilson and C. Gaffield, *Universities in Crisis: A Mediaeval Institution in the Twenty-First Century* (Montreal: Institute for Research on Public Policy, 1986); Laurence R. Veysey, *The Emergence of the American University* (Chicago: University of Chicago Press, 1965).

Second, higher education in turn is taking on more and more the structure and mission of private business. Education has internalized the structures
of business and the culture of the corporation. It has become a business.
Students have become education consumers. A discipline's majors have become its repeat customers. Admissions offices are measured by the market
share they capture. For their part, faculty have become intellectual entrepreneurs—taking their services to the highest bidders, producing and amassing
cultural capital that can be quantified on resumés that resemble bank statements or financial asset summaries. When we call teaching a profession,
today we usually mean that it is a job, not a calling. In administration, universities have become corporations—governed by people and processes that
suggest more a board room than a classroom, more a board of directors than
a genuine community of scholars. The humanities—like leisure studies, hotel
management, commercial graphics design, and, of course, business administration—have become just another one of the many enterprises of these educational corporations we call universities. As such, they have become the
humanities, incorporated—complete with middle management deans, associ-
ate deans, and department heads, fund-raisers, grant-writing assistants, public
relations specialists, and marketing experts. All of these people watch the
bottom line and count profits. They count faculty publications, course enroll-
ments, departmental credit hours, and alumni donations. And all of these
people, in committee permutations, develop strategic plans so that in the
future there will be bigger numbers to count. And humanists participate in,
legitimize, and strengthen all of it.

Third, higher education and business increasingly are entering into shared
business relationships.[12] In the language of business, these are mergers; per-

---

12. For an extensive and useful account (with extensive case studies) of the rise of university-
business relationships, see: Norman E. Bowie, *University-Business Partnerships: An Assessment*
(Lanham, Md.: Rowman & Littlefield Publishers, 1994); and, Thomas W. Langfitt, Sheldon
Hackney, Alfred Fishman, and Albert Glowasky, *Partners in the Research Enterprise: University-
Corporate Relations in Science and Technology* (Philadelphia: University of Pennsylvania Press,
1983). A briefer account is provided by Harvey Brooks, "Current Criticisms of Research Universities, *The Research University in a Time of Discontent*, ed. Jonathan R. Cole, Elinor G.
Barber, and Stephen R. Graubard (Baltimore: Johns Hopkins University Press, 1993), pp. 247–
50. Bowie, Langfitt and colleagues, and Brooks do not pay any attention to the impact of
university-business associations on the humanities. Further, these university-business partnerships in the sciences, humanities, and other fields frequently arise against a background of
increasing government and government-business influence that results from greatly increased
government funding for universities and colleges during the past fifty years. See, for example:
John W. Sommer, ed., *The Academy in Crisis: The Political Economy of Higher Education* (New
Brunswick, N.J.: Transaction Publishers, 1995); Roger E. Meiners and Ryan C. Amacher, eds.,
Federal Support of Higher Education: The Growing Challenge to Intellectual Freedom (New
York: Paragon House, 1989); Roger L. Geiger, *To Advance Knowledge: The Growth of American*

haps, in a different language, they are Faustian bargains. These associations increasingly align the interests of higher education with those of business, and increasingly assimilate the mission of educational institutions to the mission of businesses. These activities may be displayed along a spectrum from the more incidental interactions to those that fundamentally alter the structure and operations of educational institutions.

Along that spectrum, let me simply highlight five types of education/ business mergers. In the first place, for example, individual business leaders, corporations, any many foundations fund activities that further—or are thought to further—business interests. Often this support takes the form of funding for business schools and economics or business-related scientific, mathematical, engineering, and technological programs. The results include new buildings, new professorships, and new instructional and research funds. In turn, this leads to further growth in these programs and further growth in their share of resources, students, and alumni at educational institutions. There are not, for example, General Motors Professors of Religious Studies, Microsoft Professors of Comparative Literature, Wal-Mart Professors of Philosophy, or Nabisco Professors of Critical Theory. Though usually unnoticed, this has immense on-campus and off-campus consequences for the humanities. As a recent U.S. Department of Education study documented, in the last twenty years business has virtually taken over the college curriculum.[13] Making the same point more strongly and critically, Lawrence Soley describes the seduction of higher education by the military, government, and business: "The story about universities in the 1980s and 1990s is that they will turn a trick for anybody with money to invest; and the only ones with money are corporations, millionaires, and foundations. These investments in universities have

---

Research Universities, 1900–1940 (New York: Oxford University Press, 1986); Kenneth J. Arrow and Richard W. Cottle, *Education in a Research University* (Stanford: Stanford University Press, 1996); Richard J. Baker, *The Politics of Research* (Washington, D.C.: Public Affairs Press, 1966); Steven Ballard, Thomas E. James, Jr., Timothy I. Adams, Michael D. Devine, Lani L. Malya, and Mark Meo, *Innovation through Technical and Scientific Information: Government and Industry Cooperation* (New York: Quorum Books, 1989); Jonathan R. Cole, "Balancing Acts: Dilemmas of Choice Facing Research Universities" and Stephen R. Graubard, "The Research University: Notes toward a New History," *The Research University in a Time of Discontent*, pp. 1–36, 361–90. In this context, Nicholas H. Stenreck argues persuasively that a consequence of government-university associations has been the loss of academic community and loss of faculty concern with the morality of their own institutions. "Ethics and Aims of Universities in Historical Perspective," *An Ethical Education: Community and Morality in the Multicultural University*, ed. M. N. S. Sellers, pp. 9–20.

13. *The Chronicle of Higher Education*, December 1, 1995, p. A27. Business largely has taken over not simply the curriculum but also the administration of the curriculum through various simple-minded budgeting processes that directly link program support and faculty salaries to student enrollment and external funding.

dramatically led universities to attend to the interests of their well-heeled patrons, rather than those of students."[14]

In the second place, business increasingly sponsors university activities in return for advertising considerations. Like the woman in the George Bernard Shaw play—or, for those who are part of a postprint culture, like the wife in the 1993 Demi Moore/Robert Redford film, *Indecent Proposal*—it is clear the university is for sale. The only question is the exact price. At Penn State University, for example, the classic blue and white football uniforms do not sport player's names. The team, rather than the individual player, is promoted. However, the uniforms do sport a Nike Corporation patch. The team and the company are promoted—adding evidence to Nike's advertising slogan that "It must be the shoes." At Clayton State College, Delta Airlines employs about 150 students to serve its customers from a space that it has leased in the college's student center. This is so common—corporate advertising in the gym, in the labs, in the computer center, in the classroom—that it is hardly noticed any longer. Perhaps professors, like professional athletes, soon will dress in clothes covered with the patches of corporate sponsors. Worrying about this commercialization of the university, Derek Bok wondered if some things in a university should not be for sale: "But what things? And why, if they bring in money to be used for worthy academic purposes? . . . [I]t will take strong leadership to keep the profit motive from gradually eroding the values on which the welfare and reputation of universities ultimately depend."[15]

In the third place, business increasingly provides preferred customer status to colleges and universities in return for market advantage or monopoly. In return for big bucks, Penn State is a Pepsi campus. You can't find Coca Cola in any vending machine or dining facility on campus. The University of Oregon is a Taco Time—not a Taco Bell—campus. Indeed, almost every campus has—or hopes to have—such private vendor or "outsourcing" arrangements with banks, fast food restaurants, book stores, and computer makers. And, as a director of a State Council of Higher Education recently predicted, "I think it's only a matter of time before somebody outsources areas of instruction."[16]

In the fourth place, more ominously, colleges and universities increasingly enter into business partnerships that reroute educational resources and

---

14. Lawrence C. Soley, *Leasing the Ivory Tower: The Corporate Takeover of Academia* (Boston: South End Press, 1995), p. 5. Like Bowie's study, Soley's more passionate, polemical analysis ignores the humanities.
15. Derek Bok, "Universities: Their Temptations and Tensions," *Journal of College and University Law*, 1991; included in Bowie, *University-Business Partnerships*, pp. 119, 121.
16. *The Chronicle of Higher Education*, July 7, 1995, pp. A31–32.

redefine educational missions. These activities blur traditional distinctions between the public and the private, the role of government and the role of business, and the aims of business and the aims of education. As such, it is increasingly misleading to view the university as an autonomous institution and its employees as disinterested seekers of truth. Instead, it is increasingly necessary to view the university within the context of a larger system of the production and distribution of knowledge, material resources, and power—as part of a complex, interwoven system of colleges and universities, research institutes and think tanks, the media, government agencies, and corporations.[17] On campus, the most obvious, familiar manifestation of this is the university research park. Multimillion-dollar university-funded venture-capital partnerships and investment funds are more recent, less visible examples of this same development. David W. Mueller, managing partner of the AM Fund, a venture fund backed by Texas A&M University, summarizes the spirit of these enterprises that are not guided ultimately by concern with instruction or research: "We do deals because we think we're going to make money."[18] These joint university/business operations raise complex questions—questions about confidentiality, conflict of interest, profit-making ventures, the ownership of patents, faculty release time for private consulting, use of course time to address private business concerns, and the allocation of resources within the university. Faced with these sorts of problems, the University of Arizona recently terminated all direct commercialization of faculty research. By contrast, research ventures at the University of Utah, for example, result in several spin-off companies each year.[19] Here the university is not simply engaged in public service; instead, the university is engaged in self-service through projects that identify the interests of particular businesses with its own interests. Increasingly, the business of education is business. Increasingly, its professors act as entrepreneurs.

Finally, in the fifth place, other developments are under way, and lots of dollars are at stake. Many universities, libraries, and publishers are exploring the possibilities of using computer technologies to create distance education programs and virtual universities (as opposed to "campus-bound" institutions)—

---

17. For a discussion of the fundamental role of class within this system, see Stanley Aronowitz and William DiFazio, "A Taxonomy of Teacher Work," *The Jobless Future: Sci-Tech and the Dogma of Work* (Minneapolis: University of Minnesota Press, 1994), pp. 226–63. Calling the existence of a community of scholars a fiction, they conclude: "While in earlier periods it was necessary to 'penetrate the veil' of ideology of knowledge for knowledge's sake to reveal the underlying economic and political function of universities with respect to the larger social system, the overwhelming power of business as a moral pursuit increasingly makes this deconstructive work superfluous" (p. 263).

18. *The Chronicle of Higher Education*, May 17, 1996, pp. A37–38.

19. Ibid., July 21, 1995, pp. A33–34.

siteless, bookless educational institutions that provide virtual education to students and their terminal lives. New York University, for example, has begun to offer a graduate program entirely through an interactive electronic network. A group of young scholars, in part dismayed by the tough academic job market, now are planning to establish Virtual Online University, an institution entirely on the Internet. A recent study, "Using Information Technology to Enhance Academic Productivity," commissioned by Educom, a consortium of hundreds of colleges and companies committed to increasing the use of technology in higher education, concludes that in an increasingly knowledge-based economy, traditional colleges and universities must exploit new technologies or "other nontraditional providers of education will be quick to do so." Although the study notes that this new technology is most useful for transmitting "codified knowledge" and is not appropriate for teaching "meaning and value" or "culture and philosophy," it is clear that its recommendations uncritically presuppose meanings and values that are antithetical to the humanities and humane cultures.[20] At the same time, with public funds and private funding from publishing companies that produce educational media, governors of eighteen Western states and territories have agreed to explore the creation of a "virtual university" that would deliver courses and award degrees across the region through state "franchises." Moreover, some of these governors have suggested that this "alternative university" should award academic credit for knowledge gained on the job or from commercial tutorials on the Internet. Complaining that the certification of what is learned still is in the hands of the university, Colorado Governor Roy Romer observed: "People are learning all over, in places that are not part of accredited universities. . . . We're coming into the age where that is going to be blown apart."[21] Perhaps this will lead to the private or public franchising of education—McEducation—that will leave only a handful of universities (like airlines or fast food chains) whose products are delivered globally by a small workforce of producers (and a larger service economy) that can perform business office functions and deliver information. While this information, I stress again, does not constitute and cannot contain the core of the humanities, it is not difficult to imagine tomorrow's virtual students being asked if they want a little humanities with their education—being asked, in effect, "Do you want fries with that?"

Though quibbling humanists generally have not recognized it or done much about it, the rise of Edu-business—the usurpation of education by

---

20. William F. Massy and Robert Zemsky, "Using Information Technology to Enhance Academic Productivity," Educom National Learning Infrastructure Initiative, 1996
21. *The Chronicle of Higher Education*, November 22, 1995, pp. A19, A21. See also a follow-up report, June 11, 1996, pp. A30–31.

business and the transformation of education into business—has rendered the humanities marginal, impotent, and culturally unimportant. Looking ahead, it also presents the humanities with several limited options.

The first option—really more a default mode—is to pursue business as usual. This is a recipe for cultural irrelevance—what Dewey called a "shrinking classicism." It cedes the humanities to the professional humanists: They write books and journal articles for one another; they teach the many students trapped by minimal, incoherent, vestigial humanities distribution requirements; and, they teach the few "leisure class" students who have the time and money and language[22] to pursue some intellectual finishing. On this option, as their funding and numbers shrink within the college and university, and vanish altogether in "the real world" outside, humanists can console themselves that they are the keepers of genuine culture and that the barbarians sadly are already inside the gates. Moreover, the great advantage of business as usual is that it requires little effort.

Of course, humanists could forsake business as usual in order to pursue a second option. Within Edu-business, the humanities could become a booming service industry. The international banking student could gain a career edge by knowing Japanese or Spanish. The future manager may need to know some of the religious history and values of the local workers and consumers in order to achieve maximum productivity. The prospective corporate attorney may benefit from a course in logic. English composition courses could provide key skills to tomorrow's entrepreneurs who need to be not only computer-literate but also just plain literate as they navigate the information highways of the future. All this would require significant restructuring and, surely, downsizing. It could involve hostile takeovers, re-training, more "temporary" workers, and certainly some layoffs. This option—measuring the humanities and the liberal arts against the yardstick of "workplace correctness"[23]— may shock or sicken humanities purists, but it is increasingly evident in the rhetoric, if not the beliefs, of humanists on almost every campus.

There is a third option that aligns the humanities more with the consumer than the producer, more with Walt Disney than General Motors: the humanities as entertainment. A long time ago, Greek philosophers claimed that philosophy begins in wonder. Today, the *National Inquirer* instructs us that "inquiring minds want to know." Celebrity humanist scholars who now write learned essays about Madonna and feminist theory, Michael Jackson

22. See Pierre Bourdieu, Jean-Claude Passeron, Monique de Saint Martin, Christian Baudelot, and Guy Vincent, *Academic Discourse: Linguistic Misunderstanding and Professorial Power* [*Rapport Pedagogique et Communication*] (Cambridge: Polity Press, 1994 [1965]).

23. Patricia Kean, "The New Assault on the Liberal Arts," *Lingua Franca*, May/June 1993, pp. 1, 22–28.

and the politics of desire, Cindy Crawford and late capitalist productions of style, Axl Rose and the politics of diminished expectations, and "NYPD Blues" and postmodern communication are the vanguard of this movement. The movement, however, is much larger, and includes all humanists, whether politically correct or incorrect, who have given up concern with the reconstruction of practice for the fun of deconstruction of theory.

Should the humanities take the first option, remaining the harmless zoo-animals of the ivory tower? Should they pursue the second option that provides them a robust role as special skills coach for Team USA or Transnational Business? Or, should they take a third path that promises all the good times of life as a cultural court jester or epiphenomenal comic?

None of the above options is an acceptable one for education in the humanities—an education that trades in self-understanding, imagination, and self-criticism. Is a better option possible? No, not at present. Let me be very clear here. *No* better option now is available to humanists *as* humanists—in their present professional roles or current activities *as* humanists. Better options are available to many persons—including professional humanists—who are willing and able to engage the public—citizens, legislators, journalists, foundation heads, the business community, politicians, and others who do *not* determine teaching schedules, fix course prerequisites, approve research leaves, grant tenure, or award merit pay.

To note this fact is not to be pessimistic. Rather it is to be realistic. The humanities occupy an increasingly marginal position within colleges and universities, and colleges and universities play only a small educational role in society. Any philosophy that fails to address this issue fails to be genuinely pragmatic, fails to be self-reflective, and fails to do anything genuinely dangerous. The theory and the vocabulary of social democratic politics requires something both more and different. This fact must constitute a central agenda item for any genuinely instrumental and genealogical pragmatism. In the meantime, the problems that are the results of this failure—Rorty's "actual problems now being faced"—constitute an ongoing crisis in education and a crisis in society, even if to date it has meant business as usual for *postcritical* humanists, their theories, their institutions, and their investors.[24]

---

24. An earlier version of portions of this essay appeared in "The Humanities, Inc.: Taking Care of Business," *Re-Inventing the Humanities: International Perspectives*, ed. David Myers (Kew, Victoria: Australian Scholarly Publishing, 1995), pp. 3–10. These revised passages appear here with the kind permission of the editor and the publisher.

2

Do American Philosophers Exist?
Visions of American Philosophy and Culture

This chapter constitutes a seeking, an inquiring, a pursuing. It is inspired by and, I hope, recalls the spirit and vision of William James. James writes:

> Life is confused and superabundant, and what the younger generation appears to crave is more of the temperament of life in its philosophy, even tho it were at some cost of logical rigor and of formal purity.[1]

> What *you* want is a philosophy that will not only exercise your powers of intellectual abstraction, but that will make some positive connexion with this actual world of finite lives.[2]

> Knowledge about life is one thing; effective occupation of a place in life, with its dynamic currents passing through your being, is another.[3]

This is a quest, then, not for certainty or formal purity, but for connections with lives uncertain and finite, changing and situated, real. This search, assuredly, is not physically dangerous: I am not tracking the exotic beast of television's *Wild Kingdom,* exploring the immense and foreign undersea world with Cousteau, or even boldly stalking the wild asparagus and blue-eyed scallop with Euell Gibbons. I need no net or tranquilizer gun. But, if my quarry is tame, it also is elusive (if not illusive): I look for the American philosopher.

Some persons may find it simple-minded, or at least odd, to ask if American philosophers exist, particularly when this question appears to be

---

1. William James, *Essays in Radical Empiricism, The Works of William James* (Cambridge, Mass.: Harvard University Press, 1976 [1912]), p. 21.
2. William James, *Pragmatism, The Works of William James* (Cambridge, Mass.: Harvard University Press, 1975 [1907]), p. 17.
3. William James, *The Varieties of Religious Experience, The Works of William James* (Cambridge, Mass.: Harvard University Press, 1985 [1902]), p. 386.

addressed to an audience that includes philosophers. I will grant that my question is somewhat perverse, but I see no easy or simple-minded answer to it. Moreover, I doubt that the issue seems odd to persons *not* employed by colleges and universities to attend professional conferences, read and write for technical journals, and attempt to communicate to students the results of all this. (Of course, here I recognize that doubt about *whether* American philosophers exist probably is surpassed by doubt about *why* they exist.)

Accordingly, I raise this question—Do American philosophers exist?— without the aim of advancing some technical thesis. I do not wish to prove (to myself) some new argument for solipsism. I do not intend to disprove, or even doubt, the existence of others. Nor is it my plan to engage in Cartesian pseudo-pondering, at the group level, about the certainty of the existence of a whole occupation's worth of selves. I am sure, however, that many philosophers are consoled by believing that no matter how strenuously society may doubt their existence, their own doubt about their existence logically *must* vanish as it occurs. Finally, I do not ask about the existence of American philosophers in order to play with self-referential questions and seeming paradoxes. I am aware, though, that one who doubts the existence of those who do not doubt their own existence may be in for more trouble than simply being without someone to shave him.[4]

Instead, I raise this question—Do American philosophers exist?—in order to examine the relation of American philosophy both to its own vision of itself and to American culture more broadly. I seek to understand what these relationships have been, now are, and, ultimately, what these relationships now should be.

American Philosophy: Three Meanings

At the outset, it is crucial to clarify the meaning of the terms, "American philosopher" and "American philosophy." To do this, I will distinguish three senses of these terms, and I will refer to these sense as the (1) *national,* (2) *philosophical, and* (3) *cultural* senses.

In the first place, then, when we speak of American philosophers in the *national* sense, we consider American philosophers to be all those persons who are philosophers and who, as it happens, are Americans as well. In this sense, all philosophers who are Americans, regardless of their philosophical backgrounds, perspectives, and interests, are American philosophers. And, in

---

4. See W. V. O. Quine, *The Ways of Paradox and Other Essays* (Cambridge, Mass.: Harvard University Press, 1976 [1961]), p. 2.

this sense, American philosophy is simply the philosophy of Americans, philosophy in America.

Fortunately, there is a second, philosophically more interesting sense of these terms. In this second, *philosophical* sense, an American philosopher is not defined merely by nationality or place of residence, but by the presence of common attitudes, purposes, procedures, problems, terminology, and beliefs. It is in virtue of such a shared complex of features that we identify, understand, and differentiate philosophical developments, movements, communities, and images of philosophy itself. It is, moreover, the existence of such a complex of characteristics and resemblances that allows us profitably to label philosophers and philosophy as, for example, distinctively Greek, British, German, or American.

To speak of American philosophers and American philosophy in this philosophical sense is to refer to a particular and discernible unity of orientation, concern, belief, and method in a great or important portion of philosophical thought in America. Such a unity of character, we must recognize, is not a single and simple essence, some necessary and sufficient feature of American philosophy, some property present always and only in philosophy that is American. Instead, it is an identifiable configuration, a characteristic shape, a resemblance, an overlapping, an interweaving of features that, as a relational whole, constitutes the American nature of philosophers and philosophy.

What are these characteristics, these defining marks? This complex of features may be identified as the unity and continuity of belief and action.[5] For American philosophers, belief, called forth by genuinely doubtful and problematic situations, is primarily and irreducibly an instrument in, through, and for action. It is aimed at the satisfactory transformation of problems, and it is justified only in, and by, successful problem-solving action that transforms the problematic situation. In turn, it becomes, through this active process, a guide for, and an object of modification by, future action. Here belief arises within, and from, active experience, and experience, in turn, supplies an adequate method for judging belief as it functions to regulate further experience.

This general view of the philosophical character of American thinkers and American thought is widely shared by many scholars of American philosophy. A brief account of their views may serve to make clearer and more familiar the philosophical character of distinctively American philosophy. In "The Transcendence of Materialism and Idealism in American Thought," John Lachs refers to this character of American philosophy as the "primacy of action and will," a primacy which undercuts the ontological dichotomies of subject and object, matter and mind, doer and deed, individual and society—and, I might add, experience and nature, and theory and practice. Lachs

---

5. See my "Toward a Metaphysics of Experience," *Modern Schoolman* 57.4 (1980): 293–311.

writes that the entire idea of philosophy as analysis of experience into substantial and insubstantial constituents is supplanted, in American thought, by study of the dynamics by, and through, which that experience fashions a real world. American pragmatism naturalizes and eliminates the metaphysical excesses of the idealist view that experience creates a world. The focus of pragmatism, Lachs concludes, falls on "the continuing piecemeal animal and cultural creativity of the species" rather than on "some ontologically primordial indeterminate creative act": "For much if not all American thought, philosophy begins and ends with the examination of daily human practice."[6]

In this same vein, John J. McDermott, in *The Culture of Experience,* argues that American philosophy is characterized by emphasis on: primary experience and its understanding through the method of experience; the unity and rotating primacy of the speculative and the practical; and the obligation of reflection "to reconstruct experience so as to aid in the resolution of those difficulties seen to hinder growth."[7] The American philosopher's burden, McDermott states, is that of confronting and ameliorating concrete problems, such that the relevance of ideas in, and for, experience is preferred to their formalization in, and by, thought.

This parallels John E. Smith's description of American philosophy during its "most characteristic and creative period." In *Themes in American Philosophy,* he stresses the new emphasis on the roles of purpose and interest in determining the direction and importance of reflection, the new understanding of the nature of experience, and the new focus on community and the irreducibly social character of all human undertakings, from science to religion.[8]

I trust that these description supply, if not a finished portrait, an adequate and workable sketch of the character of American philosophy. That the features which constitute this character are extensively developed by Emerson, Peirce, James, and Dewey, and utilized, if less fully and consciously, by Edwards, Jefferson, Parker, Wright, Royce, Santayana, Mead, Lewis, and others I only assert at present, relying on your understanding of these writers and their work.

Now, would, or does, the occurrence of this shared complex of philosophical features mark a coincidence, a local curiosity, the result of some purely mental in-breeding? Are American philosophers and American phi-

---

6. John Lachs, "The Transcendence of Materialism and Idealism in American Thought," read at the annual meeting of the Society for the Advancement of American Philosophy, New Orleans, March 1976.
7. John J. McDermott, *The Culture of Experience: Philosophical Essays in the American Grain* (New York: New York University Press, 1976), pp. 1–17.
8. John E. Smith, *Themes in American Philosophy: Purpose, Experience and Community* (New York: Harper & Row, 1970), p. 2. See the extended discussion of Smith's views in this chapter's appendix.

losophy, understood in the philosophical sense above, labels useful to the philosophical taxonomist, but without connection to, or importance for, a broader, more inclusive American culture? This has appeared doubtful to many observers of the American scene who thus have been led to understand American philosophers and philosophy in a third, *cultural* sense. Here an American philosopher is marked not simply by residence or nationality, nor even solely by the presence of a given complex of philosophical features, but above all by a particular relation to a distinctively *American* culture or, more accurately, plural American cultures.

At this point, I realize, critics who believe that philosophy is properly defined by transcultural or culture-transcendent standards may conclude that any effort to link American philosophy to American culture is no more than an attempt to press philosophy into the service of distraction, propaganda, pride, or chauvinism. This view is unsound. If such critics simply mean that any philosophy is *multi*cultural—that it is the result of the efforts and insights of many cultures, or that it should be judged by standards which are shared or contested by more than one nation or culture—then I fully agree. However, if they mean that philosophy is *trans*cultural or nongenealogical—that it can or should be understood as an enterprise concerned with "ultimate reality" and employing eternal, ahistorical, acultural standards—then I wholly disagree. Though set forward without argument, this view now blinds many philosophers to the intrinsic and irreducible cultural connections of their own philosophies. One may come to understand these connections, and to transform them for the better, but philosophers cannot escape or "get outside" *all* cultural connections and setting. To say this is not to become distracted from Truth, Reality, Beauty, Justice, and so on; rather, it is to reject and be rid of these notions (as pure, eternal, transcendent). This does not press philosophy into the service of a particular national purpose or special-interest group. Rather, it presses *intelligence* into the service of efforts to deal with individual and community problems. This certainly does not deify one's own culture; rather it provides the critical method and vision needed for any successful ongoing reconstruction of a culture. Anyone familiar with the writings of Dewey, for example, will understand that this view of philosophy as intrinsically tied to culture promotes cultural criticism, not cultural self-glorification. As Dewey noted, "When it is understood that philosophic thinking is caught up in the actual course of events, having the office of guiding them towards a prosperous issue, problems will abundantly present themselves."[9] While it is neither possible nor desirable to specify these problems in advance or in the abstract, it is necessary that philosophers recognize and address them.

---

9. John Dewey, "The Need for a Recovery of Philosophy," *John Dewey: The Middle Works, 1899–1924*, vol. 10 (Carbondale, Ill.: Southern Illinois University Press, 1980 [1917]), p. 46.

So understood, American philosophers are nurtured by and through, arise within, formalize and reconstruct, illuminate and "fund" an identifiable and distinguishable American experience. What is essential here is the particular connection of a philosophy with its culture, of a culture with its philosophy.

In order to understand American philosophers and philosophy in this cultural sense, it is vital to grasp these connections between shared, dominant philosophical themes and pervading aspects of a culture or complex of cultures. This is, admittedly, a mammoth enterprise, only two aspects of which I will consider here. First, it is evident that philosophers who are American in the philosophical sense—philosophers of experience, purpose, action, inquiry, and community—*do* view and evaluate their own work in its intimate connection to American culture, to the particular press, immediacy, and meaning of an American experience and environment. Second, certain defining and distinguishable characteristics of that experience may be identified. I will consider briefly these two points.

In the first place, then, philosophers of a characteristically American philosophical orientation have understood their work as rooted in an identifiably American experience, have demanded that it confront and illuminate the genuine here-and-now features of this experience, and have calculated their success in terms of the extent to which they have met this challenge. From Emerson through Dewey, American philosophers have understood themselves in this manner. Emerson, in his well-know address, "The American Scholar," makes this point clear: "Our day of dependence, our long apprenticeship to the learning of other lands draws to a close. The millions that around us are rushing into life cannot always be fed on the sere remains of foreign harvests. Events, actions arise, that must be sung, that will sing themselves."[10] The American scholar, for Emerson, faces new, distinctively American experiences and culture—not abstract realities or even the customs and traditions of Europe. The American philosopher must begin and end with this experience, these actions, this rushing-into-life. The philosopher or scholar must accept, understand, reconstruct, and deepen this experience. It is because philosophy is thus tied to its culture, its time and place, that, for Emerson, it cannot ever be completed, finished. Emerson writes that "Each age it is found must write its own books; or rather each generation for the next succeeding," "for the books of an older period will not fit this." He thus instructs us to reject all inflexible philosophies, to be "Man Thinking" and not meek young men and women growing up in libraries, concerned too little with our own lives and too much with the thoughts of others. "I hate quotations," he

---

10. Ralph Waldo Emerson, "The American Scholar," *Selected Writings of Ralph Waldo Emerson* (New York: New American Library, 1965 [1837]), p. 224. See the discussion of pragmatists as the children of Emerson in chapter 5.

writes—and I stubbornly quote; instead, "tell me what you know."[11] American life-the living itself—generates and must generate, for Emerson, an American philosophy, even if it is unarticulated by the bulk of those who possess it. He observes:

> I see with joy the Irish emigrants landing at Boston, at New York, and say to myself, There they go—to school.
>
> In America we are such rowdies in church and state and the very boys are so soon ripe, that I think no philosophical skepticism will make much sensation. Spinoza pronounced that there was but one substance; yea, verily, but that boy yonder told me yesterday he thought the pinelog was God, and that God was in the jakes. What can Spinoza tell the boy?
>
> We Americans have got suppled into the state of melioration. . . . The plasticity of the tough old planet is wonderful . . . Everything has grown ductile. . . . Nationality is babyish. But stand where you are and make the best of it.[12]

George Santayana recognizes similar connections between philosophy and culture: "All traditions have been founded in practice; in practice the most ideal of them regain their authority, when practice really deals with reality."[13] It is just to this extent that traditions and theory are manifested in real and concrete practice that they escape being perfunctory and merely conventional, and "perhaps secretly despised." Santayana writes: "A philosophy is not genuine unless it inspires and expresses the life of those who cherish it."[14] Moreover, Santayana advises, a philosophy, no matter how academic and technical, must be living, must "embody a distinct vision of the universe and definite convictions about human destiny" if it is to be, fully, a philosophy."

It is from this perspective, of course, that Santayana criticizes what he calls the "Genteel Tradition in America." If measured by academic, formal, or logical criteria alone, the Genteel Tradition is without fault. Still, for Santayana, the Genteel Tradition has grown stale, and fails to make meaningful and vital the commitments, instincts, practices, discoveries—the whole living character—of American experience, of our embedded, embodied

---

11. Ibid., p. 227.
12. Ralph Waldo Emerson, "Journals and Letters," *Selected Writings of Ralph Waldo Emerson* (New York: New American Library, 1965 [1866, 1844, 1866]), pp. 178, 120, 179.
13. George Santayana, "Tradition and Practice," *Santayana on America* (New York: Harcourt, Brace and World, 1968 [1904]), p. 35.
14. George Santayana, "The Genteel Tradition in American Philosophy," *Winds of Doctrine and Platonism and the Spiritual Life* (Gloucester, Mass.: Peter Smith, 1971 [1913]), p. 187.

philosophy. The Genteel Tradition, Santayana notes, stands in sharp contrast to the pragmatic philosophy of William James, which Santayana describes as living and vital, rooted in the American subsoil, and both in sympathy with and setting fire to the moods of the dumb majority.

This is the William James, I point out, who warns us that "*it is high time for the basis of discussion in these* [philosophical] *questions to be broadened and thickened up.*" The problem, James continues, is that philosophy has "confined itself too exclusively to thin logical considerations, that would hold good in all conceivable worlds, worlds of an empirical constitution entirely different form ours." Although philosophers have treated the actual peculiarities and realities of the world as irrelevant to the content of truth, James concludes that they cannot be irrelevant: "The philosophy of the future must imitate the sciences in taking them more and more elaborately into account."[15]

Here James writes as the direct descendant of Emerson's vision of the American experience, the place of the individual in American culture, and the task for the American philosopher. He observes:

> Everything you touch is shopworn. The overtechnicality and consequent dreariness of the younger disciples at our American universities is appalling. . . . Let me repeat once more that a man's vision is the great fact about him. . . . A philosophy is the expression of a man's intimate character, and all definitions of the universe are but the deliberately adopted reactions of human characters upon it.[16]

Santayana, too, believes that a philosophy must be defined by its vision, its passion, and its culturally situated character:

> The heartiness of American ways . . . may prove fatiguing sometimes; but children often overdo their sports, which does not prove that they are not spontaneous fundamentally. . . . The atmosphere of sport, fashion, and wealth is agreeable and intoxicating; certainly it is frivolous, unless some passion is at work beneath, and even then it is all vanity; but, in that sense, so is life itself, and a philosopher who is really a philosopher will not quarrel with it on that count. . . . Isn't American life distinctly successful in expressing its own spirit?[17]

---

15. William James, *A Pluralistic Universe, The Works of William James* (Cambridge, Mass.: Harvard University Press, 1977 [1909]), p. 149.
16. Ibid., pp. 13, 14. See the discussions of James's vision in chapters 4, 8, and 15.
17. George Santayana, "Marginal Notes on Civilization in the United States," *Santayana on America*, p. 189. See the discussions of Santayana's relation to the spirit and vision of American philosophy in chapters 7 and 15.

John Dewey squarely and repeatedly addresses this same topic. There can be little question that he views his own writing in specific, and philosophy in general, as temporally and spatially located, as a product of, by, and through a definite culture, and as valuable only in terms of its cultural significance and use. In his 1948 introduction to the new edition of *Reconstruction in Philosophy,* Dewey asserts that Reconstruction *of* Philosophy now would be a more appropriate title: "For the intervening events have sharply defined, have brought to a head, the basic postulate of the text: namely, that the distinctive office, problems, and subject matter of philosophy grow out of stresses and strains in the community life in which a given form of philosophy arises, and that, accordingly, its specific problems vary with the changes in human life that are always going on."[18] For Dewey, this intrinsic, irreducible, constitutive connection of a philosophy to its culture, when acknowledged, constitutes a challenge for philosophers:

> There are human difficulties of an urgent deep-seated kind which may be clarified by trained reflection. . . . Philosophy recovers itself when it ceases to be a device for dealing with the problems of philosophers and becomes a method, cultivated by philosophers, for dealing with the problems of men. Emphasis must vary with the stress and special impact of the troubles which perplex men. Each age knows its own ills, and seeks its own remedies. . . . It is easy to be foolish about the connection of thought with national life. But I do not see how any one can question the distinctively national color of English, or French, or German philosophies. . . . I believe that philosophy in America will be lost between chewing a historic cud long since reduced to woody fiber, or an apologetics for lost causes . . . , or a scholastic, schematic formalism, unless it can somehow bring to consciousness America's own needs and its own implicit principle of successful action.[19]

Dewey is adamant that philosophers, at present as much as in the past, function in intrinsic connection to, and through, their cultures. These connections are not bonds that philosophers should seek to break so as to build a philosophy more true, pure, or eternal; rather, these connections define and constitute the context in, and through, which philosophies as definite historical occurrences have meaning and mark changes. Thus Dewey argues that there is no difference between a philosophy and its role in the history of

---

18. John Dewey, "Introduction: Reconstruction as Seen Twenty-Five Years Later," *John Dewey: The Middle Works, 1899–1924*, vol. 12 (Carbondale, Ill.: Southern Illinois University Press, 1982 [1948]), p. 256.
19. John Dewey, "The Need for a Recovery of Philosophy," pp. 46–47.

civilization: "Discover and define the right characteristic and unique function in civilization, and you have defined philosophy itself."[20]

I have sought to show that philosophers of a characteristically American philosophical orientation have understood themselves and their work in relation to a characteristically American culture. They have sought out this culture, rejected beliefs and theory not borne out in it, and grappled continually to reconstruct and ameliorate it. Moreover, I do not think that their vision of an identifiably American experience is an illusion. This leads to my second point concerning the cultural sense of "American philosopher" and "American philosophy." An eye trained on, and accustomed to, the American scene can distinguish originating and defining features of that culture—features that mark the culture as *that* culture. None of these features is the essence of American culture, unique to American culture—just as the characteristic philosophic features of American philosophy are not, any one of them, its essence. Rather, the culture, like the philosophy, is to be characterized by the peculiar, distinctive interrelations of historical events, influences, and environment.

Now, what are these features? I do not aim here to offer a complete list of such characteristics—if such is even possible. I have, moreover, no favorite, pet characteristic to push to the front of any list. Any such list, I am confident, must be a kind of list of lists. It would include, for example, the following (and much more): the observations of de Tocqueville on democracy; Perry Miller's understanding of America as an "errand into the wilderness"; Turner's perspectives on the significance and role of the frontier; the insights of Sanford on the effects of the discrepancies between European culture and the more primitive conditions of early American life; Nash's understanding of the place of wilderness in the American mind; Wills's discussion of the sources and meaning of the ideas expressed in the Declaration of Independence; and accounts of groups traditionally marginalized—from slave narratives and women's diaries of frontier life to the records of broken treaties and violence against Native Americans and waves of new immigrant groups.[21] John J. McDermott's "The American Angle of Vision," a programmatic study, provides considerable insight into the background of the six-

---

20. John Dewey, "Philosophy and Civilization," *John Dewey: The Later Works, 1925–1953*, vol. 3 (Carbondale, Ill.: Southern Illinois University Press, 1984 [1927]), pp. 5–6.

21. Alexis de Tocqueville, *Democracy in America* (New York: Doubleday, 1969 [1835]); Perry Miller, *Errand into the Wilderness* (Cambridge, Mass.: Harvard University Press, 1956); Frederick Jackson Turner, "The Significance of the Frontier in American History," *The Report of the American Historical Association*, 1893; Charles L. Sanford, *The Quest for Paradise—Europe and the American Moral Imagination* (Urbana, Ill.: University of Illinois Press, 1961); Roderick Nash, *Wilderness and the American Mind* (New Haven, Conn.: Yale University Press, 1973); and Gary Wills, *Inventing America* (New York: Doubleday, 1978).

teenth century "triple revolution"—the awareness of a new world (a new continent), the reformation (a new religion), and Copernicanism (a new cosmic order). McDermott focuses on the tension in seventeenth-century America between the reflective tradition carried from Europe and the actual natural and social environment encountered in America—"the press of environment as a decisive formulator of thought about basic structures of the world" that became "the outstanding characteristic of the American temperament." In this context, McDermott points out that "pragmatism, so often regarded as the typical American philosophical product, is but a pale reflection of an ingrained attitude affirming the supremacy of experience over thought."[22] McDermott details the effects of this dominance of experience, of this "press of the environment," in his discussion of a distinctively American view of nature and time. For my present purposes, such analyses and observations of American culture, coupled with American philosophers' own awareness of this culture and its relation to their philosophy, provide an adequate basis for understanding and identifying American philosophy in the cultural sense.

Do American Philosophers Exist?

In light of the above understanding of the national, philosophical, and cultural senses of "American philosopher" and "American philosophy," I now return to my original question: Do American philosophers exist? In the first place, American philosophers, understood in the national sense (as philosophers who happen to be Americans) clearly do exist. Indeed, they exist in record numbers, and Marlin Perkins, Jacques Cousteau, and Euell Gibbons would have no trouble tagging them and following their movements. More pipes are smoked, more out-of-fashion tweed coats are worn, more Polish notation is read, and more applicants apply for proportionately fewer teaching positions. (Perhaps the species has exceeded its carrying capacity.) While this may be of interest to the poll taker, the sociologist, or American Philosophical Association committees on membership, placement, and finance, it is not my concern here.

Still, I do think it is *possible* to argue *plausibly* that American philosophers, considered in the national sense, do *not* exist. Such an argument might parallel James's thinking in his essay, "Does Consciousness Exist?" James, of course, argued that consciousness does not exist as an entity, but does exist as a function—namely, knowing. It is more difficult, however, to give a

---

22. John J. McDermott, "The American Angle of Vision" (New York: Cross Currents, 1966), part II, p. 8.

functional, radical empiricist analysis of the existence of American philosophers than of the existence of consciousness. In the first place, it is not clear
just what function or functions constitute the American philosophers (particularly as distinct from the professor of the history of philosophy). Moreover,
whatever function this may be, there seems to be considerable evidence that
it is largely epiphenomenal and not causally efficacious—that is, it is not a
function at all but only an impotent by-product of culture. While I find this
idea intriguing and plausible, I will not develop this line of thought here.

Understood in the second, philosophical sense, American philosophy is
characterized by its focus on experience, both as a philosophic method and
as the inclusive category of being, on the continuity and unity of belief and
action in this experience, and on the function of purposeful inquiry as directed at the problems of the community. Do philosophers of this characteristic philosophical type exist today? Clearly, such philosophers once did exist.
At one time they thrived—during the so-called Golden Era or classical period, the time of Peirce, James, Royce, Santayana, Mead, and Dewey. It is
also clear, however, that these authors and their philosophical era have passed.
Do such philosophers exist at present?

There are, I am confident, some few philosophers of this distinctively
American philosophical character today. Yet two important qualifications must
be made to this affirmative answer. First, for better or worse, philosophers of
this type clearly do not constitute the majority of philosophers who are
American (by nationality); indeed, they constitute a small minority. For this
reason, reference to "American philosophy" today seems less clear and, perhaps, less useful for philosophical classification than it did in the past. Most
philosophers in America today are not American philosophers (in the second,
philosophical sense detailed above). Second, and more importantly, many of
those philosophers most familiar with and sympathetic to what is characteristically American in philosophy, despite this familiarity and sympathy, are
not, for all that, American philosophers themselves. Their own philosophy,
for better or worse, does not share this American character. Although it is
often classified as "American" in character and tradition, it is often overly
dominated by a kind of parasitic feeding on the past. Instead of American
philosophy, we often receive empty and soporific remembrances of an earlier,
so-called golden period. What is American in philosophy is the *use* of the
method of experience, not the endless cataloging of it independent of the
context of its use, nor the tedious formalization of its results into sacred
categories. What is American is the emphasis on the continuity of belief and
action *in experience,* not the mere assertion of this unity and continuity in
theory alone. What is American in philosophy is the use of inquiry to further
the purposes of individuals through the amelioration of problematic situations, not the mere analysis of the pattern of inquiry, intramural publications

on the nature of the problematic, nor scholarly comparisons of science and common sense. There is, of course, some value to these endeavors, but let us not mistake their nature. Too often, those who admire and strive for what is American in philosophy do a disservice to that philosophy and its native vision by applying their philosophical efforts to philosophy alone, and thus neglecting the larger culture. If American philosophy is to thrive again—or even survive—then it must begin again to contribute to American culture. I conclude, then, that philosophers of a distinctive American philosophical character do exist, but barely, and as an endangered species in the academic wild kingdom. They are fewer in number than is commonly thought. Santayana prophesied that the academy in America would be the death of philosophy, of *living* American philosophy, and this prediction, though not yet fully realized, may still be borne out.

If American philosophers, regarded in this second, *philosophical* sense are rare today, so too are American philosophers of the closely connected third, *cultural* sense. Few philosophers today view the origin, development, and merits of their work in intrinsic connection to American culture or the place of American culture in, and among, other cultures. Indeed, even many authors concerned with American philosophy in the philosophical sense appear deeply opposed to engaging in American philosophy of this third, cultural sort. For example, H. S. Thayer in his well-known *Meaning and Action: A Study of American Pragmatism,* writes that "climate, locale, and national boundaries are utterly irrelevant to philosophic truth" such that "in no ultimate sense is a philosophy typical of a time or a nation:" "Indeed there are mere artifices which, insofar as they affect a philosopher's vision and perhaps his language, are distractions and encumbrances that he is best rid of or made impervious to if possible."[23]

This view, ironically, is now typical of much philosophy in America at present, and affects the undertakings and blurs the vision of much academic philosophy. Whether pursuing truth and certainty in belief, ever-finer analysis of concepts and language, persuasive interpretations of great, dead thinkers, a scientistic ontology or epistemology, or the logically necessary in all possible worlds (in which, apparently, all philosophers are male), current philosophers in America characteristically pay little attention to the connections of their philosophy—its problems, distinction, and methods—to the larger culture. Similarly, they do not weigh the merits of their work by its consequences in that culture. Thus, to continue the example, Thayer thinks *the* dilemma for philosophers in America is how both to (1) remain American

---

23. H. S. Thayer, *Meaning and Action: A Study of American Pragmatism* (Indianapolis and New York: Bobbs-Merrill Company, 1973), pp. 230–31.

and (2) become fully philosophical—that is, culturally unencumbered.[24] Now this may be a dilemma, but it is a dilemma only for those who accept a view of philosophy radically different from that embedded in American philosophy of the third, *cultural* sort outlined above.

While this image of philosophy in America as acultural and, at least at its best, free of time and place, is anything but recent, it does seem closely tied to, and sustained by, the relatively recent compartmentalization, technical direction, and professionalization of philosophy in America. At present, philosophers in America largely have tried to abandon or break free from their cultural ties, as though such ties might vanish if sufficiently unacknowledged. It is clear that today virtually all philosophers in America define themselves and their work within the context of academic philosophy itself: They confront philosophical problems, maneuver philosophical distinctions and language, speak to other philosophers, and measure their success by professional standards. Few professional philosophers today actually take seriously James's remark that a person's vision is vital—or, at least, they do not take seriously that such vision is vital for the philosopher *qua* philosopher. Moreover, a vision shaped almost exclusively within the horizons of a profession is seldom directed at, or returned to, the larger cultural context. This "triumph of professionalism" is skewered by Bruce Wilshire in *The Moral Collapse of the University: Professionalism, Purity, and Alienation*[25] and detailed historically by Bruce Kuklick in *The Rise of American Philosophy*. Kuklick writes that by 1930, American philosophers were unaware or contemptuous of earlier American philosophy that once was important outside the university: "philosophy's successful practitioners were purely professional; they tended to specialize within the technical areas and even those who specialized in the practical lectured only to fellow specialists and did not apply their ideas to the real world; all popularization was suspect."[26] Kuklick concludes that philosophy's nineteenth-century role as the guide to life has been replaced by a philosophy that reflects and demonstrates the irrelevance of speculation to

---

24. Ibid., p. 230. Even those authors who declare that American philosophy is irreducibly culturally situated generally fail to demonstrate, develop, and illuminate these cultural connections and relations. When the claim that philosophy is neither insulated nor isolated from ongoing concrete human activities and culture precedes a discussion removed and remote from those activities and culture, then this claim itself surely is undermined. In this context, see John E. Smith's "Introduction," *Contemporary American Philosophy*, Second Series (New Haven, Conn.: Yale University Press, 1977).

25. Bruce Wilshire, *The Moral Collapse of the University: Professionalism, Purity, and Alienation* (Albany: State University of New York Press, 1990).

26. Bruce Kuklick, *The Rise of American Philosophy* (New Haven, Conn.: Yale University Press, 1977), p. xxiii, 565.

American life. Philosophy, of course, is not alone in all this; other disciplines have become professional, technical, and specialized. While this specialization in the natural sciences, for example, has resulted in products that are usually eagerly awaited and happily consumed by the general public, the products of professional philosophy are seldom demanded by society at large. (Of course, philosophers like to believe that their work *should* be demanded by society, and take comfort in thinking that it is the larger, popular culture that has become irrelevant—to philosophy.) Moreover, the actions of professional philosophers, carried out in a kind of self-imposed, self-deceiving cultural quarantine from society do little to generate such demand. Dewey remarked that the menial, routine character of much modern work had made the mind/body split a reality in the lives of many; the reality of this split today is enforced equally by the current nature of most philosophy in America. Santayana's advice to "lead a life of the mind," as a result, has been not so much ignored as, instead, perverted. When considered from the standpoint of American culture, then, American philosophers are a vanishing breed. The cultural environment or ecology which nurtures them has been overturned.

Should American Philosophers Exist?

I have claimed that philosophers who are characteristically American in both a philosophical and a cultural sense are few, and that American philosophy, accordingly, is seldom advocated and less often undertaken today. While this now may be a matter of profound indifference to the general public, it cannot be so for philosophers. How should philosophers judge this situation? Does the fact that American philosophers largely have abandoned their earlier concern with experience, both as subject-matter and method, and their earlier image of philosophy as intrinsically culturally connected signify progress in philosophy? Has philosophy in America become less naive, more sophisticated, more systematic, and methodologically more sound? Have recent events within the profession, the discipline, or the larger society rendered what is philosophically and culturally American in philosophy outdated, inappropriate, and irrelevant? Or, does philosophy in America need to recapture, recover, and reconstruct what has been characteristically American in its activities?

My view is this: The virtual nonexistence at present of American philosophers in the *philosophical* and *cultural* senses marks a serious failing of, and in, philosophy itself. Attempting "to forward the emancipation of philosophy from too intimate and exclusive attachment to traditional problems," John Dewey locates the recovery of philosophy not in "criticism of various solutions that have been offered" but rather in questioning "the *genuineness, under the present conditions of science and social life, of the problems"* of philosophy.[27] Today, many decades later, philosophy in America stands in even greater need of recovery, revision, and redirection. It must be rescued, in part from attachment to traditional problems, but also from more recent attachment to merely technical problems, acultural analysis, and professional self-compartmentalization. American philosophers must first recognize and then reconstruct their primary connections with their shared, separate, and contested cultures, and in so doing must strive to contribute to these cultures in America. Philosophers in America once again must become American philosophers.

As a beginning, then, this undertaking will necessitate that philosophers in America recognize that the problems, methods, and results of their enterprise are intrinsically connected to, intrinsically situated within, and ultimately assessed by the cultures in, and through, which this enterprise occurs. Why accept this view? I do not think it is possible—and, surely I am not able—to give a logically compelling, non-question begging, transcendental proof of this view—an argument that philosophy, as a human affair, necessarily and universally *must* be constituted by, and in, its cultural relations. While I find this position largely persuasive, I see no way to eliminate the bare logical possibility that philosophy somehow may transcend all cultural peculiarities and connections in understanding them. Instead, I think my view is, and can be, supported only by observing, tracing, and uncovering, case by case, the actual context and primary cultural relations of a particular philosophy. Moreover, such a genealogical undertaking, in each case, will be messy, inexact, and incomplete, for such is the nature of evidence in real inquiry.

While this procedure alone is possible, it is also difficult. It is difficult because the closeness of these cultural relations frequently and largely obscures them. They are those features which shape and guide our thinking—the backgrounds rather than the objects of thought. If Emerson is correct that each age must write its own books, then it must bring to consciousness that in experience which is habitually unconscious and implicit—the vision as well as the particular sights. It may be easier to grasp the cultural connections of a Marxist view of history, a Cartesian conception of certainty, and a Stoic notion of happiness than it is, for example, to discover such connections in our own views of human rights, the nature of mind, the definition of knowledge, the method of analysis, the nature of language, personal identity, and even the laws of logic. But to conclude that what is not seen readily is not present at all is to entertain both self-misunderstanding and a mistaken ideal of philosophy.

---

27. John Dewey, "The Need for a Recovery of Philosophy," p. 4.

This recognition of the cultural ties of philosophy is particularly difficult for us today. Our demand for, and dependence on, intellectual expertise leads to a disciplinary professionalization in which the *disciplinary approach* to a genuine problem becomes, too often and too easily, an approach to a merely *disciplinary problem*. The extensive professionalization of philosophy readily and frequently, but not necessarily, renders philosophers creatures of their discipline and a disciplinary organization of knowledges.[28] The discipline, rather than larger cultural issues and developments, comes to supply the *immediate* context of inquiry. The *ultimate*, cultural context of this inquiry then is easily ignored, and disciplinary inquiry can easily *appear* independent of other cultural forces and factors. Thus, the philosopher must strive in part to trace the workings—at once productive and confining—of philosophy as a discipline, as a profession. Although some individuals may and do succeed in this, I doubt such success can be common and frequent until professional standards are less narrowly disciplinary. Clearly, this is not now the case in professional philosophy in colleges and universities in America.

Still, in light of this recognition of cultural ties and settings, the immediate issue is transformed: The question is *not whether* philosophy in America will or will not be related intrinsically to America's cultures, but rather *what* these relations and connections will and should be. Several options are present. Philosophers in America ultimately may focus on the substantial, pressing, real problems of American individuals and groups—uncertain and changing problems of meaning and value in the lives of persons and societies. Or, philosophers may occupy themselves solely with recording and analyzing their own history, making their methods of inquiry their sole problems and subject-matter, and further refining their stock of technical distinctions, concepts, theories, and logic. Philosophers in America may judge their ultimate success in terms of their contributions to the ongoing amelioration of human problems—the resolution of conflicts, the deepening of meaning, the development of imagination, the expansion of self-understanding, and the actualization of more-inclusive ends. Or, philosophers in America may assess their work by purely formal criteria and purely professional standards. Philosophers in America may locate their procedures in experience, in the dependability of methods of inquiry as evidenced by their consequences in, and for, experience of the beliefs and theories that result from a given method. Or, they may operate by methods that aim to regulate or impose upon experience, methods that yield pronouncements about how things really are or always must be. Finally, philosophers in America may acknowledge, pursue, and reconstruct their relations with American cultures and their global positions—

---

28. See the discussion of alternatives in chapter 3.

relations that ultimately define their problems, methods, and results. Or, they may ignore or strive to overcome their time and place, seeking always the eternal, absolute, and certain, or perhaps, at least, wholly ahistorical and agenetic analysis.

One set of these options largely characterizes philosophy in America today—today when what is considered important among most philosophers is judged, by the larger society, as strikingly insignificant. The other set of options represents what has been characteristically American, philosophically and culturally, in philosophy. What is vital within this latter option is less the specifics of any given view, but more the larger purpose, orientation, and vision with which it is expressed. John Dewey gives voice to this vision:

> Reference to the primacy and ultimacy of the material of ordinary experience protects us, in the first place, from creating artificial problems which deflect the energy and attention of philosophers from the real problems that arise out of actual subject-matter. In the second place, it provides a check or test for the conclusions of philosophic inquiry; it is a constant reminder that we must replace them . . . in the experience out of which they arose, so that they may be confirmed or modified by the new order and clarity they introduce into it, and the new significantly experienced objects for which they furnish a method. In the third place, in seeing how they thus function in further experiences, the philosophical results themselves acquire empirical value; they are what they contribute to the common experience of man, instead of being curiosities to be deposited, with appropriate labels, in a metaphysical museum.[29]

Here, and more generally in all philosophy that is *philosophically* and *culturally* American in character, philosophy regularly and critically addresses the pressing problems of its time and place.

Which set of options should philosophers in America choose today? How can the choice of either set of options be defended? Is it possible to defend an image of philosophy without making use of the methods and criteria of justification of *that* image of philosophy, and so become involved in a circular procedure? The answer here, I think, is that one *cannot* defend a conception of philosophy without utilizing this conception in its own defense. (And, I have utilized such circular procedure here, I recognize.) However, this circularity is not logically vicious; rather it is historical, indicating how our demands on, and for, a philosophy shape and, in turn, are shaped by the resulting philosophy.

---

29. John Dewey, *Experience and Nature, John Dewey: The Later Works, 1925–1953*, vol. 1 (Carbondale, Ill.: Southern Illinois University Press, 1981 [1925]), p. 26.

If, then, the criteria by which we choose to do philosophy in one way rather than another are theory-relative, so too our philosophies are relative to our experience. Since Dewey, most philosophers in America largely have pursued philosophy in a philosophically and culturally non-American manner. Whatever the intramural results may be judged to be, the broadest consequence of this enterprise has been the *trivialization of philosophy in American culture.* The claim that philosophers in America ought to begin, again, to do American philosophy can be, thus, by its own admission, only an untested, yet-unadopted proposal at present. The ultimate value of this proposal and the truth of claims in its defense, must be found in the results of its acceptance and practice.

If we wait much longer, philosophers in America will find themselves *wholly* removed from the wilds of an effective place in their culture, and placed safely in the artificial environment of an academic zoo. There they can be saved from extinction, regularly (if not richly) fed, and observed by school children on brief, required school field trips that are quickly and happily forgotten.

Appendix: Philosophical Visions in America

To ask whether American philosophers exist is to ask, ultimately, about the *philosophical vision, or plural philosophical visions,* of American philosophers. In this light William James observed that "any author is easy if you can catch the centre of his vision."[30] What is the center of vision in American philosophy? Is there one? Are there multiple centers of vision? Are there so many that philosophical vision in America has no center, is de-centered? John E. Smith focuses on this issue in *America's Philosophical Vision*[31] and he thus provides an outstanding case study of visions of American philosophy and culture. For Smith, as for James, a philosophy is not merely a set of affirmations and inferences. Accordingly, we cannot capture a philosophical vision—for example, an American philosophical vision— simply by listing propositions held by its adherents. Distinctive philosophies aren't merely unique sets of doctrines. They're also expressions of *spirit,* something at once more than a set of doctrines (because it is an active stance toward life and world) and something less than a set of doctrines (because it is implicit, unconscious, and unwritten in the life of a people).[32]

---

30. William James, *A Pluralistic Universe, The Works of William James* (Cambridge, Mass.: Harvard University Press, 1977 [1909]), p. 14.
31. John E. Smith, *America's Philosophical Vision* (Chicago: University of Chicago Press, 1992). Hereafter abbreviated *"APV"* in this appendix.
32. John E. Smith, *The Spirit of American Philosophy* (Albany: State University of New York Press, 1983, revised edition), p. 187.

In this light, it is crucial to link a vision of American philosophy to a genealogy of that vision. In the case of Smith's own work, this means it is important to consider the spirit of his own writings. To do this, I focus on three points. In the first place, Smith's vision of American philosophy exhibits remarkable philosophical *pluralism* and *patience*. In this respect, Smith's work embodies the trait of receptivity that he calls a hallmark of American thought: "a broadly empirical outlook on the world,. . . a refusal to be encapsulated in one position while remaining heedless of all others. . . . a genuine concern for understanding what philosophers in other places are saying" (*APV*:196).

Smith's pluralism is everywhere evident. He aims not to demolish, caricature, or belittle views other than his own but rather to deepen understandings, make connections, and reestablish dialogue. Smith's philosophical patience is equally obvious. He turns misconceptions and misfired arguments into opportunities to restate his case: to Marxists and critical theorists who find pragmatism overly subjective, to British thinkers who view American philosophy through Russell and Ayer, and to rationalists who group Royce with Hegel and Blanshard. Philosophical generosity may never come easy, but it usually comes easier to those who can most afford it. This is what makes Smith's pluralism and patience so remarkable: he exhibits them during a virtual blackout of American philosophy, a time when American philosophy lies in the shadows of mainstream philosophy. As a result, Smith's philosophical "night vision" deserves much credit for whatever new light now shines through philosophy in America.

In the second place, Smith's successful efforts to help us see in the dark are permeated by a drive for *philosophical recovery*: this means philosophy must not continue with business as usual. The linguistic turn in modern philosophy, like the earlier but similar reflexive turn that marked the start of modern or critical philosophy, has produced no metaphilosophical certainty. Instead, it has yielded the techniques and problems of professional philosophers—who thus are understandably preoccupied with their own "occupational therapy." This therapy, I suspect Smith would agree, has not been effective: Most analytic philosophers are stuck in a state of denial, refusing to recognize the "pragmatic outcome" internal to the development of their linguistic philosophy.

Fortunately, this pragmatism doesn't need to be invented. It needs to be recovered—and the spirit of Smith's book is the melioristic spirit of the possibility of this recovery. For Smith, the philosophies of Peirce, James, Royce, and Dewey are resources for an American renaissance. They await attention, development, and use—not because they can help us do anything as unimportant, *pace* Rorty, as "overcome the tradition," but because they can help us critically clarify, investigate, and realize our ideals: "There is at present a need to focus the vision that motivated these thinkers as a way of presenting the experience of America to those across the world and of bringing to those at home a new self-consciousness of what America is and means" (*APV*:1).

In the third place, Smith's efforts to recover classical American philosophy point to an ambivalence or *dialectical emphasis on the priority of the future*. I realize that it may seem inattentive to characterize the spirit of Smith's philosophy in this way. After all, he begins by saying that American philosophy insists on the reality of time, change, and novelty, and he places great emphasis on the reality of time and the significance of the future. Moreover, he concludes by identifying attention to time and change as a defining trait and predominant fact of American thought. However, I'm not claiming that Smith is ambivalent about the centrality of time, change, and the future in classical American philosophy. Instead, I'm claiming that *his* writings express a dialectical stance toward the future—and toward philosophical traditions. Consider this: Smith says, rightly, that America "has always stressed the promise of the future over the significance of the past" (*APV*:3). Now, to the extent that Smith endorses this native vision, he too stresses the primacy and promise of the future. But, to the extent that he pursues this vision in the spirit of philosophical recovery, he equally emphasizes the past. His announced aim points us back to the future, but his actual strategy directs us forward to the past: "Back to the sources," he urges in effect. This alternating emphasis is most evident in Smith's praise of the classical American philosophers. He writes that they faced forward, engaged in novel undertakings, made original responses to problems, thought independently, and set forth new standards and ideals.

Today, how are we to recover this bold creativity through a recovery of their philosophy? Just what is it that we are to recover?

If we simply become pragmatists in theory—writing and reading about classical American philosophers, affirming the significance of the past, and, in Emerson's view, growing up in libraries—then are we really pragmatists in practice and spirit? But, if we become pragmatists in practice—confronting current problems and articulating new ideals, stressing the promise of the future, and, following Emerson, writing our own books for our own age—do we really remain pragmatists in theory and doctrine?

The spirit of Smith's essays calls forth these questions while forcing us to reject the simplistic options they present and the dichotomies they presuppose. Smith directs us to recapture American philosophy's spirit, not to repeat its doctrine. He thus calls our attention to the future by means of the past, and the dialectical spirit of his work serves both a community of hope and a community of memory. Still, I find that this very spirit must produce some anxiety and fear of inauthenticity in those who have learned from Smith.

This, of course, is no criticism of Smith's work, though it may be a criticism of the consequences that others draw from it. When we—myself included—write and speak to each other more about our vision of classical American philosophy than about our vision of our future and our culture, are we really carrying forward America's philosophical vision or are we just lowering our sights?

To the extent that Smith addresses this issue, he focuses his vision on *continuities and unities*. He emphasizes what is similar and shared by American philosophers, not what is different and disputed. He is concerned with a common American philosophical vision instead of multiple or competing ones. He seeks thematic hallmarks, and identifies American philosophy as a distinctive philosophy in terms of these shared hallmarks.

This approach supports a conception of philosophy more as spirit than as doctrine. The principal virtue of this approach is that it yields a lively overview or big picture of American philosophy. Of course, to set forth a big picture of American philosophy might appear to beg the question: Is there a big picture at all—or only many smaller pictures and peripheral visions? How many and large differences can a single philosophical vision encompass without becoming double vision or multivision?

While there may be little reason to take seriously this question in the abstract, it does have a more immediate and concrete relevance to Smith's project. This relevance is displayed in Smith's very different treatments of Royce and Santayana. For Smith, Royce occupies a central position in American philosophy and Royce receives more attention than any other thinker. By contrast, Smith excludes Santayana from the American philosophical tradition, referring to him only twice in passing (once more than to Mead!), and stating in an earlier book that the "American mind, in short, has been everything but what Santayana was and stood for."[33] While I disagree with this view of Santayana, my point here is not that Santayana is just as pragmatic as Royce, or even that American philosophers should be as receptive to Santayana as they are to Royce. Instead, it is the straightforward pragmatic point that any theory of America's philosophical vision is the product or construct of particular selective interests—and, in turn, serves particular interests.

Smith's big picture of American philosophy is rooted in his particular interests and purposes. While more might profitably be said about these purposes, their genealogy, and their effects—particularly their political and social consequences—Smith's approach is especially valuable and undeniably effective in just the sort of patient exchanges that he cultivates between American philosophy and other traditions. It may be less valuable in disputes and discussions among philosophers who largely share an American philo-

---

33. Ibid., p. xiii.

sophical vision. In any case, to raise this issue is to insist that Smith's interest in American philosophy is a characteristically American philosophical interest: It is an interest in "something other than knowing it from a theoretical standpoint" (*APV*:206).

As Smith explains, American philosophy is fundamentally concerned not simply with truth but with relevance: "Running throughout American thought . . . has been a persistent belief that thought must have an orientation in terms of purposes which serve as principles of selection for relevance." In addition to "the purely theoretical purpose of mirroring the entire universe in thought," does it address "the difference which thought and knowledge make in human life" (*APV*:205–7)? It is fitting to confront *America's Philosophical Vision* with this aspect of America's philosophical vision. Is Smith's book relevant and practical? Moreover, is American philosophy relevant and practical?

Relevance is a relation, not a property: To ask if Smith's book or American philosophy is relevant is not to ask if the book or the philosophy contains some supposed property of relevance; instead, it is to ask if the book or the philosophy meets particular purposes of particular people in particular ways. What matters is not the abstract wonder—Is Smith's vision of American philosophy relevant, or is a characteristically American philosophical vision of American philosophy relevant?—but more concrete matters—How and for whom is it relevant? In other words: Whose vision? What relevance?

Whose philosophical vision, then, is set forth in *America's Philosophical Vision* or in any other account of the vision of pragmatism or American philosophy more generally? Who is included or represented? In what ways is power exercised? Who is excluded, marginalized, or rendered as other or less than distinctively American? The answer seems clear: Smith seeks to articulate the philosophical vision of (some of) "our classical American philosophers"—Peirce, James, Royce, and Dewey. In this light, it may seem that Smith is concerned less with *America's* philosophical vision and more with the philosophical vision of a *particular handful of Americans.* Despite the volume's title—it is not, for example, "A Vision of Some American Philosophers"—Smith seems to suggest as much. He claims that the classical development of American philosophy had run its course by 1940 and been succeeded by many new interests, positions and approaches. He continues that it is impossible to view American philosophy as representing one substantive position or tradition. And, he concludes that the only way to do justice to our complex and pluralistic philosophical situation is to speak of "philosophy in America" rather than "*an* American philosophy."

Still, even for those who do not demand a neat solution to problems about the meaning of "American philosophy," this is a little unsettling and puzzling. First, what Smith *does not* say is unsettling: He does not argue that some philosophies in America are more philosophically American than others because they are more characteristic and expressive of American *life and culture*. But surely this is the sort of evidence that is needed, for example, if we are to view Royce as an American philosopher in a way in which Santayana is not, or Dewey as an American philosopher in a way in which Quine is not. Second, what Smith *does* say is a bit puzzling: If our philosophical situation, like our culture, is complex and pluralistic, then shouldn't we speak of plural philosophies in America and plural American philosophical spirits instead of "philosophy in America" or *an* American philosophical spirit? If so, can a given vision of philosophy present "the experience of America" or, instead, only the particular experience*s* of some particular Americans?

These questions have large social significance in America for concerns about representation, diversity, multiculturalism, and the politics of recognition.[34] These questions also have central intellectual importance for the relevance of a philosophy. First, they remind us that the demand for practical relevance in philosophy is a demand rooted in a particular philosophical spirit. As a result, it is hardly surprising to find that the philosophy that best meets this demand is the very philosophy that most fully expresses the philosophical spirit that gives rise to the demand.

Second, these questions remind us that there is a difference between relevance in theory and relevance in practice—"between our theoretical knowledge on the one side and the human purposes which should determine what items among that knowledge are relevant for these purposes and how that knowledge should be used" (*APV*:207). In this vein, Smith faults many philosophers for their "internalized tendency"—"the discussion by philosophers almost exclusively of what other philosophers have said or written." However, this largely is what Smith does: his essays address almost exclusively what other philosophers have said or written. In this context, there is little doubt that American philosophers exist in theory. But there also can be little doubt that the spirit of American philosophy must point philosophers toward existence in practice (and not just the practice of theory). Of course, this sort of existence cannot be demonstrated by any philosophical vision in advance of action on its behalf. Smith's book, like this book or any other book, cannot perform that action for us. But it does enable philosophers to undertake that action more intelligently. In doing so, philosophers in America may uncover and recover their own plural existences.[35]

---

34. See the discussions of identity, difference, and community in chapters 5 and 13.

35. An earlier version of portions of this essay appeared in "Do American Philosophers Exist? Thoughts on American Philosophy and Culture," *Annals of Scholarship: Metastudies of the Humanities and Social Sciences* 2.4 (1981): 65–84, followed by comments by John Wilson and Barbara Cowell, by John E. Smith, and by my reply. An earlier version of portions of the appendix appeared in "Philosophical Night Vision," *Transactions of the Charles S. Peirce Society*, 31.1 (1995): 1–10. These revised passages appear here with the kind permission of the editors and the publishers.

3

Re-Visioning Philosophy and the Organization of Knowledges

There is little life in most professional philosophy today.

Most professional philosophers, of course, strongly reject this judgment. After all, their lives are busy and the demands of their profession are large. Some are occupied earnestly with perennial philosophical problems and historical traditions. Others are occupied fashionably with new technical developments and the latest exchanges in the journals. And still others are occupied, less obliviously but no less conservatively, with pronouncements of the death of philosophy and announcements of the birth of post-philosophy.

Despite these different denials of near-death, philosophy now exists in limbo, alive but comatose. Largely withdrawn and isolated from a significant place in social life, academic philosophy (like theory in the humanities and human sciences more broadly) is sustained by an elaborate life-support system of professional practices, institutions, sanctions, and exclusions. For philosophers, the situation is precarious, all-time high membership in the American Philosophical Association notwithstanding. Santayana was right to worry that the academy might be the death of philosophy.

Still, dominant professional practices, problems, and paradigms are increasingly scrutinized and criticized today, as the arrival of recent conferences, publications, professional societies, and institutional reorganizations and arrangements make evident. Though the possibility of their containment and failure is high, these activities provide a real basis for hope for genuinely new directions. Their common premise is the claim that philosophy today must be re-visioned.

I

In formulating any philosophy, the first consideration must always be: What can we know? That is, what can we be sure we know, or sure that we know we knew it, if indeed it is at all knowable. Or have we simply forgotten it and are too embarrassed to say anything? . . . By "knowable," incidentally,

45

> I do not mean that which can be known by perception of the senses, or that
> which can be grasped by the mind, but more that which can be said to be
> Known or to possess a Knownness or Knowability, or at least something
> you can mention to a friend.
>
> —Woody Allen, *Getting Even*

As Woody Allen's "Critique of Pure Dread" may suggest, the need to re-vision philosophy is a serious matter. And, it is something that, as a beginning, philosophers (and humanists) all can know.

II

> The sort of thing the philosophers of an earlier period did is now done; in
> substance it is no longer called for. Persistence in repetition of a work that
> has little or no significance in the life-conditions (including those of physical
> science) that now exist is as sure a way as could be found for promoting
> the remoteness of philosophy from human concerns which is already tend-
> ing to alienate popular regard and esteem by reducing philosophy to a kind
> of highly professionalized busy work. In the meantime, there is a kind of
> intellectual work to be done which it is of utmost importance to mankind
> to have done, but which from the general human point of view does not
> need to be done in the name of philosophy provided only that it be done.
> From the standpoint of philosophy, that is philosophers, it may not be a
> matter of life and death but it is a matter of self-respect as well as of
> popular esteem.
>
> —John Dewey, *John Dewey Papers*

John Dewey's words are prophetic: The practice of philosophy today needs fundamental and far-reaching change. This is true not only for philosophy but for the humanities and social "sciences" as well. And it is true for a wide range of related social practices. Effective efforts to re-vision philosophy must refuse to treat it in either an intellectual or a cultural vacuum.

I will not argue extensively here for the claim that philosophy needs radical redirection. Instead, I am interested in sketching some of the implications of this claim. However, evidence of its truth is virtually omnipresent and unavoidable:

> — From popular bookstores that marginalize philosophy and identify it with
>   books on self-discovery trends, UFOs, the supernatural, how to develop
>   telekinetic powers at home in your free time, macrobiotic diets, Japanese

business theories, New Age "insights," and death as a final stage of growth;

— To public discourse and popular imagination that ignore philosophy, treating it as ancient, lifeless, trivial, endless, abstract, far less useful than technology, the sciences, and business, and far less enjoyable than *Psychology Today*, Pearl Jam, or "Wheel of Fortune";

— To colleges and universities where philosophy too often is little more than an insignificant, incoherent humanities distribution requirement for the many and an idle, culturally private language for the few;

— To philosophers themselves, who, as professional philosophers at least, typically work in the virtual self-quarantine of narrowly disciplinary problems created and sustained by institutionalized academic practices, sanctions, purifications, and exclusions.

At this point, I simply (but confidently) will rely on common experience to further multiply such instances beyond necessity.

Philosophy must be changed. As a consequence, this means that several important issues must be addressed. These questions include:

— What changes are needed in philosophy?

— What changes are actually possible at this time?

— How might these changes be accomplished?

— Who can or should make such changes?

These questions are practical, although philosophers often render them wholly theoretical. They require strenuous exercise of will as well as intellect. And, they demand action and cultural reconstruction rather than mere philosophical and literary conversation, ironic understanding, and academic solidarity.

III

If you wish to replace an official institution by another institution that fulfills the same function—better and differently—then you are already being absorbed by the dominant structure.

—Michel Foucault, *Language, Canter-Memory, Practice*

Philosophy today, Foucault argues, must be an effort that thought brings to bear on itself in an endeavor to know how it might be possible to think and live differently. To re-vision philosophy must be to see and make philosophy different, and not simply better. Thus, in the first place, needed change in philosophy today is not ultimately a matter of conceptual fine-tuning and more careful logical argument. What is needed, eventually and most centrally, is not:

— Solutions to the general problem of Being, the general problem of induction, or the general problem of other minds (which should be distinguished carefully from important specific problems concerning specific other minds);

— A merely theoretical reconciliation or conversational meeting of the minds of phenomenologists, analysts, critical theorists, pragmatists, and poststructuralists (and anyone else so fortunate as to be without professional label);

— New, improved (and not a minute too soon), universally sound proofs for the existence of God, consciousness, natural rights, ideal speech conditions, or the end of philosophy;

— Or, new logics for grasping conceptually possible worlds—sirens that beckon thinkers who find the one real world insufficiently interesting, challenging, engaging, and problematic.

In the second place, a different and re-visioned philosophy would not aim only to become, by current professional standards, merely more efficient, effective, or professional. The sort of thing ultimately needed in philosophy today is not:

— More specialists' conferences, societies, journal publications, and, I hesitate to add, books, all celebrated, endured, envied, and later exchanged into academic capital to be summarized in resumés;

— Larger and narrower research requirements, measured quantitatively and objectively, for graduate work, academic employment, renewal, tenure, and, perhaps, death with appropriate academic honor;

— Philosophy (understood here as an occupation rather than a way of living) that uncritically accepts, participates in, and legitimizes institutional arrangements that obscure public service, minimize community involvement, and weaken teaching, advising, nurturing, and mentoring;

— Or, more brilliant, bright stars (and their higher pay, prestige, and pride) in an infinitely expanding (if rapidly cooling) professional galaxy of philosophers.

Instead, change in philosophy today must be more radical, basic, and subversive. Today, philosophy's major lack is neither too little logic nor too little professionalism, neither too few answers nor too little industry Instead, there is too little vision.

IV

> The moral (or immoral) intentions in every philosophy constituted the real germ of life from which the whole plant had grown. . . . What is essential and inestimable in every morality is that it constitutes a long compulsion.
>
> —Friedrich Nietzsche, *Beyond Good and Evil*

Nietzsche may be right that each philosophy inescapably makes the world in its own image, but to re-vision philosophy must not be merely to substitute one undiagnosed myopia for another. Accordingly, the above remarks are not meant as a preface to a different (but new) set of marching orders or a different (but new) set of strategies for glimpsing reality, seeing the truth, or mastering language, nature, and other persons.

Efforts to genuinely re-vision philosophy are distinct from enterprises aimed at finally revealing the so-called "nature of philosophy" to the clear-eyed and clear-minded (who usually are simply the like-minded). Rather, to re-vision philosophy is to reject the assumption that philosophy has some one nature, waiting ready-made, self-identical, and transparent to a discovering gaze and mirroring representation. I see every reason to believe that philosophy itself is and should be as wide, pluralistic, incomplete, and messy as actual experiences, environments, cultures, and lives. A re-vision must be an affair of multiple re-vision*s*; and philosophy must be an affair of multiple, philosoph*ies*. As Margaret Fuller wrote in *The Dial*:

> Let us be wise and not impede the soul. Let her work as she will. Let us have one creative energy, one incessant revelation. Let it take what form it will, and let us not bind it by the past to man or woman, black or white.[1]

These philosophies must be critical and these visions must be engaged. Philosophy no longer can afford to look lazily where the light is best, or proclaim earnestly a theory of illumination. Instead, like successful literature, a re-visioned philosophy must help us see in the dark.

---

1. Margaret Fuller, "The Great Lawsuit: Man vs. Men, Woman vs. Women," *Selected Writings of the American Transcendentalists*, ed. George Hochfield (New York: New American Library, 1966 [1843]), p. 364.

V

> If we take the whole history of philosophy, the systems reduce to a few main types which, under all the technical verbiage in which the ingenious intellect of man envelopes them, are just so many visions, modes of feeling the whole push, and seeing the whole drift of life forced on one by one's total character and experience, and on the whole *preferred*—there is no other truthful word—as one's best working attitude.
>
> —William James, *A Pluralistic Universe*

James is right: Life is one thing and knowledge about life is another, and philosophy requires direct relations with life instead of "shop tradition" and dreary techniques alone.

In that spirit, I want to offer two initial suggestions about the need to re-vision philosophy. First, in beginning to re-vision philosophy, let us abandon (or reconstruct) sight or vision itself as the primary metaphor or discourse for change. Here I forego a lengthy and familiar survey of much of the history of philosophy as a history of: the visible; the eye; the microscope and telescope; the look; the gaze; the mirror; the detached observer; the unsoiled cultural voyeur and his (for it was his and not her) perceptions, sense data, given, "being appeared to," and "seeming to see"; and, of course, knowledge and objects of knowledge, the subjective knower and the objective known. Do you see what I mean? A different philosophy (or its self image) might successfully take as its starting point: not the eye but the whole body; not sight but all touch, contact, and motion; not the window of consciousness but the embodied mind. Visionary, clean, and unpolluted philosophical efforts to disprove the existence of the body by systematically ignoring it have not escaped contamination through abstraction. Do you feel what this means? Today, a thoroughly re-visioned, revived, full-bodied philosophy must be a kinesthetic philosophy. Such a philosophy must embody and must retrieve body, culture, and myth.

Second, let us look beyond philosophy in order to re-vision it. Efforts to re-vision philosophy ultimately must be efforts to re-vision living culture by means of philosophy. This is not an easy task today, for in philosophy "what were once vices are now habits." Philosophy now suffers chronically (if not also malignantly) from largely self-induced myopia: "Philosophical" problems, ponderings, and pronouncements now have only an incidental and irregular contact with larger, less antiseptic cultural issues, inquiry, and communication. From a cultural perspective, philosophy today is isolated and insignificant. This is a significant fact for philosophers, however, since today to be isolated or disenfranchised culturally is to have one's destiny controlled by others. And, it is a more significant fact for nonphilosophers, since today to be deprived of the fruits of broad reflection, critical inquiry, and self-examination is to lead a manipulated and malnourished life, no matter how thoroughly or frequently gross national products are consumed, produced, and reproduced.

VI

—As for us
We must uncenter our minds from ourselves;
We must unhumanize our views a little, and become confident
As the rock and ocean that we were made from.

—Robinson Jeffers, "Carmel Point," *Selected Poetry*

We have been, Jeffers warns, a little too abstract and a little too wise, and more than a little too self-contained. To re-vision, to become different, is to ask what historically possible changes in philosophy could allow it more effectively to contribute to the amelioration of cultural difficulties and human problems. And, it also must be to ask how and by whom such changes could be effected.

Responses to these questions constitute prescriptions. A re-visioned philosophy must have the courage to make such prescriptions and, above all, to act on them. Prescriptions, of course, presuppose diagnoses. To make a diagnosis in this case is to raise further issues:

— From exactly what is philosophy suffering?

— Can both symptoms and causes be identified and distinguished at this time?

— How might this be done, particularly from a position itself within philosophy?

— By whom and in the service of what interests might this diagnosis be made?

However, do these issues direct philosophy once more toward a seemingly infinite regress of abstraction—a regress from the need for prescriptions for change, to the need for diagnoses of conditions that need change, to (perhaps) the need for examinations of the truth conditions of such diagnoses, and so on? Any such necessary abstractions must be connected to the immediate, concrete, and political issues from which they arise and which they, in turn, partially preform.

But, abstract or not, re-visioning philosophy must be less a matter of proof and more a matter of collecting observations, making and remaking proposals, piecemeal resistance, and reconstructive action.

VII

i would not want t be bach. mozart. tolstoy. joe hill. gertrude stein or
james dean
they are all dead. the Great books've been written. the Great sayings
have all been said
I am about t sketch You a picture of what goes on around here
sometimes. tho i don't understand too well myself what's really
happening. i do know that we're all gonna die someday an that
no death has ever stopped the world.

—Bob Dylan, *The Words and Music of Bob Dylan*

You don't need a weatherman to know which way the wind blows,
Dylan sang. This much is evident: In philosophy today, new winds of change
are replacing older, often stagnant, winds of doctrine. These fresh changes in
philosophical theory are all for the good, I think, though many non-Dylanesque
philosophers now await—or, worse yet, hope to be—famous forecasters. These
reconstructions or changes with*in* the practices of philosophy must be extended to reconstructions or changes *of* the practices of philosophy. Accordingly, I want to suggest that a re-visioned philosophy must include at least the
following.

First, *pluralism*, increasingly a trait of the formal organizational structure of professional philosophy, *must be internalized*. The immensely valuable pluralism of professional associations and programs remains too much
a pluralism of representation, too largely a pluralism by partition, too frequently a pluralism of indifferent specialists, too often mere plurality. We all
know that, for example, attendance at professional meetings, attendance at
particular sessions at those meetings, voting for office holders and policies,
and membership in more specialized professional societies tend to follow
philosophical party lines. This means that pluralism in philosophy (and, again,
the humanities more generally) is more formal than real. This "separate but
equal" diversity has benefits, of course, but it also has drawbacks. Professional pressures tend naturally and powerfully toward specialization, and a
re-visioned philosophy must include institutionalization of counterforces to
these pressures.

Second, philosophers long concerned with achieving the unity of theory
and practice in their philosophies *must make at least an equal effort to combine theory and practice in their lives*. This means that critical theory and
practice must be joined not simply in theories but also in practices. Put
simply, whatever they preach, philosophers must practice it. As Santayana put
it, philosophy must be "honest." If philosophies do not evidently inform,
enrich, expand, deepen, and pervade the lives of individual philosophers,

there is every reason for the larger culture to view philosophy as an idle game, rigorous self-deception, or just another way to make a living. (This certainly does not mean that all—or any!—philosophy must become what now is called "applied philosophy." It does mean that philosophy must be a matter of how one lives and not simply how one thinks or collects a salary.) Philosophers, myself included, who wish to revision philosophy must look long and hard at themselves—not simply as philosophers or *homo academicus* but also and more fundamentally as persons.[2]

Third, philosophical inquiry *must become more fully and regularly cross-disciplinary and cross-professional.* John Dewey, for example, noted this long ago in distinguishing the problems of philosophy from the problems of men and women, and argued that the division of social knowledge into isolated and insulated branches of learning is a measure of their backwardness and their aloofness from the physical sciences. There is little need to argue this point, for we all are aware of the intellectual divisions and subdivisions of knowledges. We are all aware of the extraordinary efforts and resources philosophers waste trying to protect philosophy and its borders, trying to keep philosophy tidy and pure, and seeking to dismiss differing perspectives simply because they are not "philosophical." And, finally, in spite of ourselves, we all are aware of the intellectual and personal narrowness this produces. Obviously, life is cross-disciplinary and, accordingly, inquiry also should be.

VIII

You are not big enough to accuse the whole age effectively, but let us say you are in dissent. You are in no position to issue commands, but you can speak words of hope. Shall this be the substance of your message? Be human in this most inhuman of ages. . . . But I warn you, do not expect to make many friends. As for the Unspeakable—his implacable presence will not be disturbed by a little fellow like you.

—Thomas Merton, *Raids on the Unspeakable*

Having said this at the outset of *Raids on the Unspeakable*, Thomas Merton nonetheless does conclude with words of hope. His advice to poets, though missing from lists of required reading for virtually all philosophy and literature courses today, remains insightful and timely. It bears repetition at some length, particularly to philosophers:

---

2. Pierre Bourdieu, *Homo Academicus* (Stanford, Calif.: Stanford University Press, 1988).

Collective life is often organized on the basis of cunning, doubt, and guilt. True solidarity is destroyed by the political art of pitting one man against another and the commercial art of estimating all men at a price. On these illusory measurements men build a world of arbitrary values without life and meaning, full of sterile agitation. To set one man against another, one life against another, one work against another, and to express the measurement in terms of cost or of economic privilege and moral honor is to infect everybody with the deepest metaphysical doubt. Divided and set up against one another for the purpose of evaluation, men immediately acquire the mentality of objects for sale in a slave market. They despair of themselves because they know they have been unfaithful to life and to being, and they no longer find anyone to forgive the infidelity.

Yet their despair condemns them to further infidelity: alienated from their own spiritual roots, they contrive to break, to humiliate and to destroy the spirit of others. In such a situation there is no joy, only rage.

We stand together to denounce the shame and the imposture of all such calculations.

If we are to remain united against these falsehoods, against all power that poisons man, and subjects him to the mystifications of bureaucracy, commerce and the police state, we must refuse the price tag. We must refuse academic classification. We must reject the seductions of publicity. We must not allow ourselves to be pitted one against another in mystical comparisons—political, literary or cultural orthodoxies. We must not be made to devour and dismember one another for the amusement of their press . . .

Let us remain outside "their" categories.[3]

This raises a critical issue: In light of philosophers' widespread recognition of the artificiality and the drawbacks of the separation and insulation of branches of human and social learning from one another, why then do they continue so often to act so as to sustain and reinforce this separation and insulation? In part this question is historical: it seeks the conditions which gave rise to several mutually isolated branches of teaching, research, and professional institutions and practices. In part the question is moral and political: it asks what interests are served, who is excluded, what is produced, and who and what are legitimized. And, in part it is psychological: it concerns individual motives in the face of this apparent weakness of will. Failure to address these questions in practice renders most philosophical discussions about the cross-disciplinary character of philosophy impotent. This failure also renders most

---

3. Thomas Merton, *Raids on the Unspeakable* (New York: New Directions, 1965) [1964], pp. 157–58.

academic discussions of community ironic. Until philosophers and other humanists at least begin to change their own practices of inquiry and the institutions in, and through, which this inquiry is conducted, it seems unlikely that their inquiry will contribute to the creation of community.

As a result, in the fourth place, re-visioning philosophy *must involve subversion of existing disciplinary formations of knowledges and existing departmental formations of administration.* Though many, these changes would include: undermining existing departmental divisions of instruction, research, budgets, and faculty appointments within colleges and universities; unsettling entrenched disciplinary and so-called interdisciplinary (as opposed to counter-disciplinary) divisions and structures of knowledge maintained, for example, by learned organizations and societies, conferences, journals, and other forums; and undermining existing professional systems of sanctions, recognitions, rewards, incentives, and exclusions (and their underlying assumption of individual accomplishment and preference for the production of scholarly texts).

Fifth, this means that a re-visioned philosophy *must involve rethinking and restructuring the meaning and practice of professionalism in philosophy.* It is clear that the practices, institutions, and sanctions that constitute professionalism in philosophy (and, once more, the humanities more generally) today only seldom contribute substantially and by design to the production of important new knowledge or the transmission of these critical insights to the public. This is not to suggest that philosophy must become "unprofessional," but only that it must be professional in a different and more self-reflective, self-critical, and self-regenerative manner. Indeed, given philosophy's traditional concern with self-knowledge, philosophers' overwhelming lack of attention to, and acceptance of, the professional and institutional contexts of their own work is striking. Ultimately, effective efforts to address these issues must involve nothing less than a rethinking of the nature and goals of education in our culture and the place of philosophy in that education. This is not to suggest that philosophers have all the answers needed to open the supposedly closed-up American mind (or checkbook), but only that current realities make philosophers' considerable silence and inaction on these professional and public issues irresponsible.

This means that philosophy must address and reach a broader audience. Again, John Dewey made this point in discussing the necessary conditions for the formation of a genuine public and the transformation of a great society into a great community: Scholarly books and technical journals alone are an inadequate means of public communication of the results of social inquiry. Effective communication is as important for the creation and education of the public as effective inquiry. Effective communication in turn requires dissemination. The mode of presentation is decisive in dissemination (and hence successful communication). We all know learned, informed, even ground-breaking thinkers who cannot communicate to others—or, at least, to certain others. On the other side, we all know "great communicators" with nothing to say.

Granted this point, again a different, more difficult issue arises: In light of this recognition of the importance of presentation for communication and dissemination, why do most philosophers (including popular teachers) continue to present the results of their inquiries almost exclusively in ways that address a very small and specialized audience, receiving little attention, much less understanding, and virtually no social reaction? As suggested above, this issue raises important questions that are historical, political, and psychological.

No matter how these questions are answered, however, they point to the need for change now. Without such change, philosophers in practice have only inadequate ways to communicate what they have to say. Accordingly, in the sixth place, if a re-visioned philosophy is to be a genuinely public philosophy, and if philosophers are to be public educators, then philosophy *must develop an effective public voice*. It must invent and utilize new, more effective forms of communication. This task is both re-creative and subversive. It would require that philosophers: address different, broader audiences; invent, utilize, and sanction different media to do so; and, seek to dislodge and empower rather than merely to prove and disprove. This does not mean, of course: that all philosophers must rush to imitate Oprah Winfrey, Phil Donahue, Howard Stern, or Beavis and Butthead; that philosophy journals must become more like *USA Today* or *People*; or that philosophers should form a philosophy television network—*PTV*—modeled on the popular *MTV*. It does mean that philosophers must take more and different steps to ensure that they do not talk *always and only* to themselves. At this point, the potential for public dissemination of the results of philosophical scholarship through television, videos, tapes, community meetings, the internet, special events, magazines, and newspapers are still largely professionally unimportant and, so, largely unexplored.

Seventh and finally, if philosophy can begin to do this, then it may contribute to bridging the gaps between school and the so-called "real world," between the popular and the intellectual, and, more generally, between social theory and practice. Re-visioning philosophy *must involve reforming social institutions*. In the face of increasing environmental degradation, a widening gap between rich and poor, unaccountability within complex organizations, continuing international tensions and religious wars, and personal lives dominated by aimless routine, mere entertainment, and what poet Robert Penn Warren in *Democracy and Poetry* called "self de-creation,"[4] philosophy must

---

4. Robert Penn Warren, *Democracy and Poetry* (Cambridge, Mass.: Harvard University Press, 1975).

not continue *simply to talk* about (respectively) the unity of experience and nature, the social contract and social equality, moral autonomy and personal authenticity, the unity of humankind, and self-fulfillment. To do so (whether from a utopian or positivistic angle) is to send a clear, bright message to even the most supposedly dim students and citizens that philosophy is one thing and social reality is something else. And to do so is to fail to realize the significant (if limited) critical and transformative potential of philosophy.

A re-visioned philosophy must not allow itself to become absorbed by its culture—no matter how safe, comfortable, or "professional" this may be. Philosophers who engage in re-visioning philosophy must not allow themselves to fail, in William Carlos Williams's words, "to embody knowledge," to be responsible persons as well as responsible philosophers.[5] To do this is to struggle. As Frederick Douglass pointed out: "Power concedes nothing without demand. It never did and it never will."[6] Human beings live as humans, John Dewey wrote, only in the imagination. Now it is time that philosophers do so as well.

Appendix: Re-Visioning the Organization of Knowledge

Any effort to re-vision philosophy, of course, takes place in an institutional context—or, rather, many different institutional contexts. American colleges and universities, for example, have different missions, self-understandings, available resources, and administrations. At almost all these institutions, however, the intellectual vision and organization of knowledge is *disciplinary*. Correspondingly, the administrative organization of these disciplinary knowledges is *departmental*.

Typically, knowledge is divided into, and constituted by, specific intellectual disciplines (such as philosophy, literature, history, religion, studies of languages, and so on). These disciplines, the primary units of intellectual organization, may be grouped together to form larger intellectual divisions (such as the humanities, sciences, social sciences, and arts). And, they may be subdivided into fields of specialization (such as epistemology, metaphysics, logic, ethics, aesthetics, and so on). These disciplines (and their combinations and subdivisions) are so common and so fixed today that they readily

---

5. William Carlos Williams, *The Embodiment of Knowledge* (New York: New Directions, 1974 [1928]).
6. Frederick Douglass, cited in *Philosophy Born of Struggle,* ed. Leonard Harris (Dubuque: Kendall/Hunt, 1983 [1857]), p. v.

appear to be ahistorical "natural kinds." Even "interdisciplinary" teaching
and research that appear to unify, cut across, or in other ways violate this
disciplinary organization usually merely utilize, reinforce, and further legitimize this disciplinary organization by assuming, and proceeding from, the
intellectual primacy of disciplines.[7]

This disciplinary organization of knowledge is not, of course, "natural."
It does not reflect an independent reality; rather, it manufactures a reality.
Disciplinary organization produces, distributes, and enforces disciplinary
knowledges and their objects.

This intellectual organization and creation of knowledges by, and into,
disciplines most frequently is mirrored by an administrative organization of
knowledge by, and into, departments. Almost every college and university offers
courses and appoints faculty in departments that correspond to intellectual disciplines. That portion of knowledge that falls into the discipline of philosophy,
for instance, typically is supposed to be researched and taught by professors of
philosophy appointed to departments of philosophy and supported by a philosophy department budget. As a result of this structure, battles for more faculty,
students, grants, and money generally are fought along departmental lines (and
along subdepartmental lines when issues are subdisciplinary, and along divi-
sional or college lines when issues are supradisciplinary). And, battles over the
scope and primacy of disciplines—Should Marx most properly be taught by
philosophers? Should specific philosophy courses be made part of general
education requirements? Should a new faculty appointment be made in philosophy or elsewhere?—thus are battles over the scope and primacy of departments. "Interdepartmental" programs or units—such as humanities centers
and institutes—that appear to be exceptions to this pervasive departmental
organization frequently do participate in this organization by presupposing
(and then seeking to bridge) the administrative primacy of the several departments involved.

To consider the possibility of re-visioning this organization of knowledge is in large part at present to consider the possible critical function of
these humanities centers and institutes in unsettling disciplines and departments, undoing their effects, and remaking their creations.

Of course, this assumes that the present disciplinary and departmental
organization of knowledges *ought* to be changed. I think this assumption is
correct. The existing standard disciplinary and departmental organization of
knowledges has several seriously negative consequences. First, this organization supports a self-misunderstanding of the humanities as primarily exten-

---

7. See, for example, Stephen Jay Kline, *Conceptual Foundations for Multidisciplinary Thinking*
(Stanford, Calif.: Stanford University Press, 1995).

sive bodies of disciplinary knowledges (that students may come to possess and so be "culturally literate," and that meritorious faculty can single-handedly invent, patent, and own for an indefinite tenure). However, while constituting big bodies of knowledge, the humanities are constituted by the power to illuminate who we are, the power to imagine who we might be, and the power to develop the abilities needed to realize our ideals.

Second, this organization of knowledge gives rise to and sustains problems and issues in the humanities that simply are not genuine (though they may be thoroughly scholarly). This leaves students skeptical of any connection between the humanities and real life, and skeptical about the value of education in the humanities. The fundamental subject matter of the humanities is human life and, in this light, particular humanities disciplines must not investigate disciplinary pseudo-problems, but instead must address human issues from a variety of disciplinary approaches and perspectives.

Third, failure to recognize this leads to the intellectual fragmentation of the humanities and their academic isolation from one another (as well as from other studies). This is not due simply to specialization. Rather, the problem originates in assumptions and practices that attempt to match aspects and dimensions of human life to intellectual disciplines and academic departments. This allows humanists, deluded but happy, to view their own discipline as intellectually most basic or superior, and their own interests as canonical. (In this regard, humanists have been slow at best to incorporate into their educational institutions the insights of much contemporary genealogical work in the humanities that undermines disciplinary separations and unearths historical bases of traditional exclusions and standards of evaluation. In practice, most humanists have looked to climb up the disciplinary ladder rather than kick it away.) This is passed on to students who often find little connection among humanities disciplines and their respective jargons. Unlike their counterparts in the natural sciences who must include study of sciences outside their major, humanities majors often need take few humanities courses in disciplines other than their major.

Fourth, the organization of knowledge into these separate disciplines and its administration by departments withdraws the humanities from public discourse. This is a special problem for a democracy, since self-government requires the self-development at which the humanities aim.

Given these problems, can alternative organizations of humanists, such as humanities centers and humanities institutes, do anything effective? In many cases, I believe they can, although the reorganization of knowledge in the humanities rarely has been an explicit goal of such groups. Instead, typically these centers and institutes are committed centrally to furthering humanistic research, improving teaching in the humanities, and providing public and scholarly programs. In this way, humanities centers and institutes usually are revisionist rather than re-visionary. But if they can further strengthen the status quo, so they often can contribute to an institutional reorganization of knowledge.

The basic issue is rather simple: Will humanities centers and institutes allow humanists to play familiar disciplinary games a little better, or will they contribute to the end of these games and the beginning of new ones? New games? How? By doing what? Basically, humanities centers and institutes can and need to play a subversive, counter-institutional role. They should not be "interdisciplinary" or "interdepartmental," but instead counter-disciplinary and counter-departmental.

To accomplish this task (and avoid institutional containment and the sometimes-misguided wishes of administrators for research dollars, star scholars, and prestige—to become, in short, more like the sciences), humanities centers and institutes need to utilize aggressively their resources on two fronts. First, they need to help enable their own faculty, students, and administrators—long habituated to disciplines and departments (and so often not the least bit interested in any possible change)—to rethink their own work and then do different work. This involves the recognition that disciplinary divisions do not merely reflect their subject matter, but rather constitute it. And it involves the recognition that departmental divisions have intellectual consequences as well as administrative and political ones. This means, for example, that there is a need for these centers and institutes to support development of courses that do not seek to combine disciplinary approaches, but rather aim to undermine and marginalize them. Further, it means funding research projects and public programs that are not set forth in the terms of disciplinary assumptions and standards. Moreover, it means rethinking traditional knowledge, its production, and its politics (including issues of gender, race, culture, and texts, as well as notions of originality, individual research, and ownership of scholarship). Finally, it means rethinking the practices of distribution requirements, major requirements, departmental budgets, and the role of departments in faculty personnel decisions.

At the same time, humanities centers and institutes must pursue this agenda outside as well as inside their own institutions. They must pursue this agenda with journal editors and reviewers, publishers, agencies that award grants and fellowships, colleagues at other educational institutions, boards of professional associations, politicians, and prospective donors. This amounts to an infiltration tactic. I think it is unlikely that efforts to redirect knowledge at a given institution can succeed unless those efforts are matched and supported by changes within the whole network of forces that now determine professional success and legitimacy.

To say that humanities centers and institutes should take up a subversive philosophy—that they should unsettle and infiltrate—may appear hopelessly and wholly negative. It is, I admit, thoroughly negative in two senses. First, it views negating, resisting, or undermining disciplines and departments as necessary for any successful re-visioning and reconstruction of knowledges in the humanities. Second, it amounts to a wariness to specify or detail any alternative positive organization of knowledge from within a standpoint thoroughly pervaded by disciplines and departments. In a larger sense, though, this view expresses a positive task and hope for humanities centers and institutes, the departments with which they work, the institutions in which they are housed, and the disciplines they address. Though the prospects for containment are high, humanities centers and institutes can be effective institutional forums for the ongoing critical self-transformation of educational institutions.[8]

---

8. An earlier version of portions of this essay appeared in "Revisioning Philosophy," *Philosophy Today*, vol. 33.3 (1989): pp. 264–75. These revised passages appear here with the kind permission of the editor and the publisher.

4

Pragmatism versus Fundamentalism

Pragmatism: Making Connections

Believing in philosophy myself devoutly, and believing also that a kind of new dawn is breaking upon us philosophers, I feel impelled . . . to try to impart to you some news of the situation.[1]

—William James,
Pragmatism: A New Name for Some Old Ways of Thinking

Philosophy is supposed to be important to *you*. It is supposed to matter. It is supposed to enrich and stimulate imagination. It is supposed to foster and deepen vision. It is supposed to substitute wonder and the love of wisdom for dogmatism, prejudice, and the unexamined life. In sum, it is supposed to make a difference in the way *you* lead your life every day. As William James put it, philosophy is supposed to make some important, positive connection with *your* actual life and world.

Of course, even many beginning students of philosophy realize that too often this is not the case. As they register for philosophy courses to fulfill degree requirements, sit through philosophy lectures like inmates doing time, and plod through philosophy books on the way to nothing more than a final paper or exam, they understand almost at once that frequently something has gone wrong. Many times they quickly find large gaps and little connection between the pretend "problems of philosophy" and the actual problems of life. Frequently they rapidly note the poverty and paucity of philosophical positions in comparison to the richness and plurality of real experiences. And often they immediately recognize the differences between the theoretical "justifications" of philosophy and practical problem-solving and experimentation.

As a result, philosophy not infrequently seems unimportant, artificial and contrived, practically worthless, and virtually void of vision. As William James observed, the world of philosophy and philosophy professors is usually simple, logical, clean, and noble. Its classic architecture, James wrote, expresses purity and dignity: "It is a kind of marble temple shining on a hill . . . a class sanctuary in which the rationalist fancy may take refuge from the intolerably confused and gothic character which mere facts present. It is no *explanation* of our concrete universe, it is another thing altogether, a substitute for it, a remedy, a way of escape"[1]. As a result, many philosophers, in turn, seem at these times to be nothing more than sophistic pickpockets and tenured thieves, employed by colleges and universities to steal time and squeeze life from anyone who comes too close.[2]

Most students in this situation, of course, just turn off. They turn away from philosophy, and they turn toward the "real world." A few students, however, suspend their disbelief and their disinterest, set aside their own experience and practical concerns, and, at least as long as philosophy class lasts, just fake it. Some of those who do so long enough, fully enough, and well enough may become philosophy majors, philosophy Ph.D.s, or philosophy professors. Along the way, they may even lose sight of the fact that they are faking it, and may find their days and their thoughts earnestly occupied by eternal Forms, rational proofs for the existence of God, universal doubt, transcendental deductions, the verification principle, the question of Being, the "is/ought" gap, the problem of other minds, or any of the other supposedly general problems or theoretical puzzles of philosophy.[3]

This approach to the problems of philosophy has proven to be a recipe for irrelevance. As William James bemoaned in the final paragraph of *A Pluralistic Universe*, philosophers behave "as if the actual peculiarities of the world that is were entirely irrelevant to the content of truth."[4] However, as James immediately added, the actual peculiarities of the world—*your* experiences, *your* practical affairs, *your* purposes and daily activities—"cannot be irrelevant" and must be taken into account by "the philosophy of the future."

---

1. William James, *Pragmatism: A New Name for Some Old Ways of Thinking*, *The Works of William James* (Cambridge, Mass.: Harvard University Press, 1975 [1907]), p. 18. Hereafter abbreviated *"P"* in this chapter.
2. See the discussion of fear of time—"chronophobia"—in chapter 9.
3. These philosophers, like an anonymous reviewer of an earlier version of this essay, may suspect that these remarks are intended to shock. My aim, however, is simply to describe, and my observations are rooted in, and convey written and verbal comments of undergraduate philosophy students at several leading public and private institutions. I realize, of course, that many philosophers—like my anonymous reviewer—may report that these observations are "very far from the reactions which most of us philosophy teachers notice in new students." My concern, however, is not with what most philosophy teachers notice about their students. Rather, it is with what a significant number of philosophy students (and students who never take any philosophy courses) notice about too much philosophy and too many philosophy teachers.
4. William James, "Conclusions," *A Pluralistic Universe* (Cambridge, Mass.: Harvard University Press, 1977 [1909]), p. 149. Hereafter abbreviated *"APU"* in this chapter.

Looking toward that future, James urged young people to take to heart pragmatism's commitment to gather philosophic conclusions only from "the *particulars of life*."[5]

Now James offered far more than a mere hint about all this. He offers *you* a philosophical promised land full of life, a full-blown, radical, practical, living alternative to traditional philosophies. This alternative is pragmatism. Pragmatism occupies a central place in classical American philosophy and in American thought and culture more broadly. William James, in turn, occupies a central place in the development of pragmatism.

Eager critics will charge, of course, that the very notion of a genuinely pragmatic philosophy is absurd or, at best, naive. "Pragmatic philosophy," they will object, is a contradiction in terms—an oxymoron similar to "military intelligence," "easy listening music," "safe sex," "low taxes," or "gourmet fast food." Being pragmatic or practical, they will assert, is something totally different from being philosophical. These objections, however, are not new. James was aware of them. He heard them all. In fact, he voiced them himself. In the opening chapter, "Philosophy and Its Critics," of his last book, *Some Problems of Philosophy*, James rehearsed these hostile objections against philosophy. On behalf of all bored students and critics of philosophy, James wrote: "Philosophy is dogmatic, and pretends to settle things by pure reason, whereas the only fruitful mode of getting at truth is to appeal to concrete experience"; and, "philosophy is out of touch with real life, for which it substitutes abstractions."[6] In reply, James noted that these objections are historically valid: In the past, most philosophies have been dogmatic and abstract. However, James continued, in the future, it is possible for philosophy to be different because "no reason appears why philosophy should keep aloof from reality permanently." Instead, philosophy may become as experimental and undogmatic "as the most empirical science," and "may get into as close contact as realistic novelists with the facts of life."[7]

In order to reconnect with reality—with *your* experience, *your* life, *your* concerns—philosophy must become pragmatic. This is a big task, but we do not have to start from scratch. The pragmatism of William James awaits recovery and development by each of us—by *you*. William James made philosophy pragmatic. The pragmatic question, then, is this: *How* did he do it?

---

5. From this advice, James draws conclusions that differ sharply from those of Richard Rorty. See the discussion of pragmatism and Rorty in chapter 1.
6. William James, "Philosophy and Its Critics," *Some Problems of Philosophy* (Cambridge, Mass.: Harvard University Press, 1979 [1911]), pp. 18–19.
7. Ibid., p. 19.

Practice

> Few people have definitely articulated philosophies of their own. But almost everyone has his own peculiar sense of a certain total character in the universe, and of the inadequacy fully to match it of the peculiar systems that he knows. They don't just cover *his* world. . . . [H]e and we know offhand that such philosophies are out of plumb and out of key and out of "whack," and have no business to speak up in the universe's name.
>
> —William James, *Pragmatism*

James made philosophy pragmatic by reversing the commitments and orientation of traditional philosophies. He emphasized: practice, consequences, and the outcomes of beliefs (rather than theory, pure reason, and authority in advance of results); purpose, effort, and the realization and frustration of aims (rather than disinterested contemplation, speculation, and intelligence divorced from action and experiment); and pluralism, novelty and change, and difference and variation (instead of absolutism, finality, sameness, certainty, and neat categories of thought that sanitize all the messiness of real life). Pragmatism, then, takes *practice, purpose, and pluralism* seriously.

This isn't impossibly difficult, despite the fact that few philosophers have been able to do it themselves or to understand how James did it. As James observed in his landmark book *Pragmatism*, "great expertness" in professional or technical philosophy is not required, for philosophy does not sit in judgment of the feelings and lives of ordinary people. Instead, it is just the opposite: "The finally victorious way of looking at things will be the most completely *impressive* way to the normal run of minds" (*P*:25).

Moreover, this isn't something completely different or novel. It represents a generalization or extension or improvement of a familiar attitude—an empirical or experience-centered attitude. James thus titles pragmatism "a new name for some old ways of thinking." He does note, however, that philosophers may find this way of thinking to be radically new: "A pragmatist turns his back resolutely and once for all upon a lot of inveterate habits dear to professional philosophers. He turns away from abstraction and insufficiency, from verbal solutions, from bad *a priori* reasons, from fixed principles, closed systems, and pretended absolutes and origins. He turns towards concreteness and adequacy, towards facts, towards action, and towards power" (*P*:31).

In order to make philosophy pragmatic, the first step is to turn toward *practice* and to make it central. There are three aspects to this. First, James insisted that philosophical problems must originate in practical activities, actual events, concrete situations, and real experiences—"the particulars of life." This ensures that the problems of philosophy are drawn from experience, rather than forced artificially upon it. In order to ensure that philosophy does not end up aloof from reality, it must begin in reality and in real problems—and real problems are particular problems, somebody's or some group's problems, *your* problems.

This advice is clear and simple, but revolutionary in its results. James warned us that we must not accept that so-called philosophical problems really are genuine problems just because philosophers have called them problems. Unlike class reading lists and professors' writing assignments, genuine problems cannot be simply handed out and received as something ready-made. Instead, they are genealogical. As James pointed out, calling something a problem does not, by itself, make that thing a problem. Genuine problems must arise within experience; situations become problem situations for us in, and through, our experiences. Unlike classroom discussion topics, real problems cannot be simply imposed externally on experience.

Consider, then, some supposed philosophical problems: the problem of appearance and reality; the problem of induction; the mind/body problem; the problem of free will and determinism; the prisoner's dilemma; Zeno's paradoxes; the problem of evil; and so on. These problems may seem distant, abstract, irrelevant, anything but compelling, and mere esoteric make-believe. If this is not the case, then the pragmatist must show how these problems arise from, and are rooted in, practice. As James so often did throughout his writings, the pragmatist must demonstrate the practical beginnings of these problems, if they are to be considered genuine problems. If this is not the case with some philosophical problems, then the pragmatist must identify and dismiss these "problems" as pseudo-problems. To pursue such a pseudo-problem, a problem with no practical origin, is merely to pretend to do philosophy, to take a holiday from the real world, and, at best, to engage in what James called "intellectual gymnastics." Charles Peirce succinctly made much the same point before James: "Let us not pretend to doubt in philosophy what we do not doubt in our hearts."[8] And John Dewey made this point after James: "Reference to the primacy and ultimacy of the material of ordinary experience protects us, in the first place, from creating artificial problems which deflect the energy and attention of philosophers from the real problems that arise out of actual subject-matter."[9]

Pragmatism makes practice central in a second way: Just as philosophical problems have practical origins, so too philosophical theories and positions have practical consequences—consequences in practice. But pragmatists

8. Charles Sanders Peirce, *Collected Papers* (Cambridge, Mass.: Harvard University Press, 1978 [1868]), p. 157 [*CP* 5:265].

9. John Dewey, *Experience and Nature, The Later Works of John Dewey, 1925–1953*, vol. 1 (Carbondale, Ill.: Southern Illinois University Press, 1981 [1925]), p. 26.

do not simply claim that a given philosophy has practical consequences. They make practice central in a more far-reaching and important way: For pragmatists, the practical consequences of a philosophy constitute the meaning of that philosophy. The meaning of a philosophy is to be found in its practical consequences; these consequences are that philosophy's practical meaning—and, as James observed, for us there is no meaning other than practical meaning. James identified "the pragmatic method" as the effort to determine the meaning of a philosophy by tracing its practical consequences. There can be no difference, James wrote, "in abstract truth that doesn't express itself in a difference in concrete fact and in conduct consequent upon that fact, imposed upon somebody, somehow, somewhere, and somewhen." Accordingly, James concluded, "The whole function of philosophy ought to be to find out what definite difference it will make to you and me, at definite instants of our life, if this world-formula or that world-formula be the true one" (*P*:30).

This means that different world-formulas or philosophies, if they really are different, must have or make for different practical consequences. If there are no differences in practical consequences, the theories are not really different and there is nothing really at stake. James put it this way: "What difference would it practically make to anyone if this notion rather than that notion were true? If no practical difference whatever can be traced, then the alternatives mean practically the same thing, and all dispute is idle. Whenever a dispute is serious, we ought to be able to show some practical difference that must follow from one side or the other's being right" (*P*:28).

James emphasized that this pragmatic method stands for an attitude rather than any particular results. The attitude it stands for is radically empirical and practical: "*The attitude of looking away from first things, principles, 'categories,' supposed necessities; and of looking towards last things, fruits, consequences, facts*" (*P*:32). Though shot through with this practical attitude, the pragmatic method does not, by itself, stand for any special results in philosophy; it does not, by itself, answer philosophical questions. Consider: Is materialism or idealism correct? Is Christianity, Hinduism, or atheism true? Is beauty subjective or objective? Are there natural laws or just human laws and conventions? Is reality one or many? Is the empiricist or the rationalist correct? Pragmatists argue that it is impossible to answer these questions, impossible to know which (if any) view is true, unless and until we can determine the meaning, the practical meaning, of these views. (This is why, James explained, so many philosophical disputes are interminable in the absence of the pragmatic method.) By directing us to the practical consequences that would follow from a given view's being true, pragmatism prepares us to investigate and experiment whether or not these consequences in fact do hold or exist. Until we grasp a philosophy's practical meaning—what

James called its "cash value"—we cannot assess it. Pragmatism provides that practical meaning, and as such it "appears less as a solution, then, than as a program for more work. . . . *Theories thus become instruments, not answers to enigmas, in which we can rest*" (*P*:32). This, of course, is wonderful news for philosophers and philosophy students fed up (but not well nourished) by a steady diet of the assumptions, intuitions, introspections, stipulations, contemplations, deductions, certainties, abstractions, generalizations, and overarching systems of practice-free philosophies.

This suggests a third way in which practice is central to pragmatism. Just as practice supplies the origin of philosophical problems and the meanings of different philosophical views, so too it provides the test of a philosophy's truth. What is the difference—the practical difference—between an idea or belief or philosophy that is true and one that is false? (To ask this question is simply to apply the pragmatic method to the notion of truth.) True ideas, beliefs, and philosophies work in practice: They have cash-value, they lead, they guide; they are verified, assimilated, corroborated (*P*:97). True ideas are effective instruments in practice. They satisfy: "*ideas (which themselves are but parts of experience) become true just in so far as they help us to get into satisfactory relation with other parts of our experience. . . .* Any idea upon which we can ride, so to speak; any idea that will carry us prosperously from any one part of our experience to any other part, linking things satisfactorily, working securely, simplifying, saving labor; is true for just so much, true in so far forth, true *instrumentally*" (*P*:34).

Truth, then, is not found by theorists or discovered by the inactive. Instead, it is made by practitioners, created through action. This is a revolutionary insight: The pragmatist point here is not merely that we find out what is true through practice, action, or experiment; instead, it is that our practice, action, and experiment constitute, construct, manufacture, make truths. Truths are results or outcomes of practical actions; they do not exist independently from, or antecedently to, these actions. Ideas become true—become verities—through practical processes of verification—processes that lead us in agreeable, progressive, harmonious, satisfactory ways. In a famous passage, James proclaimed: "The truth of an idea is not a stagnant property inherent in it. Truth *happens* to an idea. It *becomes* true, is *made* true by events. Its verity *is* in fact an event, a process: the process namely of its verifying itself, its veri-*fication*. Its validity is the process of its valid-*ation*" (*P*:97).

This focus on practice is at once a focus on the future. Unlike traditional philosophies that "face backward to a past eternity," James observed, pragmatism faces forward to an open future: "pragmatism shifts the emphasis and looks forward into facts themselves. The really vital question for us all is, What is this world going to be? What is life eventually to make of itself?" No present truth is immune from revision, modification, or complete abandonment due to the results of future practices, experiment, and inquiry. No present truth can prescribe wholly future practice. Although truths are built up from previous truths, they cannot legislate future experiences: "beliefs at any time are so much experience funded. But the beliefs are themselves parts of the sum total of the world's experience, and become matter, therefore, for the next day's funding operations" (*P*:107–8, 62). The truth of any idea, belief, or philosophy is simply a truth relative to particular practices of particular persons in particular places at particular times. To fail to understand this is to convert philosophy into abstract fantasy.

Purpose

> Let me begin by reminding you of the fact that the possession of true thoughts means everywhere the possession of invaluable instruments of action; and that our duty to gain truth, so far from being a blank command from out of the blue, or a "stunt" self-imposed by our intellect, can account for itself by excellent practical reasons.
>
> —William James, *Pragmatism*

Pragmatism locates philosophy's origin, meaning, and test of truth in practice. And, for pragmatists, if philosophy is centrally and irreducibly practical, practice is centrally and irreducibly purposeful. To make philosophy pragmatic, it is necessary to take purpose seriously.

James presents us with a biological account of human nature that focuses on purpose. Practices have purposes: Human organisms pursue purposes, have interests, project ends, and establish goals, and strive to fulfill those purposes, satisfy those interests, act to attain those ends, and work to meet their goals. We engage in many, many different activities—from dribbling a basketball to buying groceries, from changing the oil in a car to driving drunk, from talking with friends to joining the army, from reading a philosophy assignment to taking vitamins, from sewing a quilt to trying not to make eye contact with street people, or from playing a flute solo to sharing a kiss—and these many different activities are efforts to fulfill many different purposes.

If we could immediately, effortlessly, and uniformly fulfill all our various purposes, there would be no reason at all to reflect, to inquire, or to philosophize. Sadly, our experience demonstrates that this is not the case. In order to more regularly and fully satisfy our interests, we need to think—and, frequently, to think before, during, and after we act. Thinking thus has a practical or instrumental value. For pressing, practical reasons, "we must find a theory that will work; and that means something extremely difficult; for our theory must mediate between all previous truths and certain new experiences" (*P*:104).

In this context, from his earliest writings to his last, James set forth not simply a practical or instrumental account of truth, but also a practical or instrumental account of the mind. Calling all concepts "teleological instruments"[10] and calling the mind "an essentially teleological mechanism," James explained that "I mean by this that the conceiving or theorizing faculty . . . functions *exclusively for the sake of ends* that . . . are set by our emotional and practical subjectivity altogether."[11] Guided by practical purposes and emotional ends, mind is selective and picks out and pays attention only to certain portions of reality, its reality: "The human mind is essentially partial. . . . Man always wants his curiosity gratified for a particular purpose."[12] Selection—attending to some things and ignoring others—is omnipotent, James held: It is "the very keel on which our mental ship is built" so that "each of us literally *chooses*, by his ways of attending to things, what sort of a universe he shall appear to himself to inhabit" and what sort of "being he shall now resolve to become."[13]

For James, human activities, including the activities of the mind, are purposeful. The success or failure of our activities can be judged only in relation to these purposes and the means available to realize them. We cannot determine whether our efforts have attained an aim unless we know what that aim is and what alternatives might lead to that same aim. Thus, in assessing our activities, we must focus not simply on practical results but on practical results in relation to particular purposes, and on practical results in relation to the means that brought about these results. For example, suppose I spend a weekend building a low picket fence. I'm more likely to succeed if I use effective instruments—in this case, a shovel, level, and treated lumber work better than a small trowel, the naked eye, and green wood. Was I successful? It depends—on my purpose. If I intended to create a safe play area for a toddler, then perhaps I was successful. If I intended to keep jumping deer out of my garden, then perhaps I failed. Or suppose I journey to New York City for Christmas vacation. This may be very satisfying if my goal is to visit

10. William James, "The Sentiment of Rationality, " *Essays in Philosophy* (Cambridge, Mass.: Harvard University Press, 1978 [1879]), p. 56.
11. William James, "Reflex Action and Theism," *The Will to Believe and Other Essays in Popular Philosophy* (Cambridge, Mass.: Harvard University Press, 1979 [1881]), pp. 94–95.
12. William James, "Great Men and Their Environment," *The Will to Believe and Other Essays in Popular Philosophy*, p. 165.
13. William James, "The Stream of Thought," "Memory," and "Attention," *The Principles of Psychology*, vol. 1 (Cambridge, Mass.: Harvard University Press, 1981 [1890]), pp. 276, 640, 401, 277.

museums and see new theater productions. It may not work so well if I seek warm weather and inexpensive relaxation and solitude.

The consequences of this rather simple point are far-reaching for philosophy. In the first place, James reminded us that philosophy is a practice. It is one of the things we do. As such, like any other activity, it is undertaken with certain interests and on behalf of certain purposes. In order to evaluate its success or failure, we must make constant reference to those interests and purposes. We do this regularly with most of our actions: Is the fence well-built? Was the vacation trip a success?

Philosophers, by contrast, traditionally have not addressed or acknowledged, or worse yet, have concealed, the selective interests that have guided their philosophizing. Selective interests, however, do not cease to operate simply because they are unacknowledged. Instead, failure to recognize and state a philosophy's purpose renders it opaque, distant, and curious—as a museum piece might appear to school children who do not know a tool's use but nonetheless vaguely suspect the item is, or was, a tool of some sort. What purposes is Plato attempting to fulfill through his theory of the Forms? What interest and focus are at work in Leibniz's account of monads? What aims led Marx to view history in terms of a materialist dialectic? What are the purposes that Heidegger advances in *Being and Time*, and what "partiality" and selective attention underlie these concerns? James called on philosophers—he calls on *you*—to make clear purposes: "No concept can be a valid substitute for a concrete reality except with reference to a particular interest in the conceiver."[14] John Dewey drove home this same point approximately fifty years later: "selective emphasis, choice, is inevitable whenever reflection occurs. This is not an evil. Deception comes only when the presence and operation of choice is concealed, disguised, denied. Empirical method finds and points to the operation of choice as it does to any other event. . . . Whatever enters into choice, determining its need and giving it guidance, an empirical method frankly indicates what it is for; and the fact of choice, with its workings and consequences, an empirical method points out with equal openness."[15]

In the second place, we do not philosophize simply to know the truth or to arrive at true ideas. True ideas are means to realize given ends, not ends themselves; they are instruments for reaching particular goals, not final goals themselves. We do not philosophize in order to have true theories; rather we strive to philosophize truthfully in order to fulfill practical

---

14. William James, "The Sentiment of Rationality," *Essays in Philosophy*, p. 56.
15. Dewey, *Experience and Nature*, p. 34.

purposes—practical purposes apart from which there is no truth at all. As James observed: "The possession of truth, so far from being here an end in itself, is only a preliminary means toward other vital satisfactions. . . . True ideas would never have been singled out as such, would never have acquired a class-name, least of all a name suggesting value, unless they had been useful from the outset in this way" (*P*:98). Here James showed us that truth does indeed matter—but as an instrument within a philosophy, not as an end in life: "all our theories are *instrumental*, are mental modes of *adaptation* to reality, rather than revelations or gnostic answers to some divinely instituted world-enigma" (*P*:94). Some ideas and philosophies, like some garden implements and travel itineraries, are better instruments than others. They are not better in themselves, but better in relation to particular purposes and better in guiding us to satisfaction of those purposes. Purely objective, interest-free, or purpose independent truth, James demanded philosophers to confess, "is nowhere to be found:" "The trail of the human serpent is thus over everything" (*P*:37).

In the third place, this means that there is nothing mystical or otherworldly or abstract or esoteric about truth. True ideas are simply good ideas—and this goodness is a relation that involves a particular purpose, just as good shovels and good vacations are good not by themselves but only in relation to particular persons and their particular purposes. James summarized: For pragmatists, truth "is simply a collective name for verification-processes, just as health, wealth, strength, etc., are names for other processes connected with life, and also pursued because it pays to pursue them. Truth is made, just as health, wealth and strength are made, in the course of experience" (*P*:104). Accordingly, James classified truth as a kind or subset of goodness. It is simply "*one species of the good:* . . . *The true is the name of whatever proves itself to be good in the way of belief, and good, too, for definite, assignable reasons*" (*P*:42). Logic and epistemology, then, are subsets of ethics, and philosophy's ultimate concern is not with the nature of truth and how to know it, but with the nature of the lives we should lead—the nature of the life *you* should lead—and how to live it.[16] To hold tight to a different view, "wedded by education and tradition to the abstractionist manner of thought,"[17] is to engage in a process that it does not pay to pursue, as any honest student knows.

---

16. See the discussion of these issues in the context of James's radical empiricism and moral philosophy in chapters 8 and 15.
17. William James, "A Dialogue," *The Meaning of Truth* (Cambridge, Mass.: Harvard University Press, 1975 [1909]), p. 159.

Pluralism

> There is no complete generalization, no total point of view, no all-per-
> vasive unity, but everywhere some residual resistance to verbalization,
> formulation, and discursification, some genius of reality that escapes
> from the pressure of the logical finger, that says "hands off," and claims
> its privacy, and means to be left to its own life. . . . Philosophy must pass
> from words, that reproduce but ancient elements, to life itself, that gives
> the integrally new.

> —William James, "A Pluralistic Mystic"

We engage in practices with purposes. These purposes and their results are
local, varied, different, and multiple. Pragmatism is not a philosophy of practice
and purpose; it is a philosophy of plural practice*s* and plural purpose*s*. To make
philosophy pragmatic, it is necessary to take pluralism seriously.

Traditional philosophies have emphasized the eternal, the absolute, the
fixed, the precise, the general, the common, the same, and the one. They have
sought synthesis, completeness, finality, and system. James resisted all of
this. In response, he championed finitude, relativity, change, vagueness, particularity, individuality, difference, and plurality. He declared himself a friend
of the concrete, the incomplete, the imperfect, and the messy—in short, a
friend of real experiences and real lives. Life exceeds logic (*APU*:148) and
experience boils over our categories and neat theories (*P*:106).

Two facts seem obvious. First, to a large extent, an individual's experience is shared; our desires and hopes, fears and worries, joys and sufferings,
beliefs and doubts, and values and meanings frequently are also at work—
sometimes a lot and sometimes a little—in the lives of other persons. Second,
against this backdrop the experiences of different individuals simply are different. Experience is irreducibly and intrinsically subjective, individual, and
plural. In philosophy (and in other reflections), we may talk about Experience
or Life or Being or Reality or the Environment or the World, but these are
simply groupings of unique experiences, individual lives, multiple beings,
different realities, many environments, and plural worlds.

The philosophical consequences of these facts are less obvious. James
spelled out three points of special significance. First, any adequate philosophy
must make room for the real differences among individuals. These differences
cannot be ignored, declared unreal, or somehow eliminated by transcendental
tricks. Quoting an "unlearned carpenter," James observed that there are very
few differences among people, "but what little there is, *is very important*."[18] We

---

18. William James, "The Importance of Individuals," *The Will to Believe and Other Essays in
Popular Philosophy*, p. 191.

must make room for these differences in philosophy; indeed, we must make them central. To say that one theory is more satisfactory than another is to say that it is more satisfactory for some individual, recognizing that "individuals will emphasize their points of satisfaction differently" (*P*:35). "We are invincibly parts" (*APU*:23), James declared, and so "our account of truth is an account of truths in the plural" (*P*:104). Truths must be as plural as the experiences in which they function: "No two of us have identical difficulties, nor should we be expected to work out identical solutions."[19]

Accordingly, there is no reason to expect or demand less pluralism from our philosophies than we encounter in our lives. The notions of a single real truth, a single correct set of values, or a single accurate philosophy are neat, clean, and familiar—and, perhaps, reassuring. They provide a basis for all sorts of absolutist agendas. James showed us how to kick this bad habit.

Second, philosophy must make room for possible, as well as for actual, differences among persons. It must be pluralistic about the future as well as the present. This means that philosophy must be open-minded and fallibilistic. It cannot close itself off from the future. It cannot offer guarantees or proclaim the last word. It must "bide its time," and be ready to revise its conclusions from day to day: "It may be voluminous, and even luminous, but it "never can be *final*."[20]

This does not mean that philosophy must have a crystal ball or anticipate the future. Nor does it mean that a philosopher must somehow speak for everyone (or from nowhere). It does mean that philosophy must not pretend to legislate the future in advance or exclude the perspectives of others: "The philosophic attempt to define nature so that no one's business is left out . . . is sure in advance to fail. The most a philosophy can hope for is not to lock out any interest forever. No matter what doors it closes, it must leave other doors open for the interests which it neglects" (*APU*:19). Pragmatism is the embodiment of this open-door spirit on life. There may be final papers and final exams, but there can be no final philosophy.

Third, of course, this may not be very appealing or satisfying to professional philosophers and self-righteous, would-be saviors who long have been in the business of shutting doors and who have developed sophisticated, clever door-shutting techniques and vocabularies. James recognized this: Pluralism, in falling back on a hardy "willingness to live without assurances or guarantees . . . is bound to disappoint many sick souls whom absolutism

---

19. William James, "Conclusions," *The Varieties of Religious Experience* (Cambridge, Mass.: Harvard University Press, 1985 [1902]), p. 384. See the discussion of this point's implications for community in chapter 13.
20. William James, "The Moral Philosopher and the Moral Life," *The Will to Believe and Other Essays in Popular Philosophy*, pp. 157, 159.

can console."[21] To these persons, pragmatism has only a this-worldly human-ism, a radical empiricism to offer: "For pluralistic pragmatism, truth grows up inside of all the finite experience. They lean on each other, but the whole of them, if such a whole there be, leans on nothing. All 'homes' are in finite experience; finite experience as such is homeless. Nothing outside of the flux secures the issue of it. It can hope salvation only from its own intrinsic promises and potencies" (*P*:125).

To those who find this troubling, James offered simply further pluralism and toleration—"Each attitude being a syllable in human nature's total mes-sage, it takes the whole of us to spell the meaning out completely."[22] But to those who cannot tolerate this pluralism, fallibilism, and humanism, James offered a warning: "Hands off: neither the whole of truth nor the whole of good is revealed to any single observer, although each observer gains a partial superiority of insight from the peculiar positions in which he stands. Even prisons and sick-rooms have their special revelations. It is enough to ask of each of us that he should be faithful to his own opportunities and make the most of his own blessings, without presuming to regulate the rest of the vast field."[23] The remedy for pluralism, then, is more pluralism, just as the remedy for pragmatism is more, not less, pragmatism.

Things in the Making: Justifying Pragmatism

> What really exists is not things made but things in the making. Once made, they are dead, and an infinite number of alternative conceptual decompositions can be used in defining them.
>
> —William James, *A Pluralistic Universe*

William James is dead. His pragmatism, however, is not dead, despite the repeated efforts of clever scholars—some friendly, some hostile, and some just indifferent—to squeeze all the life out of it, to turn it into something already wholly made, to decompose it. As I write this essay, I do not want it to become simply another entry in the already massive conceptual decom-position of James and pragmatism. It may be difficult, I realize, to escape this fate: "When you have broken the reality into concepts you never can recon-struct it in its wholeness" (*APU*:116). To escape this fate, if possible at all,

---

21. James, "The Absolute and the Strenuous Life," *The Meaning of Truth*, p. 124.
22. James, "Conclusions," *The Varieties of Religious Experience*, p. 384.
23. William James, "On a Certain Blindness in Human Beings," *Talks to Teachers on Psychol-ogy: and to Students on Some of Life's Ideals* (New York: Henry Holt, 1928 [1902]). p. 269.

you have to consider pragmatism not so much just in terms of what you know, but in terms of how you live.

In this context, to present the pragmatism of William James as a radical alternative to traditional thought and as a genealogical philosophy of practice, purpose, and pluralism is one thing; to present a justification for this philosophy is something else. As a result, important questions—pragmatic questions—still remain: Is pragmatism true? Was James right? Is pragmatism justified? Who cares, and why does it matter—why does it matter to *you*?

In the end, I think, James presents *no* justification for his philosophy of pragmatism—at least no justification of the traditional sorts. He sets forth this philosophy, he clarifies it, he expands it, he contrasts and compares it to other views, he addresses misunderstandings, he lays out its implications, he pursues some of its applications, he discusses consequences of its adoption, and he situates it within the history of philosophy and contemporary work. But, despite all this, he does not justify pragmatism. He presents no overarching system of valid inferences or sound argument, decisive new evidence, or self-evident propositions.

I also have no proof or ready-made justification of pragmatism to offer to *you*—something cooked up since the death of James. I think there is *no* such compelling or final proof. You should, I believe, stop asking for one, stop turning pages looking for one, and stop trying to think up one.

This is not a measure of failure. It is a measure of consistency and practicality. James held that there can be no *theoretical* justification of a philosophy—pragmatism or any other philosophy. A philosophy's justification, for James, is a practical matter. It is something to be made in one's life—in *your* life—and not found in a class lecture, a journal article, or the pages of a philosophy book (even this one). (In fact, the whole idea of a worldview that becomes justified simply through the arguments sets forth in a book or lecture is a rather comical idea! This comedy, of course, is tediously familiar to many students who have been presented with various fine formal arguments and theoretical proofs for various philosophies, but who nonetheless find themselves not the least bit able or willing to actually live by those philosophies in the "real world.")

For pragmatism, the justification of any philosophy is a function of the consequences of adopting it. What difference does it make? Does it work? A philosophy can be justified only in light of these practical consequences—not before or in advance of the facts, but only after and in full view of the facts of practice. Pragmatism renders philosophy practical, then, only to the extent to which it renders practice—*your* life—more satisfactory. This task, in turn, awaits *your* action. My advice is straightforward: Don't wait any longer. No philosophy assignment is more important, and James sets before you no other conclusion.

Appendix: Fundamentalism and the Empire of Philosophy

In the concluding chapter of *A Pluralistic Universe*, William James wrote:

> Everything you can think of, however vast or inclusive, has on the pluralistic view a genuinely "external" environment of some sort or amount. Things are "with" one another in many ways, but nothing includes everything, or dominates over everything. The word "and" trails along after every sentence. Something always escapes. "Ever not quite" has to be said of the best attempts made anywhere in the universe at attaining all-inclusiveness. The pluralistic world is thus more like a federal republic than like an empire or kingdom.
>
> —William James, *A Pluralistic Universe*

What are the implications of this pluralist insight for philosophy, education in philosophy, and the profession of academic philosophy? More specifically:

A. *What* constitutes a pluralist philosophy department?

B. *Why* constitute a pluralist department?

C. *How* might a pluralist department be constituted?

A. What Constitutes a Pluralist Philosophy Department?

On the surface, this question may appear to be a request for a *descriptive definition* or sociological report on the profession. What do professional philosophers mean when they say that a department is, or is not, "pluralist?" How do they use this term or understand this notion?

I posed (in writing) these questions to a diverse group of two dozen department chairs in American colleges and universities. Not surprisingly, I received (in writing and by telephone) a diverse group of two dozen responses (with a sampling error approaching 100%), including the following:

1. "The bottom line is that a pluralist department is a department that can't or won't do logic or science. Pluralists are fuzzy and fear math."

2. "A pluralistic department is a *broad* department. But this is simply not an issue anymore—*all* departments are pluralistic, teaching, for example, Searle *and* Dennett, Rawls *and* Dworkin, Quine *and* Davidson, and so on."

3. "Quite simply, a Continental, history-oriented department. Easy question."

4. "The defining mark of a pluralist department is that some members of the department believe other members don't simply hold philosophical positions that are mistaken but—and this is the key—actually fail to hold

philosophical positions or address philosophical issues at all. A pluralist department is a nice old liberal idea but in reality it is just a place for hatred, envy, jealousy, disappointment, manipulation, and pettiness. Unfamiliarity breeds contempt!"

5. "We can hardly be expected to know—for there are only four or five semipluralist departments in the country. By contrast there are dozens of departments in denial, in sustained self-deception. What constitutes a pluralist department—well, conditions very different from the ones we now have!"

And, finally, in a more administrative bent:

6. ". . . will, vision, money and a good Dean. Mostly a pluralist department is constituted by a department chair who *each* day resembles God on a good day."

These observations are telling, though, with James, we should glimpse the word "and" trailing after every sentence. Illuminating if "ever not quite," these remarks, like other more extensive evidence, indicate that "pluralism" has divergent meanings and contested uses in professional philosophy today. As a consequence, it may be tempting to tidy things up by offering a *stipulative* (rather than descriptive) *definition*. Craving a certain sort of clarity, we thus may ask: What are the necessary and sufficient conditions of a philosophy department's being a pluralist philosophy department? And we thus may proceed to fill in the blank: A philosophy department is a pluralist philosophy department *if and only if* _____.

To put the issue in this way, of course, is to risk conscription in the service of the empire of philosophy. Any such approach to the issue, if it is to avoid such service, must be both genealogical and pragmatic. It must explicitly acknowledge: (1) the historical events that give rise to this issue; (2) the forces and selective interests that guide it and are served by it; and (3) the individual and institutional arrangements that result from and are produced by it. This project points us toward many questions. For example, when and why did the identification of philosophers, departments of philosophy, and organizations of philosophers as pluralist, nonpluralist, or antipluralist arise? How and by whom has this development been sustained, directed, and transformed? What or whose interests have been and are served or frustrated by this process? What impact has this had on individuals, departments, and the profession? And, is consideration of these questions a mark of subversion, reconstruction, official marginalization, or more perfect containment?

These questions require specification of contexts. To ask what constitutes a pluralist philosophy department is to ask different questions—plural questions—in different situations. What, for example, makes a philosophy department's undergraduate or graduate curriculum, degree requirements, or teaching pluralist? What makes a department's search process or budget priorities or system of merit pay pluralist? What makes the editorial policies of a departmentally affiliated philosophy journal or university press pluralist? What makes an entire department faculty—taken collectively, as a department—pluralist?

Having raised these questions and issued these cautions, let me directly answer (rather than duck) the question at hand. In doing so, I focus on a philosophy department's faculty. Question: What constitutes a pluralist philosophy department? Answer: A philosophy department with a philosophically diverse and philosophically pluralist faculty. A philosophy department is a genuinely pluralist department if and only if its faculty members hold multiple, wide-ranging, different philosophical positions and, at the same time, share a philosophical commitment to pluralism on ontological, epistemological, moral, and other issues.

To be genuinely pluralist, then, a philosophy department must satisfy two requirements. In the first place, its faculty must have philosophical differences from one another—differences about philosophical problems, methods, traditions, arguments, positions, and philosophy itself. These differences must range widely across the scope and history of philosophy—more widely, suffice it to say, than from Quine to Davidson. A department cannot be genuinely pluralist if its faculty largely are philosophically interchangeable (even though these faculty members individually all may be pluralists). Of course, with the possible exceptions of one-person departments and departments shaped by institutional orthodoxies, it is not difficult for most departments to satisfy this requirement. Philosophers typically have no difficulty in disagreeing with one another.

However, while a faculty with philosophical differences may be a necessary condition for a pluralist department, it is not a sufficient condition. Here it is crucial to distinguish between mere plurality (mere multiple philosophies—something commonplace) and genuine pluralism (multiple pluralist philosophies—something very rare). Philosophical difference among individual departmental faculty constitutes a plurality of philosophies within a department. This is a default mode for many departments. It yields a philosophically plural faculty—and, often, one in which unfamiliarity indeed does breed contempt. It does not yield a faculty of pluralists. It produces little philosophical empires at war with one another, but no philosophical republics. It nourishes philosophers who believe there are two kinds of philosophy—one's own philosophy and philosophies that are wrong. By itself, such difference is not enough to establish pluralism.

A faculty of pluralists, however, is another matter. In the second place, a plurality of philosophers in a given department constitute a pluralist department only to the extent that those philosophers are philosophical pluralists.

A member of such a department must believe that nothing—not even one's own philosophy—includes everything. As such, a pluralist is committed not simply to a plurality of experiences, beliefs, commitments, and ways of life, but also to the irreducible plurality of realities, truths, goods, and human natures.[24] Members of a pluralist department, then, view their philosophical plurality as philosophically (and not just pedagogically) valuable. Moreover, this value must be expressed in practice as well as theory: A constitutive mark of a genuinely pluralist department is that its members do not seek to dominate all others, eradicate or treat as inferior all philosophical differences, or demand complete philosophical agreement on behalf of their little empires. A pluralist department—admittedly very different from many existing departments—is constituted by faculty who think and act as members of an intellectual republic.

B. Why Constitute a Pluralist Philosophy Department?

Now, it might be supposed that any attempt to explain *what* constitutes a pluralist philosophy department must be no more than a preface to a more important attempt to explain *how* to constitute a pluralist department. Afterall, in the abstract, pluralism seems much like motherhood, apple pie, and the flag: We almost all feel that we approve it, and we almost all pay lip-service to it almost all the time.

Today, however, pluralism is not widely endorsed; the empire has struck back. It is not clear to many philosophers and administrators that pluralism, is or should be a value for, or in, a philosophy department. This is so for two main reasons. In the first place, pluralism has become a "plastic word."[25] Like strategic planning, vision, accountability, openness, fairness, quality, and excellence, it is a ubiquitous, tyrannizing term. It has been shaped and utilized to cloak and serve almost every agenda or administration—just check any recent addresses or reports by any university president, government leader, business CEO, or professional scholarly organization. When virtually everyone talks the pluralist talk, but virtually no one who does so walks the pluralist walk, much of the talk must be regarded with a healthy dose of suspicion and skepticism.

---

24. For purposes of illustration, I take William James to be an exemplar of this pluralism: *Essays in Radical Empiricism* and *A Pluralistic Universe*, for example, develop an ontological pluralism; *Pragmatism* and *The Meaning of Truth* set forth an epistemological pluralism; *The Varieties of Religious Experience*, "The Will to Believe," "The Moral Philosopher and the Moral Life," and many other essays articulate a moral pluralism; and *The Principles of Psychology* and "The Sentiment of Rationality" present a plurality of human natures.

25. Uwe Poerksen, *Plastic Words: The Tyranny of Modular Language* (University Park, Penn.: Penn State University Press, 1995). I am indebted to Carl Mitcham for bringing this work to my attention.

In the second place, of course, not all philosophers or administrators even talk the pluralist talk. Indeed, pluralism now is a fighting creed, and the battle over pluralism in philosophy is being waged on two major fronts:

1. The first opponents of pluralism are those who believe (mistakenly) that a pluralist department is a department that attempts to be all things to all people—a departmental Noah's Ark that must find space for a couple of philosophers of every kind and pedigree.

   a. Sometimes these opponents of pluralism explain that excellence means specialization and that, in turn, specialization requires more depth and concentration than a pluralist department supposedly allows. In order to achieve quality, excellence, and high reputational rankings from colleagues at other institutions, these captains of the academy claim that philosophy departments, unlike Noah, must leave behind, for example, the frogs and bears in order to take on a couple more hedgehogs and bats (and in so doing perhaps become *the* leader of hedgehog and bat thought, the institutional dream destination, at least with tenure thrown in, of hedgehogs and bats everywhere).

   b. At other times, opponents of pluralism argue that tight budgets and scarce resources simply make pluralism unaffordable in practice. In order to "right-size" our enterprise and fit our passengers to our ship, they assert that departments simply have to leave behind some of the animals—whether the hedgehogs and bats or, as almost all hedgehogs and bats would advise in external departmental reviews, the frogs and bears.

   c. Still other opponents of pluralism claim that it now threatens to overturn "our" Western intellectual tradition, "our" cultural heritage, and "our" classics of philosophy (hedgehog and bat philosophy, and even frog and bear philosophy) in a politically correct effort to serve the demands of multiculturalism and the politics of recognition.[26] Pluralism, they charge, promotes inclusion and coverage over quality; pluralism, they fear, looks to the fashions of the day over the standards of tradition and the tests of time. On a pluralist ship, they worry that award-winning hedgehogs and bats can have no more space than scruffy panthers, pandas, and toucans

---

26. The literature here is vast. See, for example, *Multiculturalism: Examining the Politics of Recognition*, ed. Amy Gutmann, (Princeton, N.J.: Princeton University Press, 1994 [expanded edition]). In "Struggles for Recognition in the Democratic Constitutional State," his essay in this book, Jürgen Habermas made a distinction within democracies between (1) justified assimilation to the principles of a constitution and (2) unjustified assimilation to a dominant cultural form of life (p. 138). This parallels my distinction within pluralist departments between (1) a shared commitment to pluralism and (2) different commitments to a plurality of philosophies.

(once safely housed below deck). On a pluralist ship, they worry that all animals are equal.

Now, it is crucial to recognize that these views all contain some important insights. Each highlights some important new realities—realities of increasing intellectual specialization and inter-institutional competition, shrinking institutional resources, and pressing political challenges and the importance of non-Western intellectual traditions. To the extent, however, that these points are set forth *as objections to pluralism* (or pluralist departments), they rest on a pervasive but simple misunderstanding—the conflation of pluralism with maximum possible plurality, superficial coverage and breadth, and uncritical openness to all difference.

2. There is a war over pluralism on another battlefield. The battle here is largely intramural, though this war frequently is anything but civil. Using the common, seemingly accepted labels, this war pits pluralist against analyst, or Continentalist against Anglo-Americanist, or Continental philosopher against analytic philosopher.[27] Now, I want to suggest that these categories are theoretically flawed and practically ineffective—especially in the context of pluralism. There are several reasons why this is so.

   a. In small part, the problem is that this categorization suggests that analysts can't be pluralists. However, analytic philosophers can be pluralists, even if many analysts—including those who are lip-service pluralists—are not.

   b. In another small part, these familiar labels suggest that Continental philosophers can't fail to be pluralists. However, the issue of pluralism is not so easy. Continental philosophers can fail to be pluralists, even if they champion nonpluralist and exclusionary theories and practices that differ from those of their nonpluralist analytic adversaries. In this context, there may be a need for self-described pluralists

---

27. See, for example, Nicholas Rescher, "American Philosophy Today" in *American Philosophy Today and Other Philosophical Studies* (Boston: Rowman & Littlefield, 1994), p. 18. In this context, Rescher claimed as a matter of fact that "at present philosophy is a garden where 100 flowers bloom" (p. 8). This claim, I think, is false—and results from a failure to distinguish genuine *pluralism* from the mere *plurality* or "luxuriant diversity" (p. 22) of philosophies (and a failure to distinguish those philosophies that are blooming from those that are withering). In a related context, in *Pluralism: Against the Demand for Consensus* (Oxford: Oxford University Press, 1993), Rescher claimed as a matter of principle that philosophers should be pluralists— "Given the diversity of human experience, empiricism entails pluralism" (p. 77). This claim, I think, is true—even though, as students of William James well know, many philosophers avoid this "unavoidable" inference from experience to pluralism.

to pluralize their own pluralism, to render pluralism more radical and thorough-going.

c. In larger part, the Continental/analytic categorization suggests that analytic philosophers do not or cannot read Continental philosophy, and that Continental philosophers, fearing science and logic, do not or cannot engage in analysis. This is false. Analytic philosophers are able to engage important Continental texts, themes, and traditions, and should not allow themselves to be restricted by professional categories and labels from doing so. And, Continentalists, like all philosophers, analyze, distinguish, reason rigorously, and attend to language. As a result, they should not cede to others ownership of, or association with, important philosophical activities such as analysis.

d. Finally, the Continental/analytic disjunction produces categories that are incomplete—as many pragmatists, critical theorists, feminists, non-Western philosophers, and many others know first-hand.

Despite these problems, it may seem that the familiar Continental/analytic categories have rough meanings and accepted uses. The rough meanings, however, are too rough; the accepted uses are abuses. These categories obscure the most important fact. For this reason, I propose that all professional philosophers completely stop using these categories and labels—stop thinking, talking, and interacting in Continental/analytic terms. Instead, let us use more accurate labels: In the academy as in society, the opponent of the pluralist is the *fundamentalist*. A philosophical fundamentalist is simply a philosophical absolutist who is proud of being an absolutist and who believes others should adopt this same absolutism.[28] In philosophy, the fundamentalist pursues conceptual—rather than ethnic—cleansing. Pluralists, then, may analyze *or* argue *or* formalize *or* symbolize *or* interpret *or* deconstruct *or* historicize *or* critique *or* do any number of other things. However, when *any* of these activities is undertaken on behalf of ontological, epistemological, or moral absolutes, it acquires a fundamentalist, antipluralist character. There is no fundamentalist love of empire in honest love of wisdom. For this reason

---

28. After completing this chapter, I discovered William E. Connolly's most recent book, *The Ethos of Pluralization* (Minneapolis: University of Minnesota Press, 1995). Connolly's insightful concern with the critical pluralization of pluralism, his identification of fundamentalism as a "general imperative to assert an absolute, singular ground of authority"—"a fundamentalist is an American dogmatist who is proud of it" (p. 105)—and his analysis of the interplay between fundamentalism and pluralism make no reference to the pluralism and pragmatism of James or Dewey. Still, I take his insights to deeply parallel this tradition from beginning to end. And, just as James concludes "ever not quite" that "something always escapes," Connolly concludes that "there is always more political work to be done" (p. 198).

a "fundamentalist philosophy department," like "fundamentalist education," is an oxymoron; similarly, a "pluralist philosophy department" is a redundancy.[29] Pluralist philosophy departments are valuable because they promote this truth.

C. How Might a Pluralist Philosophy Department Be Constituted?

There are few, if any, pluralist philosophy departments at present. Love of empire is prevalent and powerful. But it doesn't have to be this way. What can be done? And who should do it?

In the abstract, the outlines of a solution seem obvious enough:

1. Educate pluralists in undergraduate and graduate institutions, and hire and employ them in college and university departments of philosophy;

2. Foster conditions that enable existing fundamentalist philosophers to become pluralists;

3. Stimulate pluralists to develop and sustain the common experiences, shared commitments, respect for differences, and habits of seeking alternatives that make possible pluralist cultures and climates in departments— here there is much to learn from the experiences and situations of many different individuals and departments; and,

4. Encourage the American Philosophical Association and other professional organizations critically to promote genuine pluralism (rather than mere professional plurality)— here a sustained series of programs or a "professional conversation" on pluralism would be an appropriate undertaking at present.

Of course, none of this is obvious or easy—except in the abstract. Still, this is not the place to develop at length these or other suggestions. What professional philosophy needs at present is not another executive order or even another strategic plan for pluralist reconstruction. Instead, it needs a strategic *process* of genuinely pluralist reconstruction—and any such process must involve and include multiple voices and multiple viewpoints. For now, with James, let me note simply that "something always escapes."

However, individual responsibility must not escape. Between courses and students, research and scholarship, and committees and community service,

---

29. I take the absolutism of the philosophical fundamentalist to stand in sharp contrast to the "immaturity" outlined by John Dewey as a necessary condition of education as growth. See *Democracy and Education, John Dewey: The Middle Works, 1899–1924*, vol. 9 (Carbondale, Ill.: Southern Illinois University Press, 1980 [1916]).

each one of us—you and I—has a responsibility to engage in a sustained effort to make our philosophy departments intellectual republics rather than intellectual empires. If we do not act this way, we do not *live* as pluralists.

Nothing includes everything—James was right—but in our lives each of us must include at least this much.

5

The Idols of the Twilight: Pragmatism and Postmodernism

The anxiety of influence is born then in that in order to take a given course, in order to transmit or transfer a given message, you must in advance pay for the stamp, have it punched or obliterated, have yourself taxed for this or that.

—Jacques Derrida, *The Post Card*

I am reluctant to make assessments about the type of culture that may be in store. Everything is present, you see, at least as a virtual object, inside a given culture. Or everything that has already featured once. The problem of objects that have never featured in culture is another matter. But it is part of memory and culture to be able to reactualize any objects whatever that have already featured. Repetition is always possible; repetition with application, transformation.

—Michel Foucault, "Critical Theory/Intellectual History"

To arrive at new truth and vision is to alter. The old self is put off and the new self is only forming, and the form it finally takes will depend upon the unforeseeable result of an adventure. No one discovers a new world without forsaking an old one; and no one discovers a new world who exacts guarantee in advance for what it shall be, or who puts the act of discovery under bonds with respect to what the new world shall do to him when it comes into vision.

—John Dewey, *Experience and Nature*

What are the significant relations, if any, between French postmodernists and American pragmatists? What is the same or, at least, largely shared? What is different or, perhaps, even incompatible? In the face of postmodernism, is pragmatism obsolete? Has classical American philosophy now run its prepostmodern course? Or, in the face of pragmatism, is postmodernism irrelevant? Is postmodernism still occupied with the ills of a modernism for which pragmatism long ago developed a vaccine? What, if anything, might these two groups of philosophers have to offer one another? And, what might an account of their official papers, blood lines, and relations have to offer us?

These questions have not been posed frequently, examined urgently, or answered in depth. Philosophers operating within either one of these broad traditions largely have ignored the other tradition, even though they've often been concerned with "the Generalized Other" and, more generally still, simply "the Other."

When they have been raised, these questions have been answered in a great many different ways for a great many different purposes. Some writers view postmodernism and pragmatism in terms of resemblance and identity. They locate overriding deep historical and philosophical similarities between postmodernism and pragmatism. From this point of view, for example, both postmodernism and pragmatism overturn the priorities and dualisms of much traditional modern philosophy, and critically articulate new possibilities for questioning, thinking, and being.

By contrast, some other writers view postmodernism and pragmatism in terms of discontinuity and difference. They argue that the two traditions are marked by irreducible major differences. Postmodernists who hold this view typically find pragmatists hopelessly American, fixated on science and method, and naively committed to voluntarism, individualism, humanism, and liberalism—and their accompanying, if often unrecognized, forms of subjection and domination. On this view, pragmatism has philosophical merit only as a forerunner or foreshadow of postmodernism. In turn, pragmatists who hold this view believe that postmodernists are hopelessly French, thoroughly self-consumed and academic in the worst sense of the term, and wholly ensnared by the very metaphysical theories that they seek to overcome. On this view, what is insightful in postmodernism is merely an echo or trace of pragmatism and anything but original (except in jargon), while what is genuinely original in postmodernism is merely wrong.

Perhaps a plausible case could be made for either of these two general and polemical views of postmodernism and pragmatism. Richard Rorty, for example, has made separate, somewhat inconsistent cases for both of these positions, claiming first that "we should see Dewey as having already gone the route Foucault is traveling, and as having arrived at the point Foucault is still trying to reach,"[1] and later that Dewey's pragmatism needs to be "spliced with the very different kind of criticism" provided by Foucault.[2]

---

1. Rorty, *Consequences of Pragmatism* (Minneapolis: University of Minnesota Press, 1982), p. 207.

2. Rorty, "Comments on Sleeper and Edel, *Transactions of the Charles S. Peirce Society* 21.1 (1985): 44.

Both of these views, however, are oversimplifications. The complex relations between pragmatism and postmodernism simply cannot be grasped adequately either in terms of identity or in terms of difference. Moreover, today there is no space in philosophy from which to issue with confidence any such judgment about the supposed identity or the supposed difference between pragmatism and postmodernism. Any illuminating consideration of pragmatism and postmodernism today—today when each largely is present only as an absence to the other, only under almost total erasure by the other—must create new space in which different and more valuable sorts of engagements may be possible.

It is possible, of course, that there is no room in professional philosophy for this undertaking. Foucault observed that "we have to walk in line because of the extreme narrowness of the place where one can listen and make oneself heard."[3] Accordingly, in this essay I will walk out of line; perhaps I will walk out of two lines, one Deweyan and the other Foucauldian. I do so in order to make heard deeper, richer, more complexly engaged pragmatist and postmodernist voices. My strategy is first to examine critically in turn how postmodernism has been understood by many pragmatists and how postmodernism has been viewed by many pragmatists as a challenge to pragmatic accounts of nature, self, and reason. I then consider how pragmatism in turn may be viewed as a challenge to postmodernism, and conclude by offering an outline for a *genealogical pragmatism*—a pragmatism that takes seriously the temperament of postmodernism, a genealogy that takes seriously the temperament of pragmatism. At no point do I aim to deliver a philosophical knockout punch; my goal is neither refutation nor reduction (nor simply synthesis). Instead, with Foucault, "I believe too much in truth not to suppose that there are different truths and different ways of speaking truth."[4]

Pragmatism's Postmodernism: The Quest for Identity

Instead of understanding the relations of pragmatism and postmodernism in terms of identity or difference, several philosophers recently have articulated more complex, nuanced, richer understandings of pragmatism and

---

3. Michel Foucault, "The Masked Philosopher," *Politics, Philosophy, Culture: Interviews and Other Writings, 1977–1984* (New York: Routledge, Chapman & Hall, 1988 [1983]), p. 327. In *The Twilight of the Idols*, Nietzsche notes "Now I have you, nihilist! Assiduity is the *sin* against the holy spirit. Only ideas *won by walking* have any value." (New York: Penguin Books, 1990 [1889]), p. 36.
4. Michel Foucault, "Practicing Criticism," *Politics, Philosophy, Culture: Interviews and Other Writings, 1977–1984*, p. 156. Compare William James's statement that the pragmatic "account of truth is an account of truths in the plural." *Pragmatism, The Works of William James* (Cambridge, Mass.: Harvard University Press, 1975 [1907]), p. 104.

postmodernism. These philosophers, motivated by rather different concerns but perhaps all influenced more by pragmatism than postmodernism, include Kai Nielsen, Vincent Colapietro, and John Ryder.[5] All stress three points:

1. Pragmatism and postmodernism have much in common, including being antimetaphysical, antirepresentational, and antifoundational.

2. Postmodernism differs from pragmatism in important ways that constitute critical challenges to pragmatism and, for example, pragmatic accounts of reason, self, and nature.

3. Pragmatism successfully meets the challenges of postmodernism and, as such, is philosophically preferable to postmodernism.

I am sympathetic to these claims and, even more so, to the pragmatism that underlies them. Still, against this background of agreement, I have some serious reservations and countersuggestions. I intend these critical remarks to

---

5. I focus on the following three insightful essays: Kai Nielsen, "Peirce, Pragmatism and the Challenge of Postmodernism," Transactions *of the Charles S. Peirce Society*, 29, #4, pp. 513–560; Vincent Colapietro, "The Vanishing Subject of Contemporary Discourse: A Pragmatic Response," *The Journal of Philosophy* 87.11 (1990): 644–55; and John Ryder, "The Use and Abuse of Modernity: Postmodernism and the American Philosophic Tradition," *The Journal of Speculative Philosophy* 7.2 (1993): 92–102. See my direct replies to these essays: "Can Pragmatism Appropriate the Resources of Postmodernism?," *Transactions of the Charles S. Peirce Society* 29.4 (1993): 561–72; "Subjects Constructed, Deconstructed, and Reconstructed," *The Journal of Philosophy* 87.11 (1990): 655–57; and, "Postmodernism: Old and New," *The Journal of Speculative Philosophy* 7.2 (1993): 103–9; © 1993 by The Pennsylvania State University; reproduced with changes by permission of The Pennsylvania State University. See also these analyses of pragmatism and postmodernism: Kai Nielsen, *After the Demise of the Tradition: Rorty, Critical Theory, and the Fate of Philosophy* (Boulder, Colo.: Westview Press, 1991); David Ray Griffin, John B. Cobb Jr., Marcus P. Ford, Pete A. Y. Gunter, and Peter Ochs, *Founders of Constructive Postmodern Philosophy* (Albany: State University of New York Press, 1993); Robert Cummings Neville, *The Highroad around Modernism* (Albany: State University of New York Press, 1992); Giles Gunn, *Thinking Across the American Grain: Ideology, Intellect, and the New Pragmatism* (Chicago: University of Chicago Press, 1992); Ralph Sleeper, "The Pragmatics of Deconstruction and the End of Metaphysics" in *Philosophy and the Reconstruction of Culture: Pragmatic Essays After Dewey,* ed. John J. Stuhr (Albany: State University of New York Press, 1993); Kathleen M. Wheeler, *Romanticism, Pragmatism, and Deconstruction* (Oxford: Blackwell, 1993); Honi Fern Haber, *Beyond Postmodern Politics: Lyotard, Rorty, Foucault* (New York: Routledge, 1994); Frank J. Macke, "Pragmatism Reconsidered: John Dewey and Michel Foucault on the Consequences of Inquiry," *Recovering Pragmatism's Voice: The Classical Tradition, Rorty, and the Philosophy of Communication*, ed. Lenore Langsdorf and Andrew R. Smith (Albany: State University of New York Press, 1995); John Patrick Diggins, "Conclusion: Poststructuralism and America's Intellectual Traditions," *The Promise of Pragmatism: Modernism and the Crisis of Knowledge and Authority* (Chicago: University of Chicago Press, 1994).

be constructive, or reconstructive, and seek by means of this criticism to extend or radicalize pragmatism.

Even these pragmatists who seek to understand postmodernism not simply in terms of its identity with, or difference from, pragmatism often characterize postmodernism in inadequate ways. This inadequacy manifests itself in four interrelated ways. First, pragmatist accounts of postmodernism often are *overly general*, if not downright inaccurate. Ryder, for example, links Kierkegaard, Nietzsche, Heidegger, Wittgenstein, Lyotard, Dewey, and Sellars by means of a supposedly single "postmodernist sensibility." Similarly, Nielsen fails to note (though he must notice) that just as there is a "lot of distance" between Peirce and Dewey or between Nagel and Rorty, there also is a "lot of distance" between Lyotard and Foucault, or Kristeva and Deleuze, or between many other pairs of contemporary French theorists. In the same vein, while Colapietro declares that postmodernism is not a "monolithic position," he uses the term "postmodernism" (and also, interchangeably, the term "poststructuralism") to refer to the thought of Derrida, Foucault, Lacan, Lyotard, and many others. This seems too sweeping and unconvincing: Do Lacan and Deleuze, for example, really employ a shared paradigm of language and philosophy? Are the styles and methods of Derrida and Lyotard, for instance, really substantially the same? Just how similar are the political analyses of Foucault and Baudrillard? The danger here, of course is that pragmatists (like many other thinkers) readily may come to use the term "postmodernism" as a blanket category for a sort of French "other"—a single other that does not include the necessary distinctions between the work of philosophers who differ from one another in many respects. I find it about as useful to group together, say, Foucault, Derrida, Lacan, Lyotard, and Baudrillard as postmodernists as it would be to group together without distinction, say, Moore, Carnap, Wittgenstein, Rawls, and Davidson as analytic philosophers. In this context, Foucault's exasperated remark seems appropriate: "I do not understand what kind of problem is common to the people we call post-modern or post-structuralist."[6] Furthermore, this same issue arises within the different works of many individual so-called postmodernists. As Foucault again asks: "[D]o

---

6. Michel Foucault, "Critical Theory/Intellectual History," *Politics, Philosophy, Culture: Interviews and Other Writings, 1977–1984,* pp. 33–34. In turn, David Hoy has commented that "In contrast to Lyotard's stance, a Foucauldian postmodern would not need to be an advocate of postmodernism. I think that Foucault was a consistent postmodern in that he would never have called himself a postmodern." David Couzens Hoy, "Foucault: Modern or Postmodern?," *After Foucault: Humanistic Knowledge, Postmodern Challenges,* ed. Jonathan Arac (New Brunswick, N.J.: Rutgers University Press, 1988), p. 38.

you think I have worked like that all those years to say the same thing and not be changed?"[7] The other side of this issue is just as problematic: Postmodernists may come to use the term "pragmatism" as a catchall label for a sort of American "other"—a caricature that fails to note the crucial differences among the philosophers so grouped. Again, I find it about as useful to group, say, Emerson, Peirce, Dewey, Lewis, and Rorty together as pragmatists as it would be to identify Kierkegaard, Husserl, Schutz, Sartre, and Gadamer as phenomenologists. In this context, Dewey's observation seems on the mark: The term "pragmatism" almost always is employed in philosophy by persons who find the use of this label an easy alternative to the work of becoming attuned to a new kind of thought.

Second, many pragmatic accounts of the relations between pragmatism and postmodernism are *overly abstract*. These accounts often detach analytically philosophical temperaments, questions, methods, and positions from the larger cultural contexts in which they arise and function. As such, they unintentionally reduce philosophies to complexes of propositions ripe for the plucking from books and journals that thus seem to set forth views from nowhere and no time. However, don't time and place have intrinsic import for, to, and in philosophy? Are the different realities, for example, of Dewey's New York City in 1929, Heidegger's Freiburg in 1939, Foucault's Paris in 1968, and Rorty's Virginia in 1995 philosophically irrelevant? Shouldn't philosophy take its own cultural contexts seriously? To omit this—even with the good intentions of Ryder, Nielsen, Colapietro, and others—is to offer a paradigmatically analytic reading or checklist of pragmatism and postmodernism, a reading of both as free-floating and unconnected to history, politics, economics, science, technology, and so on. Of course, pragmatists engaged in this sort of reading may find it easier, as Colapietro puts it, to "reformulate" and, once reformulated, to "respond" to the apparent insights or shortcomings of a philosophic tradition other than their own. Although methodologically easier, this sort of reformulation may be a recipe for distortion and oversimplification. Moreover, this whole approach is foreign both to postmodernism—to projects of deconstruction and genealogy—and to pragmatism—to projects of inquiry and criticism. Both postmodernists and pragmatists insist on the irreducibly temporal, spatial, social, contextual character of human subjects, languages, thoughts, experiences. Both insist that they themselves must be approached, interpreted, assessed, and appropriated from this perspective. At one level, Colapietro in particular seems to recognize and agree with this point: He asserts insightfully the inseparability of "symbolization and context" as a defining

---

7. Michel Foucault, "The Minimalist Self," *Politics, Philosophy, Culture: Interviews and Other Writings, 1977–1984* [1983], p. 14.

feature of pragmatism. At another level, however, he seems willing to separate symbolization from context: His "pragmatic response" to French
postmodernism neither identifies nor locates the cultural context(s) of
postmodernism. To fail to do this is in effect to employ a noncontextual
notion of philosophy and a Cartesian notion of the self (who philosophizes).
In practice, this reinscribes in philosophy this Cartesian self and its authority by means of a context-free analysis of postmodern theories—theories
that seek, ironically, to erase those very notions of the self and context-free
analyses.

Third, many pragmatic accounts of pragmatism and postmodernism are
overly modernist. For example, Ryder sets forth a brief, overarching master
account of philosophy through its classical, modern, and postmodern periods—ending with three waves or generations of postmodernists that include,
remarkably, Jefferson, Emerson, Peirce, and Rorty. Similarly, Nielsen con-
structs a grand metanarrative or metaconversation—with a cast of characters
from Peirce to Heidegger, Austin to Habermas, Carnap to Freud, and Quine
to Lyotard—that tells us how history has gone and what it is finally to gain
human emancipation or, at least, to be left with the honest hope (if not the
reality) of such emancipation. These narratives perform a foundationalist
epistemological function that is at odds with both pragmatism and
postmodernism. Moreover, these narratives are unconvincing as histories of
philosophy in at least two respects:

(a) To view pragmatism as an early model of postmodernism—Jefferson and
Emerson and Peirce as postmodernists!—is to mistake both the history
of pragmatism and its contemporary philosophic significance.

(b) To view postmodernism as a wholesale rejection of modernism is to
misunderstand the origins and claims of postmodernism. As Foucault has
repeatedly claimed, postmodernism cannot be seen simply as
antimodernism.[8] In this same vein, Lyotard has argued that the postmodern
is a precondition of the modern and that the postmodern is the modern
at its beginning rather than its end. Arguing that the postmodern is a
component of the modern, Lyotard identifies the postmodern as "that
which, in the modern, puts forward the unpresentable in presentation
itself; that which denies itself the solace of good forms, the consensus of
a taste which would make it possible to share collectively the nostalgia
for the unattainable; that which searches for new presentations, not in

---

8. Nielsen, calling postmodernism "the very hallmark of modernity," falls victim to the opposite
extreme, and thus is led to claim that many analytical philosophers would find most postmodernist
claims plainly true and little more than platitudinous commonplaces ("Peirce and the Challenge
of Postmodernism," pp. 548–49).

order to enjoy them but in order to impart a stronger sense of the unpresentable."[9]

Any master narrative that views postmodernism as a refutation of modernism, and pragmatism as a variety of postmodernism is a modernist abuse of both pragmatism and postmodernism.

Finally, the comparative studies by many pragmatists of pragmatism and postmodernism often are *overly theoretical*—or, too little practical. To put this a different way, such studies are too close to Rorty and too far from James and Dewey.[10] Rorty declares that philosophy is clever conversation. Taken as an account or prescription about philosophy, I think this is dead wrong; but, taken as an account or description of Rorty's own work, I think it is right on target. As a result, Rorty gives us pragmatist theory without pragmatist politics; he is Dewey now fully kept or quarantined inside the academy. Ryder, Colapietro, and Nielsen, for example, all come very close to viewing philosophy as conversation. They weave many major twentieth-century thinkers into a grand narrative without in the end connecting this conversation to the life experiences and problems that gave rise to it. What are the origins and products of postmodernism or pragmatism? What interests do these philosophies serve? And, what is the "cash-value" of the pragmatist response to the challenge of postmodernism? Why and how, if at all, does this matter outside the academy? Dewey, of course, claimed that these sorts of genealogical, practical questions supply a first-rate test of the value of any philosophy: Does it yield conclusions that when referred to ordinary experiences and predicaments, render them more significant, more luminous to us, and make our dealings with them more fruitful? For postmodernists and pragmatists, these issues cannot be mere afterthoughts.

Pragmatism's Postmodernism as a Challenge:
Nature and Objective Reality

Many pragmatists have sought not only to identify postmodernism, but also to characterize postmodernism as a challenge to pragmatism. Agreeing that this is so, these pragmatists have understood this supposed challenge in different ways. Ryder, for example, views postmodernism as a challenge to a pragmatist conception of nature. Colapietro focuses on postmodernism as

---

9. Jean-François Lyotard, *The Postmodern Condition: A Report on Knowledge* (Minneapolis; University of Minnesota Press, 1984 [1979]), pp. 79, 81.
10. See the discussion of Rorty and Dewey in chapter 6.

a challenge to a pragmatist conception of the self, subjectivity, and agency. Nielsen understands postmodernism as a challenge to pragmatic notions of reason and the rational fixation of belief. All agree that pragmatism meets the challenge(s) of postmodernism. These reassurances to pragmatists, I think, are in part misplaced.

In a challenging, important analysis, John Ryder claims that post-modernism is committed to some form of pluralism or relativism that amounts to an "abuse" (rather than use) of modern philosophy. It is this abuse, Ryder, contends, that makes it impossible for postmodernism to sustain or justify or give substance to any political vision of progress or emancipation, or any metaphysical account of nature or reality. The philosophic basis of this abuse, Ryder asserts, is postmodernism's faulty logic. Postmodernists, Ryder holds, make an invalid inference from the denial of objective knowledge to the denial of knowledge of objectively determinate traits of nature—the nature that we see and bump into. He explains that postmodernists conclude that knowledge of the objective traits of nature is impossible (or, further, that it makes no sense even to attribute objective determinate traits to nature) on the basis of their belief that objective knowledge of nature is impossible given that cognition is irreducibly perspectival and inherently creative. However, this argument, Ryder concludes, is a *non sequitur* because the belief that there can be no objective knowledge does not entail the belief that that there can be no knowledge of the objectively determinate traits of nature: "The fact that I see through eyeglasses, or that I see from some spatial perspective, does not mean that I cannot see what is there. . . . Postmodernism is correct, in other words, in its rejection of nonperspectival 'objective' knowledge, but it is incorrect in its associated claims that there are no objective traits of nature or that if there are such traits they cannot be known."[11]

This argument raises many issues. I think that Ryder pinpoints but does not pursue the most important issue when he observes that both pragma-tism—he calls pragmatism one of "the many postmodernist traditions"—and postmodernism have established irrefutably that "human activity, experience, is in some ways (and it would remain to be specified in which ways) creative of the worlds in which we live."[12] Now, American pragmatists set forth a metaphysics of *experience* and, in so doing, view experience as world cre-ative in a stronger sense than would be allowed by Ryder and many American naturalists and realists who set forth a metaphysics of *existence*.

However, this issue aside, there are three problems here. First, postmodernists simply do not make the argument that Ryder attributes to

---

11. Ryder, "Use and Abuse of Modernity," pp. 100–1.
12. Ibid., p. 98.

them. There is no textual basis for attributing to postmodernism the inference that Ryder rejects. The postmodernist point, I think, is not an "inference" resulting in the denial of the possibility of knowledge of objectively
determinate traits of nature, but rather an outright rejection of the meaning-
fulness and coherence of this very notion of objectively determinate traits
of nature (and a rejection of all modernist issues of subjectivity and objectivity that this notion makes possible). Second, I do not see how this
point constitutes an "abuse" of modernity. Ryder seems to conclude that it
is an abuse because he (with Buchler and other naturalists, perhaps) assumes some sort of realist/naturalist view of the world. Even if this assumption is correct, to use it in this argument in this way against postmodernism
simply begs the question. Third, in this context, I cannot understand how
bumping into or walking through doors yields knowledge of "where the
door objectively is." It seems to yield knowledge of where the door *interactively* or *transactionally* or *radically empirically* is. I take this to be one
of the lessons of the theories of experience of those well-known
"postmodernists," William James and John Dewey! As James observed,
reality supposedly independent of experience "seems a thing very hard to
find": Reality is "what we make of it. It is fruitless to define it by what it
originally was or by what it is apart from us."[13] I take this to be one of the
reasons that many postmodernists, like many pragmatists, ignore and reject
wholesale intramural realist/antirealist disputes still fashionable in other
sorts of philosophy today. As a result, postmodernism may constitute a
challenge to traditional empiricist, realist, or naturalist notions of nature
and objective reality, but it poses no such challenge to a radically empiricist
pragmatism, a pragmatism that is itself deeply critical of traditional empiricism, realism, and naturalism.

Pragmatism's Postmodernism as a Challenge:
Self, Subjectivity, and Agency

Like Ryder, Vincent Colapietro views postmodernism as a challenge to
pragmatism. In contrast to Ryder's view of postmodernism as a challenge to
supposedly pragmatic notions of nature and objective reality, Colapietro views
postmodernism as a challenge to pragmatic notions of the self and subjectivity.[14] He argues that both contemporary French postmodernism and classical
American pragmatism decenter, displace, and replace Cartesian accounts of

---

13. James, *Pragmatism*, pp. 119, 117.
14. Colapietro, "Vanishing Subject."

consciousness, subjectivity, and reference. In this respect, these two philosophical traditions are importantly similar. For Colapietro, the similarities
stop there, however. He claims that the postmodernists deconstruct the Cartesian self by means of an account of language that renders problematic the
self's agency and language's denotative function—hence the "vanishing subject" of postmodernism. On the other hand, Colapietro continues, pragmatists
provide an equally radical but more successful critique of modern thought
and culture. According to Colapietro, their account of self, nature, and communication permits appropriation of postmodernists' insights about subjectivity for pragmatic purposes of cultural reconstruction, instead of mere textual
deconstruction.

To say all this, of course, as Colapietro rightly notes, is not to "translate"
postmodernism into pragmatism, or *vice versa*. Moreover, if Colapietro asks
pragmatists to respond to postmodernist analyses of subjectivity—to speak
French—he primarily calls on postmodernists to respond to pragmatist insights about agency and meaning—to become pragmatists. This invitation to
conversion has deep roots in the history of pragmatism: Dewey called pragmatism a Copernican Revolution, and James compared it to the Protestant
Reformation, naming it the philosophy of the future and detailing the stages
through which it would pass on the way to eventual triumph. Colapietro
employs this strategy effectively, and I trust that my admiration for his work
will not be obscured by my critical focus here.[15]

Stating that there are important differences among postmodernists,
Colapietro focuses on Derrida in discussing postmodernist "decentering the
subject/overthrowing the father." This focus, however, is limited, and contains only one passage by Derrida. Elsewhere, Colapiertro always mentions
Derrida in connection with other postmodernists, and makes clear that he
considers Derrida to be a "representative figure" of postmodernism more
generally. In this light, the question becomes: For Colapietro, what exactly
does Derrida represent? Does Derrida represent only (a) the decentering of
Descartes's view of the self—a decentering that Colapietro accepts? No. For
Colapietro's purposes, this characterization must be too narrow. Derrida must
represent more than this if he is to function as a representative figure of
postmodernism because, as Colapietro rightly observes, there is nothing distinctively postmodern about decentering the Cartesian self. Does Derrida,

---

15. In a recent unpublished essay, "Fateful Ruptures and Fragile Reconciliations," delivered to
the American Philosophical Association Eastern Division meetings in 1994, Colapietro advocates
a "dialectical critique" in which pragmatism and postmodernism may avoid "disingenuous compromise and unwarranted vilification." In this context, he cites my genealogical pragmatism as
an exemplary instance of this approach.

then, represent (a) the decentering of the Cartesian self by means of (b) a particular account of language, via Saussure, "as a self-contained yet self-de(con)structive system of differences" which in turn makes possible (c) a particular (and distinctively postmodern) alternative account of human subjects (that Colapietro rejects)? Yes: This is what Derrida represents for Colapietro. But Derrida can perform this representative function only if other postmodernists share (b) his view of language and his relation to structuralism, and (c) his view of subjectivity. Colapietro seems to assume that this is so, but he presents no evidence for this assumption. I think this assumption is anything but self-evident. Derrida's post cards and Foucault's genealogies, for example, strike me as very different projects.

In part for this reason, I think it is far preferable to talk about the vanishing *self* or vanishing *substance* or, with William James, the vanishing *consciousness* of contemporary discourse—but not the vanishing *subject*. In postmodernism, it is this metaphysical self, substance, or consciousness that vanishes through deconstruction and differentiation. The subject, in contrast, is historically situated and constituted.[16] Thus, Derrida claims that differences are historical through and through (as long as "history" is not understood as any sort of final differentiation): "Differences . . . are the effects produced . . . that do not have as their cause a subject or substance, a thing in general, or a being that is somewhat present and itself escapes the play of difference."[17] Similarly, Foucault explained the objective of his work as the creation of "a history of the different modes by which, in our culture, human beings are made subjects."[18] In postmodernism, then, historical *subjects*, their care and technologies, far from vanishing, are the focus of archaeology and genealogy. Expressing his skepticism and hostility toward the notion of a sovereign, founding, universal, omnipresent self, Foucault denied that the self is a self-identical substance:[19] "I believe, on the contrary, that the subject is constituted through practices of subjection, or, in a more autonomous way, through practices of liberation, of liberty, as in Antiquity, on the basis, of course, of a number of rules, styles, inventions to be found in the

16. See especially Jacques Derrida, "Structure, Sign, and Play in the Discourse of the Human Sciences, *Writing and Difference* (London: Routledge and Kegan Paul, 1979 [1967].

17. Jacques Derrida, *Speech and Phenomena* (Evanston, Ill.: Northwestern University Press, 1973 [1967]), p. 141.

18. Michel Foucault, "Subject and Power," in Hubert L. Dreyfus and Paul Rabinow, eds., *Michel Foucault: Beyond Structuralism and Hermeneutics*, 2nd ed. (Chicago: University of Chicago Press, 1983), p. 208.

19. Michel Foucault, "The Ethic of Care for the Self as a Practice of Freedom: An Interview with Michel Foucault on January 20, 1984," in *The Final Foucault*, ed. James Bernauer and David Rasmussen (Cambridge, Mass.: MIT Press, 1988 [1984]), p. 10.

cultural environment."[20] Genealogy, for Foucault, is the study of these practices—"a form of history which can account for the constitution of knowledges, discourses, domains of objects, etc., without having to make reference to a subject which is either transcendental in relation to the field of events or runs in its empty sameness throughout the course of history."[21]

Given this view of the subject, why does Colapietro claim that postmodernists tend "to obscure and even to deny human agency"? How does this happen? It does not happen simply because they, like pragmatists, reject the Cartesian self. In the concluding section of the essay, Colapietro asserts that it happens "because of their [postmodernists'] view of language." But how does a postmodern view of language entail or lead to a denial of human agency? How does it leave the "status of the self-as-agent in doubt"? How does it deny "recognition of selves as sources of innovation and resistance"? (Did Foucault really deny this?)

These questions are scarcely addressed, but they are central to Colapietro's thesis. Colapietro *seems* to think that the loss of agency stems from postmodern dissolution of "commonsense" links between language and reality—a dissolution that leaves discourse wholly self-referential. If so, three questions remain.

1. Do postmodernists dissolve links between language and reality (and its real selves)? Or, like pragmatists, do they rather transform links between language and reality, dissolving only a transcendent, self-identical, self-present, and language-independent reality?

2. Does such a dissolution necessarily lead to a denial of agency? Or, again like pragmatists, do postmodernists affirm the existence of agency— particular cultural productions, formations, and self-understandings?

3. What sort of agency is thus repudiated? Is it the agency or "centers of experience" that may result from, in, and by meaningful organism/environment transactions? Or, once more with pragmatists, do postmodernists instead deny only traditional metaphysical accounts of agency—agency that results from meaningful organism/environment or subject/object transactions that are not themselves understood as products of agency?

Colapietro begins his essay by claiming that pragmatists must appropriate fundamental postmodern "insights into subjectivity," and ends by concluding that postmodernists, like pragmatists, "illuminate the practices,

---

20. Michel Foucault, "An Aesthetics of Existence," in *Politics, Philosophy, Culture: Interviews and Other Writings, 1977–1984* [1984], pp. 50–51.
21. Michel Foucault, "Truth and Power," *Power/Knowledge: Selected Interviews and Other Writings, 1972–1977* (New York: Pantheon Books, 1980 [1977]), p. 117.

discourses, and institutions in and through which embodied agents make practical decisions." I agree, and that is why I find Colapietro's further conclusions puzzling. Given postmodern illuminations of embodied agency, there is no reason to judge, as Colapietro does, that viewing agency as socially constructed within a system of differences necessarily renders the self "reduced" or "passive." Moreover, this view of agency seems to me no more opposed to common sense than James's radical empiricism, Dewey's individualism and democratic faith, or Mead's social behaviorism. As a result, postmodernism may constitute a challenge to traditional modern philosophies of the subject, but it poses no such challenge to a pragmatism trained on the incapacities of modern philosophy, a contextualizing, historicizing pragmatism of plural subjects.

Pragmatism's Postmodernism as a Challenge: Reason, Critique, and the Fixation of Belief

Like Ryder and Colapietro, Kai Nielsen also views postmodernism as a challenge to pragmatism. While he believes that both postmodernism and pragmatism hold some version of holistic antifoundationalism, he views postmodernism as a challenge—indeed, an "onslaught"—to pragmatism or any other *critical* theory of truth, reason, and inquiry. Drawing on what he takes to be the most uncompromising formulation of this position in the writings of Baudrillard, Nielsen views postmodernism as the rejection of truth, reason, critique, and validity. For postmodernism, Nielsen holds, these notions are unbelievable myths and oppressive social realities:

> There is no way validly to distinguish between reason and rhetoric. It is an illusion, claims Baudrillard, to believe that we can fix belief, criticize existing beliefs or past beliefs, from some superior vantage point of truth, reason, or scientific method. Both Marxism and pragmatism, he contends, fall into this error as fully as do the philosophies of the grand metaphysical tradition. . . . But in reality the very idea of an Archimedean point, an absolute historically non-contingent standard of critical appraisal is incoherent.[22]

By contrast, Nielsen believes that Peirce and Peircean pragmatism give hope to professional philosophers whose beliefs and self-images are challenged by postmodernism: "hope" for a "criterion of cognitive or at least factual significance." This hope seems to me to be a longing for foundations. It is a longing that most pragmatism—Dewey's pragmatism if not Peirce's

---

22. Nielsen, "Peirce and the Challenge of Postmodernism," pp. 519, 521.

pragmaticism—and most postmodernism has abandoned. Perhaps it is difficult to give up this hope, as Foucault observed: "It is understandable that
some people should weep over the present void and hanker instead, in the
world of ideas, for a little monarchy."[23] For those people, as Rorty notes by
reference to Peirce, there are still "philosophical slop-shops on every corner"
that sell supposedly objective beliefs and advertise values central to the very
structure of the universe.[24]

Postmodernism and pragmatism, however, play no part in these shops'
transactions. But this does not mean that they abandon criticism or proclaim its impossibility. Nielsen seems to believe that cultural criticism
requires some form of epistemological foundationalism; he seems to believe that an antifoundationalist, antiessentialist, antirepresentationalist,
antimetaphysical, historicist, holist criticism is a contradiction in terms.
Because he believes that postmodernism shows us once and for all that
there is no such foundation, he concludes that there can be no criticism—
even as he ends by stating his hope for "a criterion of cognitive or at least
factual significance, so that we could somehow gain a more adequate
understanding of our world."[25]

To realize his hope, there are two possible strategies available to Nielsen.
To employ the first strategy, we would have to retain the belief that criticism
requires foundations, but reject the view that postmodernism and pragmatism
are antifoundational. From the standpoint of pragmatism, this would require
abandoning pragmatism for pragmaticism, and setting forth an account of
Peirce as a foundationalist. This, of course, is exactly how modernists on both
sides of the Atlantic Ocean have appropriated Peirce, and it is exactly why
Peirce can be pressed into the service of modernism in ways in which James
and Dewey cannot. From the standpoint of postmodernism, this strategy would
require interpreting attacks on foundationalism as themselves forms of
foundationalism. In discussing Nielsen's position, James Jakob Liszka employs just this strategy to argue that Nielsen's antifoundationalism is just a
displacement of foundationalism: "What Nielsen wants, Derrida would say, is
a foundation without a foundation, which is the classical formula of reversal
in deconstruction: the foundation is not a foundation and the non-foundation
is a foundation." "When the Derridaean carnival is over," Liszka concludes,
"we will return to a purged form of foundationalism."[26]

---

23. Foucault, "The Masked Philosopher," p. 330.

24. Richard Rorty, "Trotsky and the Wild Orchids," *Wild Orchids and Trotsky: Messages from
American Universities*, ed. Mark Edmundson (New York: Penguin Books, 1993), p. 49.

25. Nielsen, "Peirce and the Challenge of Postmodernism," p. 556.

26. James Jakob Liszka, "Good and Bad Foundationalism," *Transactions of the Charles S.
Peirce Society* 29.4 (1993): 574.

This strategy is little more than clever equivocation about the meaning of foundationalism. As such, it begs the question about the possibility of nonfoundationalist criticism: It asserts without argument that attacks on foundationalism must be foundational; it denies without argument that a claim may have a foundation in the sense that it has a rational basis even though it does not have a foundation in the sense that it has direct warrant. As a result, this strategy is neither promising nor plausible.

A second strategy is available. To employ it, we would have to reject Nielsen's belief that criticism requires foundations, while retaining the view that postmodernism and pragmatism are antifoundational. This strategy is eminently reasonable: It proves possibility by pointing out actuality; it shows that criticism without foundations is possible by demonstrating that criticism without foundations has been actualized. Criticism without foundations: Read *Freedom and Culture* or *Discipline and Punish*. This strategy directs us to pragmatism: to thoroughgoing genetic analyses of liberal values of freedom, individualism, and reason; to radical attacks on economic determinism, our money culture, and the production of its accompanying business mind; to careful studies of major social institutions, including the school, the museum, and the church; and to striking new views of philosophy as criticism, inquiry, and vision. This strategy also directs us to postmodernism: to detailed genealogies of the cultural production of subjects, discourses, and regimes; to sophisticated accounts of the nature of power and its relation to interpretation, rationalities, and knowledges; to penetrating analyses of the nature of the self and to bold conceptions of philosophy as criticism, concept creation, and countermemory. In this light, postmodernism may constitute a challenge to foundationalist philosophies, but it poses no such challenge to a pragmatism committed to a genuinely experiential fixation of belief. On this score, the only challenge that postmodernism presents to pragmatism is the same challenge that pragmatism presents to postmodernism: a wealth of insights awaiting critical consideration. At present, this is an opportunity more than a challenge.

Pragmatism as a Challenge to Postmodernism: Hope, Will, and Ideals

> Farewell to an idea. . . . The cancellings,
> The negations are never final. The father sits
> In space, wherever he sits, of bleak regard,
> As one that is strong in the bushes of his eyes.
> He says no to no and yes to yes. he says yes
> To no; and in saying yes he says farewell.
>
> —Wallace Stevens, "The Auroras of Autumn"

Although many have viewed postmodernism as a challenge to pragmatism, few have viewed pragmatism as a challenge to postmodernism. Perhaps pragmatists, exhausted after a century of defending themselves against seemingly endless waves of linguistic, analytic, positivistic, absolutist, idealistic, materialistic, dualistic, scientistic, and therapeutic theorists, have lacked the necessary energy to go on the offensive. Or perhaps pragmatists, increasingly contained within, and by, the university, its increasing professionalization and specialization, and a disinterested commercial culture, have lacked the necessary incentive.[27] Or finally and more accurately, I think, perhaps pragmatists—meliorists in a global culture seemingly marked less and less by a melioristic mood—have lacked the necessary audience.

In any case, while we may debate whether or not we live in a philosophically postmodern condition, we surely do not live in a philosophically pragmatic one. If Dewey is correct in his observation that we are living in the twilight of a time of transition, then it is clear that pragmatists are not among the idols of this twilight. Instead, from philosophy to literary theory and cultural studies, the postmodernists are our idols. At present, the darlings of the academy are not Emerson, Peirce, James, Royce, Dewey, Santayana, and Mead. Instead, they are Nietzsche, Foucault, Derrida, Lacan, Deleuze, Lyotard, and Baudrillard.

Why is this? The answer lies not so much in matters of doctrine—sharply differing views of nature, self, or reason, for example—as in matters of style and spirit—sharply differing temperaments and wills. Postmodernism is the expression of a deconstructive temperament. It is dark and brooding, suspicious, and accusatory. It seeks to destabilize, delimit, defer, demystify, denaturalize, decolonize, delegitimize, and dethrone. It uncovers, interrogates, and interrupts. Rejecting the death of the will, recounted most fully by John Barth in *The End of the Road*,[28] postmodernism is the expression of a *will to oppositionality*, a demand for difference and the exhilaration of change. At work perhaps most fully in the sometimes playful work of Derrida on speech, writing, and meaning, this will to difference, is expressed most seriously and self-consciously by Foucault:

---

27. See the discussion of the "business mind" and the Humanities, Inc. in chapter 1.
28. John Barth, *The End of the Road* (New York: Bantam Books, 1969 [1958]). As Joe tells Jake in this novel, "when you say good-bye to objective values, you really have to flex your muscles and keep your eyes open, because you're on your own. It takes energy; not just personal energy, but cultural energy, or you're lost. Energy's what makes the difference between American pragmatism and French existentialism—where the hell else but in America could you have a cheerful nihilism, for God's sake" (p. 47).

[The subject] is not a substance; it is a form and this form is not above all or always identical to itself. . . . And it is precisely the historical constitution of these different forms of subject relating to games of truth that interest me.[29]

The main interest in life and work is to become someone else that you were not in the beginning. If you knew when you began a book what you would say at the end, do you think that you would have the courage to write it? What is true for writing and for a love relationship is true also for life. The game is worthwhile insofar as we don't know what will be the end.[30]

But, then, what is philosophy today—philosophical activity, I mean—if it is not the critical work that thought brings to bear on itself? In what does it consist, if not in the endeavor to know how and to what extent it might be possible to think differently, instead of legitimizing what is already known? . . . The object [is] to learn to what extent the effort to think one's own history can free thought from what it silently thinks, and so enable it to think differently.[31]

The movement by which, not without effort and uncertainty, dreams and illusions, one detaches oneself from what is accepted as true and seeks other rules—that is philosophy The displacement of received values and all the work that has been done to think otherwise, to do something else, to become other than what one is—that too is philosophy.[32]

In contrast, pragmatism is the expression of a reconstructive temperament. It is more cheerful and hopeful, trusting, and affirming. It seeks to recover, reassess, realize, readjust and reconcile, redescribe, reinvent, redirect, and realign. It inquires, ameliorates, and articulates ideals for action. Also (but differently) rejecting the death of the will, pragmatism is the expression of a *will to intimacy*, a demand for harmony and the exhilaration of ideals. At work perhaps most fully in Dewey's always earnest writings on experience and community, this will to intimacy—to plural intimacies—is expressed most directly and self-consciously by James:

For a philosophy to succeed on a universal scale it must define the future *congruously with our spontaneous powers*. . . . A philosophy whose prin-

29. Foucault, "The Ethic of Care for the Self as a Practice of Freedom," p. 10.

30. Michel Foucault, "Truth, Power, Self: An Interview with Michel Foucault, October 25, 1982," *Technologies of the Self*, ed. Luther H. Martin, Huck Gutman, and Patrick H. Hutton (Amherst, Mass.: University of Massachusetts Press, 1988), p. 9.

31. Michel Foucault, *The Use of Pleasure* (New York: Pantheon Books, 1985 [1984]), p. 9. Writing about Foucault, Deleuze puts this same point this way: "Thought thinks its own history (the past), but in order to free itself from what it thinks (the present) and be able finally to 'think otherwise' (the future)." Gilles Deleuze, *Foucault* (Minneapolis: University of Minnesota Press, 1988 [1986]), p. 119.

32. Foucault, "The Masked Philosopher," p. 330.

ciple is so incommensurate with our most intimate powers as to deny them all relevancy in universal affairs, as to annihilate their motive at one blow, will be even more unpopular than pessimism. . . . If we survey the field of history and ask what features all great periods of revival, of expansion of the human mind, display in common, we shall find, I think, simply this: that each and all of them have said to the human being, 'The inmost nature of the reality is congenial to *powers* which you possess.'[33]

This is the philosophy of humanism in the widest sense. Our philosophies swell the current of being, add their character to it. They are part of all that we have met, of all that makes us be. . . . Remember that one of our troubles with [absolutism] was its essential foreignness and monstrosity—there really is no other word for it than that. Its having the all-inclusive form gave to it an essentially heterogeneous nature from ourselves. . . . The all-form or monistic form makes the foreignness result, the each-form or pluralistic form leaves the intimacy undisturbed.[34]

In the end it is our faith and not our logic that decides such questions, and I deny the right of any pretended logic to veto my own faith. I find myself willing to take the universe to be really dangerous and adventurous, without therefore backing out and crying "no play." I am willing to think that the prodigal-son attitude, open to us as it is in many vicissitudes, is not the right and final attitude towards the whole of life. I am willing that there should be real losses and real losers, and no total preservation of all that is. I can believe in the ideal as an ultimate, not as an origin, and as an extract, not the whole. When the cup is poured off, the dregs are left behind forever, but the possibility of what is poured off is sweet enough to accept.[35]

Our contemporary mind having once for all grasped the possibility of a more intimate *weltanschauung*, the only opinions quite worthy of arresting our attention will fall within the general scope of what may roughly be called the pantheistic field of vision, the vision of God as the indwelling divine rather that the external creator, and of human life as part and parcel of that deep reality. . . . From a pragmatic point of view the difference between living against a background of foreignness and one of intimacy means the difference between a general habit of wariness and one of trust.[36]

In the hands of Royce and Dewey, this will to intimacy informs a distinctively pragmatic social philosophy of community and democracy. This

---

33. William James, "The Sentiment of Rationality," *The Will to Believe and Other Essays in Popular Philosophy, The Works of William James* (Cambridge, Mass.: Harvard University Press, 1979 [1882]), pp. 70–71, 73.
34. James, *A Pluralistic Universe, The Works of William James* (Cambridge, Mass.: Harvard University Press, 1977 [1909]), p. 144.
35. James, *Pragmatism*, p. 142.
36. James, *Pluralistic Universe*, p. 19.

intimacy is not a metaphysical fact—something actual. Rather, it is a social ideal—something possible. Achieving this ideal—really living against a background of intimacy—requires social action. Reworking Peirce's doctrine of signs into a method of interpretation on behalf of this social ideal, Josiah Royce located the salvation of intimacy in the action of community and a new provincialism: "the salvation of the world, will be found, if at all, through uniting the already existing communities of mankind into higher communities, and not through merely freeing the peoples from their oppressors, or through giving them a more popular government, unless popular government always takes the form of government by the united community, through the united community, and for the united community." This higher, great community, Royce argued, must be a pluralist community, a community of differences, a community that finds "no place for that sort of internationalism which despises the individual variety of nations and which tries to substitute for the vices of those who at present seek merely to conquer mankind, the equally worthless desire of those who hope to see us in future as 'men without a country.' " There can never be a genuinely great community or spiritual body, Royce concluded, "unless that body . . . has its many members."[37] Calling consciousness of this communal life and its implications the very idea of democracy, John Dewey stressed that "*the end of democracy is a radical end*," an "end not realized in any country at anytime," an end that requires sweeping economic, political, legal, and cultural change: "A democratic liberalism that does not recognize these things in thought and action is not awake to its own meaning and to what that meaning demands."[38] The extent to which this democratic faith—this faith in community, harmony, and intimacy— is justified, Dewey and all pragmatists hold, can be determined only after (and not before) sustained action on its behalf.

Perhaps it is not surprising to find this sort of melioristic faith in the pragmatists, in the children of Emerson. And perhaps it is not surprising to

---

37. Josiah Royce, *The Hope of the Great Community* (Freeport, N.Y.: Books for Libraries Press, 1967 [1916]), pp. 49–50, 51. There are two superb extended discussions of Royce's social philosophy: John J. McDermott, "Josiah Royce's Philosophy of the Community, " *American Philosophy*, ed. Marcus G. Singer (Cambridge: Cambridge University Press, 1985), pp. 153–76; and John E. Smith, *Royce's Social Infinite: The Community Interpretation* (New York: Liberal Arts Press, 1950).

38. John Dewey, "Democracy is Radical," *John Dewey: The Later Works, 1925–1953*, vol. 11 (Carbondale, Ill.: Southern Illinois University Press, 1987 [1937]), pp. 298–99. For an extended discussion of Dewey's notions of community and democracy, see my "Democracy as a Way of Life," *Philosophy and the Reconstruction of Culture: Pragmatic Essays After Dewey*, ed. John J. Stuhr (Albany: State University of New York Press, 1993), pp. 37–58.

find little or no such melioristic faith in most of the postmodernists, in the children of Nietzsche. Thus Lyotard, writing on the meaning of "post" in "postmodernism," observes our lack of intimacy, the decline in our confidence in the principle of general human progress, and our lack of fit with our culture. After two bloodstained centuries in which both liberalism and Marxism stand accused of crimes against humanity, we now are alert to the signs of "an opposing movement": "It is no longer possible to call development progress. . . . We are like Gullivers in the world of technoscience: sometimes too big, sometimes too small, but never the right size."[39]

Perhaps, however, it is the pragmatists—more cheerful and hopeful, more trusting, and more affirming—who are, if not the idols of our twilight, the real children of Nietzsche, the real children of the twilight of the idols:

> To stay cheerful when involved in a gloomy and exceedingly responsible business is no inconsiderable art: yet what could be more necessary than cheerfulness? Nothing succeeds in which high spirits play no part. Only excess of strength is proof of strength.[40]

Pragmatism's challenge to postmodernism is the challenge to become cheerful in Nietzsche's sense. This is anything but—and must not be confused with—the challenge to postmodernism made by its communitarian critics, neopragmatic would-be prophets, and other Enlightenment blackmailers.[41] Instead, it is the challenge to make explicit the notion of progress already embedded in postmodernism's own suspicion and rejection of earlier notions of progress. It is the challenge to recognize that postmodernists are engaged in action even when they are engaged in the interrogation or interruption of action. It is the challenge to recognize the formations of subjects, the discourses of rationalization, and the perspectival political

---

39. Jean-François Lyotard, *The Postmodern Explained: Correspondence 1982–1985* (Minneapolis: University of Minnesota Press, 1993 [1985]), pp. 77–79. Compare John Dewey: "It is no longer possible to hold the simple faith of the Enlightenment that assured advance of science will produce free institutions by dispelling ignorance and superstition:—the sources of human servitude and the pillars of oppressive government." *Freedom and Culture, John Dewey: The Later Works, 1925–1953*, vol. 13 (Carbondale, Ill.: Southern Illinois University Press, 1988 [1939]), p. 156.

40. Friedrich Nietzsche, "Foreword," *Twilight of the Idols*, p. 31. Foucault remarked that "I do not believe there is a single Nietzscheanism. There are no grounds for believing ours is any truer than others." "Critical Theory/Intellectual History," p. 31.

41. Richard J. Bernstein asks whether many of Foucault's critics engage in "Enlightenment blackmail" and seeks to develop an alternative critical response to Foucault's work. *The New Constellation: The Ethical-Political Horizons of Modernity/Postmodernity* (Cambridge, Mass.: MIT Press, 1992), pp. 152–66.

ideals at work in postmodernism's own will to oppositionality. Finally, it is the challenge to refrain from privileging this oppositionality and differences among subjects.

When postmodernism does privilege oppositionality and difference, it commits "the fallacy of selective emphasis" detailed by Dewey.[42] This is a seductive error, offering us, now fortified by an appreciation of difference, the easy solace of traditional idealism: self-transformation and self-transcendence (and becoming other than what one is) through self-understanding and self-awareness. Now this self, as postmodernism has shown, is not a self-contained individual, a wholly self-identical and autonomous agent, or an essentially private or inaccessible-to-others consciousness. Instead, it is a culturally-embedded, embodied, practicing subject—Mead's irreducibly "social self,"[43] Dewey's fully "live creature."[44] (By giving the subject a practical function, Dewey noted, pragmatism avoids subjectivism—"an old story in philosophy; a story that began in Europe and not in America."[45])

As a result, any demand for difference and any personal will to oppositionality must be rooted not simply in an individual subject but in social subjects, subjects in societies, subjects in associations of intimacies—associations that may or may not constitute communities in the pragmatist sense of that term. There can be no politics of pure, privileged difference; deconstruction is politically "undecidable" or underdetermined.[46] Pragmatism thus challenges postmodernism to become political, to situate and localize wills to oppositionalities in social practices of resistance, transformation, and reconstruction, and to create space within experience for the possibility of those practices, as well as their contestation. This is a challenge to employ genealogy on behalf of its own intimate values. As Foucault observed: "Critique doesn't have to be the premise of a deduction that concludes: This then

---

42. John Dewey, *Experience and Nature*, *John Dewey: The Later Works, 1925–1953*, vol. 1 (Carbondale, Ill.: Southern Illinois University Press, 1981 [1925]), p. 34. Hereafter abbreviated "*E&N*; *LW* 1."

43. George Herbert Mead, *Mind, Self, and Society: From the Standpoint of a Social Behaviorist* (Chicago: University of Chicago Press, 1934), especially chapters 18–29.

44. John Dewey: *Art as Experience*, *John Dewey: The Later Works, 1925–1953* (Carbondale, Ill.: Southern Illinois University Press, 1987 [1934]), especially chapters 1–3.

45. John Dewey, "The Development of American Pragmatism" in *John Dewey: The Later Works, 1925–1953*, Vol. 2 (Carbondale, Ill.: Southern Illinois University Press, 1984) p. 20.

46. I discuss this point in greater detail in a review of Michael Ryan's *Marxism and Deconstruction: A Critical Articulation*, in *Philosophy and Literature* 8.2 (1984): 291–92. Though her major targets include neither Derrida nor Ryan, in the final chapter of her *Beyond Postmodern Politics: Lyotard, Rorty, Foucault*, Honi Fern Haber develops similar reservations about the politics of difference and the "negative aspects" of the "law of difference."

is what needs to be done. It should be an instrument for those who fight, those who resist and refuse what is."[47]

The challenge of pragmatism to postmodernism is political: It is the challenge to become genuinely instrumental. Of course, here there is reason for a certain cheerfulness, as Foucault realized: "My optimism would consist rather in saying that so many things can be changed, fragile as they are, bound up more with circumstances than necessities, more arbitrary that self-evident, more a matter of complex, but temporary, historical circumstances than with inevitable anthropological constants."[48] This optimism, pragmatists would remind postmodernists once more, is the possession of a social self, not an autonomous individual. It is not "my" optimism or oppositionality; however fragile, arbitrary, or temporary, it is *our* optimism and *our* oppositionality.

Toward a Genealogical Pragmatism

> And out of what one sees and hears and out
> Of what one feels, who could have thought to make
> So many selves, so many sensuous worlds,
> As if the air, the mid-day air, was swarming
> With the metaphysical changes that occur,
> Merely in living as and where we live.
>
> —Wallace Stevens, "Esthetique du Mal"

The most important challenge of postmodernism to pragmatism is *not* the one that has occupied Nielsen, Colapietro, Ryder, and many others pragmatists. The issue is not whether pragmatism can avoid the destructive, deconstructive criticisms that postmodernism raises against the philosophical tradition. This appears as a significant challenge to pragmatism only to persons who, unlike Nielsen, Colapietro, and Ryder, do not grasp pragmatism's deep attacks on: the problems and methods of modern philosophy, whether idealist or materialist, antirealist or realist; metaphysics, First Philosophy, dualisms of all sort (like those employed by Rorty) and what Dewey termed "the epistemology industry"; scientism and rosy notions of progress and optimism (as opposed to meliorism); and a wide range of ideological and

---

47. Michel Foucault, "Questions of Method," *The Foucault Effect: Studies in Governmentality*, ed. Graham Burchell, Colin Gordon, and Peter Miller (Chicago: University of Chicago Press, 1991 [1980]), p. 80.
48. Foucault, "Practicing Criticism," p. 156.

institutional roadblocks to the achievement of genuine individuality, community, and democracy as a way of life.

Instead, the real challenge of postmodernism to pragmatism is the challenge to recognize and critically consider the differences, distances, destructions, violence, interests, agonies, and foreignness at work in pragmatism's own will to intimacy. This is the challenge to make explicit the exclusions, oppositionalities, and single-mindedness embedded in pragmatism's own notions of community, inquiry, and pluralism. It is the challenge to pragmatists to recognize the delimitations and violence of all ideals, and to remain open to multiple deconstructions of their own ideals even as they engage in the reconstruction of those ideals. It is the challenge to recognize the formations of subjects, the discourses of rationalization, and the perspectival political differences at work in pragmatism's own will to intimacy. Finally, it is the challenge to refrain from privileging in a final or closed manner this intimacy, association, and community among subjects.

It is simply not possible (for pragmatists, postmodernists, or anyone else), however, to refrain from privileging (if only provisionally) particular intimacies, associations, and communities.[49] Recalling both Emerson's remark that "society is everywhere in conspiracy against its members" and his advice to "accept the place the divine providence has found for you, the society of your contemporaries, the connection of events," Dewey claims that

---

49. This is a point that simply has not been understood by many recent postmodernist and some recent feminist critics of community who propose a supposed politics of difference. One very influential example of this misunderstanding is Iris Marion Young's "The Ideal of Community and the Politics of Difference," *Social Theory and Practice* 12.2 (1986). It is noteworthy that Young appears either entirely unfamiliar with, or entirely unconcerned with, the notion of community developed by the classical pragmatists. Judith M. Green, drawing on this notion and the pragmatist tradition, provides careful criticism and a corrective to Young in her "The Diverse Community or the Unoppressive City: Which Ideal for a Transformative Politics of Difference?," *Journal of Social Philosophy* 26.1 (1995): 86–102. Haber develops a parallel criticism of Young in the final sections of her *Beyond Postmodern Politics: Lyotard, Rorty, Foucault.* Like Young but unlike Green, Haber appears unaware of the classical pragmatist tradition, and thus concludes with a "suggestion" long ago not simply suggested but developed at length by the pragmatists: "the subject of oppositional struggle is subjects-in-community and not the subject in isolation; nor is it no subject at all" (p. 134). Feminist criticisms of notions of community in the works of more recent "communitarian" theorists (as opposed to pragmatists), however, surely are on target. See, for example: Jean Bethke Elshtain, "Feminism, Family, and Community," *Dissent* 29.4 (1982): 442–49; Marilyn Friedman, *What Are Friends For? Feminist Perspectives on Personal Relationships and Moral Theory* (Ithaca, N.Y.: Cornell University Press, 1993); Amy Gutmann, "Communitarian Critics of Liberalism," *Philosophy and Public Affairs* 14:3 (1985): 308–22; and Jane Mansbridge, "Feminism and Democratic Community," *Nomos XXXV: Democratic Community*, ed. John W. Chapman and Ian Shapiro (New York: New York University Press, 1993), pp. 339–75.

even though the acceptance of the notion of a society fixed in its institutions does destroy difference and conspire against individuality, still " 'the connection of events,' and 'the society of your contemporaries' as formed of moving and multiple associations, are the only means by which the possibilities of individuality can be realized."[50] Moreover, as Dewey noted, this sort of selective use and emphasis is inevitable—making the universalization of oppositionality or commitment to pure difference impossible:

> There is no mystery about the fact of association, of an interconnected action which affects the activity of singular elements. There is no sense in asking how individuals come to be associated. They exist and operate in association. If there is any mystery about the matter, it is the mystery that the universe is the kind of universe it is. Such a mystery could not be explained without going outside the universe. And if one should go to an outside source to account for it, some logician, without an excessive draft upon his ingenuity, would rise to remark that the outsider would have to be connected with the universe in order to account for anything in it.[51]

It is only immature and undisciplined minds, Dewey claimed, that believe in supposedly unconnected actions that issue from supposedly particular, separate beings. This belief, he argued, is destroyed by the advance of intelligent criticism that "transforms the notion of isolated one-sided acts into acknowledged interactions" (*E&N; LW* 1:324). It is possible, however, case by case and time after time, to fail to acknowledge this selective emphasis, to fail to critically (if piecemeal) inspect it, and to fail to take up, or even allow others to take up, oppositional perspectives on this emphasis. Arguing that pragmatism must pursue a "genetic method," Dewey is committed to just this sort of genealogical criticism that refuses "to be diverted into absurd search for an intellectual philosopher's stone of absolutely wholesale generalizations, thus isolating that which is permanent in a function and for a purpose, and converting it into the intrinsically eternal, conceived either (as Aristotle conceived it) as that which is the same at all times, or as that which is indifferent to time, out of time." Dewey continued:

> Selective emphasis, choice, is inevitable whenever reflection occurs. This is not an evil. Deception comes only when the presence and operation of choice is concealed, disguised, denied. . . . An empirical philosophy is in

50. John Dewey, *Individualism: Old and New, John Dewey: The Later Works, 1925–1953*, vol. 5 (Carbondale, Ill.: Southern Illinois University Press, 1984 [1930]), p. 122.
51. John Dewey, *The Public and Its Problems, John Dewey: The Later Works, 1925–1953*, vol. 2 (Carbondale, Ill.: Southern Illinois University Press, 1984 [1927]), p. 250.

any case a kind of intellectual disrobing. We cannot permanently divest ourselves of the intellectual habits we take on and wear when we assimilate the
culture of our time and place. But intelligent furthering of culture demands
that we take some of them off, that we inspect them critically to see what they
are made of and what wearing them does to us. (*E&N; LW* 1:33–34, 40)

A disrobed pragmatism is a genealogical pragmatism, a pragmatism that
disrupts, "eventalizes,"[52] and problematizes. It is also a pragmatism that sus-
pects itself, that critically inspects its own methods, including logic and science. For this reason, it is a pragmatism closer to Dewey's *Experience and
Nature, Freedom and Culture*, and *The Public and Its Problems* than to his
Logic: The Theory of Inquiry. In *Logic*, Dewey sets forth an account of
inquiry that appears distant from (though in the end, I think, plausibly may
be interpreted as consistent with) intellectual disrobing, genealogy, difference, and oppositionalities. Dewey defines inquiry as "the controlled or directed transformation of an indeterminate situation into one that is so
determinate in its constituent distinctions and relations as to convert the elements of the original situation into a unified whole," and formulates a pattern or process of inquiry that begins with an indeterminate situation and
moves to the institution of a problem and the determination of a problem-
solution through reasoning in which facts have operational status.[53] This account
of inquiry attaches too little importance to the roles of difference and
oppositionalities. First, any present—an indeterminate situation—requires a
history of that present: For whom is the situation indeterminate? In relation
to what interests is it indeterminate? How did it become indeterminate? And
what does the indeterminate situation render determinate and produce? Second, any problem—the partial transformation by inquiry of the indeterminate
into the problematic—requires a genealogy of that transformation: Whose
problem is "the" problem? By what mechanisms and disciplines is this problem formulated? On behalf of what interests is this problem, rather than some
other problem, formulated? And within what cultural productions of discourses and subjects does this determination of a problem and service of
interests take place? Third, any determination of a problem-solution—the
examination of the "functional fitness" of possible resolutions—requires an
analysis of exclusions: Who decides whether a "resolved unified situation"
has been reached? How is this control exercised? What interests does this
control serve or frustrate? And whom does it subjugate or liberate, whom
does it constitute?

52. See Foucault, "Questions of Method," p. 78ff.
53. John Dewey, *Logic: The Theory of Inquiry, John Dewey: The Later Works, 1925–1953*
(Carbondale, Ill.: Southern Illinois University Press, 1986 [1938]), pp. 108–22.

Dewey does not embrace openly these sorts of questions in his *Logic*, and thus he pays no explicit attention, for example, to issues of race, ethnicity, gender, age, class, sexual orientation, body—to issues of difference and identity and matters of power. The subject of his pattern of inquiry readily appears as an abstract universal self, a subject from no place and no time.[54] Yet, in analyzing objectivity not as the opposite of all bias but rather as a particular sort of bias, and in stressing the operational character of facts, Dewey's own account of inquiry prepares and leads us to ask just these questions and to focus on particular, different, historical subjects. Asking what is meant by calling facts operational, rather than self-sufficient or complete, Dewey replied that facts are selected and described for a purpose—"namely statement of the problem involved in such a way that its material both indicates a meaning relevant to resolution of the difficulty and serves to test its worth and validity."[55] A pragmatism that refuses to forget that facts are selected rather than self-sufficient must not forget to attend to the differences and oppositionalities inherent in all such selection, including its own.

Understood in this light, genealogical pragmatism is, as Dewey defines philosophy, "inherently criticism"—"criticism become aware of itself and its implications." As such, a philosophy "becomes in effect a messenger, a liaison officer, making reciprocally intelligible voices speaking provincial tongues, and thereby enlarging as well as rectifying the meanings with which they are charged." This goal, of course, has often not been realized:

> The difficulty is that philosophy, even when professing catholicity, has often been suborned. Instead of being a free messenger of communication it has been a diplomatic agent of some special and partial interest; insincere, because in the name of peace it has fostered divisions that lead to strife, and in the name of loyalty has promoted unholy alliances and secret understandings. One might say that the profuseness of attestations to supreme devotion to truth on the part of philosophy is matter to arouse suspicion. . . . Truth is a collection of truths. (*E&N*; *LW* 1:298, 302, 306–7)

Because truth is a collection of truths, a genuinely genealogical pragmatism must recognize that the philosopher-messenger who enlarges the meanings contained in provincial tongues is also a messenger who speaks a provincial tongue—a different, but still provincial tongue. Similarly, pragmatism must recognize that a philosopher-messenger of free communication is an agent of some special interests—special and partial, though not necessarily insincere, unholy, or secret.

---

54. See the discussions of time in chapters 9 and 10.
55. Dewey, *Logic: The Theory of Inquiry*, p. 116.

Striving too much to realize the different truths, provincial meanings, and enlarged values that criticism may discriminate, this philosophy refuses to embrace the logic of the death of the will: that because there is no reason—no universal, total, absolute, foundational justification—for doing one thing rather than another, therefore there is sufficient reason for doing nothing at all. And (perhaps unfashionably today) striving too much for the possibilities of intimacies implicated within different truths and oppositional values, this philosophy refuses to embrace the logic of the will to difference: that because there is no reason—no universal, total, absolute, foundational justification—for being the person whom one is, therefore there is sufficient reason for becoming merely different, for taking up merely oppositional stance toward the person one is at present and toward others. Instead, as genealogy, pragmatism embraces the logic of the will to intimacy, plural and provisional intimacies: that because there is no reason to think fuller individuality and fuller community are impossible, therefore there is sufficient reason for undertaking the reconstruction of experience by means of intelligent criticism—criticism that is always partial, perspectival, and provisional.

As an idol of our twilight, such a pragmatism is a *hard* philosophy. Perhaps too hard. As Dewey notes in the final lines of *Experience and Nature*, many may find it treason to view philosophy as the critical method of developing methods of criticism. Have these persons put pragmatism on trial for treason? Perhaps so. But as Dewey observes, "life itself is a sequence of trials" (*E&N*; *LW* 1:326). As James observes: "Be not afraid of life"[56]

A maxim from *The Twilight of the Idols*: "Let us not be cowardly in the face of our actions!"[57] In pragmatism, the joy of becoming—a joy that encompasses reconstruction and intimacy as well as destruction and oppositionality—is not an eternal or inexhaustible joy. It is, however, the only joy.

---

56. William James, "Is Life Worth Living," *The Will to Believe to Believe and Other Essays in Popular Philosophy*, p. 56.
57. Friedrich Nietzsche, *The Twilight of the Idols*, p. 33. The "eternal joy of becoming" is discussed most explicitly in the final section of "What I Owe the Ancients," p. 121.

II

Experience

6

Rorty as Elvis: Dewey's Reconstruction of Metaphysics

What is metaphysics? Does it have a distinctive aim, method, or subject-matter? Is metaphysics, or a metaphysics of experience, possible? If possible, is it necessary? What is the status of seemingly endless metaphysical disagreements? Are they speculative, imaginative, confessional, or empirical? What values, interests, and institutions do particular metaphysical systems serve, participate in, and promote?

Moreover, do questions about the nature of metaphysics even matter any longer? Do they have any non-antiquarian importance in an age of postmodern theories and global production and consumption practices? Does metaphysics today have any "cash value" at all? Or are philosophers who still deal in metaphysics simply the junk bond traders of the academic world? Is the very notion of "pragmatic metaphysics" at best nostalgia and at worst a contradiction in terms? Worse yet, is mere consideration of these issues simply an indication of a pressing need for therapy?

Metaphysics as Disease: Rorty's Dewey

> Barely to note and register that contingency is a trait of natural events has nothing to do with wisdom.
>
> —John Dewey, *Experience and Nature*

Richard Rorty provides a familiar and influential set of responses to these questions in his discussions of John Dewey's metaphysics, the place of this metaphysics in Dewey's philosophy more generally, and the similarities between Dewey and some of Rorty's other favorite post-Kantian writers such as Heidegger, Habermas, Foucault, and Derrida. For Rorty, metaphysics is a bad habit that Dewey effectively criticized but couldn't quite completely kick. It is a disease that Dewey never fully beat, a disease often manifest as science-envy and method-mania. However, Dewey is not alone. Rorty finds the symptoms of this disease almost everywhere in recent philosophy. It is a virtual epidemic. Its victims—in the spirit of Rorty, I label them Metaphysicians Anonymous—include many major twentieth-century writers who all became infected by the very disease they sought to cure.

Rorty's diagnosis of Dewey has wavered a bit through the years, although his view of metaphysics has not. First, in a 1976 comparison of Dewey and Heidegger, "Overcoming the Tradition," Rorty seems to give Dewey—but not Heidegger—a clean bill of health. Dewey's philosophy, Rorty claims, holds that metaphysics has exhausted its potentialities and reached its end. It turned away from metaphysics and all the special problems of philosophy; it turned to the ordinary world and the everyday problems people face. In contrast, Rorty claims, Heidegger turned toward a new path for philosophy, a path he hoped would open "if we detach ourselves from the problems of men and are still; in that silence we may perhaps hear the words of Being. Which of these attitudes one adopts depends on how devoted one is to the notion of 'philosophy.' "[1]

Rorty sides with Dewey against Heidegger, perhaps (as Rorty himself suggests) because of the philosophers he had been reading and the jargon that he fancied at the time. Accordingly, he concludes that we should not criticize Heidegger "for wanting something *strenger als das Begriffliche:*"

> Few of us do not. If he is to be criticized, it is for helping keep us under the spell of Plato's notion that there is something special called "philosophy" which it is our duty to undertake. . . . By offering us "openness to Being" to replace "philosophical argument," Heidegger helps preserve all that was worst in the tradition which he hoped to overcome. (*CPr*:54)

Second, in 1977, a year later, Rorty's diagnosis of Dewey has a different emphasis. Dewey's case appears far more serious. Metaphysics infects much of Dewey's work, and amputation is indicated. In "Dewey's Metaphysics," Rorty writes:

> Dewey set out to show the harm which traditional philosophical dualisms were doing to our culture, and he thought that to do this job he needed a metaphysics—a description of the generic traits of existence that would solve (or dissolve) the traditional problems of philosophy, as well as open up new avenues for cultural development. I think that he was successful in this latter, larger aim; . . . Dewey's mistake . . . was the notion that criticism of culture had to take the form of a redescription of "nature" or "experience" or both. (*CPr*:85)

---

1. Richard Rorty, *Consequences of Pragmatism* (Minneapolis: University of Minnesota Press, 1982), pp. 53–54. Hereafter abbreviated "*CPr*."

Dewey, Rorty judges, provides no illuminating account of the generic, pervasive traits of experience, culture, or nature. This task is impossible. Instead, Dewey offers great provocative suggestions for overcoming and playfully experimenting with our intellectual past. Rorty concludes that Dewey helps us set aside the spirit of seriousness evident in traditional philosophy:

> For the spirit of seriousness can only exist in an intellectual world in which human life is an attempt to attain an end beyond life, an escape from freedom into the atemporal. The conception of such a world is still built into our education and our common speech, not to mention the attitudes of philosophers toward their work. But Dewey did his best to help us get rid of it, and he should not be blamed if he occasionally came down with the disease he was trying to cure. (*CPr*:87–88)

Third, three years later, in his 1980 "Method, Social Science, and Social Hope," Rorty describes a virtually disease-free Dewey, a Dewey already waiting at the end of the post-metaphysical route now traveled by many Continental writers. For Rorty, the destination of this philosophical journey is human solidarity without transcendental human subjects; it is liberalism without Truth, Reality, or Eternity. Because Dewey reached this point long ago, contemporary philosophers who focus on "discourse," "textuality," and the "hermeneutic circle" do nothing radically new or significantly different, even though their jargon sounds a little less dated and musty to us:

> But the difference in jargon should not obscure the common aim. This is the attempt to free mankind from Nietzsche's "longest lie," the notion that outside the haphazard and perilous experiments we perform there lies something (God, Science, Knowledge, Rationality, or Truth) which will, if only we perform the correct rituals, step in to save us. (*CPr*:208)

Fourth, by 1985, partially in response to strong criticism, Rorty offers his most bleak diagnosis of Dewey's philosophy. Metaphysics seems widespread and malignant in Dewey. Rorty rejects Dewey's theory of experience, his theory of inquiry, and all the "dregs" of his philosophy. Linking Dewey's views of science and method to both Aristotle and Carnap, Rorty rejects Dewey's steadfast view that there is a constructive cultural task for philosophy:

> What Dewey was good at, in my view, was seeing how the dregs of old philosophical and religious ideas were still part of the common sense of the American public. What we had better be good at, I think, is seeing how the dregs of Deweyan thought—all that stuff about scientific method—have permeated the common sense of the American public of our own day and have themselves become a "cake of convention" which needs to be pierced.

That is why I think that the pragmatist strain in American philosophy, if it is to be of any use in our public life, needs to be spliced with the kind of criticism of contemporary social science found in Habermas and Foucault.[2]

As a result, Rorty concludes that Dewey's self-image is not usable by his heirs. We must forsake his metaphysics and conception of philosophy. We must trade in his "experimental" philosophy for new "poetic" theories and descriptions.

Don't Be Cruel: Rorty as Elvis

The king is gone but he's not forgotten
This is the story of a Johnny Rotten
It's better to burn out than it is to rust
The king is gone but he's not forgotten

—Neil Young and Jeff Blackburn, "My My Hey Hey"

These diagnoses of Dewey's metaphysics are deeply and thoroughly mistaken. They constitute both (1) misreading and (2) misuse of Dewey. Nonetheless, they are instructive because they highlight the sharp contrast between, on the one hand, Dewey's pragmatism and its focus on the reconstruction of culture and, on the other hand, Rorty's "neo-pragmatism" and its focus on the deconstruction of theory.

1. Rorty misreads Dewey. Rorty is right, of course, that Dewey does oppose philosophical dualisms and does criticize traditional cultural practices. This is Dewey the cultural critic who Rorty wants to appropriate; this

---

2. Richard Rorty, "Comments on Sleeper and Edel," *Transactions of the Charles S. Peirce Society* 21.1 (1985): 44. This response is part of a remarkable "Symposium on Rorty's *Consequences of Pragmatism*" that includes an introduction by John J. McDermott and papers by Ralph Sleeper, "Rorty's Pragmatism: Afloat in Neurath's Boat, But Why Adrift," and Abraham Edel, "A Missing Dimension in Rorty's Use of Pragmatism." See my discussion of these issues in the context of pragmatism and postmodernism in chapter 5. Several other critical essays and reviews address these issues, including: James Campbell, "Rorty's Use of Dewey," *Southern Journal of Philosophy* 22.2 (1984); Thomas Jeannot, "On Co-opting Pragmatism in the Debate about Foundations: Dewey, Rorty and Whitehead," *Transactions of the Charles S. Peirce Society* 23.2 (1987); and, John J. Stuhr, "Review of Rorty's *Contingency, Irony, and Solidarity*," *The Personalist Forum* 5.2 (1989). Konstantin Kolenda offers a very different, positive reading of Rorty in his *Rorty's Humanistic Pragmatism* (Tampa: University of South Florida Press, 1990), as does David L. Hall in his *Richard Rorty: Prophet and Poet of the New Pragmatism* (Albany: State University of New York Press, 1994). See also Rorty's replies to criticism in *Rorty and Pragmatism: The Philosopher Responds to His Critics*, ed. Harman J. Saatkamp (Nashville: Vanderbilt University Press, 1995).

is the Dewey who resembles Rorty. Moreover, Rorty is right that Dewey does seek to set forth a description of the generic features of experience and does develop a general theory of inquiry. This is Dewey the metaphysician and logician who Rorty wants to ignore or reject; this is the Dewey who does not resemble Rorty. Beyond these generalizations, however, Rorty's reading of Dewey is flawed. Consider simply three points.

(a) Rorty's 1976 claim that Dewey turns away from philosophy and toward the problems of men and women is either false or overly general. It is false insofar as it presupposes that Dewey is concerned *either* with philosophy *or* with human problems. This simply is a false dichotomy. It is overly general insofar as it fails to distinguish among conceptions of philosophy as different as those of Plato, Aquinas, Descartes, Hegel, and Dewey. It is an invalid generalization to infer that Dewey turned away from any and all philosophy because he turned away from some conceptions of philosophy.

(b) Rorty's 1977 assessment that Dewey's metaphysics is only an "occasional" disease simply is not supported by Dewey's writings. Perhaps Rorty's difficulty here, as he himself later suggests, stems from too little homework and systematic study of Dewey.[3] In any case, Dewey's metaphysics pervades his cultural criticism and is inseparable from it. In fact, Dewey rejects any sharp split between metaphysics and cultural criticism—a distinction that Rorty wants to discover or produce so that he then can abandon or dismantle it. The "metaphysics" of *Experience and Nature*—the account of precariousness, continuity and history, qualitative immediacy, mediation and instrumentality, meaning and communication, body-mind, and criticism itself—is borne out by and informs, for example, in turn, *A Common Faith*, *The Quest for Certainty*, *Art as Experience*, *Logic: The Theory of Inquiry*, *The Public and Its Problems*, *Individualism: Old and New*, and *Democracy and Education*. Whatever else it is, Dewey's "metaphysical" description of the generic features of experience definitely is not "an attempt to attain an end beyond life, an escape from freedom into the atemporal." Any careful reader must realize that this runs counter to the word and the spirit of Dewey's philosophy. Amazingly, Rorty, the self-styled philosopher of contingency, fails to recognize that Dewey's description of experience is a theory of that contingency—and anything but its denial. As a result, Rorty repeatedly announces his discovery of a condition that Dewey long ago not only recognized but described in depth. It is no surprise that Rorty's "discovery" and conquest of a contingent philosophical New World is hardly news to its pragmatic native inhabitants.

(c) Both his 1980 praise and 1985 criticism provide further evidence that Rorty misreads Dewey in terms of categories that Dewey's philosophy

---

3. Rorty, "Comments on Sleeper and Edel, p. 39.

itself outstrips. Although Rorty has heralded "linguistic" and "narrative" turns in philosophy, his view of Dewey's metaphysics only retraces a Cartesian path. (Perhaps Rorty should not be criticized for succumbing to the disease he hopes to cure!) For Rorty, philosophers must be either metaphysical constructionists or deconstructionists. That is, they may seek "seriously," "scientifically," and methodically to escape life by constructing some ritual or general account of Reality. Or, they may converse "playfully," "artistically," and poetically so as to affirm contingency by deconstructing metaphysical systems, performing "haphazard experiments," and piercing "cakes of convention." However, Dewey is neither traditional metaphysician nor brave new antimetaphysician. The key point here is that Dewey's account of the generic traits of experience—an account that he identifies as a species of criticism— is, at once, a reconstruction of metaphysics itself.

2. Rorty misuses Dewey. Rorty's misreading of Dewey is significant because it supports and underlies a broad misuse of Dewey within the academy. This misuse is obscured by Rorty's surface invocation of Dewey's central commitments—for example, growth, communication, liberal individualism, democratic community, and human solidarity. At a deeper level, however, Rorty and Dewey differ immensely. Consider again three points.

(a) Ironically, Rorty enlists Dewey in order to narrate and promote the very dualisms that Dewey ceaselessly criticized and replaced—dualisms such as public/private, fact/value, and self/society. This is most obvious in Rorty's campaign in *Contingency, Irony and Solidarity* to resurrect a foundational split between the private and public dimensions of life.[4] This project makes clear that Rorty is the great philosophical dualist of our day. For example, he posits that there are two kinds of philosophical thinkers: historicists (such as Kierkegaard, Marx, Baudelaire, Mill, Proust, and Dewey) and nonhistoricists (such as Plato and Descartes).[5] And, there are two kinds of historicists: those concerned with private perfection (such as Kierkegaard, Nietzsche, Heidegger, and Foucault!) and those interested in public life (such as Marx, Dewey, Habermas, and Rawls). Rorty never *defends* these dualisms, unless repetition of a claim counts as support for that claim. This is remarkable because it is not clear that there is *any* cultural evidence to support these tidy separations. Even when Rorty promises to make belief in these dualisms plausible, he only demonstrates that it is not theoretically inconsistent to affirm both such

4. Richard Rorty, *Contingency, Irony, and Solidarity* (New York: Cambridge University Press, 1989). Hereafter abbreviated "*CIS*."

5. To a large extent, Rorty's division of philosophical thinkers into historicists and nonhistoricists parallels his later division of humanities instructors into knowing, debunking teachers and charismatic, inspiring teachers. See his "The Necessity of Inspired Reading," *The Chronicle of Higher Education*, 42.22 (February 9, 1996): A48.

dualisms and certain humanistic, liberal views about public life. All this is ironic (though not in Rorty's special sense of that term) for two reasons. First, this dualism functions as just the sort of foundational Truth that Rorty rightly rejects in the works of many other philosophers. Second, most of the historicist writers Rorty discusses themselves reject this dualism. At the very least, Rorty needs to address rather than sidestep their views.

There is another crucial dualism in these essays. For Rorty, there are two kinds of philosophical methods or procedures: the arguments of common sense and the descriptions of intellectuals. Rorty rejects common sense and traditional argumentation, and instead proceeds by literary criticism, description, and redescription—by sweeping stories about the histories of philosophy and literature. Rorty seems to view common sense as hopelessly narrow and naive, and he characterizes philosophy-by-argument as hopelessly tied to foundationalist epistemologies, transcendental metaphysics, and supposed final, essential vocabularies. By contrast, he advocates philosophy-by-redescription, and awards it the "ironist" seal of approval. Ironist philosophers, Rorty explains, are "never quite able to take themselves seriously because always aware that the terms in which they describe themselves are subject to change, always aware of the contingency and fragility of their final vocabularies, and thus of their selves" (*CIS*:73–74). However, it does seem that ironist philosophers take one another very seriously. In fact, as Rorty describes them, they seem downright clubby: "So our doubts about our own characters or our own culture can be resolved or assuaged only by enlarging our acquaintance. The easiest way of doing that is to read books, and so ironists spend more of their time placing books than in placing real live people" (*CIS*:80). Ironists, Rorty continues, take literary critics as their moral advisers because these critics have large ranges of acquaintances—they "have been around." This may be so, but it is instructive to note that at least in one important and distressing respect, ironists and traditional metaphysicians are alike. Although they differ about the reality of contingency, both *fear* contingency. For Rorty, contingency is dangerous, threatening, humiliating; it suggests that life is futile. As a result, literary criticism does for ironists what the search for universal moral principles aimed to do for metaphysicians.

Rorty's timid political agenda is a central consequence of this ironist fear of contingency. Of course, Rorty does not view his own politics in this way. Rorty describes himself as a liberal concerned with solidarity, and defines liberals as people who believe that "cruelty is the worst thing they do." This is a vague, minimalist account of liberalism, and it is a distressing account because it seems that liberalism for Rorty is almost exclusively a matter of belief rather than social action. But Rorty is not concerned with providing a deeper definition of liberalism or more effective strategies for liberal action. Instead, he wants to show that (public) liberalism is compatible in practice with (private) ironism. And, of course, it turns out that they are compatible. A liberal person can abhor cruelty while holding ironist beliefs that there is no foundational reason to oppose cruelty. Rorty writes: "What matters for the liberal ironist is not finding such a reason but making sure that she *notices* suffering when it occurs. Her hope is that she will not be limited by her own final vocabulary when faced with the possibility of humiliating someone with a quite different final vocabulary" (*CIS*:93). While this all sounds pleasant, eminently humane, and well-intentioned, it is remarkably reactionary in practice. The practical political difficulties do not lie with Rorty's ironism (which is neither as novel nor as startling as Rorty seems to think). Rather, the difficulties here lie with Rorty's passive and smug brand of liberalism. Rorty's liberals are intellectuals who safely read one another's books in an effort to expand their capacities to notice suffering and cruelty. This may be necessary, but it is not enough. Rorty separates liberalism from practical action, and he offers us textual redescription in the place of social reconstruction. In so doing, he confines liberalism to the academy—whether an academy of ironists or metaphysicians. This political timidity is virtually omnipresent: "One can easily imagine an ironist badly wanting more free-dom, more open space, for the Baudelaires and the Nabokovs, while not giving a thought to the sort of thing Orwell wanted: for example, getting more fresh air down into the coal mines, or getting the Party off the backs of the people" (*CIS*:88–89). The political, public issue, of course, is not simply what we might *think* about. It is about what we actually do.

Action aside, Rorty claims that philosophy is increasingly useless even for thinking about public issues. The novelist, Rorty asserts (though not in a novel), is better able to help us imaginatively attend to "the springs of cru-elty" in our own lives. This leads Rorty to a correct but hardly startling conclusion: The future is "up for grabs" (*CIS*:184). This humanist conclusion pinpoints Rorty's central difficulties in two ways. First, if the future really is "up for grabs," then the notion of a single, nondualistic vision of private perfection *and* human solidarity cannot be dismissed as a theoretical impos-sibility, as Rorty does. In this sense, Rorty's judgment of Nabokov should be applied to Rorty's own work: His best insights "are the ones which exhibit his inability to believe his own general ideas" (*CIS*:168). Second, if the future is "up for grabs," then any sort of private life or personal lifestyle that in-cludes no practical commitment to social action cannot be judged a form of "private perfection."

Here it is clear that Rorty wholly fails to grasp Dewey's insights about the social character of the self and the reciprocal relation between genuine individuality and community. While Rorty proclaims that "there is no way to bring self-creation together with justice at the level of theory" (*CIS*:xiv), Dewey just does it: "It is absurd to suppose that the ties which hold together ["the mental and moral structure of individuals, the pattern of their desires and purposes"] are merely external and do not react into mentality and character, producing the framework for personal disposition."[6]

(b) Rorty's dualistic philosophy and account of other philosophers result from a more extensive misuse of Dewey. In turn, this larger misuse arises from Rorty's either/or misreading of Dewey's metaphysics—either as essentialist ritual or as deconstructive play. It is precisely because Dewey understands philosophy (including metaphysics) as inquiry (neither ritual nor play) that he maintains that there is a constructive moral, educational task for philosophy. Rorty concludes that this amounts to scientism. However, this is an invalid inference based on an overly narrow view of inquiry. After all, Dewey constantly links inquiry and the art of communication, calling Walt Whitman the "seer of democracy." By contrast, Rorty detaches art and his favorite novelists from inquiry and scientists. As a result, Rorty's conversations, narratives, redescriptions, and vocabularies are both as speculative and as final as the metaphysics he abhors. As such, they may be clever confessions or hopes, but they are nothing more.

(c) In one sense, of course, Rorty's point is that there is nothing more that philosophy might be. However, this view is equivocal and masks Rorty's most important misuse of Dewey. Dewey would agree with Rorty: Philosophy can't transcend the contingency of life; this is the *metaphysics of contingency* that Dewey and Rorty share, although Rorty does not recognize it. However, Dewey would disagree with Rorty: Philosophy can perform a constructive critical function; this is the *politics of contingency* that Dewey and Rorty do not share, as Rorty's discussion of liberalism reveals. He takes a liberal to be a person for whom "cruelty is the worst thing they do" (*CIS*:74), and posits two groups (surprise!) of liberals. Metaphysical liberals arrogantly seek transcendental proofs of the immorality of cruelty so that we will not act cruelly. By contrast, Rorty's preferred nonmetaphysical ("ironist") liberals sensitively seek only to recognize and portray cruelty, so that we better may avoid it. Rorty thus offers an ultimatum to liberals: Proceed by metaphysical proof or by supposedly nonmetaphysical redescription. Neither of these choices include inquiry or criticism in Dewey's sense. Why should this matter? It matters because, in the absence of a critical metaphysics of contingency, Rorty is able only (though confidently) to tell us *what* he thinks we should do. But, he is not able to tell us *why* to do it or *how* to do it. To ask liberals *why* we shouldn't be cruel need not be to ask for any transcendental proof. It is a request for liberals to support intelligently their commitments. It is a

---

6. John Dewey, *Individualism: Old and New, John Dewey: The Later Works, 1925–1953*, vol. 5 (Carbondale, Ill.: Southern Illinois University Press, 1984 [1930]), p. 81.

request for criticism—what Dewey calls "criticism of criticism." This request may not be important to like-minded liberal professors who converse principally with one another, but it has been and continues to be important in real struggles and larger cultures. Moreover, to investigate *how* to avoid cruelty need not be to mouth timeless transcendental principles. It is inquiry into the conditions upon which concrete social relations depend at given times and places. This work too is crucial, at least outside the classroom. Without this criticism and inquiry, Rorty can provide only impotent liberal rhetoric. This is fine for rhetorical purposes, but not for reconstruction of philosophical theory or political practice. From the standpoint of these important purposes, Rorty is the Milli Vanilli of liberalism, merely lip-syncing the old Elvis refrain: "Don't Be Cruel."

Metaphysics as Inquiry and Criticism

> Any theory that detects and defines these [generic] traits [manifested by existences of all kinds] is therefore but a ground-map of the province of criticism, establishing base lines to be employed in more intricate triangulations.
>
> —John Dewey, *Experience and Nature*

To grasp Dewey's views, it is necessary to resist the temptation to interpret his metaphysics in terms of dualistic issues and stances that he explicitly rejects. This means, more specifically, that it is not useful to ask if Dewey is a metaphysician or an anti-metaphysician, a metaphysician or a post-metaphysician, a metaphysical system builder or a deconstructionist. In reconstructing metaphysics, he occupies neither position. Moreover, it is not illuminating to ask if Dewey is a naturalist or an idealist, an empiricist or a rationalist, a realist or an antirealist. In criticizing the presuppositions that give rise to these pairs of theories, he accepts neither view.

In place of these issues, let me raise three central questions. First, for Dewey, what is the nature of metaphysics? What is Dewey's understanding or conception of the subject-matter and method of metaphysics? Second, in this light, what is Dewey's actual metaphysics? When Dewey undertakes metaphysics as he understands it, what are the results? Finally, for Dewey, what is the practical significance, if any, of this metaphysics?

1. What is metaphysics for Dewey? Scholars typically respond to this question by pointing to Dewey's comments that metaphysics is the study of the generic, irreducible, pervasive features of existence, and, as such, is the ground-map of criticism. What does this mean? Negatively, it means that metaphysics is neither certain nor final; it is concerned neither with ultimate

origins nor with ultimate ends; and, it is neither a foundation nor an alternative to science or literature. Stated positively, as a beginning, it means that metaphysics is a particular sort of inquiry. As inquiry, metaphysical investigations are historical reflective responses to culturally located problematic situations. It is methodologically experimental, incomplete, and self-corrective (to the extent that it is corrective). As inquiry, metaphysics differs from the various inquiries of special sciences in the generality of its subject-matter. It is concerned with irreducibly pervasive "traits of the very existences with which scientific reflection is concerned" in a manner that "frees these traits from confusion with ultimate origins and ultimate ends—that is from questions of creation and eschatology."[7] (Thus freed, it seems to me that metaphysics is not a study of "paradigms" of existence. Because it is concerned with generic traits, Dewey's metaphysics is more democratic: All existences, as existences, equally are exemplars of existence. Similarly, it seems to me that there is no single class of experiences that provides or constitutes a key to metaphysical inquiry. There are many equally legitimate entrances into Dewey's metaphysics: Aesthetic experience, religious events, economic activities, scientific experiments, school routines, social practices, and many others.)

2. In light of this general understanding of metaphysics as inquiry, a second central issue arises: What is Dewey's metaphysics? That is, what for Dewey are the generic and pervasive features of reality? What is his ground-map of criticism? I have argued elsewhere that an adequate response to this question requires an account of Dewey's views about precariousness, eventfulness, historicality, continuity, quality, logiscibility, and sociality.[8] I want to focus here on only one central aspect of this account: More broadly, what is the subject matter of Dewey's metaphysics? Depending on the passages that one selects, there seems to be evidence for several different answers, including existence, nature, experience, culture, and reality. Does Dewey, then, offer us a *metaphysics of existence* as some scholars contend or a *metaphysics of experience* as others, including myself, claim?

Moreover, what hangs on this issue of interpretation? Is all this merely a temperamental or terminological difference? I suspect that differing responses to these questions in fact do reflect different temperaments among sympathetic and informed readers. Those who worry about any "metaphysics

---

7. John Dewey, "The Subject-Matter of Metaphysical Inquiry" in *John Dewey: The Middle Works, 1899–1924*, vol. 8 (Carbondale, Ill.: Southern Illinois University Press, 1979 [1915]), pp. 6, 13.

8. See my *John Dewey* (Nashville, Tenn.: Carmichael & Carmichael, 1991) and "Introduction to John Dewey" in *Classical American Philosophy: Essential Readings and Interpretive Essays* (New York: Oxford University Press, 1987).

of experience" are concerned to distance Dewey from Kant, idealism, and subjectivism. They want to link him to naturalism and realism, and emphasize that experience falls within nature. By contrast, others who reject any "metaphysics of existence" are concerned to distance Dewey from Santayana, contemporary realism, and objectivism. They want to link him to radical empiricism, radical social theory, and a will to intimacy.[9] They stress the transactional nature of experience and the transformative function of communication.

However, the issue is not merely temperamental. Although each side in this dispute can locate many passages in support of itself, there does seem to be overwhelming textual evidence that Dewey believes precariousness, continuity, quality, and sociality, for example, are generic traits of experience—where experience is understood as a transaction, as "double-barreled," as the irreducible unity of subject and object, organism and environment, foreground and background. This means in part that the generic and pervasive traits that Dewey discusses are not traits of existence—where existence is understood as ontologically independent of experience (and not simply prior to or other than experience). To think otherwise, as Rorty does in his criticisms of Dewey, is to miss Dewey's insistence on the primary, irreducible transactional character of experience, and the irreducible connections between meaning and existence. This is radical empiricism, and not idealism or naturalistic realism: Experience constitutes reality. To think otherwise is to hold a view that Dewey labels not so much false as meaningless. Responding often to misunderstandings of his position, Dewey makes this point over and over:

> And, of course, when events-without-meaning are referred to, that very fact brings them within the field of thought and discourse, and in so far confers meaning upon them, if only the meaning of being without meaning. One could go further: to refer to anything as an *event* is in so far to ascribe character or nature and hence a meaning to it.[10]

> The conditions which antecede experience are, in other words, already *in transition* towards the state of affairs in which they are experienced. . . . [K]eep in mind the fact of *qualitative-transformation-towards,* and keep in mind that *this* fact has the same objective warrant as any other assigned trait.[11]

9. See the discussions of Dewey and Santayana in chapter 7, radical empiricism in chapters 8–10, and the will to intimacy in chapter 5.

10. John Dewey, "Meaning and Existence," *John Dewey: The Later Works, 1925–1953*, vol. 3 (Carbondale, Ill.: Southern Illinois University Press, 1984 [1928]), p. 88.

11. John Dewey, "Reality as Experience," *John Dewey: The Middle Works, 1899–1924*, vol. 3 (Carbondale, Ill.: Southern Illinois University Press, 1977 [1906]), p. 101.

... books, chairs, geological ages, etc., are experienced ... *as* existent at other times than the moments *when* they are experienced.[12]

As a result, Dewey's philosophy not only contains no metaphysics of existence, but, as Santayana understood, is incompatible with such a metaphysical stance. Put more cautiously: If Dewey did intend to develop a metaphysics of existence, surely he failed in the end. In fact, he never began. There simply is no list or account in Dewey's writings of generic traits of existence independent of experience. Indeed, as Dewey notes, any attempt to provide such an account must be self-defeating because it would link immediately and intrinsically such existence with experience, with meaning and value. Moreover, if this sort of account—a list of experience-free, generic features of existence—could be located in Dewey's work, then Rorty would be correct to place Dewey squarely and unsuccessfully in the tradition that he, like Heidegger, sought to overcome.

3. There is a more important, more practical reason to insist that experience is the subject-matter of Dewey's metaphysics. For Dewey, metaphysics is not simply a particular kind of inquiry. It also is a particular kind of criticism, because Dewey defines philosophy as criticism and because metaphysics is a particular branch of philosophy. As criticism, metaphysics is concerned with values, and values occur wholly within experience. If experience is not the ultimate subject-matter of metaphysics, then metaphysics can perform no critical function. This is why a radical empiricist theory of experience matters in practice.

Just as the core of Dewey's reconstruction *in* metaphysics is his theory of the generic traits of experience, so the core of his reconstruction *of* metaphysics is his characterization of it as criticism, as discriminating judgment and appraisal of values. Dewey, recognizing that this view may seem baffling, notes that metaphysics may appear all "analysis and definition" and may seem "to have nothing to do with criticism and choice, with an effective love of wisdom" (*E&N*; *LW* 1:308).[13] How then can metaphysics establish "base lines" and be a "ground-map" of criticism?

(a) In its traditional forms, metaphysics is not criticism. In this sense, Dewey's characterization of metaphysics is more future prescription than description of the history of philosophy. Traditional metaphysics either proclaims that ideal values already are real, and exist secure in a realm of Being independent of unsure human efforts on their behalf in the natural world. Or

12. John Dewey, "Pure Experience and Reality: A Disclaimer," *John Dewey: The Middle Works, 1899–1924*, vol. 4 (Carbondale, Ill.: Southern Illinois University Press, 1977 [1907]), p. 120.
13. John Dewey, *Experience and Nature, John Dewey: The Later Works, 1925–1953*, vol. 1 [*E&N*; *LW* 1] (Carbondale, Ill.: Southern Illinois University Press, 1981 [1925]), p. 309.

it proclaims that ideal values cannot be realized, and exist in a realm of Being forever cut off from experience and nature.

(b) Such assurances and foundations are foreign to criticism. For Dewey, metaphysics provides no blueprint or timetable. It is merely a general orientation. It seeks to identify the general features of situations upon which particular realizations of particular values depend. The more sure one is that the world is of such and such a character, Dewey writes, the more one is committed to try to conduct life upon the basis of that character assigned to the world; thus "to note, register and define the constituent structure of nature is not then an affair neutral to the office of criticism" (*E&N*; *LW* 1:315). As such, metaphysics is not simply a prelude to criticism; it is criticism, judgment and appraisal of goods in thought and action.

This general orientation supplies useful direction in concrete situations. Dewey's own work provides evidence of this utility. It is manifest in the connections, for instance, between: his account of the pervasively qualitative character of experience and his more specific theory of art and aesthetic experience; in his account of the generic precariousness of experience and his more specific analyses of the religious dimension of experience and traditional philosophers' "quest for certainty"; and, his account of the irreducibly social character of experience and his more specific views of individuality, freedom, and community.

(c) Understood in this light, metaphysics is incomplete and always unfinished. It is neither "First Philosophy" nor "Last Philosophy." Instead, it must be always underway: the insight into generic existence "is itself an added fact of interaction, and is therefore subject to the same requirement of intelligence as any other natural occurrence; namely, inquiry into the bearings, leadings and consequences of what it discovers" (*E&N*; *LW* 1:310). More importantly, for Dewey, this sort of metaphysics happens to be as untried as it necessarily must be unfinished. As a result, writers like Rorty appear more pre-metaphysical than post-metaphysical. Having rightly discarded some bad metaphysical maps, Rorty tries to convince us that no ground map is needed. This makes for interesting reading, but it obscures the issue at hand for philosophy. This issue is not one of conversation, edification, or redescription. Redescription by any other name is neither criticism nor inquiry. Instead, the task at hand is the critical reconstruction of our values, and inquiry into the conditions upon which these values depend. Though we will hear the words of Dewey instead of "the word of Being," on this issue Rorty is silent.[14]

---

14. An earlier version of portions of this essay appeared in "Dewey's Reconstruction of Metaphysics," *Transactions of the Charles S. Peirce Society*, 28.2 (1992): 161–76. These revised passages appear here with the kind permission of the editor and the publisher.

7

Experience and the Adoration of Matter: Santayana's Unnatural Naturalism

Criticism arises out of the conflict of dogmas.... Dogma cannot be abandoned; it can only be revised in view of some more elementary dogma which it has not yet occurred to the sceptic to doubt.

—George Santayana, *Scepticism and Animal Faith*

Introduction: Two Men Who Look Very Much Alike, Especially One of Them

In his critical review of *Experience and Nature,* George Santayana labels John Dewey's metaphysics "half-hearted" and "short-winded" naturalism. Santayana observes critically that pragmatists are naturalists only by accident, "when as in the present age and in America the dominant foreground is monopolized by material activity; because material activity . . . involves naturalistic assumptions, and has been the teacher and the proof of naturalism since the beginning of time." He concludes: "Naturalism in Dewey is accordingly an assumption imposed by the character of the prevalent arts; and as he is aware that he is a naturalist only to that extent and on that ground, his naturalism is half-hearted and short-winded."[1]

In his reply to this attack, Dewey characterizes Santayana's naturalism as "inarticulate, a kneeling before the unknowable and an adjuration of all that is human," and locates Santayana's philosophy in "a hang-over of an intellectual convention which developed and flourished in physics at a particular stage of history." Calling Santayana's version of naturalism "broken-backed," Dewey writes:

---

1. George Santayana, "Dewey's Naturalistic Metaphysics," *Journal of Philosophy* 22.12 (1925): 673–88. This review is included as an appendix in *John Dewey: The Later Works, 1925–1953,* vol. 3 (Carbondale, Ill.: Southern Illinois University Press, 1984), pp. 374–75. Hereafter abbreviated "DNM" in this chapter.

It is in virtue of what I call naturalism that such a gulf as Mr. Santayana puts between nature and man—social or conventional man, if you will—appears incredible, unnatural and, if I am rightly informed as to the history of culture, reminiscent of supernatural beliefs. To me human affairs, associative and personal, are projections, continuations, complications, of the nature which exists in the physical and prehuman world. There is no gulf, no two spheres of existence, no "bifurcation." For this reason, there are in nature both foregrounds and backgrounds, heres and theres, centres and perspectives, foci and margins. If there were not, the story and scene of man would involve a complete break with nature, the insertion of unaccountable and unnatural conditions and factors.[2]

This testy confrontation between two of America's greatest philosophers is hardly unknown. Unfortunately, its philosophical importance is seldom grasped. This argument between Santayana and Dewey over the meaning and worth of naturalism in philosophy is more than a quibble over a label and the ownership rights to it. Instead, it constitutes a source of fundamental importance for a proper understanding of the worldviews of both Santayana and Dewey. It is also a striking example of an important feature and function of characteristically American philosophy in general—a valuable function often inadequately fulfilled in professional philosophy in America today.

Dewey and the Dominance of the Foreground

The significance of this Santayana-Dewey exchange cannot be grasped without a clear understanding of the positions involved. This is a difficult undertaking. Indeed, it is one at which Santayana himself failed in large part. Santayana understands naturalism to be that "spontaneous and inevitable body of beliefs involved in all animal life." This naturalism includes the beliefs of children who identify themselves with their bodies, and are interested in animals and "mechanical contrivances and in physical feats." In short, it is that body of beliefs which "covers the whole field of possible material action

---

2. John Dewey, " 'Half-Hearted Naturalism'," *John Dewey: The Later Works, 1925–1953*, vol. 3 (Carbondale, Ill.: Southern Illinois University Press, 1984 [1927]), pp. 74–75. This essay, originally published in the *Journal of Philosophy* 24.2 (1927): 57–54 is a reply to Santayana's "Dewey's Naturalistic Metaphysics" and to Frank Thilly's "Contemporary American Philosophy," *Philosophical Review* 35.11 (1926): 522–38. Thilly's review also is included as an appendix in *John Dewey: The Later Works, 1925–1953*, vol. 3, pp. 385–400. Hereafter abbreviated "HHN" in this chapter.

to its uttermost reaches." It is in this "material framework" or "world of naturalism," Santayana continues, that philosophers (and all people) labor: In relation to this naturalism, "philosophical systems are either extensions (a supernatural environment, itself natural in its own way, being added to nature) or interpretations (as in Aristotle and Spinoza) or denials (as in idealism)." Philosophical systems, that is, with all words, feelings, ideas, spirit, poetries, theologies, and so on, are "hung" on this material framework or universe of action. The "natural place" of such things is secondary and epiphenomenal.

Accordingly, naturalism breaks down, for Santayana, when the mental or spiritual "are taken to be substantial on their own account, and powers at work prior to the existence of their organs, or independent of them." In this sense, Santayana characterizes naturalism as anti-metaphysical: "Now it is precisely such disembodied powers and immaterial functions prior to matter that are called metaphysical. . . . To admit anything metaphysical in this sense is evidently to abandon naturalism" ("DNM": 368–369).

In this light, Santayana recognizes (and endorses) a strong naturalist strain in Dewey's work. He notes:

> It would be hard to find a philosopher in whom naturalism, so conceived, was more inveterate than in Dewey. He is very severe against the imagination, and even the intellect, of mankind for having created figments which usurp the place and authority of the mundane sphere in which daily action goes on. The typical philosopher's fallacy, in his eyes, has been the habit of hypostatizing the conclusions to which reflection may lead, and depicting them to be prior realities—the fallacy of dogmatism. . . . Here is a rude blow dealt at dogma of every sort: God, matter, Platonic ideas, active spirits, and creative logics all seem to totter on their thrones; and if the blow could be effective, the endless battle of metaphysics would have to end for lack of combatants. ("DNM": 369)

However, for Santayana, in the end Dewey can not deliver an effective, final blow against metaphysics because his naturalism is not complete, consistent, or thoroughgoing. Calling Dewey "the devoted spokesman of the spirit of enterprise, of experiment, of modern industry," Santayana holds that Dewey's philosophy also contains an equally strong antinaturalistic strain. As a result, Santayana concludes, Dewey's philosophy is metaphysical—antinaturalism disguised as naturalism.

Now, what is this antinaturalistic strain in Dewey's work? According to Santayana, it flows from Dewey's "choice" of "events"—I prefer the term "activity"—"to be his metaphysical elements," a choice that Santayana insightfully links to Dewey's sympathetic study of Aristotle. As a result, Santayana charges, Dewey "grafts something consciously actual and spiritual

upon the natural world" ("DNM": 372), and then treats this immaterial foreground of nature as the dominant reality, as constitutive of nature. Against
this *"dominance of the foreground,"* Santayana sets forth his own view, the
view that he takes to be naturalism proper:

> In nature, there is no foreground or background, no here, no now, no moral
> cathedra, no centre so really central as to reduce all other things to mere
> margins and mere perspectives. A foreground is by definition relative to some
> chosen point of view to the station assumed in the midst of nature by some
> creature tethered by fortune to a particular time and place. If such a fore-
> ground becomes dominant in a philosophy naturalism is abandoned. Some
> local perspective or some casual interest is set up in the place of universal
> nature or behind it, or before it, so that all the rest of nature is reputed to be
> intrinsically remote or dubious or merely ideal. This dominance of the fore-
> ground has always been the source of metaphysics. ("DNM": 373–74)

In opposition to all metaphysical philosophies of the foreground,
Santayana sets forth his own epiphenomenal materialism as genuine naturalism. This naturalism names the "circle of material events" "to which all
minds belonging to the same society are responsive in common" unless they
are "stupid and backward."[3] As he explains in his discussion of naturalism in
Dominations and Powers:

> Most of the critics of naturalism retain their animal faith in the physical theatre
> of life into which, however, they wish to insert their own moral energy, and
> perhaps other spiritual forces as continual remodellers of matter. This is an old
> and familiar conception, but its very naturalness renders it treacherous. . . . Life
> and spirit are not the cause of order in the world but its result.[4]

In a characteristically beautiful passage that could serve as an executive
summary of his own brand of naturalism, Santayana briefly sketches this
epiphenomenalism in which spirit is the by-product of matter:

> Of course, no earthly flame is so pure as to leave no ashes, and the highest
> wave sinks presently into the trough of the sea; but this is true only of the
> substance engaged, which, having reached a culmination here, continues in
> its course; and the habit which it then acquired may, within limits, repeat the
> happy achievement and propagate the light. One torch by material contact
> may kindle another torch; and if the torches are similar and the wind steady,

---

3. George Santayana, *Realms of Being* (New York: Scribner's, 1942 [1937]), p. vi. Hereafter
abbreviated *RB* in this chapter.
4. George Santayana, "Naturalism," *Dominations and Powers* (New York: Scribner's, 1950), pp.
8–9.

the flames, too, may be similar and even continuous; but if anyone says that the visible splendor of one moment helps to produce that of another, he does not seem ever to have seen the light. It will therefore be safer to proceed as if the realm of actual spirit had not been broached at this point, and as if the culminations recognized were only runs or notes discoverable in nature, as in the cycle of reproduction or in sentences in discourse. ("DNM":373)

Santayana's point, then, is this: Dewey's philosophy *essentially* is one in which the immaterial and "unnatural"—events, histories, situations, qualities, uses and endings, preparations and culminations—are ontologically dominant and primary; it is a philosophy of the flame rather than the torch. This antinaturalistic philosophy may appear naturalistic and may take up the language of naturalism simply because it just happens that the foreground of twentieth-century America, and so Dewey's twentieth-century American philosophy, is "monopolized by enterprise and material activity" and the accompanying natural-istic assumptions. Santayana identifies the philosophy of America—"the philoso-phy by which American live, in contrast to the philosophies which they profess"—as a "philosophy of enterprise" that "moves in the infinitely extensible boyish world of feats and discoveries—in the world of naturalism" ("DNM":370). As such, this naturalism, no matter how fashionable or American, is only "half-hearted" and "short-winded." Santayana concludes, it is the romantic and meta-physical reduction of nature to experience, of the world to a story or history, and of reality to humanity: "The luminous fog of immediacy has a place in nature; it is a meteorological and optical effect, and often a blessing. But why should immediacy be thought to be absolute or a criterion of reality?" The remedy for this idolatry of the immediate, Santayana advises, is to be found in "trusting in the steady dispensations of the substance beyond" ("DNM":384). As he states at the conclusion to his "Preface" to *Realms of Being*:

It is so simple to exist, to be what one is for no reason, to engulf all questions and answers in the rush of being that sustains them. Henceforth nature and spirit can play together like mother and child, each marvellously pleasant to the other, yet deeply unintelligible; for as she created him she knew not how, merely by smiling in her dreams, so in awaking and smiling back he somehow understands her; at least he is all the understanding she has of herself. (*RB*: xix)

Santayana and the Adoration of Matter

Although I think this is not the case, suppose for the moment that Santayana has fully understood Dewey's position. Why is that position philo-sophically objectionable or flawed? Why is spirit always the result and never the cause of order? Why must nature and spirit remain deeply unintelligible?

To what extent does Santayana address this issue without simply begging the question?

At the outset, it is important to recognize that Dewey's philosophy, like that of Santayana or anyone else, surely was influenced in many ways by the culture in which it arose, the culture in which it functioned, and the culture to which it was addressed. It is less sure that the dominant, primary feature of this culture was, or is, its commercialism and industrialism in business. Experimentalism in science, democracy in government, and individualism in social life, for example, seem no less crucial. In any case, the further claim that Dewey's philosophy is an attempt to justify all aspects of this commercialism and culture of enterprise is simply unfounded rhetoric and misreading. Dewey's later political writings make this especially clear, but even his early and middle works cannot be read as uncritical endorsement of American economic, political, and social policies.

More important still, a philosophy—even a supposedly "half-hearted" naturalism—cannot be rejected *merely* by noting those cultural factors, objectionable or not, which helped shape or mark the character of its author. If Santayana's analysis of Dewey's position is to be accepted as a non-question-begging criticism of that philosophy—as Santayana intends—then Santayana's own, alternative brand of naturalism must be adequately set forth and developed. The weakness of Dewey's view is not simply self-evident, even in Santayana's boyish "world of naturalism." If there is a fatal weakness in Dewey's metaphysics of experience, it is a weakness only in relation to criteria supplied by the background of nature that is Santayana's own philosophy.

Santayana attempts to avoid this point by means of an interwoven two-part strategy. In the first place, both in setting forth his own views and in attacking the views of others, he repeatedly claims that he operates without *any* metaphysics at all, that his philosophical system is not in any way metaphysical. He makes this point succinctly in the preface to *Scepticism and Animal Faith*, arguing that metaphysics is the result of a confusion of just those realms of being that he carefully distinguishes:

> Metaphysics, in the proper sense of the word, is dialectical physics, or an attempt to determine matters of fact by means of logical or moral or rhetorical constructions. . . . It is neither physical speculation nor pure logic nor honest literature, but (as in the treatise of Aristotle first called by that name) a hybrid of the three, materialising ideal entities, turning harmonies into forces, and dissolving natural things into terms of discourse. Speculations about the natural world, such as those of the Ionian philosophers, are not metaphysics, but simply cosmology or natural philosophy. Now in natural philosophy I am a decided materialist— apparently the only one living; and I am well aware that idealists are

fond of calling materialism, too, metaphysics, in rather an angry tone, so as to cast discredit upon it by assimilating it to their own systems. But my materialism, for all that, is not metaphysical. I do not profess to know what matter is in itself. . . . But whatever matter may be, I call it matter boldly, as I call my acquaintances Smith and Jones without knowing their secrets.[5]

This, however, will not do—at least, not all by itself. Now, if Santayana chooses to hold that the notion of a metaphysics of the experiential foreground is a redundancy and the notion of a metaphysics of the natural background is a contradiction in terms, of course, he is free to stipulate the meaning of "metaphysics" in this way. Similarly, if he chooses to hold that his own views about experience, nature, and reality constitute a "cosmology" or a "natural philosophy" (rather than any "metaphysics"), he is again free to stipulate the meaning of these terms in this way. In this case, Santayana's criticism of Dewey's metaphysics rests on the philosophical adequacy of his own natural philosophy (rather than the adequacy of his own, alternative "metaphysics"). This is simply a terminological shift (though one that means a great deal to Santayana), and the question remains: In criticizing Dewey, what are Santayana's underlying materialistic presuppositions and how are they justified? What justifies Santayana's materialism or naturalism, his cosmology or natural philosophy?

This is a pressing question because merely to note (or stipulate) the difference between a metaphysics of experience and nature and a natural philosophy of spirit and matter is not thereby to establish the philosophical superiority of the latter to the former. Here Santayana relies on the second element of his two-part strategy. In the second place, then, he claims that his naturalism *cannot* be justified by reason as skeptical philosophers have demanded; however, he adds that his naturalism *need not* be justified by animal faith (which presupposes this naturalism) as agents at work in the world never cease to realize. Thus, Santayana holds that philosophy has no honest answer to the skeptic; a thoroughgoing philosophical demand for rational justification leads to "ultimate scepticism." In contrast, Santayana locates his naturalism in an "animal faith" that he describes as "inevitable." He thus identifies himself as a dogmatist or dogmatic naturalist. In "The Scope of Natural Philosophy" in *Realms of Being*, for example, he writes that while (his) natural philosophy may be rejected in theory, it cannot be rejected in practice. He asserts: We all *"must* conceive a surrounding world":

---

5. George Santayana, *Scepticism and Animal Faith* (New York: Charles Scribner's Sons, 1923), pp. vii–viii. Hereafter abbreviated *S&AF* in this chapter.

Of course the belief that I can communicate with other minds, and that the reports reaching me signify an experience of theirs over and above my own, is a part of this extraordinary compulsory assumption which I make in living; the assumption that I am surrounded by a natural world, peopled by creatures in whom intuition is as rife as in myself: and as all my concern in perception and action turns on what those external things may do, so half my interest in my own thoughts turns on what other people may be thinking. It is not the task of natural philosophy to justify this assumption, which indeed can never be justified. Its task, after making that assumption, is to carry it out consistently and honestly, so as to arrive, if possible, at a conception of nature by which the faith involved in action may be enlightened and guided. (*RB*: 193–95)

At other times, Santayana stresses that there is a kind of evidence or experiential basis or "justification" for this animal faith, evidence that makes possible a sort of existential intimacy that is a hallmark concern of pragmatism.[6] He writes:

If experience, undergone, imposes belief in substance, experience studied imposes belief in nature. . . . As experience remodels my impulses, I assume that the world will remain amenable to my new ways . . . making nature a single and quasi-personal entity, bound tragically to its past, and pledged more or less wilfully to a particular future. . . . What evidence is there for the existence of nature in this sense of the word? If I speak of the universe at large, there can be no evidence. . . . Evidences for the existence of nature must be sought elsewhere, in a region which a monadologist would regard as internal to each monad, in that the substances posited by me in obedience to my vital instincts seem to me to behave as if they were parts of nature. Nature is the great counterpart of art. What I tuck under my pillow at night, I find there in the morning. Economy increases my possessions. People all grow old. Accidents have discoverable causes. There is a possible distinction between wisdom and folly. But how should all this be, and how could experience, or the shocks that punctuate it, teach me anything to the purpose, or lend me any assurance in life not merely a reinforced blindness and madness on my part, unless substance standing and moving in ordered ways surrounded me, and I was living in the midst of nature? (*S&AF*: 235–36)

Respect for matter, Santayana says, is the beginning of wisdom (*RB*: 396–97).[7] Naturalism, for Santayana, is this respect for matter:

---

6. See the discussion of this intimacy in chapter 5, and the discussion of Santayana and death in chapter 15.

7. Dewey draws a very different conclusion from virtually the same premises. Thus, for example, he claims that "experience, if scientific inquiry is justified, is no infinitesimally thin layer or foreground of nature. . . . The very existence of science is evidence that experience is such an

Thus the notion of an independent and permanent world is an ideal term used to make and as it were to justify the cohesion in space and the recurrence in time of recognisable groups of sensations. This coherence and recurrence force the intellect, if it would master experience at all or understand anything, to frame the idea of such a reality. If we wish to defend the use of such an idea and prove to ourselves its necessity, all we need do is to point to that coherence and recurrence in external phenomena.[8]

If Santayana is right that we must conceive a surrounding world, why must it be the world as he conceives it? If Santayana is right that we must view ourselves as living in the midst of nature, why must we view this nature as he does? And, if Santayana is right that we may point to coherence and recurrence in phenomena, why must we understand these phenomena as external, independent, and permanent? As a self-professed dogmatist, Santayana does not address these questions. His position is dogmatic precisely because he assumes without argument that his—and only his—particular brand of naturalism is justified and, in turn, claims both that this assumption itself can never be justified by any argument or theory and, at the same time, that this theoretically unjustified assumption can never be abandoned in life or practice. As a result, it might seem that there is nothing more to be said. Santayana himself remarks: "I would rather be silent than use some people's language; I would rather die than think as some people think."[9]

Dewey, however, seeking a genealogy of this dogmatism, rather than its proof, does find something more to say. He thus begins:

But even a dogmatist may be asked the grounds for his assertion, not, indeed, in the sense of what proof he has to offer, but in the sense of what is presupposed in the assertion, from what platform of beliefs it is propounded. I can not think that Santayana supposes that it is self-evident to others or to himself that nature is of the sort mentioned. The sweep and import of the statement is the more striking in that Santayana professes to

---

occurrence that it penetrates into nature and expands without limit through it." *Experience and Nature, John Dewey: The Later Works, 1925–1953*, vol. 1 (Carbondale, Ill.: Southern Illinois University Press, 1981 [1925]), pp. 11, 13. This difference is a measure of the philosophical distance between Santayana's materialism and Dewey's pragmatism. Henry Samuel Levinson has suggested that one of the pragmatic strains in Santayana's philosophy is his assertion that things are "historical all the way down." "Santayana's Pragmatism and the Comic Sense of Life," *Overheard in Seville* 6 (1988): 17. (See also his *Santayana, Pragmatism, and the Spiritual Life* [Chapel Hill: University of North Carolina Press, 1992].) Against this view, it seems to me that one of the nonpragmatic strains in Santayana's philosophy, evidenced by the passages included here, is his view that things are "material" (rather than historical) all the way down.
8. George Santayana, *The Life of Reason, or The Phases of Human Progress*, rev. ed. (New York: Scribner's, 1953 [1905]), p. 25.
9. Ibid., p. 197.

operate without any metaphysics. . . . Since knowledge of nature is not the ground for Santayana's statements as to its character, their ground, I take it, is negative and antithetic; the traits denied are those which are characteristic of human life, of the scene as it figures in human activities. Since they are found where man is, they are not, it would seem, attributable to anything but man; nature, whatever else it is or is not, is just something which does not have these traits. In short, his presupposition is a break between nature and man; man as anything more than a physically extended body, man as institutions, culture, "experience." ("HHN":74)

What does Santayana presuppose in propounding his naturalism as the one true, genuine naturalism? From what platform of beliefs does he address us? Moreover, what exactly does Santayana's "world of naturalism" "spontaneously and inevitably" commit us to believe? In most general terms, Santayana's brand of naturalism commits us to an ontological dualism of causally efficacious body and epiphenomenal mind, a dualism of objects and subjects, nature and consciousness, matter and spirit, torch and flame. Santayana presupposes this dichotomy: the active material world or background framework—the separate chunks of space in distinct bits of time; and, consciousness or spirit, constituted by intuitions—the epiphenomenal foreground that binds, unifies, and makes meaningful the realm of active matter.

Given this dualism, it is interesting to note that, contrary to his own admittedly dogmatic pronouncements, Santayana most often accounts for the life of spirit not in terms of an epiphenomenal foreground or dressing of a primary reality, but as an ongoing inclusive unity of spirit *and* its products or world by which it is known. His accounts of reason in art, religion, science, government, and social practice—the "life of reason"—are accounts of spirit as activity, in the sense in which Aristotle understands the term as a temporal unity of means and end, of act and product, of subject and object. When Dewey, the radical empiricist, uses the term, "experience," he is employing this same notion.

What then is Santayana's account of matter, the organ of spirit and the foundation of his naturalism? In smiling back at nature, what does spirit understand matter to be? Santayana often avoids giving us an account of the material world, or rather his account is not an account at all. He writes that this realm is unknowable and wholly without character. Encountering matter, he suggests, is a shock; it is a speechless kneeling before the unknown infinite, the unknown other. In his terminology, it is the totally indeterminate and formless counterpart of essence. As distinct from substance, it is a mark of the supposed unintelligibility of existence, of the fact that there is this existence rather than some other existence or no existence at all. Moreover, the essence of matter, of course, is not matter itself, but matterless and uninstantiated. Matter is a nature-less and unknowable surd. Nature, the field of material action, is thus unnatural or nonnatural. At least for humans, it is without nature or character. As such, it cannot be grasped by mind. Here Santayana's naturalism reveals itself as unnatural.[10]

This account clearly is inadequate and unacceptable. If matter is, as Santayana says, without form or character and is thus unknowable, the identification and designation of the realm of matter or "natural world" is without meaning or justification. Indeed, even for animal faith, there can be no evidence or import of such existence, for it is without connection to the foreground of human life. Moreover, it is not clear how something that we cannot know and characterize can be characterized, by Santayana himself, in terms of a contrast to spirit and foreground. Santayana's version of naturalism thus seems little more than a confusion, an idolatry of matter—an idolatry "reminiscent of supernatural beliefs," in Dewey's view ("HHN": 74).

It is crucial to recognize that Santayana invents, rather than discovers, this naturalism. It is possible to believe consistently in the existence of a surrounding world and at the same time to deny all dualisms of matter and spirit. It is possible to believe consistently that we live and act in the midst of nature and at the same time to believe that our lives are themselves "a portion of nature, an integral portion, and that nature is not just the dark abysmal unknown postulated by a religious faith in animality" ("HHN": 76). And it is possible to point to coherence and recurrence in our experience and at the same time "bring together on a naturalistic basis the mind and matter that Santayana keeps worlds apart." Concerning this endeavor, Dewey adds: "That success is impossible, given Santayana's premises, I am quite aware. But why not change the premises?" ("HHN":79).[11] Faith in nature need not be the adoration of matter. The unintelligibility of existence is an unintelligibility *within* experience. The shock of the real is a shock *within* experience. Faith in nature may be faith in the nature *of* our experiences, nature *in* our experience, experience as the background *of* nature.

This faith need not be dogmatic. It must be courageous. It is also circular: It moves from experience as the source of a view of nature to nature as

---

10. For a sympathetic interpretation of this issue, see John Lachs's discussion of Santayana's realm of matter in his *George Santayana* (Boston: Twayne Publishers, 1988), pp. 71–74. Lachs briefly provides a more critical assessment later in the same book, pp. 138–40.

11. In his moving *Obscenity, Anarchy, Reality* (Albany: State University of New York Press, 1996), Crispin Sartwell embraces and develops Santayana's premises. With Santayana, Sartwell writes that the experience of shock establishes realism. In contrast, with Dewey, I hold that the experience of shock establishes radical empiricism—the reality of that which is shocked as much as the reality of that which does the shocking. It is only in this way that Santayana and Sartwell can account for the self as an animal or agent in a field of action rather than as a pain-free spectator external to a more fundamental realm of being. See the development of this radical empiricist account of experience in chapters 8, 9, and 10.

the source of evidence for that view of experience. As Dewey writes in "Nature in Experience," a 1940 response to critics who had not learned the lessons of his reply to Santayana:

> That this circle exists is not so much admitted as claimed. It is also claimed that the circle is not vicious; for instead of being logical it is existential and historic. That is to say, if we look at human history and especially at the historic development of the natural sciences, we find progress made from a crude experience in which beliefs about nature and natural events were very different from those now scientifically authorized. At the same time we find the latter now enable us to frame a theory of experience by which we can tell how this development out of gross experience into the highly refined conclusions of science has taken place.[12]

Experience-and-Nature

In any adequate account of nature, nature must be knowable and must have form or character. Nature must have a nature. Naturalism must reject any sharp existential dichotomy between matter and form, matter and spirit, matter and life, matter and essence. Although he frequently claims that matter is featureless and unknowable—a claim that must be contained in any philosophy to which he will award the title of naturalism—Santayana's own brand of naturalism, despite his strong pronouncements, often does not contain this claim. Indeed, Santayana's own naturalism often constitutes an alternative to this claim. However, Santayana appears unable to recognize fully this alternative. Vehemently opposed to idealism, Santayana seems to believe that materialism is the only alternative. Similarly, insightfully aware of the fact that Dewey is not a materialist, Santayana appears to conclude that Dewey therefore must be an idealist. In contrast, Dewey is concerned to develop an alternative metaphysics that differs from both materialism and idealism. In a typical passage, Dewey thus observes:

> Presentation of a view of experience which puts experience in connection with nature, with the cosmos, but which would nevertheless frame its view of experience on the ground of conclusions reached in the natural sciences, has trouble in finding ways of expressing itself which do not seem to lead into one or the other of these historically sanctioned alternative perspectives.[13]

---

12. John Dewey, "Nature in Experience," *John Dewey: The Later Works, 1925–1953*, vol. 14 (Carbondale, Ill.: Southern Illinois University Press, 1988 [1940]), p. 143.
13. Ibid., p. 142.

Santayana's inability to self-consciously frame such a view, and his own confusion and inconsistency on this point is especially evident in his discussions of matter and substance. Dewey seizes on this problem:

> In discussing specific matters he often suggests that he shares the belief of the ordinary man that human experience, adequately safeguarded by a normal organism and a proper equipment of apparatus and technique, may afford dependable indications of the nature of things that underlie it; that we do not merely fall back on an "animal faith" that there is some adorable substance behind, but that we come to reasonable terms with its constituents and relations. If one generalizes this position, then the main features of human life (culture, experience, history—or whatever name may be preferred) are indicative of outstanding features of nature itself—of centres and perspectives, contingencies and fulfillments, crises and intervals, histories, uniformities, and particularizations. This is the extent and method of my "metaphysics."
>
> I find two movements and two positions in Santayana which are juxtaposed, but which never touch. In his concrete treatments of any special topic when a matter of controversy to which traditional school labels are attached is in abeyance, he seems genuinely naturalistic; the things of experience are treated not as specious and conventional, but as genuine, even though one-sided and perverse, extensions of the nature of which physics and chemistry and biology are scientific statements. . . . But when he deals with a system of thought and finds it necessary to differentiate his own system from it, his naturalism reduces itself to a vague gesture of adoring faith in some all comprehensive unknowable in contrast with which all human life—barring this one gesture—is specious and illusory. ("HHN":81)

Santayana's more informative account of matter emerges in discussions of specific issues and concrete problems, particularly in *Scepticism and Animal Faith*, *The Realms of Being*, and *The Life of Reason*, where the "world of naturalism" frequently functions as the world of substance, and where substance is understood as the union of a specifying and determining form, and a slice of constitutive and creative material action or energy. Here the combination of essence and matter is the constitution of a particular existent. Here neither essence nor matter exist independently and self-sufficiently. This world of substance is the reality or material of our daily lives. It is the stuff of our loving, hating, striving, obtaining, failing, encountering, remaking, and dying. But this material or stuff that is our lives is not "matter" in Santayana's special, ontological sense of the term. Instead, this matter is the creative source or producing agent of this natural world of substance; form is the resource from which this creative material action selects or "picks out." The union of these factors is the natural world of substance. Matter and substance, then, constitute Aristotle's *energeia*,

Dewey's "experience," an active unity of producing and product, of doing and deed.

Just as Santayana describes spirit in terms of its fruits in our natural world, so he accounts for matter most successfully in terms of its consequences and establishments in our environment. In *The Realm of Matter,* for instance, it is clear that matter is neither self-enclosed nor without character. Rather, it is the context in which we act, a context that presupposes, and is presupposed by, our actions and purposes. It is the unified, continuous, spatiotemporal milieu that surrounds, supports, and includes us. In this vein, Santayana goes so far as to say that there is no substance, no existence, that is essentially independent of this field or context of action. This active reality, of course, is strikingly "unnatural" in Santayana's professed dogmatic understanding of naturalism. In these moments, the philosopher—Santayana—is greater than his mask—materialism.[14]

Exactly why it might be appropriate to apply the label, "matter," to nature understood as a field of action is not clear. Santayana's masked motives and "pigeonholes into which every philosophy must go" are not my concern here. Nor is it my concern to detail the two strains of naturalism in Santayana's thought. I *am* concerned to indicate that his "whole-hearted" naturalism is empty and inadequate. It is also important to see that the second strain of naturalism, although very confused and only at most sporadically self-conscious, is whole-heartedly "half-hearted." Despite its confusions and inconsistencies, it is this strain of naturalism that is the source of Santayana's most successful and insightful prose writing.

This naturalistic strain or position, of course, is developed in greater detail, consistency, and self-awareness by Dewey. Santayana, in his "half-hearted" naturalistic moments, writes that all existence or substance is constituted by an agent in a field of action. Dewey writes that existence is constituted by selective interest in a context or background. He calls this transactional existence "experience" and, later, "culture," and thus struggles to differentiate his meaning of the term from that of "orthodox British mentalism." This experience, according to Dewey, is eventful, historical, qualitative, practical, meaningful, and social. Moreover, it is "world-constitutive": There is nothing which can meaningfully be said to be existence which is not intrinsically a feature or aspect of experience. Existence or nature is, as Santayana noted, experience (and not experienc*ing*) deployed. To so much as refer to existence or background reality unconnected with human experience is to connect that existence to experience; this connection, moreover, is as

---

14. See George Santayana, "The Mask of the Philosopher," *Soliloquies in England and Later Soliloquies* (New York: Scribner's, 1922), p. 160.

real a feature of a given existent as any other feature. Experience, for Dewey as for James, is "double-barreled": it includes the processes of experiencing and the objects of that experiencing. Experience is transactional: it is an inclusive unity and continuity of subject and object, of producer, process, and product.

In this light, radical empiricism simply is radical naturalism. In Dewey's writings, this radical naturalism gives no ontological dominance or privilege to the experiential foreground. However, this foreground of experience—experiencing—does have ontological parity or equality with the background of experience—the experienced, nature. In this nonidealistic, nonmaterialistic, inclusive understanding of experience, Dewey unites what Santayana separates. Throughout *Experience and Nature*, Dewey asserts that the human situation or foreground falls wholly within nature. As such, nature is understood not only as the object of experiencing, but the activity which is the union of experiencing and the subject-matter experienced.

We are now in a position to grasp the philosophical and larger social importance of a "half-hearted" naturalism which understands reality in terms of unified, continuous, ontologically irreducible activity.[15] To identify this reality, with Dewey, as experience, is to profess naturalism in such a way as to call attention to the reality of human undertakings, the efficacy of human purposes, and the need for human intelligence. To do this is to remind all philosophers that their undertakings arise from within, and must be evaluated in terms of, this environment of daily social practice. Philosophers must see to it that their philosophies mark an enlightenment and enrichment of that daily living. The task here is not simply to conceive of a surrounding world. Instead, it is to render, bit by bit, that world increasingly intelligent. It is to make, bit by bit, Santayana's "mother" intelligible to "her children." This concern has been a trademark of many of America's best philosophers, regardless of the labels that they have applied to their own work.

A naturalistic philosophy which focuses on this concern becomes a genuine philosophy of experience. As such, as Santayana notes, this philosophy removes "external compulsions." It also removes external supports, and forces us to be responsible for the intelligent piecemeal reshaping of our lives and their backgrounds. In Santayana's language, it forces us to be artists

---

15. In *Individualism: Old and New*, for example, Dewey writes: " 'Naturalism' is a word with all kinds of meanings. But a naturalism which perceives that man with his habits, institutions, desires, thoughts, aspirations, ideals and struggles, is within nature, an integral part of it, has the philosophical foundation and the practical inspiration for effort to employ nature as an ally of human ideals and goods such as no dualism can possibly provide." *John Dewey: The Later Works, 1925–1953*, vol. 5 (Carbondale, Ill.: Southern Illinois University Press, 1984 [1930]), p. 114.

rather than metaphysicians: "An absolute perfection, independent of human nature and its variations, may interest the metaphysician; but the artist and the man will be satisfied with a perfection that is inseparable from the consciousness of mankind, since it is at once the natural vision of the imagination, and the rational goal of the will."[16]

Like much of Santayana's work that moves beyond the adoration of nature to its possibilities within our lives and its demands on our wills, Dewey's philosophy frequently is an inspiring example of this natural vision of the imagination. In *Art as Experience*, for example, aesthetic experience is not only described but recovered, made accessible, extended, and deepened. In *A Common Faith*, the religious nature of our lives is not merely noted or defined, but liberated from supernaturalism and expanded so as to pervade the farthest reaches of daily transactions. Such a "naturalism of the foreground" is a whole-hearted humanism: It is a philosophy in which the focus on natural ends is directed by, and in turn directs us to, the always incomplete work of achieving moral ends.

Against the relentlessly returning darkness, the illumination provided by such a philosophy may be only small and temporary comfort. When this philosophy's flame flickers and its wick burns low, the soul, longing for brighter exposure, may dream of torches or stars that burn brilliantly forever. In these moments, philosophers first thought of matter.[17]

---

16. George Santayana, *The Sense of Beauty* (New York: Scribner's, 1896) p. 266.

17. Compare Santayana, "Atmosphere," *Soliloquies in England and Later Soliloquies*, p. 13. An earlier version of portions of this essay appeared in "Santayana's Unnatural Naturalism," *Two Centuries of Philosophy in America*, ed. Peter Caws (London: Blackwell, 1980), pp. 144–50. These revised passages appear here with the kind permission of the editor and publisher.

8

Socrates and Radical Empiricism

The Practical Need for Theory

In the *Myth of Sisyphus,* Camus observes that "in that race which daily hastens us toward death," "we get into the habit of living before acquiring the habit of thinking."[1] Here, of course, Camus does not mean to stress the primacy of experience over reflection; rather, like John Dewey, he is distinguishing a life of minimum and incidental thinking from a life that results from continuous, regulated, reflective inquiry. We normally act, Camus asserts, without first adequately thinking about our actions, and so our lives come to be fashioned by situation and circumstance instead of consistent, coherent planning. By contrast, the character of Sisyphus, always lucid, always conscious, is exceptional. Most of us, our shoulders to the rock and ever straining forward, are so busy pursuing the good life that we rarely even pause to consider what such a life is.

This refusal to think about the values of, and in, our actions would be of no consequence if we could continuously lead the good life without contemplating its nature. If desires were followed naturally, regularly, and effortlessly by satisfaction, there would be no cause for philosophical pondering about the nature of the good life. Reflection would serve no pragmatic function, and philosophical contemplation indeed would be useless.

Unfortunately, a short course in experience harshly teaches us that this is not the case. It is only too often that we suffer from the lack of past thought. We often find ourselves now unable to obtain that which we desire, or discover that we have labored only to obtain that which is not what it seemed once. We discover that we desire mutually exclusive ends, and experience even wider conflicts between our own goals and those of other individuals.

---

1. Albert Camus, "The Myth of Sisyphus," *The Myth of Sisyphus and Other Essays* (New York: Vintage Books, 1955 [1942]), p. 7.

Philosophers, of course, are thought commonly to suffer not from such a refusal to think, but rather from a refusal to act, to live, to do. They often seem to have acquired the habit of thinking only to lose the habit of living. Granted that much philosophy *is* remote from daily living as William James and other American philosophers repeatedly charge, so too much of daily life is distant from rational self-examination and its fruits. We must study the good, no doubt, but we must study it, as Aristotle points out, not simply to know it but to live well. James thus rightly contrasts knowledge about life with effective, dynamic living.

Socratic Questions

This practical need for philosophical reflection on the goods at which our actions aim is dramatized in Plato's *Euthyphro*. Here the character of Euthyphro reveals himself a master of thoughtless deed. He acts without sufficient thinking: He charges his father with impiety although, it turns out contrary to his boasts, he is ignorant of what piety is. By his own admission, a person who acts in such ignorance is not worth much. After his first attempts at defining piety are shown quickly by Socrates to be inadequate, Euthyphro defines piety as that which is pleasing to, or loved by, all the gods. In the discussion that follows, Socrates leads the unwitting Euthyphro to admit that this definition also fails. Although virtually all students of philosophy are familiar with the exchange between Socrates and Euthyphro, I want to look carefully from a pragmatic perspective at its structure in order to avoid Euthyphro's apparent errors.

Solely for the purpose of argument, Socrates accepts Euthyphro's definition of piety as that which all the gods love, and proceeds to show that, given this definition, a contradiction is entailed. Socrates asks: "Do the gods love piety because it is pious, or is it pious because they love it?"[2] Socrates then argues, against Euthyphro, that piety cannot be pious because it is loved by the gods since nothing is (essentially) what it is because of its relations to other things. Socrates points out that being loved (or being led, being carried, or being seen) is the effect of someone actively loving (or leading, carrying, or seeing), and is not the cause of anything's being what it is—for example, of piety's being pious. Next, Socrates asserts that the gods may love the pious, but this causes the pious to be loved, and does not make it pious because it is loved.

---

2. Plato, *Euthyphro*, trans. F. J. Church, trans. rev. Robert D. Cumming (New York: Bobbs-Merrill, 1956), p. 11.

Socrates then shows Euthyphro that if piety is loved by the gods because it is pious, then piety is not the same thing as that which the gods love. Socrates argues that if piety is defined as that which is loved by all the gods (as Euthyphro now defines it), then it follows (by substitution) that piety is what is loved by all the gods because it is that which is loved by all the gods. But, Socrates has just shown that nothing is loved because it is loved, but rather is loved because someone loves it. Socrates concludes that what is loved by the gods is loved because they love it, while the pious is loved by the gods because it is pious. Since the cause of the gods' love of that which they love is not the cause of their love of that which is pious, what is loved by all the gods and piety are "opposite things, and wholly different from each other."[3]

In sum, Socrates argues as follows:

1. Assume, as Euthyphro claims, that piety is defined as that which is loved by all gods.

2. If piety is defined as that which is loved by all the gods, then either piety is loved by the gods because it is pious, or piety is pious because it is loved by all the gods.

3. It is not the case that piety is pious because it is loved by all the gods (since being loved is an effect of someone actively loving, and is not the cause of anything being what it essentially is).

4. Therefore, if piety is defined as that which is loved by all the gods, then piety is loved by all the gods because it is pious.

5. If piety is loved by all the gods because it is pious, then the pious and that which is loved by all the gods are essentially different things (since if the pious were that which is loved by all the gods, then piety would be loved by all the gods because it is loved by all the gods, and this is not the case).

6. But the claim that piety and that which is loved by all the gods are essentially different contradicts the initial assumption; therefore, piety is not defined properly as that which is loved by all the gods (and so Euthyphro is mistaken).

This argument is valid. Moreover, since Euthyphro readily agrees to the truth of steps 2, 3, and 5, he is led to abandon his claims to being able to define piety and to being wise in such matters. More generally, Socrates' argument, if sound, demonstrates not only that Euthyphro is mistaken in this case, but that piety—or, apparently, goodness, justice, honesty, beauty, courage, and so

---

3. Ibid., p. 13.

on—logically cannot be defined by a *relation* to something else, some action, some person, or some or all gods. Whether some persons or gods love piety—or, again, goodness, justice, honesty, beauty, courage, and so forth—are pious, desire to be pious, are bored thinking about piety, and so on, is irrelevant to what piety itself is.

Euthyphro's apparent problems should temper popular judgment that philosophers think too much and act too little. Surely it is better to continue thinking with Socrates than to act rashly and unknowingly with Euthyphro. Perhaps, however, we can learn from Euthyphro, and can escape repeating his apparent errors.

William James and Radical Empiricist Ethics

In the "Moral Philosopher and the Moral Life," William James *seems* not to have learned from Euthyphro's difficulties. James defines goodness in terms of relations—relations between sentient, conscious demand or desire, and the objects which satisfy that demand or desire. James writes that "*the essence of good is simply to satisfy demand*," that "everything which is demanded is by that fact a good," and that so far as someone "feels anything to be good, he *makes* it good" (and "it *is* good, for him"). Continuing, James claims that "goodness, badness, and obligation must be *realized* somewhere in order really to exist and that "neither moral relations nor the moral law can exist *in vacuo*," independent of a mind that feels them.[4]

James thus appears to have inherited all of Euthyphro's difficulties. Indeed, perhaps the plight of James is worse, for Socrates is no longer present. We might imagine, then, the conversation between James and Socrates to be the following:

James: What are you doing in the Dean's Office, Socrates?

Socrates: I have been charged with failure to publish. But what brings you here, James?

James: I wish to leave a copy of my essay, "The Moral Philosopher and the Moral Life," in which I define the nature of goodness.

Socrates: Tell me then, most pragmatic of men, what is goodness and what is not-goodness, for I am eager to become your pupil and learn.

James: I say that goodness is that which a sentient being finds to satisfy demand.

---

4. William James, "The Moral Philosopher and the Moral Life," *The Will to Believe and Other Essays in Popular Philosophy*, *The Works of William James* (Cambridge, Mass: Harvard University Press: 1979 [1891]), pp. 153, 146, 145.

Socrates: Let us examine this statement. Consider this: Is goodness found by sentient beings to satisfy demand because it is good, or is it good because a sentient being finds it to satisfy demand?

James: Say what?

The Socratic line of questioning in this discussion, though imaginary, is evident, and would parallel the argument that Socrates presents to Euthyphro. Socrates would argue that goodness cannot be good because it is found to satisfy demand by a sentient being, since nothing essentially is what it is because of its relation to other things. Socrates would then point out that being found to satisfy demand is the effect of someone actively being satisfied, and is not the cause of anything's being what it essentially is. A sentient being may find that that which is good satisfies demand, but this only demonstrates that that which is good does happen to satisfy demand. Socrates then would show James that if goodness is found by sentient beings to satisfy demand because it is good, then goodness and that which is found to satisfy demand are not the same thing. If they were the same, then goodness would be found to satisfy demand by sentient beings because it is found to satisfy demand by sentient beings. This claim, however, has just been rejected.

Briefly, again, Socrates would argue as follows:

1. Assume, as James asserts, that goodness is defined as that which a sentient being finds to satisfy demand.

2. If goodness is defined as that which a sentient being finds to satisfy demand, then either goodness is that which a sentient being finds to satisfy demand because it is good, or goodness is good because it is that which a sentient being finds to satisfy demand.

3. It is not the case that goodness is good because it is that which a sentient being finds to satisfy demand (since something's being found to satisfy demand is an effect or result of someone's actively being satisfied, and is not the cause of anything's being what it essentially is).

4. Therefore, if goodness is defined as that which a sentient being finds to satisfy demand, then goodness is that which a sentient being finds to satisfy demand because it is good.

5. If goodness is that which a sentient being finds to satisfy demand because it is good, then goodness and that which a sentient being finds to satisfy demand are different things (since if goodness were that which a sentient being finds to satisfy demand, then goodness would be that which a sentient being finds to satisfy demand because it is found to satisfy demand, and this is not the case).

6. But the claim that goodness and that which a sentient being finds to satisfy demand are different things contradicts our initial assumption above; therefore, goodness is not defined as that which a sentient being finds to satisfy demand (and so James is mistaken).

This argument, again, is valid. If one accepts the truth of steps 2, 3, and 5, the argument must be accepted and James' line of thinking must be rejected.

I think it is highly doubtful, though, that James would or should accept as true steps 2, 3, and 5. How would James, the radical empiricist, reply to this Socratic cross-examination? How would his responses differ from those of Euthyphro? In raising these questions and pursuing these issues, my purpose, of course, is not to develop some acultural, ahistorical criticism of Socrates and Plato. Rather, I am interested in generating a dialogue between James and Socrates so as to illuminate an originating and important view of reality, experience, and the good life present in much characteristically American philosophical thought. In particular, I am interested in making clear how this thought undercuts and redirects certain traditional philosophical concerns rooted in an earlier complex of philosophical assumptions. In doing so, I recall James's own words:

> I saw that philosophy had been on a false scent ever since the days of Socrates and Plato, that an *intellectual* answer to the intellectualist's difficulties will never come, and that the real way out of them, far from consisting in the discovery of such an answer, consists in simply closing one's ears to the question.[5]

At the onset of the discussion with James, as with Euthyphro, Socrates poses a key question: Is goodness that which a sentient being finds to satisfy demand because it is good, or is goodness good because it is that which a sentient being finds to satisfy demand? Euthyphro apparently is intent on deciding which of these alternatives he should pick and which he should avoid, and does not object to this sort of question. In contrast, James would object to, and would reject, this central question because of his denial of a fundamental assumption necessary for the intelligibility of the question itself. James, then, "closes his ears" to Socrates; the Socratic questions are discarded rather than answered. Of course, this is a characteristic response of American philosophers to many traditional philosophical problems. "Intellectual progress," Dewey wrote in "The Influence of Darwinism on Philosophy,"

---

5. William James, *A Pluralistic Universe*, *The Works of William James* (Cambridge, Mass: Harvard University Press: 1977 [1909]), p. 131.

"usually occurs through sheer abandonment of questions. . . . We do not solve them: we get over them."[6]

What is this fundamental Socratic assumption that James denies? As a beginning, we should note that Socrates finds it meaningful to predicate an individual instance—a property, a character, a quality—of a class of instances, even when the class is composed of individuals of the type being predicated of the class. That is, Socrates assumes that it is meaningful to predicate the property of being pious of piety, and so asks why piety is pious. (See step 2 of the first argument above.) Similarly, Socrates would assume that it is meaningful to predicate the property of being good of goodness, and so would ask why goodness is good. (See step 2 of the second argument above.) Is this meaningful? The answer to this question depends on the resolution of a complex metaphysical issue. My aim here is not to settle this issue, but rather to point out that Socrates' line of questioning presupposes a certain sort of answer to this question.

Stated most generally, Socrates' questions, of course, logically presuppose a metaphysical theory such as Plato's Theory of Forms (although the Socrates of *Euthyphro* may not have appealed to or developed fully this theory). What is important here is not arguments for the existence of a realm of Forms, accounts of the possibility of knowledge of these Forms, or explanations of their relations to particulars, but rather the implicit rejection and assumption of unintelligibility of an alternative understanding of morality *as relational*.

This is evident in Socrates' original question: Socrates believes that if goodness is that which a sentient being finds to satisfy demand, then *either* goodness is that which a sentient being finds to satisfy demand because it is good, *or* goodness is good because it is that which a sentient being finds to satisfy demand. Socrates offers two options. James rejects both of these options, and articulates an alternative account. James thus denies (the truth of step 2 in the above arguments, and so) the soundness of Socrates' entire argument.

Stated more specifically and directly, Socrates assumes that nothing—piety, goodness, and so on—is what it is essentially in virtue of its relation to something else. The contrast between Socrates' Platonic metaphysics and James's radical empiricism could not be sharper. Socrates would argue that goodness cannot be good because it is found to satisfy demand by a sentient being, for he thinks that, in general, any relation some X has to some Y is not, or does not constitute, what X is essentially. Euthyphro also believes, or is led to believe, this, and that is why he abandons the view that piety is pious

---

6. John Dewey, "The Influence of Darwinism on Philosophy," *John Dewey: The Middle Works, 1899–1924*, vol. 3 (Carbondale, Ill.: Southern Illinois University Press, 1977 [1909]), p. 14.

because the gods love it when Socrates convinces him that being what the gods love is a *relation* that piety has to the gods' act of loving. Now the assumption is clear: Socrates, and with him Euthyphro, simply assume that while piety—or presumably goodness—may stand in a certain relation to the gods' love, piety itself is not defined by, or constituted by, this relation since piety itself is not a relation of any sort. Put more generally, the assumption is this: Things may have relations, but relations never essentially constitute things.

This assumption, made by Socrates and many later philosophers, including critics of both pragmatism and postmodernism, is explicitly denied by James, the radical empiricist.[7] James does not assert that goodness stands in some relation to that which is found to satisfy demand, or to the demand for satisfaction. Rather, he asserts that goodness *is* that relation. Goodness is the relation between a sentient being and some object which satisfies its demand; goodness is the satisfying/satisfied relation.

In *Essays in Radical Empiricism*, James writes that radical empiricism

> *does full justice to conjunctive relations,* without, however, treating them as rationalism always tends to treat them, as being true in some supernal way, as if the unity of things and their variety belonged to different orders of truth and vitality altogether.[8]

James views goodness as this sort of experienced, real relation, as an "affair of relations." These relations are primarily and essentially neither subjective nor objective, neither aspects of conscious demand nor the content of that demand. They have no such "inner duplicity":

> I refer here to *appreciations,* which form an ambiguous sphere of being, belonging with emotion on the one had, and having objective "value" on the other, yet seeming not quite inner nor quite outer. (*ERE*:18)

It is this metaphysical stance, this view of the reality of relations, of pure experience, that provides the metaphysical basis for James's remarks in "The Moral Philosopher and the Moral Life." We must remember this radical empiricism if we are to understand James's remarks about mind and demand creating and making goods. James is not, in response to Socrates, advocating a subjectivism or idealism; rather he is undercutting the dualism of subject/

---

7. See the discussions of postmodernism and objective reality in chapter 5, Rorty's linguistic idealism in chapter 6, and Santayana's naturalism in chapter 7.

8. William James, *Essays in Radical Empiricism, The Works of William James* (Cambridge, Mass.: Harvard University Press, 1976 [1912]), p. 23. Hereafter abbreviated "*ERE*" in this chapter.

object that is the basis of the idealism/realism dispute. Goodness, for James, is no more a "property" of the experiencing subject than it is a "property" of the experienced object; it *is* this relation, primary, irreducible, and not yet analyzed by later reflection.

James makes this explicit in his essay "The Place of Affectional Facts in a World of Pure Experience." He writes that he will try to show the erroneousness of the popular view of experiences of pleasure, pain, fear, anger, beauty, comicality, preciousness, and so on as being "purely inner facts." Instead, he continues, these experiences illustrate the *relational* character of affectional facts:

> "[S]ubjectivity and objectivity are affairs not of what an experience is ab-originally made of, but of its classification. Classifications depend on our temporary purposes. For certain purposes it is convenient to take things in one set of relations, for other purposes in another set. (*ERE*:71)

This reinforces the discussion in "Does 'Consciousness' Exist?," about *assigning* the nature of values:

> Sometimes the adjective wanders as if uncertain where to fix itself. Shall we speak of seductive visions or of visions of seductive things? Of wicked desires or of desires for wickedness? Of healthy thoughts or of thoughts of healthy objects? Of good impulses, or of impulses toward the good? (*ERE*:18)

John Dewey and Radical Empiricist Inquiry

This radical empiricist thinking underlies "The Moral Philosopher and the Moral Life." James makes this evident by explicit reference to goodness and badness as "moral relations." (Although "The Moral Philosopher and the Moral Life" preceded James's development of radical empiricism, I think this moral theory presupposes radical empiricism, much as *Euthyphro* temporally but not logically preceded Plato's development of the Theory of Forms.) However, although James's radical empiricism underlies and is evident in his own writings on ethics, many of the implications of radical empiricism for moral theory were most fully developed by John Dewey. Moreover, in linking radical empiricism to inquiry, Dewey transformed James's radical empiricist ethics:

> The fundamental trouble with the current empirical theory of values is that it merely formulates and justifies the socially prevailing habit of regarding enjoyments as they are actually experienced as values in and of themselves. It completely side-steps the question of regulation of these enjoyments. . . . To say that something is enjoyed is to make a statement about a fact, something

already in existence; it is not to judge the value of that fact. . . . But to call
an object a value is to assert that it satisfies or fulfills certain conditions. . . .
The fact that something is desired only raises the question of its desirability;
it does not settle it.[9]

Dewey insists that values are consequences, rather than antecedents of
inquiry. As a result, he emphasizes that any effective reconstruction of democracy, education, logic, and experience—the reconstruction of our entire
culture—requires inquiry. In these situations, the subject-matter of inquiry is
social rather than physical; it is human action, social organization, and values,
rather than chromosomes and genes, quarks and quasars, and heavy water and
fusion. Accordingly, all social inquiry—whether focused on child abuse, drug
use, housing needs, consumer wants, or world peace—presupposes that values properly can be made the subject-matter of inquiry. Of course, Dewey
recognizes that today values are only rarely and haphazardly the result of
inquiry. Instead, ethics is usually treated as something wholly subjective,
emotional, relative, neither right nor wrong, and incapable of rational, public,
experimental examination. Dewey notes this fact, bemoans it, and views it as
a positive opportunity for philosophy to do now for moral inquiry what it did
three centuries ago for physical inquiry:

> It is a favorite idea of mine that we are now in the presence of an intellectual
> crisis similar to that of the seventeenth century. Then the crisis concerned
> the free creation of new ideas regarding physical nature, ideas that formed
> the points of departure for new ways of observing and interpreting physical
> phenomena. Now the crisis concerns the initiation of new hypotheses re-
> garding man, regarding the nature and significance of those human associa-
> tions that form the various modes of social phenomena.[10]

According to many earlier and many contemporary philosophers, however, the metaphysical split between objective facts and subjective values
makes any such experimental inquiry into values impossible. The mark of
this supposed impossibility is what philosophers have called the "is/ought
gap." This so-called "gap" is thought to be a logical gap: the idea is that
statements of fact—"is" statements, judgments that such and such is the
case—never by themselves logically lead to or warrant any statements of

---

9. John Dewey, *The Quest for Certainty, John Dewey: The Later Works, 1925–1953*, vol. 4
(Carbondale, Ill.: Southern Illinois University Press, 1984 [1929]), pp. 207–8. Hereafter abbreviated "*QC; LW* 4" in this chapter.
10. John Dewey, "Philosophy," *John Dewey: The Later Works, 1925–1953*, vol. 5 (Carbondale,
Ill.: Southern Illinois University Press, 1984 [1929]), p. 177.

value—"ought" statements, judgments that such and such is good or ought to be done. This supposed problem has led many earlier philosophers to pursue one of two strategies. Some have tried valiantly and cleverly to "bridge" the is/ought gap by showing that there are some statements of fact, or facts about reason or language, that logically entail some statements of value. Others, noting the sleight of hand in these efforts, have declared the gap between fact and value too wide to cross. And so, they have declared themselves skeptics, nihilists, tyrants, or subjectivists—positions that are far less comfortable in practice than in theory.

Not surprisingly, taking up a radical empiricist position, Dewey pursues neither of these strategies. Instead, he declares the supposed split between fact and value abstract and artificial—like other philosophical dualisms of experience and nature, mind and body, thought and action, child and curriculum, and individual and society. But philosophies that begin with a separation of fact and value are not simply indefensible theories. In addition, they have terrible practical consequences. By excluding values from the legitimate subject-matter of inquiry, such theories make, or at least allow, values to become the subject-matter of other, unintelligent and undemocratic social procedures such as authority, custom, force, self-interest and class-interest, and the pressures of immediate circumstances.[11] Dewey concludes: "Thus we are led to our main proposition: *Judgments about values are judgments about the conditions and the results of experienced objects; judgments about that which should regulate the formation of our desires, affections and enjoyments*" (*QC*; *LW* 4:211–12).

Value statements are statements about certain sorts of facts; values are certain sorts of experienced facts. This shifts the problem. The issue is no longer one of how to put fact and value back together again. Instead, it is one of analyzing from within experience the nature of values—or, as Dewey sometimes calls them for emphasis, "value-facts."

Thus, like James (and perhaps more fully than James), Dewey's ethics is radically experiential or naturalistic in the sense that he views valuing as something an organism does in response to its environment. These responses are matters of liking and disliking, of being satisfied or unsatisfied, of attraction or aversion, of seeking or avoiding, of enjoying or suffering. In the absence of sentient life and its reflective strivings, values do not exist. Moreover, living beings do not simply passively discover values; instead, they create and recreate values. Values are not revealed so much as made. Intimacy is not a "given" or ready-made; where it exists, it is a "taken" or achievement.

---

11. See the discussions of community and democracy in chapters 13 and 14.

Agreeing with James that values are relations—that the goodness or badness of something simply is an experienced relation in a particular situation to particular desires of a particular person—Dewey stresses the link between desire and intelligence. Accordingly, he is careful to point out that fulfillments of desires and enjoyments do not by themselves constitute values. Instead, values are objects of desires only when those desires have been informed, and transformed by, experimental inquiry. Earlier self-proclaimed "empirical" theories of valuation have not been sufficiently radical; they have failed to recognize that the sheer fact that something is desired does not establish that the thing is desirable—that it actually is valuable. So, to say that some thing or action is good is to say that inquiry has established its existential relations:

> If we know the conditions under which the act of liking, of desire and enjoyment, takes place, we are in a position to know what are the consequences of that act. The difference between the desired and the desirable, admired and the admirable, becomes effective at just this point. Consider the difference between the proposition "That thing has been eaten" and the judgment "That thing is edible." The former statement involves no knowledge of any relation except the one stated; while we are able to judge of the edibility of anything only when we have a knowledge of its interactions with other things sufficient to enable us to foresee its probable effects when it is taken into the organism and produces effects there. . . . Enjoyments that issue from conduct directed by insight into relations have a meaning and a validity due to the way in which they are experienced. (*QC; LW* 4: 212)

Since inquiry secures and intensifies enjoyments, and so transforms them into values, its pragmatic worth is beyond calculation. As a result, Dewey thinks it is ironic that we so far have failed to formulate a theory of values based on experimental, experiential inquiry:

> The time will come when it will be found passing strange that we of this age should take such pains to control by every means at command the formation of ideas of physical things, even those most remote from human concern, and yet are content with haphazard beliefs about the qualities of objects that regulate our deepest interests; that we are scrupulous as to methods of forming ideas of natural objects, and either dogmatic or else driven by immediate conditions in framing those about values. There is, by implication, if not explicitly, a prevalent notion that values are already well known and that all which is lacking is the will to cultivate them in the order of their worth. In fact the most profound lack is not the will to act upon goods known but the will to know what they are. (*QC; LW* 4: 214)

To meet this lack, Dewey formulated his radically empiricist theory of valuation,[12] from which two especially important consequences follow. First, ends framed without inquiry into the means necessary for their realization are foolish and irrational. Nothing is intrinsically good. Nothing is self-evidently good. Second, ends framed without inquiry into their role as means to further ends are shortsighted and harmful. Nothing is a final good. Nothing is a complete good. Through inquiry, foolish and shortsighted action may be avoided. Through inquiry, we may come to understand both our existing problem situation and the likelihood that a particular course of action on behalf of a particular end-in-view will address that problem and "do away with conflict by directing activity so as to institute a unified state of affairs" (*TV; LW* 13: 221-22).

From this radical empiricist perspective, three central questions in ethics can be resolved. These questions are: Are values subjective? Are values relative? Does the end justify the means?

First, are values subjective? Following James, Dewey answers with a resounding "No." Neither propositions about value nor values themselves are subjective. Propositions about values refer to existential relations between an organism and its environment. The truth or falsity of these propositions depends upon the presence or absence of the stated relations. For example, the truth or falsity of a mother's claim to prize her child depends upon objective facts of experience—her actual desires and her actual activity. Similarly, the truth or falsity of a vacationer's appraisal of a canoe trip depends upon objective facts of experience—the actual extent to which projected means efficiently secure the prized end of relaxation. Thus, propositions about values are, in part, propositions about individual persons or subjects, but there is nothing peculiarly subjective about the propositions. In this vein, Dewey notes that propositions about potatoes are not, for that reason, starch-filled propositions. And, like propositions about values, values themselves are not subjective. They are experienced, transactional relations between—or through—organism and environment. The goodness of water for a thirsty person is neither a bare fact about the water or the person. It is a fact about an experienced relation that irreducibly includes both organism and environment, subject and object.

In this light, are values relative? According to one form of ethical relativism, values are relative to individuals in the sense that whatever anyone believes is valuable therefore is valuable for him or her. On this view, values are relative to individual beliefs. A radical empiricist theory of valuation

12. John Dewey, *Theory of Valuation, John Dewey: The Later Works, 1925–1953*, vol. 13 (Carbondale, Ill.: Southern Illinois University Press, 1988 [1939]), pp. 191–251. Hereafter abbreviated "*TV; LW* 13" in this chapter.

exposes the silliness and danger of this view. This view is silly because values do not depend simply on what one thinks, but rather upon the actual nature of a person and his or her actual situation. The fact that a person believes, perhaps passionately and totally, that eating sand will satisfy a great thirst, for example, does not make eating sand in this situation refreshing, quenching, or satisfying. This view is dangerous since it implies that prejudices unsupported by experience may nonetheless be maintained as truths by those who choose to do so. History provides serious examples of this sort of prejudice that involve class, race, gender, religion, ethnicity, nationality, and physical abilities.

Dewey's radical empiricism supports a different sort of relativism. According to Dewey, values are relative to persons and situations, not to beliefs. Since values are relations that exist between the desires and activities of an organism and its environment, differences or changes in the organism or the environment make for different values. A good meal, for example, means different things to a newborn infant and an Olympic athlete in training. This form of ethical relativism—a point of agreement between Dewey and Santayana—goes hand in hand with Dewey's commitments to individualism and growth. But it is at odds with all armchair ethics. It means that we cannot rely upon blanket principles, formulated once and for all, in leading our lives. It means we must engage in inquiry and action in order continuously to have the self-knowledge and knowledge of nature needed to satisfy our desires and to have satisfactory desires.

This relativism sheds light on a further traditional issue: Does the end justify the means? In discussing this issue, Dewey recalls Charles Lamb's essay on the origin of roast pork. In this story, a house in which pigs were kept burns down. While searching through the remains, the owners burn their fingers and bring them to their mouths to cool them. Enjoying the taste and wanting more, they set about building houses, enclosing pigs in them, and burning them down. Only when the end prized is appraised in terms of means employed, Dewey observes, is this absurd:

> In such situations enjoyment of the end attained is itself valued, for it is not taken in its immediacy but in terms of its cost—a fact fatal to its being regarded as "an end-in-itself," a self-contradictory term in any case. . . . The conception involved in the maxim that "the end justifies the means" is basically the same as that in the notion of ends-in-themselves; indeed, from a historical point of view, it is the fruit of the latter, for only the conception that certain things are ends-in-themselves can warrant the belief that the relation ends-means is unilateral, proceeding exclusively from ends to means. . . . It thus discloses in a striking manner the fallacy involved in the position that ends have value independent of appraisal of means involved and independent of their own further causal efficacy. (*TV; LW* 13: 227-28, 229)

This fallacy, Dewey notes, is everywhere evident in our society, particularly in our unwillingness to confront critically economic realities:

> [U]pon the whole, economics has been treated as on a lower level than either morals or politics. Yet the life which men, women and children actually lead, the opportunities open to them, the values they are capable of enjoying, their education, their share in all the things of art and science, are mainly determined by economic conditions. Hence we can hardly expect a moral system which ignores economic conditions to be other than remote and empty. Industrial life is correspondingly brutalized by failure to equate it as the means by which social and cultural values are realized. That the economic life, thus exiled from the pale of higher values, takes revenge by declaring that it is the only social reality, and by means of the doctrine of materialistic determination of institutions and conduct in all fields, denies to deliberate morals and politics any share of causal regulation, is not surprising. (QC; LW 4: 225)

The alternative is social life marked by experimental inquiry into values. A radically empiricist moral philosophy articulates the theory of this valuation. The wide-scale adoption in practice of this theory would constitute a genuine "Copernican revolution," one that still awaits our action.

Socrates or Radical Empiricism?

The adoption in theory of this radically empiricist ethics requires rejection of the fundamental assumptions that underlie the questioning that Socrates and many of his successors employ. James and Dewey reject these assumptions. Should we? Should we side with Socrates, or with James and Dewey? This question, of course, raises difficult issues not simply in moral theory but also in metaphysics and epistemology. In doing so, it makes evident how philosophers have come to be accused of too much thought and too little action.

Addressing fully these issues may require an eternity, just as rolling the rock occupies Sisyphus forever. But as James recognized, despite philosophers' best efforts to escape time,[13] no eternity is available to us. We, each of us, must make our fate our own, and must do it here and now, in this life. James's view of such a life is plausible and promising. In virtue of its radical empiricist base, it provides responses to Socratic questions that undercut those questions and redirect our philosophic concerns.

---

13. See the discussions of time in chapters 9 and 10, and death in chapter 15.

As such, James's ethical theory supplies guidelines for radical empiricist practice. First, on this view, the good life consists in *creating* continuous, self-constituting, and self-sustaining relations with our natural and cultural environment. It consists neither in steadfast, simplistic obedience to rules, nor in the achievement of supposed "pure" knowledge of an eternal, unchanging "essence" of good. This is what James means when he denies the possibility of a dogmatic ethics made up in advance.

Second, these relationships must be not only constructed, but continually *reconstructed* as both self and environment evolve; as experience is neither static nor merely repetitive, attainment of the good life is neither final nor certain. There can be no "final truth" in ethics, James tells us. The good life, then is not the result of our action, but is the action itself—when the values that arise from our actions are continually directed intelligently so as to be realized in them.

Third, just as living the good life involves the continual reconstruction and amelioration of our relations with our environment, so too our *understanding* of the good life, of the ideal itself, must be reconstructed continually. As James, Dewey, and other American philosophers have stressed, values not affirmed and reaffirmed in, and by, experience simply cease to be values. While we may undertake actions on the basis of values sustained by the past or acclaimed by others, this basis is not authoritative, fixed, or infallible. No values escape the demand of continuing reconfirmation in, and by, experience.

Fourth, as such, the good life requires exercise of the ability to make decisions that are mutually supporting and sustaining, that form a coherent lifestyle, that *reconstruct the self and actively remake the environment*. The ongoing mutual adjustment of self and environment demands adjustments of, and in, the environment as well as the self. The good life requires transformative social actions, and so reconstruction of values likely and regularly may require reconstruction in society.

Fifth, for James, the good life consists in the achievement of *inclusiveness and intimacy*, the construction of a harmony of desires and purposes. There is no objective standard of goodness, but there are intersubjective, transsubjective standards that direct us to "awaken the least sum of dissatisfactions" and to count highest those ideals that "prevail at the least cost" and destroy "the least possible number of other ideals" and differences.[14] (This returns us to the first guideline and its emphasis on the creation of values and the rejection of abstract rules and maxims—including utilitarianism, which, in opposition to radical empiricist ethics, would advocate the "hideous" course

---

14. James, "The Moral Philosopher and the Moral Life," p. 155.

of sacrificing "lost souls" in order to achieve maximum utility given *existing* demands.)

To omit either this reflection or this action is to fall far short of the good life. And, to fail to incorporate critically these features of experience into philosophy is to invite questions about the existence and worth of philosophy, and the need for the habit of thinking. It is to ensure, moreover, that philosophers will speak only to themselves—a fate, unlike the rock of Sisyphus, that perhaps cannot be surmounted simply by scorn.[15]

---

15. Camus, "The Myth of Sisyphus," p. 90.

An earlier version of portions of this chapter appeared in "Socratic Questions and Radical Empiricist Ethics," *Transactions of the Charles S. Peirce Society* 20.1 (1984): 38–50. In that form, this chapter was awarded the first Douglas Greenlee Prize by the Society for the Advancement of American Philosophy. These revised passages appear here with the kind permission of the editor and the publisher.

9

Chronophobia

Introductions

Order: There is something orderly about a chapter that begins with an introduction, at least with one and only one introduction. Multiplying introductions beyond the normal order, but not beyond necessity, I hope, I begin with three introductions.

1. In Hong Kong a couple of years ago, the concierge at a British luxury hotel one day posted this announcement (in the Queen's English) in the hotel lobby near the elevator: "Dear guests: Today the lift is out of order, so you will be unbearable." No doubt: When it comes to time, we aren't stoics; we can't bear things being out of order. Now, does saying that the elevator is out of order simply give us factual information about the elevator itself? Or does it signal a relation between the elevator in its current state and the typical desires or interests or values of most hotel guests? In reflecting about order, shouldn't we now abandon the long-standing subject/object dualism, and, in insisting on the unity of subject and object, must we not reject all simple dualisms of order and disorder. Isn't the notion of order irreducibly a normative notion? Can anything be out of order or unordered except in its relation to demands made by an ordering subject? Isn't a state of affairs that is out of order, disorderly, or chaotic simply a state of affairs that is ordered, or in order, in a manner that we do not desire? To proclaim order is to judge. To proclaim chaos is to extend order.

2. Washington, Adams, Jefferson, . . . What is the next item in this ordered series? Red, purple, blue, green, yellow, . . . What is the next item in this ordered series? 2, 4, 6, 8, . . . What is the next item in this ordered series? Old, new, borrowed, . . . What is the next item in this ordered series? Are these questions too easy? Are the ordering principles too obvious? Consider: 1, -5, 102, 1.25, 69,008, . . . What is the next item? Perhaps the answer again is obvious: 3 is the next item; only 3 could be the next item in the ordered series 1, -5, 102, 1.25, 69,008, 3, 104, 106, -2, and so on. Here, of course, the ordering principle is that the first item is 1, that the second item is the result of subtracting 6 from the first item, that the third item is reached by

165

adding 107 to the second item, that the fourth item is 100.75 less than the third item, and so on. If I ask you about this series of items later—if I repeat the series and ask you many times—will you know the right answer? Will you learn the ordering principle? Will you experience this order? Isn't a state of affairs that is without order simply a state of affairs that is ordered in an unfamiliar or dangerous way? To establish order is to achieve familiarity and safety. To confront chaos is to begin to establish new order.

3. Suppose a philosopher wanted to champion chaos or to argue against order. Would we demand a valid (orderly) argument? True (orderly) premises? Grammatical (orderly) propositions? Shared (orderly) meanings and a common (orderly) vocabulary? I think so. Three introductions? Probably not. Isn't the attempt to argue against or overcome order the discovery that one is commanded to engage in acts of ordering, that one is ordered to order? Isn't all traditional epistemology, metaphysics, and moral theory a set of marching orders that cannot be evaded? Doesn't epistemology command: "Think in order!"? Doesn't metaphysics command: "Be in order!"? And, doesn't moral theory command: "Live in order!"? Indeed, doesn't all thought command: "Come to order!"? "What we cannot speak about we must pass over in silence," Wittgenstein wrote at the close of his *Tractatus*.[1] A nice try! However, this is simply another marching order, because the fact is that to speak about that which we must pass over in silence—to speak about it even this much—is to speak volumes. About that which we say we cannot speak, we must already have said too much. Moreover, as R.E.M., the musical group, has declared insightfully (to all would-be Wittgensteins) on their recording *Out of Time*: About that which we say too much, we haven't said enough.[2]

Toward a Genealogy of Fear

In his *Rommel Drives on Deep into Egypt*, a book of short poems published in 1970, almost twenty years before his suicide, Richard Brautigan included "The Memoirs of Jesse James:"

> I remember all those thousands of hours
> that I spent in grade school watching the clock,
> waiting for recess or lunch or to go home.
> Waiting: for anything but school.
> My teachers could easily have ridden with Jesse James
> for all the time they stole from me.[3]

---

1. Ludwig Wittgenstein, *Tractatus Logico-Philosophicus*, trans. D. Pears and B. McGuiness (London: Routledge & Kegan Paul, 1974 [1921]), p. 74.
2. See R.E.M., "Losing My Religion," *Out of Time* (Warner Brothers, #26496–4, 1991), track 2.
3. Richard Brautigan, *Rommel Drives on Deep into Egypt* (New York: Dell, 1970), p. 4.

Like Brautigan's teachers, most theorists and virtually all philosophers have made careers riding with Jesse James, stealing our time and leaving us only eternity, leaving us supposed salvation, leaving us the True, the Real, and the Good. Waving their theories like so many sawed-off shotguns, these time thieves long ago perfected the Hollywood Western routine: "This is a hold-up. Give me all your valuables. Don't move or I'll shoot." Wait to go home, and don't move.

Like America's Wild West, philosophy's Wild West was, and still is, full of dangerous characters, deliberate masterminds, and desperate men who would rather die with (their books and) their boots on than do time. Western philosophers, awaiting Hollywood casting: Plato and Augustine as Jesse and Frank James seeing visions and hearing divine orders to steal people's this-worldly savings by robbing banks; Immanuel Kant as Butch Cassidy blowing up trains on time and hiding out with his Hole-in-the-Wall gang of transcendentalists; Soren Kierkegaard as Billy the Kid stopping stagecoaches and preaching to his victims before shooting them; and, G. E. Moore, A. J. Ayer, and Bertrand Russell as the Clanton brothers spending rustling profits in a saloon and toasting their conception of "the Ideal"—"what things are such that, if they existed *by themselves*, in absolute isolation, we should yet judge their existence to be good."[4] Don't move.

This is the history of philosophy in the West. This is Western philosophy—waiting for recess, waiting for anything.

Was Jesse James brave? He worried and frightened and killed people, but was he courageous? Were Richard Brautigan's teachers—our teachers—or even many of us ourselves (not you, of course, but perhaps someone else nearby)—valiant? They wasted and stole and killed time, but were they courageous? Most Western philosophers say little, if anything, about courage. In his *Nicomachean Ethics*, however, Aristotle discussed courage at length. He listed it as the first virtue, defined it, and identified possession of it as a necessary condition for the possible possession of all other virtues. Recall his words:

> [Courage] is a mean concerning matters that inspire confidence and fear. . . . It chooses and endures what it does because it is noble to do so or base to refuse. But to seek death as an escape from poverty, love, or some other painful experience is to be a coward rather than a man of courage. For to run away from troubles is softness, and such a man does not endure death because it is noble but because he is fleeing from evil.[5]

---

4. George Edward Moore, *Principia Ethica* (London: Cambridge University Press, 1966 [1903]), p. 187.
5. Aristotle, *Nicomachean Ethics*, trans. M. Ostwald (New York: Bobbs-Merrill, 1962), pp. 71–72 (1116a10–a15).

To seek escape from painful experience is to be a coward, Aristotle said.
Isn't to seek order in the face of chaos to seek escape? Isn't to understand that
we are ordered to order—that we cannot escape order—also to seek escape?
And isn't such understanding the favored form of escape of traditional Western philosophers? As musician and master dialectician Bob Dylan might have
pointed out to these traditional Western thinkers—from Plato's philosopher-
king to Hegel's master and slave—when it comes to achieving escape through
understanding the impossibility of escape, it is time to realize "there's no
success like failure, and that failure's no success at all."[6]

If courage is rare in life, its deficiency, cowardice, is anything but rare.
Today confidence is in short supply, and many fears are widespread. We all
are familiar with them, even those of us with fingerprints of our children, car
alarm devices, home security systems, gated communities, and concealed
weapons permits designed for escape, designed to order, designed to protect
our bodies and our property from a modern (or postmodern) day Jesse James.
We each wrestle with some of these fears day by day as best we can, and we
observe them over and over in the lives of others. These commonplace phobias include (but are not limited to): fear of heights and fear of open spaces;
fear of flying, fear of falling, and fear of failing; fear of fire and fear of water;
fear of isolation and fear of crowds; fear of the new, the strange, and the
different; fear of crime and fear of war; fear of darkness; fear of disease; and,
of course, fear of death.

In philosophy, as in life, there are many pervasive phobias. These fears
produce and sustain, and in turn are strengthened by, the familiar projects,
prejudices, and perspectives of much of Western philosophy. In epistemology
and logic, in metaphysics, and in moral theory, they include: fear of the vague
and the inexact; fear of the uncertain, the ungrounded, and the unfounded;
fear of the emotional, the noncognitive, and the ineffable; fear of the feminine
and fear of the body; fear of the defeasible, the fallible, and the revisable; fear
of the individual, the incomplete, the local, the particular, and the partial; fear
of the inconsistent, the arbitrary, and the unordered; fear of the plural, the
relative, and the contingent; fear of change and impermanence; and, again,
fear of death.

Of course, most Western philosophers do not acknowledge these fears—
even though these fears play originary and fundamental roles in their philosophies. Instead, philosophers: ignore them (like business executives who
automatically turn newspaper pages past the obituaries to the stock market
reports); deny them (like children who tell their friends that they do not sleep
with night-lights); rationalize them (like abusive, violent husbands who have

---

6. Bob Dylan, "Love Minus Zero/No Limit," *Bringing It All Back Home* (Columbia, #CS9128,
1965), track 4.

convinced themselves that their wives deserve to be battered); or, cover up or hide them (like self-righteous people who attempt to disguise their fear of homosexuality as love of Jesus).

Western philosophers have demonstrated no confidence in their fears, and so have sought not to live with them, but rather to escape from them— as Santayana has pointed out, in the classic tradition by understanding them, and in the Romantic tradition by eluding them.[7] As a result, Western philosophers have not acknowledged, much less confronted or examined deeply, their fundamental fears, and we in turn have come to accept what most of them, from the ancient Greeks to the present, have told us about philosophy. They have told us: Philosophy begins in wonder; everyone desires to know; and, philosophy, after all, is love of wisdom and commitment to truth. Accordingly, we have become habituated to asking certain questions about philosophies: What meanings do they clarify? What insights do they illuminate? What truths do they embody? What arguments do they advance, on what evidence do they draw, and what justification do they have?

Now, as Santayana observed in "The Genteel Tradition in American Philosophy," "to covet truth is a very distinguished passion. Every philosopher says he is pursuing the truth, but this is seldom the case." As Bertrand Russell has suggested (and Santayana recalled approvingly), philosophers often fail to reach the truth because they often do not desire to reach the truth. We may declare that we seek the True, the Real, or the Good, but simply pronouncing that we have this desire does not make the desire exist, just as failing to acknowledge a fear does not make that fear vanish. Philosophers, Santayana continued, usually are apologists absorbed in defending vested illusions and eloquent ideas:

> Like lawyers or detectives, they study the case for which they are retained, to see how much evidence or semblance of evidence they can gather for the defence, and how much prejudice they can raise against the witnesses for the prosecution for they know they are defending prisoners suspected by the world, and perhaps by their own good sense, of falsification. They do not covet truth, but victory and the dispelling of their own doubts. What they defend is some system, that is some view about the totality of things, of which men are actually ignorant. No system would have every been framed if people had been simply interested in knowing what is true, whatever it may be. What produces systems is the interest in maintaining against all comers that some favourite or inherited idea of ours is sufficient and right.[8]

---

7. George Santayana, "The Genteel Tradition in American Philosophy," *Winds of Doctrine: Studies in Contemporary Opinion* (New York: Scribner's, 1913), p. 199.
8. Ibid., pp. 197–99.

In this light, perhaps we must begin to tell a different story about philosophy. Perhaps philosophy begins not simply in wonder, but rather in worry, anxiety, and apology; perhaps everyone desires not simply knowledge, but instead safety and security; and perhaps philosophy means less a sort of love and more a sort of fear. This perspective is practical and genealogical, and directs us to ask different questions about philosophies: What problems do they construct? What, and whose, interests do they seek to advance? What forces do they bring to bear or put in play? Above all, from what fears do they arise and develop?

Chronophobia

These questions obviously could be approached in many ways. One could focus on the fears at work, explicitly or implicitly and consciously or unconsciously, in the writings of a particular philosopher—Plato, or Leibniz, or Hegel, for example. Or one could concentrate on the fears at work in a particular theory or doctrine—Plato's theory of Forms, Leibniz's monadology, or Hegel's phenomenology of spirit, for example. Or one could analyze similarly the particular phobias linked to the works of a particular cluster or school of philosophers—the ancient Greeks, the rationalists, or the German Idealists, for instance. Or, one could display the fears at work in a particular branch of philosophy throughout its history in the West—epistemology, metaphysics, or moral theory, for example.

This last strategy has been employed in a limited but effective manner by several twentieth-century philosophers. For example, John Dewey's *The Quest for Certainty* is a brilliant genealogical analysis and critique of traditional epistemology (in philosophy, science, and the arts) from Plato to the present. Published two years after Heisenberg set forth his indeterminacy principle, Dewey's examination of epistemology was not motivated by an interest in attacking or defending a particular theory, and he did not propose any new solutions to old problems. Instead, he called on philosophy to give up epistemology, to completely close down what he called the rusting "epistemology industry," and to dissolve (rather than solve) ancient, outdated epistemological problems. Accordingly, he wasn't interested in the different views that loom large and divide traditional epistemologists into competing camps—for example, skeptics and mystics, empiricists and rationalists, sensationalists and transcendentalists, realists and antirealists, truth-as-correspondence and truth-as-coherence theorists, and so on. Instead, he was more interested in the common, shared, pervasive problems that these different views all seek to address. In other words, he was struck not by the fact that epistemologists have disagreed about *solutions* to central problems in epistemology; instead, he found it much more striking that they have agreed with one another about the central *problems* themselves.[9]

How did these problems arise? In turn, what are their consequences? What and who's interests are advanced or created in this process? We live in a world of hazards, dangers, and perils. We fear uncertainty and long for security. Action cannot provide us this security in practice; its results are inherently uncertain. Can thought provide us this security in theory? This "quest for certainty," a quest that can be fulfilled only in pure knowing, has defined and constituted traditional epistemology:

> [In practical activity] no complete assurance is possible. All activity, more- over, involves change. . . . Hence men have longed to find a realm in which there is an activity which is not overt and which has no external conse- quence. "Safety first" has played a large role in effecting a preference for knowing over doing and making. With those to whom the process of pure thinking is congenial and who have the leisure and the aptitude to pursue their preference, the happiness attending knowing is unalloyed; it is not entangled in the risks which overt action cannot escape. . . . The quest for certainty is a quest for a peace which is assured, an object which is unquali- fied by risk and the shadow of fear which action casts.[10]

The same fears and insecurities that made epistemology a "quest for certainty" made metaphysics a "search for the immutable." If knowing—or a special, philosophical form of knowing—is to yield certainty, then the objects of knowing must be invariant, fixed, eternal, and real independently of, and antecedent to, our efforts to know them. Our beliefs cannot be certain unless their objects are permanent. And since the objects of this world are not permanent, metaphysics (unlike physics, for example) must be concerned with "a higher realm of fixed reality of which alone true science is possible," "a higher and more ultimate form of Being than that with which the sciences of nature are concerned." Given this conception, Dewey summarized:

> The realm of the practical is the region of change and change is always contingent; it has in it an element of chance that cannot be eliminated. If a thing changes, its alteration is convincing evidence of its lack of true or complete Being. What *is*, in the full and pregnant sense of the word, is

---

9. For an extended discussion of Dewey's philosophy as an alternative to traditional philosophi- cal dualisms, see the first chapter of my *Experience and Criticism: John Dewey's Pragmatism* (Nashville, Tenn.: Vanderbilt University Press, 1998).
10. John Dewey, *The Quest for Certainty, John Dewey: The Later Works, 1925–53*, vol. 4 (Carbondale, Ill.: Southern Illinois University Press, 1984 [1929]), pp. 6–7. Hereafter abbrevi- ated (*QC; LW* 4) in this chapter.

always, eternally. It is self-contradictory for that which *is* to alter. If it had no defect or imperfection in it, how could it change? That which becomes merely *comes* to be, never truly is. . . . Thus the depreciation of practice was given a philosophic, an ontological justification. (*QC; LW* 4: 16)

But if the depreciation of practice has been given both an epistemological and an ontological (or metaphysical) justification, the origin of this depreciation of practice lies, paradoxically, in practice itself.[11] The practical perils we face far outstrip our practical abilities. But these perils are no match for our theoretical abilities. As Dewey observed, "in the absence of actual certainty in the midst of a precarious and hazardous world, men cultivated all sorts of things that would give them the feeling of certainty. And it is possible that, when not carried to an illusory point, the cultivation of the feeling gave man courage and confidence and enabled him to carry the burdens of life more successfully" (*QC; LW* 4: 26–27). But belief in a super-sensible, transphenomenal, immutable reality is insufficient; by itself, it allays no fears and gives rise to no courage. Just as epistemic certainty must go hand in hand with ontological immutability, so too ontological immutability must go hand in had with ethical ideality. Instead of understanding the good as the possible outcome of our actions—goods that are contingent and actions which may not succeed—it is far safer to understand the good as real—ultimately or really Real—independent of, and prior to, our action. If the Real is to allay our fears, the real must be Ideal. In a scary world, what could be better than Ideals that come prepackaged with their own ultimate Reality? One-hundred percent contingency-free: There is no need to imagine the possibilities for such an intellectual marketing campaign; the history of Western philosophy supplies us with the actuality.

This, Dewey noted, has been the chief aim of traditional philosophies: "to show that the realities which are the object of the highest and most necessary knowledge are also endowed with the values which correspond to our best aspirations, admirations, and approvals." This is pathetic, and would strike us as curious, Dewey speculated, if it were not so common to seek consolation by "projecting a perfect form of good into a realm of essence, if not into a heaven beyond the earthly skies, wherein their authority, if not their existence, is unshakable":

> Thus the object of philosophy is to project by dialectic, resting supposedly upon self-evident premises, a realm in which the object of completest cognitive certitude is also one with the object of the heart's best aspiration. The fusion of the good and the true with unity and plenitude of Being thus becomes the goal of classic philosophy. (*QC; LW* 4: 27–28)

---

11. See the discussion of practice and pragmatism in chapter 4.

The quest for certainty and the search for the immutable, I believe, are simply the epistemological and the metaphysical phases or dimensions of the *pursuit of order*—an essentially normative, critical, moral undertaking. Philosophers have sought (and in their metaphysical systems pretended to find) an immutable reality (the Real). Why have they wanted this? Because they've wanted certainty, and without ontological permanence, certainty is impossible. And so philosophers have embarked on (and in their epistemological systems pretended to return successfully from) a quest for certainty (the True). But why have they wanted this? Because they want moral order, and without epistemological certainty, moral order cannot be guaranteed. And so philosophers have pursued (and in their systems of morals pretended to reach) moral order (the Good). But, at last, why have they wanted this?

This is not a simple question, but it is possible to state the answer briefly: fear of time—what I shall call *chronophobia*. The search for the immutable, the quest for certainty, and the pursuit (or invention) of moral order—the principal enterprises of traditional Western philosophy—are simply philosophical formalizations of familiar responses to familiar fears: the fear of time; the fear that some Jesse James is always victimizing us; the fear that our lives are just temporal streams, brief and finite passings, precarious comings and sure goings, journeys with ends but without destinations; the fear that goals will never be attained, that satisfactions will not last, that failings will never be corrected, and that missed opportunities are missed forever; the fear that self-actualization is simply self-depletion, self-exhaustion, self-consumption, self-destruction, and, perhaps, self-distraction; the fear that going to conferences, reading books, playing with children, talking with neighbors, eating dinner, and driving to work are just so many familiar ways of dying and so many familiar instances of disorder wrought by time. Chronophobia is evident in the fear of uncertainty—time will overturn our knowledge and our truths; manifest in the fear of impermanence—time will undo the reality we encounter and the particular world in which we live; and, above all, constituted by the fear of disorder—time will expose our values as wholly local, contingent, fleeting, and merely autobiographical. Chronophobia is fear of moral chaos. Even as we find ourselves ordered to order, we fear disorder—unwanted or unfamiliar order—and search not for truth but for order, for system (or mathematical equation), and for safety—running away from disorder like a coward, like Jesse James.

Chronophobia's Moral Imperative: From Chaos to Order

The workings of chronophobia are nowhere more important than in the realm of moral theory, and in the moral *systems* that are its products. It is crucial to understand that these systems all are remarkably similar, despite the fact that most philosophers, like most textbook anthologies and college lectures, focus on the differences among these theories, inventing labels by which to differentiate and pigeonhole various accounts. I will not rehearse all this here: Suffice it to say for present purposes that *intramural* issues have loomed large. For example, is an action good because of the consequences it brings about, the intentions that gave rise to it, or the character of the agent who performed it? Is the foundation of morality provided by the word or nature of God, human nature or evolution, the requirements of Pure Reason, or social goals? Is morality known by humans through faith, deductive argument, experience, intuition, social experiment, custom, or a fellow-feeling? And does morality require us always to do unto others as we would have them do unto us, act always so as to treat all rational beings as law-giving members of a kingdom of ends, act always so as to maximize happiness, or act at all times according to the dictates of one's station in life?

No doubt the different responses to these questions are important for many purposes but, to repeat, viewed in a larger context, these various theories are remarkably similar. All traditional moral theories are systems of order. They all are imperatives to order. They are a command—or order—for order. Let me be very precise about this: Traditional moral theories are systems of *order*, virtual recipes and handbooks for producing order from chaos, in the *three primary senses of the notion of order*:

1. They establish order in the sense of an *arrangement* or *sequence*.

2. They establish order in the sense of a *regulation* or *direction*; and,

3. They create an order in the sense of a *rank* or *class*, and differentiate a moral class from other classes outside, and foreign to, this order.

Let me very briefly explicate these three points.

1. All moral theories specify or characterize the moral life and its development. In the face of hazards, difficulties, and disarray, such a life has a certain *sequence* or *arrangement* or care[12] to its moments. It is arranged in a certain way. It is ordered, for example, so that calculations of utility or calculations of rational universality or calculations of actions that form virtuous habits or calculations of divine teachings precede and inform action. To live morally is to live in a certain way rather than others, to arrange one's actions in a particular manner or order, to order one's lifestyle, to care for oneself in a prescribed way. A moral life is the ordered expression of a moral order. A moral life is a life of arrangement.

---

12. See Michel Foucault, *The Care of the Self: The History of Sexuality*, vol. 3, trans. R. Hurley (New York: Pantheon Books, 1986 [1984]), especially pp. 37–68.

2. This lifestyle arrangement issues from a principle of action. All moral theories establish order in this second sense: They constitute a *regulation* or *direction*. They command: Act always so as to maximize happiness; act always so as to be willing that your maxim of action become a universal law; act always so as to obtain the mean (relative to your nature); always do unto others as you would have them do unto you. Moral theories, then, establish order in the sense of regulation. Moreover, they hold this regulation to be a transtemporal, universal order in the sense of a regulation that binds always, binds at all times. As Nietzsche remarked, all morality is a command, a long compulsion: "You shall obey—someone and for a long time."[13] (Here I want to note that it is interesting that traditional chronophobic moral theory assumes the identity of the agent remains unchanged over time, that the passage of time is not intrinsic irreducibly to the identity of the agent.) A moral principle of action, then, regulates. A moral principle is the ordered direction of an agent by, or in harmony with, a moral order. A moral principle is a principle of regulation.

3. Action undertaken on behalf of this principle defines a moral *rank* or *class*. All moral theories establish order in this third sense: They determine moral rank. Manufacturing dualisms, they produce and distinguish: the saved from the damned; the virtuous from the unvirtuous; the selfless from the selfish; the rational and consistent from the irrational and inconsistent; in short, the moral agents from the immoral. For virtually all moral theorists, of course, moral theory does not distinguish the happy from the unhappy. Instead, because happiness depends upon the contingencies of this world, moral theories distinguish instead those who are worthy of being happy from those who are not worthy of happiness. Moral rank is a consequence of moral lifestyle or arrangement directed by a moral regulation. Happiness may be something we cannot secure or fully regulate, but membership in the moral class that deserves happiness can be secured. Have no fear, but pick your moral system as carefully as you would pick your lawyer.

In philosophy, at least, this is how the West was won: A moral theory establishes moral order through (and as):

1. The articulation or description of a moral lifestyle or life-arrangement;

2. The proclamation of an overarching regulation or principle of action, adherence to which gives rise to this lifestyle; and,

3. An identification of the moral classes and rank that action on this principle establishes.

---

13. Friedrich Nietzsche, *Beyond Good and Evil: Prelude to a Philosophy of the Future*, trans. W. Kaufmann (New York: Vintage Books, 1966 [1886]) p. 102.

In practical terms, the purpose of moral theory is the production and guarantee of moral order—of a given moral order, a given moral arrangement and regulation and ranking.

In the face of practical uncertainties, changes, and problems (no two of which are ever just alike) and in the face of competing, mutually exclusive options for action (none of which we can foresee wholly or keep open), a moral theory is a security blanket, a happy diversion, a sort of conceptual Prozac for chronophobia. For chronophobics, moral theory functions as an anesthetic. As such, it is just what the frontier-town doctor (of philosophy) ordered: "That leg is going to have to come off, Zeke. Here—bite down on this"; "No one could have seen it was going to work out this way, Slim. Now let's get some rest before sun-up"; "Jesus, Bart, you shot Jesse! Can I buy you a drink?"

Traditional Western moral theory, however doesn't deliver the required goods—moral order that is ontologically permanent and epistemically certain. Traditional moral theories, of whatever brand or variety, all say too much, and do too little, for their own behalf. This is strikingly evident in two main ways. First, as skeptics, relativists, and nihilists have long known, no moral theory can justify itself on its own terms. No moral theory can legitimate the order it commands, although, of course, most moral theories command that their orders are legitimate. Put differently: No moral theory can provide a non-question-begging argument on its own, and for its own, behalf. Philosophers have tried to do this by appealing, for example, to God, human nature, rationality, societal welfare, evolution, nature, and language and universal speech conditions. They're still trying to do this, apparently convinced that one can no more have too many "proofs" of ethical systems than one can have "proofs" of the existence of God. However, these so-called proofs of morality are little more than the sideshow freaks and curiosities displayed in Buffalo Bill's traveling Wild West Show. Honest philosophers, philosophers who haven't been put on retainer by some high-paying moral system, realize that none of this is authentic even though it may sometimes be entertaining enough to be worth the price of admission for a short visit.[14] In formal terms, all these "proofs" require premises, and although these premises may be self-evident in a psychological sense to those who hold them, they never can be self-evident in an epistemic sense.

---

14. Adorno's insight about the culture industry applies to much of Western philosophy and its marketing campaign for moral order: Even philosophers who see through moral theory apparently feel compelled to use its products. See Max Horkheimer and Theodor W. Adorno, *Dialectic of Enlightenme.it* (New York: Continuum, 1982 [1944]). See also the discussion of this point in the context of the humanities and higher education in chapter 1.

To justify these premises requires either another proof—and here an infinite regress (with no fractal self-similarity) begins—or an appeal to the conclusion of the argument in which the premises appear—and here a vicious circularity begins.

This same failing of moral theory on its own grounds can be seen in a second way. From a practical standpoint, from the standpoint of so-called applied ethics, no moral theory can rationally compel anyone who rejects its premises. This is why, for example, moral arguments (such as those now surrounding abortion and euthanasia) generate much heat but little light. No moral theory rationally can require persons who hold other theories to convert.

Moral theory commands order: Live this way! In return for obedience to this command, it promises order: arrangement, regulation, rank. But the inability of any moral theory to justify itself leaves us with just as much disorder or chaos at the level of theory as we have at the level of life. Which moral arrangement or lifestyle should I adopt? Which moral direction and regulation should I follow? And, which moral rankings and classes really exist, which are "natural kinds?" To be forced to ask these questions is to be forced to live without a fixed or sure moral order, forced to live with time. For chronophobics, to realize honestly the disorder in our order, is to be forced to live courageously.

It is worth stressing here that none of this should give nihilists or antimoralists—whose views I call the ethics of disorder—any cause for celebration. Self-styled critics of all morality, in the end, formulate their own moral orders. They characterize and recommend a way of life, identify its guiding principle or drive, and, on this basis, determine rank (such as Nietzsche's herd and master classes or Kierkegaard's esthetic, ethical, and religious lives). Traditional wholesale criticisms and attacks on moral theory are only games of substitution, though sometimes brilliantly self-reflexive games of substitution. They merely replace one moral order by another, replace the would-be moralist with the would-be immoralist, and replace one sort of obedience with another—and for a long time. This is just another script to cast: Nietzsche as Judge Roy Bean, the hanging judge, declaring himself the law on this side of the border from now on. Turn in your guns. Don't move.

From Moral Order to Temporal Relations

Developing relativity theory in philosophy years before its development in physics, William James, in his brilliant book *A Pluralistic Universe*, asserted: "We humans are incurably rooted in the temporal point of view. The eternal's ways are utterly unlike our ways."[15] If we are going to philosophize—to think and speak and write—as irreducibly temporal creatures, we need to make a fresh start. Courage must turn us away from traditional philosophies and their intramural differences. Any such turn, however, is not a turn toward chaos or disorder. This is impossible. Still it is a turn away from the moral order of traditional moral theory—a single order, a permanent order, a sure order, and an order revealed to, discovered by, or waiting for us. It must be a turn to moral relations—plural relations, finite relations, uncertain relations, changing relations, and relations *made* by our orderings (in the sense in which making values differs from finding values).

Such a philosophy would be an irreducibly temporal philosophy, a philosophy that takes moral orders to be temporal relations, that takes moral arrangements, directions, and rankings to be temporal matters. James set forth the outlines of such a philosophy in his rich essay "The Moral Philosopher and the Moral Life." Here James set forth a radically empirical stance that rejects all subject/object and fact/value dualisms:

> How can one physical fact, considered simply as a physical fact, be "better" than another? Betterness is not a physical relation. . . . Goodness, badness, and obligation must be *realized* somewhere in order really to exist; and the first step in ethical philosophy is to see that no merely inorganic "nature of things" can realize them. Neither moral relations nor the moral law can swing *in vacuo*. Their only habitat can be a mind which feels them. . . . Moral relations now have their *status*, in that being's consciousness. So far as he feel anything to be good, he *makes* it good. It is good, for him.[16]

This radical empiricism makes possible a radically humanistic and pluralistic ethic.[17] Asking "what particular consciousness in the universe can enjoy this

---

15. William James, *A Pluralistic Universe* (Cambridge, Mass.: Harvard University Press, 1977 [1909]), p. 23. To many tradition-minded philosophers, this insistence on the temporal appears to be a denial of time's reality—that is, a denial of time's existence independent of temporal subjects. These "temporal realists," still hypnotized by subject/object and idealism/realism dualisms, are unable even to identify accurately, much less assess critically, a pragmatic pluralism. See, for example: Peter K. McInerney, *Time and Experience* (Philadelphia: Temple University Press, 1991), especially pp. 34–47 and 206–26; or M. Matsumoto, "Time: Being or Consciousness Alone?—A Realist View," *The Study of Time*, vol. 2., ed. J. T. Fraser and N. Lawrence (New York: Springer-Verlag, 1975), pp. 206–15. An awareness of the importance of pragmatism for a theory of time, and of a pragmatic theory of time for moral theory, may be found in the writings of Charles Sherover. See, for example: "Time and Ethics: How is Morality Possible?," *The Study of Time*, vol. 2, pp. 216–30; and *The Human Experience of Time: The Development of Its Philosophic Meaning* (New York: New York University Press, 1975), especially pp. 347–437.
16. William James, "The Moral Philosopher and the Moral Life," *The Will to Believe and Other Essays in Popular Philosophy, The Works of William James* (Cambridge, Mass.: Harvard University Press, 1979 [1897]) pp. 145–46.
17. The radically empiricist ethic is outlined in chapters 4, 8, and 15.

prerogative of obliging others to conform to a rule which it lays down?,"
James replied:

> Various essences of good have thus been found and proposed as bases of the
> ethical system. . . . No one of the measures that have been actually proposed
> has, however, given general satisfaction. . . . [S]o that, after all, in seeking
> for a universal principle we inevitably are carried onward to the most uni-
> versal principle—that the essence of good is simply to satisfy demand. The
> demand may be for anything under the sun. There is really no more ground
> for supposing that all our demands can be accounted for by one universal
> underlying kind of motive than there is ground for supposing that all physi-
> cal phenomena are cases of a single law. The elementary forces in ethics are
> probably as plural as those of physics are.[18]

This moral pluralism has important consequences. A moral theory that
understands moral order in terms of plural, uncertain, changing relations,
demands, and satisfactions, leads us to realize that:

1. All order, time's arrow included, is relative to, and constituted by, an
   ordering subject, and both this subject itself and the subject's universe,
   the only universe about which a subject may think or speak, are inescapably ordered and irreducibly temporal (and, so, anything but "nowless").[19]

2. No order is more complex, developed, hierarchically advanced, or better
   than another,[20] except in relation to the interests and values of some such
   subject.

3. The achievement of relative stability, the rise of entropy, or the resolution of conflict do not establish or advance or indicate a higher or more
   perfect order, but only a different order, an existentially other order
   (though perhaps, and this would be part of its difference or otherness, a
   more desired one).

The further development of each of these points requires courage. Collectively, these claims steer us away from much traditional philosophy and its
quest for certainty, its search for the immutable, and, above all, its pursuit of
moral order. Instead, they direct us toward pragmatism and its fallible inquiry

---

18. William James, "The Moral Philosopher and the Moral Life," pp. 151–52. In the context of
physics, consider also Nietzsche's remark thirteen years earlier: "It is perhaps just dawning on
five or six minds that physics, too, is only an interpretation and exegesis of the world (to suit
us, if I may say so!) and *not* a world-explanation" (*Beyond Good and Evil*, p. 21).
19. See J. T. Fraser, "Human Temporality in a Nowless Universe," *Time and Society* 1.2 (1992):
pp. 159–73.
20. Much the same point is articulated in an largely parallel manner, but from the perspective
of social science, by Barbara Adam, *Time and Social Theory* (Cambridge, U.K.: Polity Press,
1990), pp. 161–65.

and piecemeal justification through practice, its pluralistic universe, and its moral relativity.

To pursue this path is to take time seriously. This direction, I repeat, requires considerable courage. Our chronophobia will tempt us to run away like cowards. Our chronophobia will attempt to make us unbearable puritans rather than pragmatic stoics. In his novel *The Last Puritan*, Santayana wrote: "Its a wretched world, a wretched world . . . and the worst part of it is that nobody can live in it forever."[21] Santayana was right, and so chronophobia will point us toward some other world, less wretched and more bearable, filled with other times and places, filled with forever. It will turn us away from really living in this world—living not so much as a self "in" time or "in" history, but rather living as a series of events, as a constellation of temporal relations, as a history.

Chronophobia: Do you see it happening? As we begin again to think and speak, it arises again—for isn't this a new arrangement?[22] As we call for courage, it spreads again—for isn't even this call for courage now simply a new regulation? And, as we seek to overcome it, chronophobia conquers us— for isn't any diagnosis and prescription a new ranking on behalf of a new class, a new philosophy?

Waiting for recess, waiting for anything, waiting long after the death of the last puritan, long after the last puritan has asserted "that sin exists, that sin is punished, and that it is beautiful that sin should exist to be punished,"[23] Richard Brautigan, in his poem, "We stopped at perfect days," wrote:

> We stopped at perfect days
> and got out of the car.
> The wind glanced at her hair.
> It was as simple as that.
> I turned to say something—[24]

He ends with a dash, ends without speaking about the unspeakable. He ends in time—

Order: There is something orderly about a chapter that ends with a conclusion, at least with one and only one conclusion.

---

21. George Santayana, *The Last Puritan* (New York: Scribner's, 1936), p. 287. See also the discussion of Santayana in chapter 15.
22. In a book significantly shaped by pragmatism, James Gouinlock writes in defense of pluralism: "Integral to pluralism is a certain conception of virtue, and virtue is the condition of maintaining a steady and ordered life. . . . The virtues of a pluralistic point of view might not find universal endorsement, but they will provide confidence, not necessarily certainty, for their possessor." *Rediscovering the Moral Life: Philosophy and Human Practice* (Buffalo: Prometheus Books, 1993), pp. 290, 296.
23. Santayana, "The Genteel Tradition in American Philosophy," p. 194.
24. Brautigan, *Rommel Drives on Deep into Egypt*, p. 41.

10

Taking Time Seriously

Time in Theory and Time in Life

It is not uncommon for academic authors to introduce their work by saying that their readers will be presented with, for example, the first volume (complete with references to ten earlier essays) of a four-volume work now in progress. This serves at least two purposes. First, it proclaims the author's self-understanding as an active, productive researcher (Deans and personnel committees: take notice!) and a thinker with far too deep and numerous thoughts to be conveyed fully in a few pages. This is the "I'm out of time before I begin" Ploy: So many profound things for me to say, so little future time in which to say them. Second, it warns the readers to remember that any claims that might seem intellectually suspect actually are thoroughly correct and very profound—and surely would appear that way if the readers only had the time and talent to gain access to the author's work in its entirety (Insomniacs: take notice). This is the "You're out of time before I begin" Ploy: So much essential background for you to acquire, so little past time in which to have gained it.

This chapter, I hope, foregoes these too-familiar academic ploys that jointly allege a poverty of time (whether the author's future or the readers' past). Instead, I begin with a commonplace: *There is no time like the present.*

Of course, studies of time and the present—time in theory—and practices of time and the present—time in life—are very different and, frequently, quite separate. Moreover, they may be separate from one another in theory in ways that differ from their separateness in practice. Awareness of these differences often leads to general skepticism about the pragmatic value of studies of time. What practical difference do they make? In the familiar phrase of William James, what, if anything, is their "cash-value?"

Let me briefly provide a concrete illustration of this skepticism. I mentioned to my neighbor, a physician, that I was writing a chapter on time. A bit perplexed, she asked me if I usually failed to meet writing deadlines. I explained that the chapter was on the *topic* of time. At this, she became a bit more perplexed and suggested that I might as well miss my deadlines: "Studies of time can't tell you anything that will make a difference. If you don't already know about time, no essay or book is going to help. If you already do know, there is no need for another essay or book. People can write essays that are abstract or trivial, but when they finish, people will still hope and remember, prosper and suffer, change and die—already aware of time in ways no lecture or book can produce." She concluded, "And I thought you were a pragmatist!"

I have a lot of sympathy for this sort of skepticism about theory and theorists—at least in the humanities and human sciences. Still, I do not think that it is a contradiction in terms to take time pragmatically. To do so involves two tasks. First, the skeptic about the pragmatic value of the study of time does get one thing right: the temporal quality of experience is ontologically pervasive and primary; moreover, it is ineffable. (This last point has been understood much better by many artists than by most philosophers.) In this light, to take time pragmatically in theory requires the critical articulation of a genuinely temporalist theory of experience—a temporalist metaphysics of qualitative experience. Second, the skeptic about the pragmatic value of the study of time gets one thing wrong: An honest, unflinching awareness of time as a generic, pervasive trait of experience has far-reaching practical consequences for individual, community, and social action. (This point has been understood much better by many pragmatic and phenomenological philosophers than by most social scientists.) In this context, to take time pragmatically is to set forth a politics of time that outlines intelligent ends and the means for their ongoing realization in a manner consonant with the irreducible temporality of experience. In this chapter, I address briefly these two issues.

A Pragmatic Metaphysics of Life and Time

At present, there is a need not to invent from scratch but to recover and reappropriate a pragmatic theory of time. The main features of such a theory are set forth richly and suggestively in the classical American philosophical tradition—in the works of Charles Peirce, William James, Josiah Royce, George Santayana, George Herbert Mead, and, above all, John Dewey. Dewey called problems of time "the most fundamental" in philosophy, and throughout his long life addressed these problems in detail in many books and articles, including: *Experience and Nature*; *Reconstruction in Philosophy*; *The Quest for Certainty*; "Time and Individuality"; "Events and the Future"; and, "Events and Meanings."

The centerpiece of this work is Dewey's mature theory of experience, and it is this theory that contains his clearest and most comprehensive account of time. At the outset, it is crucial to understand that Dewey does not use this word "experience" in any of its traditional or ordinary senses. For Dewey, experience is not to be understood subjectively—as the inner or private states of an experiencing subject. Nor is it to be understood objectively—as the outer or external condition of an object experienced. Moreover, it is not even to be understood interactively—as a combination of subject and object that exist as such independently of their interaction with one another.

For Dewey, the subject/object dualisms so dear to the hearts of materialists and idealists, realists and antirealists, and empiricists and rationalists, are merely metaphysical fictions. Dewey replaces these metaphysics of fictional subjective and/or objective substances with an organic, holistic metaphysics of temporal activity or process. From this standpoint, the dualisms of traditional philosophies are merely distinctions made by reflection for assorted practical purposes. These dualisms may have a functional or useful status (and they may not!), but never an ontological status. If we fail to understand this, we merely make up problems. This creates a gap between, on the one hand, philosophy and the theoretical pseudo-problems of philosophers and, on the other hand, life and the real practical problems of men and women. Thus, in *Knowing and the Known* Dewey advises philosophers to stop spending their time creating dichotomies (such as subject and object, self and society, experience and nature, mind and body, and so on) and then trying to unify and bring together the divisions they have invented. This whole enterprise, Dewey warns, is artificial: "On the basis of fact, it needs to be replaced by consideration of the conditions under which they occur as distinctions, and of the special use served by these distinctions."[1]

Instead, taking his lead from Darwin, Heisenberg, Maxwell, Einstein, Peirce, and William James, Dewey views experience in a radically empirical way. This approach is oriented to the evolutionary, transient, uncertain, and open, rather than the supposedly eternal, permanent, secure, and closed. Experience is " 'double-barreled' in that it recognizes in its primary integrity no division between act and material, subject and object, but contains them both in an unanalyzed totality. 'Thing' and 'thought,' as James says in the same connection, are single-barreled; they refer to products discriminated by reflection out of primary experience."[2] For Dewey, then, experience is a process in which subject and object are temporally unified and constituted as

---

1. John Dewey, *Knowing and the Known* in *John Dewey: The Later Works, 1925–1953*, vol. 16 (Carbondale, Ill.: Southern Illinois University Press, 1989 [1949]), p. 248. For a more recent analysis of the ways in which these traditional philosophical dualisms plague social science as well as the humanities and natural sciences, see Barbara Adam, *Time and Social Theory* (Oxford: Polity Press, 1990). Although framed without explicit awareness of Dewey and pragmatism, Adam's treatment of these dualisms is remarkably Deweyan.

2. John Dewey, *Experience and Nature, John Dewey: The Later Works, 1925–1953*, vol. 1 (Carbondale, Ill.: Southern Illinois University Press, 1981 [1925]), pp. 18–19. Hereafter abbreviated "*E&N; LW* 1" in this chapter.

partial features and relations within this ongoing, unanalyzed totality. Experience is an ontologically primary temporal unity: "An organism does not live *in* an environment; it lives by means of an environment. . . . The processes of living are enacted by the environment as truly as by the organism; for they *are* an integration."[3]

Dewey constantly struggled to arrive at adequate language to express this point about experience. He thus abandoned the term "interaction" in favor of "transaction," trying to stress that the parties in a transaction are defined by their interrelation and have no independent existence. Late in his life, near ninety, he even considered abandoning the term "experience" in favor of the word "culture" to designate the "inclusive subject-matter" that modern philosophy breaks up into dualism.

Of course, this is not meant as a finished portrait of Dewey's view of experience, but I trust that it is an adequate working sketch.[4] It is meant to function as a point of entry for the development of a Deweyan, pragmatic account of time. Dewey understood metaphysics as the description of the generic and pervasive features of experience. Given Dewey's general view of experience, then, what are the generic and pervasive features of experience?

For Dewey, *experience is intrinsically and irreducibly temporal*. Equally important, *time is intrinsically and irreducibly experiential*. From the standpoint of pragmatism, to deny either of these two claims is to fail to take time seriously. That is, any notion of time as supposedly *wholly* independent of experience—whether this notion of time is intuitive, mystical, scientistic, or other—is nonsensical and literally meaningless. For all pragmatists about life and time, this means that there are no timeless realities or existents.

In the context of this pragmatic *temporal account of experience* and reciprocal *experiential account of time*, I want to develop five key points. First, *experience is intrinsically and irreducibly social*. Moreover, since time is intrinsically and irreducibly experiential, all *time is social*. Dewey thus argues that the social is *the* inclusive philosophic idea, and that there is no existence ontologically independent of the sociotemporal. There is, for example, no existence which is physical, organic, or mental and not also social as well. This is so because the physical, organic, and mental are not levels of being ontologically separate from experience, but rather features of, and within, experience distinguished for various purposes:

---

3. John Dewey, *Logic: The Theory of Inquiry*, *John Dewey: The Later Works, 1925–1953*, vol. 12 (Carbondale, Ill.: Southern Illinois University Press, 1986 [1938]), p. 32.
4. I provide fuller treatments of Dewey's view of experience in *John Dewey* (Nashville, Tenn.: Carmichael and Carmichael, 1991) and *Experience and Criticism: John Dewey's Pragmatism* (Nashville: Vanderbilt University Press, 1998).

Timeless laws, *taken by themselves*, like all universals, express dialectic intent, not any matter of fact existence. . . . They are out of time in the sense that
a particular temporal quality is irrelevant to them. If anybody feels relieved
by calling them eternal, let them be called eternal. But let not "eternal" be
then conceived as a kind of absolute perduring existence or Being. It denotes
just what it denotes: irrelevance to existence in its temporal quality. These
non-temporal, mathematical or logical qualities are capable of abstraction, and
of conversion into relations, into temporal, numerical and spatial order. As
such they are dialectical, non-existential. (*E&N*; *LW* 1:148–149)

For pragmatists, then, the universe is a sociotemporal universe through
and through, and all temporality is qualitatively sociotemporality.
Sociotemporality, that is, is not merely one among many levels of time. It is
not a container that encloses other levels of time. Experience does not cover
or surround nature; rather, it penetrates and permeates nature. For Dewey (but
not for Santayana), "experience, if scientific inquiry is justified, is no infinitesimally thin layer or foreground of nature." Instead, experience "reaches
down into nature; it has depth. It also has breadth to an indefinitely elastic
extent. It stretches. That stretch constitutes inference. . . . The very existence
of science is evidence that experience is such an occurrence that it penetrates
into nature and expands without limit through it" (*E&N*; *LW* 1:4).[5]

At this point, it is worth noting that this pragmatic emphasis on the ontological primacy of temporality as qualitatively social temporality and the accompanying rejection of ontological hierarchies seem to stand in sharp contrast to J.
T. Fraser's account of "nowless universes" and his well-known and influential
theory of time as a nested hierarchy of unresolvable, creative conflicts.[6] For
pragmatists, a "nowless universe," is either a useless ontological abstraction or a
reflective distinction (with useful, but not ontological, status) made from within
our now-filled universe. Either way, a "nowless universe" is no "universe" at all.

Dewey thus argues that the social is *the* inclusive philosophic idea, and
that there is no existence ontologically independent of the sociotemporal,[7]

---

5. See the discussion of Dewey's and Santayana's naturalisms in chapter 7.
6. J. T. Fraser, "Human Temporality in a Nowless Universe," *Time and Society,* 1.2 (1992):
159–73; "Toward an Integrated Study of Time," *The Voices of Time,* 2nd ed., ed. J. T. Fraser
(Amherst: University of Massachusetts Press, 1981), pp. xlv–xlviii; *Time: The Familiar Stranger*
(Amherst: University of Massachusetts Press, 1987), chapters 3 and 4; and "The Individual and
Society," in *The Study of Time*, vol. 3, ed. J. T. Fraser, N. Lawrence, and D. Park (New York:
Springer-Verlag, 1978), pp. 419–42. See also Adolph Grunbaum's account of becoming as mind-
dependent: "The Status of Temporal Becoming" in *The Philosophy of Time*, ed. R. Gale (London:
Macmillan, 1968), pp. 322–54.
7. John Dewey, "Meaning and Existence," *John Dewey: The Later Works, 1925–1953,* vol. 3
(Carbondale, Ill.: Southern Illinois University Press, 1984 [1928] p. 88. In the same volume, see
also "The Inclusive Philosophic Idea," pp. 41–54.

though, of course, there was in the past existence before the beginning of social life and there may be in the future existence after the end of social life.[8] Thus, when Fraser notes that our experience of time's passage "is a notion that we must bring to physical science as living beings" since "it cannot be extracted from what is known about time in the physical world,"[9] Dewey would reply that if the physical world is a world without time's passage, then it is a world without time and, thus, is an abstraction and not an existential "world" at all.

This line of thought has been voiced repeatedly by other pragmatists. Dewey's colleague, George Herbert Mead, for example, in his brilliant but neglected extended analysis of "the social nature of the present," writes that a scientific object is "an abstraction of that within experience which is subject to exact measurement."[10] In a sweeping essay that ranges from Galileo, Kant, and Rousseau to Einstein, Lorentz, and Minkowski, Mead argues that emergent social life marks not an additional level or kind of temporality but a penetration or permeation or *transformation* of temporality: That is, "we recognize that emergent life changes the character of the world just as emergent velocities change the character of masses." Life "extends its influence to the environment about it."[11]

By contrast, the abstract conception of a timeless universe eliminates human life, its influence, and, paradoxically, the phenomenon of relativity now often thought to support such an abstract conception of time: "If at this point there were no time, there could be no temporal perspectives, and, if reality could be located at such a temporal zero point, the experiences of relativity would be just what it was in an instant of no temporal spread."[12] This sort of point has been made by more recent philosophers who write in a broadly pragmatic vein. For example, in his "Introduction" to a collection of essays on postmodernism, pragmatism, and process philosophy, David Ray Griffin critically examines Fraser's hierarchical theory of time from the perspective of philosophers such as Peirce, James, and Whitehead, and asserts that we need not, and must not, speak of a "genesis" of time. Griffin argues that Fraser's view, as Fraser himself seems to Griffin in some respects to admit, is self-contradictory and commits Whitehead's "fallacy of misplaced concreteness"—misidentifying the products of thought as existents prior to

8. John Dewey, "Reality as Experience," *John Dewey: The Middle Works, 1899–1924*, vol. 3 (Carbondale, Ill.: Southern Illinois University Press, 1977 [1906]), p. 101.
9. J. T. Fraser, *Time: The Familiar Stranger*, p. 222.
10. George Herbert Mead, *The Philosophy of the Present* (LaSalle, Ill.: Open Court, 1932), p. 141.
11. Ibid., pp. 234–35.
12. George Herbert Mead, *The Philosophy of the Act* (Chicago: University of Chicago Press, 1972 [1938]), p. 236.

and independent of that thought.[13] However, as Mead concludes, the genuinely experimental scientist, apart from unwarranted philosophic bias, "is not a positivist" and has no inclination to build up a universe out of abstract scientific data: "The reference of his data is always to the solution of problems in the world that is there about him, the world that tests the validity of his hypothetical reconstructions."[14]

This need for ongoing reconstruction points to a second aspect of a pragmatic theory of time: Experience is *eventful, always changing, active, precarious, and hazardous.* Even that which is stable and fixed is merely stable relative to specifiable changes, and is not absolutely stable or permanent. As G. J. Whitrow has remarked, "The essence of time is its transitional nature, and no theory of time can be complete that does not account for the fact that everything does not happen at once."[15] Traditional philosophers (and many contemporary thinkers) often deny this in their explicit and implicit quests for certainty—their attempts through theory alone to make life, meaning, and values timeless and safe, eternally prevailing over the instability of actual life. This denial takes the form of converting precarious ideals that may be realized (if realized at all) only through temporal action and without advance guarantee into fixed actualities realized only in metaphysical theories of existence sure and fixed prior to action. In longing for a perfect or safe world, that is, philosophers have claimed ultimate reality for their values, and have turned the goals of experience into the antecedently existing causal conditions of that experience itself. Despite this, experience—the unity of experiencing subject and experienced object—is undeniably precarious, changing, unsettled. The stablest thing we can speak of is not free from the many conditions set to it by other things. It is subject to continual tests imposed upon it by surroundings which are only in part compatible and reinforcing. As Dewey says succinctly, "Every existence is an event" and objects are complexes of events: "Nothing but unfamiliarity stands in the way of thinking of both mind and matter as different characters of natural events in which matter expresses their sequential order and mind the order of meanings in their logical connections and dependencies" (*E&N; LW* 1:66).

Third, *experience is continuous.* Experience is not only eventful; it undergoes change itself. That is, experience is not simply a succession or seamless sequence of events. Rather, these events themselves have temporal connections and relations—connection directly experienced and immediately real. Experience is connected, conjoining and disjoining, resisting and yielding, modifying

---

13. David Ray Griffin, *Founders of Constructive Postmodern Philosophy* (Albany: State University of New York Press, 1993), pp. 12–14.
14. Mead, *Philosophy of the Act,* p. 62.
15. G. J. Whitrow, "Time and the Universe," in *The Voices of Time,* p. 581.

and being influenced, organized and confused, planned and surprising. Connections, changes, continuities, relations, changing-in-the-direction-of, and being-in-transition-toward are pervasive experienced features of experience. Events interact and transform one another. Each event itself not only passes, but undergoes change and altering. Whatever influences the changes of other things or features of experience is itself changed. Variation or continuous change is a feature of each event. For example, Dewey notes that an indispensable character of anything that may be termed an event is "a qualitative variation of parts with respect to the whole which requires duration to display itself." Every event is a passing into and out of other things in such a way that a later occurrence is an integral part of the character or nature of present experience—of the so-called "specious present."[16] Every present is a presence of a past no longer present and a future not yet present. This is what Charles Sherover aptly has called the "spread" of time that "takes my perspective of future and selected recall of the relevant past into constituting what I take to be the present situation."[17] Temporal continuity, like precariousness, then, is an experienced fact. It also constitutes a postulate or methodological starting point from the perspective of which experienced facts are facts. In an important sense, that is, the temporal continuity of experience cannot be denied. All efforts at denial must always link that which is being denied—continuity—with the rest of experience—with the experience of naming and understanding in the denying itself. Each denial of continuity, then, only serves to establish additional connections and continuities. Thus, any theory that sets up a breach of continuity, a complete rupture, is not so much false as nonsensical, absurd, and meaningless.[18]

Experience, however, is not merely changing and continuous. In the fourth place, *experience is historical*. Experience is not, that is, an undifferentiated flow or mere happening of events. Rather, experience itself consists of experiences, affairs with beginning and endings, initiations and consummations. Life is an affair of affairs, a "thing of histories, each with its own plot, its own inception and movement toward close, each having its own particular rhythmic movement."[19] These existential ends of experiences, of

16. John Dewey, "Events and the Future, " *John Dewey: The Later Works, 1925–1953*, vol. 2 (Carbondale, Ill.: Southern Illinois University Press, 1984 [1926]), pp. 62, 66. Charles Sherover supplies a thoroughly pragmatic account of time and continuity in his "Perspectivity and the Principle of Continuity" in *The Study of Time*, vol. 4, ed. J. T. Fraser, N. Lawrence, and D. Park (New York: Springer-Verlag, 1981), pp. 136–46.

17. Charles Sherover, "Time and Ethics: How Is Morality Possible," in *The Study of Time*, vol. 2, ed. J. T. Fraser and N. Lawrence (New York: Springer-Verlag, 1975), p. 225.

18. John Dewey, "Nature in Experience," in *John Dewey: The Later Works, 1925–1953*, vol. 14 (Carbondale, Ill.: Southern Illinois University Press, 1988 [1940]), pp. 141–54.

19. John Dewey, *Art as Experience, John Dewey: The Later Works, 1925–1953*, vol. 10 (Carbondale, Ill.: Southern Illinois University Press, 1987 [1934]), pp. 42–43.

course, are not final or moral ends *for* experience (as traditional teleological philosophies and religions hold), but only ends-in-view (and means to them) *within* experience. Nor do they amount to fate (as mechanists hold), but only orders within historical events—orders that we potentially can control so as to achieve particular ends and deepen the significance of our experience. Temporal order or succession is one such example. Importantly, this view of experience as overlapping temporal histories permits both humanists and scientists together to "apprehend causal mechanisms and temporal finalities as phases of the same natural processes, instead of as competitors where the gain of one is the loss of the other" (*E&N; LW* 1:83).

Fifth, this natural process, *experience, is qualitatively temporal.* Within and shot through each experience there is a self-sufficient, wholly immediate, individual quality that renders an experience just the experience that it is, that particular experience—that meal, that snowstorm, that philosophy lecture, and so on. To characterize experience as qualitatively temporal is to assert that experience is not merely a continuous, changing process or relational whole.[20] Instead, in every experience "there is something obdurate, self-sufficient, wholly immediate, neither a relation nor an element in a relational whole, but terminal and exclusive" (*E&N; LW* 1:74). Temporal quality, Dewey adds, "as such is final; it is at once initial and terminal; just what it is as it exists" (*E&N; LW* 1:82). This temporal qualitativeness or brute is-ness of experience has not been grasped by many traditional philosophers who have understood experience primarily or exclusively in terms of knowing and cognitive relations. In contrast to these writers, Dewey repeatedly stresses the irreducible, infinitely plural, undefinable, indescribable temporal qualities of experience from his early *Psychology*[21] to *Essays in Experimental Logic*[22] through *Experience and Nature* and later works. Thus he writes:

> Many modern thinkers, influenced by the notion that knowledge is the only mode of experience that grasps things, assuming the ubiquity of cognition, and noting that immediacy or qualitative existence has no place in authentic science, have asserted that qualities are always and only states of consciousness. It is a reasonable belief that there would be no such thing as "consciousness" if events did not have a phase of brute and unconditioned "isness," of being just what they irreducibly are. Consciousness as sensation, image

20. In the remainder of this section and the next section, I draw on my analysis of Dewey's view of quality and its place in his philosophy of experience, "Dewey's Notion of Qualitative Experience," *Transactions of the Charles S. Peirce Society* 40.1 (1979): 68–82.

21. John Dewey, *Psychology, John Dewey: The Early Works, 1882–1898*, vol. 2 (Carbondale, Ill.: Southern Illinois University Press, 1975 [1887]), especially pp. 75–136.

22. John Dewey, *Essays in Experimental Logic, John Dewey: The Middle Works, 1899–1924* (Carbondale, Ill.: Southern Illinois University Press, 1980 [1916]), especially pp. 331–35.

and emotion is thus a particular case of immediacy occurring under complicated conditions. And also without immediate qualities those relations with which science deals would have no footing in existence, would be . . . relations that do not relate. (*E&N; LW* 1:75)

It is important to understand that *all* experience is qualitatively temporal. Despite the suggestions of many commentators,[23] Dewey's position is not dualistic: Experience is not either had *or* known, primary *or* reflective. Rather, all experience, including reflectings and knowings, is temporally qualitatively had and unified; even experience which mediates—that is, *performs* the function of mediation—is itself immediate—that is, *exists* and is experienced as irreducibly temporally qualitative and brute.

This point has several crucial implications. In the first place, the qualitative aspect of experience is not an object of knowledge. It is not *known* but *had*. It is the brute "is-ness" of experience, the defining mark of a given transaction, and the basis for pointing to a given experience as the unique experience that it is—*that* meal, *that* storm, *that* long chapter. This temporal quality, Dewey stresses, is neither emotional nor intellectual—because these terms name distinctions made by reflection on experience. Indeed, much to the dismay of traditional philosophers who conflate knowledge about life with life itself, Dewey says that this qualitative dimension of experience cannot be known or communicated since the objects of knowledge are mediate rather than immediate; they concern the relations among experiences and not the immediate quality of experience. If existence in its immediacy could speak, Dewey says, "it would proclaim 'I may have relatives but I am not related' " (*E&N; LW* 1:75). Of course, we both can, and do, know that experience is qualitative—know that we directly experience temporal quality—but we must not confuse our knowledge about this characteristic of experience with the characteristic itself. Thus Dewey writes that although in reflection and discourse we must distinguish and emphasize various features or properties of an experience, "yet the experience was not a sum of these different characters; they were lost in it as distinctive traits."[24] The temporal qualitativeness of experience may *become* the subject of reflection—of an-

---

23. See, for example, the following. G. Watts Cunningham, "The New Logic and the Old," *Journal of Philosophy* 36.21 (1939): 565ff.; W. Thomas, "Dewey's Doctrine of the Situation," *Journal of Philosophy*, 50.22 (1953): 581ff.; A. Visalberghi, "Remarks on Dewey's Conception of Ends and Means," *Journal of Philosophy*, 50.24 (1953): 759ff.; D. J. O'Conner, "Indeterminate Situation and Problem in Dewey's Logical Theory," *Journal of Philosophy* 50.24 (1953): 753ff.; P. Welsh, "Some Metaphysical Assumptions in Dewey's Philosophy," *Journal of Philosophy* 51.25 (1954): 861ff.; D. Piatt, "Immediate Experience," *Journal of Philosophy* 25.18 (1928): 477ff.; A. O. Lovejoy, "Time, Meaning, and Transcendence," *Journal of Philosophy* 19.19 (1922): 505ff.; D. Drake, "Dr. Dewey's Duality and Dualism," *Journal of Philosophy* 14.24 (1917): 660ff.
24. Dewey, *Art as Experience*, p. 44.

other experience with its own immediate temporal quality—but that quality itself is *not* known. To know anything, we must go beyond what is immediately present by transforming, mediating, and relating it to other things. The frightening situation known is not the frightening situation immediately and qualitatively encountered. A particular experience as it occurs simply is; that particular experience, as it is connected by later reflection to things beyond itself, becomes a sign and refers.

In the second place, the temporally qualitative character of experience is not something subjective, for experience is not something subjective. Neither is it objective. Temporal quality is neither *in*, nor *of*, just the organism or just the environment. Rather temporal qualities belong as much to the thing experienced as to the experiencing subject. They belong to the entire, unified situation or transaction that is the unity of organism and environment. To ask, then, whether qualities are mental or physical, subjective or objective, is to misunderstand the nature of the experience which is qualitative. Again, we must be careful not to mistake the results of our inquiry for existents independent of, and antecedent to, this inquiry. In this context, in *Experience and Nature* Dewey explains:

> The qualities were never "in" the organism; they always were qualities of interactions in which both extraorganic things and organisms partake. When named they enable identification and discrimination of things to take place as means in a further course of inclusive interaction. Hence they are as much qualities of the things engaged as of the organism. For purposes of control they may be referred specifically to either the thing or to the organisms or to a specified structure of the organism. (*E&N*; *LW* 1:198–99)

He stresses this same point in his *Logic*:

> The pervasively qualitative is not only that which binds all constituents into a whole but it is also unique; it constitutes in each situation an *individual* situation, indivisible and unduplicable. Distinctions and relations are instituted *within* a situation. . . . The universe of experience surrounds and regulates the universe of discourse but never appears as such within the latter.[25]

In the third place, then, temporal qualities are experienced. As such, they are not only sensory qualities (qualities that are typically classified according to the organ of apprehension), but pervasive, directly-had tertiary qualities (qualities concerning pleasure and pain). Dewey stresses that experience really is indeterminate, settled, distressing, cheerful, dull, exciting, foreign, or familiar. Temporal qualities of pleasure and pain pervade experience:

---

25. Dewey, *Logic: The Theory of Inquiry*, p. 74.

"Empirically, things are poignant, tragic, beautiful, barren, harsh, consoling, splendid, fearful; are such immediately in their own right and behalf" (*E&N*; *LW* 1:82). The termination of an experience marks the termination of its temporal quality, and in this sense different temporal qualities "obstruct" one another in their immediacy, inclusiveness, and unity. If we designate this unified temporal quality in psychological terms, Dewey writes, we say that it is felt. However, so designated, this feeling is not subjective: "Anything that can be called feeling is objectively defined by reference to immediate quality: anything that is a feeling, whether of red or of a noble character, or of King Lear, is some immediate quality when that is present as experience."[26] This quality defines the *meaning* of a feeling, and the feeling, in turn, names a particular *relation* of quality. Thus, for example, a situation may be constituted by a pervading temporally qualitative anger. However, in this case, the experience is angry; the situation itself is angry. Anger is not an experience-independent object of awareness for a subject, and this anger is not ontologically separate from such a situation. Of course, as Dewey points out, in *another* situation, anger may appear as a separate, detached, distinct term, identified by reflection as a feeling or emotion:

> But we now have shifted the universe of discourse, and the validity of the terms of the latter depends upon the existence of the direct quality of the whole in a former one. That is, in saying that something was *felt* not thought of, we are analyzing in a new situation, having its own immediate quality, the subject-matter of a prior situation; we are making anger an object of analytic examination, not being angry.[27]

In the fourth place, finally, Dewey thus distinguishes carefully temporal quality from temporal order, and rightly holds temporal quality to be ontologically more fundamental—an immediate, ineffable feature of all experience. Temporal order, on the other hand, is not immediate. It is the result of reflection, a matter of science, a consequence of inquiry into the conditions upon which occurrence of particular temporal qualities depend. But temporal order does not explain, or explain away, temporal quality. The temporal quality and presentness of experience cannot be reduced to temporal order. This qualitative character of experience, as all neighborhood skeptics know whether or not they've ever studied pragmatism or any other philosophy, cannot be

---

26. John Dewey, "Peirce's Theory of Quality," *John Dewey: The Later Works, 1925–1953*, vol. 11 (Carbondale, Ill.: Southern Illinois University Press, 1987 [1935]), p. 94.
27. John Dewey, "Qualitative Thought," *John Dewey: The Later Works, 1925–1953*, vol. 5 (Carbondale, Ill.: Southern Illinois University Press, 1984 [1930]), p. 248.

captured fully in later reflection on experience (no matter how "phenomeno-logical" the reflection):

> Immediacy of existence is ineffable. But there is nothing mystical about such ineffability; it expresses the fact that of direct existence it is futile to say anything to one's self and impossible to say anything to another. Dis-course can but intimate connections which if followed out may lead one to *have* an existence. Things in their immediacy are unknown and unknowable, not because they are remote or behind some impenetrable veil of sensation of ideas, but because knowledge has no concern with them. For knowledge is a memorandum of conditions of their appearance, concerned, that is, with sequences, coexistences, relations. Immediate things may be *pointed* to by words, but not described or defined. (*E&N*; *LW* 1:74–75)

Thus, as this outline of an experiential view of time and a temporal view of experience indicates, in practice as in pragmatic theory, there really is no time like the present. As Dewey notes in "Time and Individuality," an essay originally presented as part of a public lecture series on "Time and Its Mys-teries," this is "genuine time."[28]

Brute Misunderstandings

The novelty and scope of Dewey's view of experience as temporally qualitative have led many commentators to misunderstand it. More specifi-cally, many commentators have claimed that there is a fundamental unintel-ligibility, ambiguity, and inconsistency in Dewey's position. Careful analysis of the misunderstandings contained in these claims may help to illuminate further Dewey's actual position.

In an influential essay, Richard J. Bernstein, for example, writes that there is a shift in Dewey's discussion of quality—a shift from a "phenomeno-logical" level to a "metaphysical" level. This shift, Bernstein thinks, is ille-gitimate and unfounded. He writes that there seems "to be little relation between the type of quality which is characteristic of experiential transactions and the type of quality which is claimed to be a characteristic of other natural existence."[29] When Dewey discusses experiential transactions—the "phenom-enological" level—Bernstein believes that he emphasizes that qualities are

---

28. John Dewey, "Time and Individuality," *John Dewey: The Later Works, 1925–1953*, vol. 14 (Carbondale, Ill.: Southern Illinois University Press, 1988 [1940]), pp. 98–114.
29 Richard J. Bernstein, "John Dewey's Metaphysics of Experience," *Journal of Philosophy*, 58.1 (1961): 7.

active, capable of mediation and transformation, and able to become enriched and funded with meaning. However, when Dewey discusses natural existence—the "metaphysical" level—Bernstein claims that he characterizes qualities as brute, unconditioned, and unmediated. He concludes:

> The nature of quality, then, appears to be radically different in these two contexts. The distinguishing feature of experienced quality is that it can be mediated and funded. But when Dewey switches to discuss quality as an intrinsic possession of existences which do not necessarily enter into experiential transactions, he insists that qualities are unconditioned, they are precisely what is unmediated.[30]

Bernstein may be correct in claiming that this view is an "unholy alliance" of idealist and realist doctrines or strains. However, he surely is incorrect in attributing this view to Dewey. In the first place, it is worth noting that there is no inconsistency in the first part of the position sketched by Bernstein. This position holds simply that there is something that "*can be* transformed and mediated, enriched and funded with meaning," *and* that there *is* also something that is brute, unmediated, and not in the process of being transformed or funded. The first "something" certainly may *be* the second something, because there is nothing inconsistent about something being capable of being—that is, becoming—mediated, transformed, related, and funded at a given future.[31] Indeed, this unity in continuity is the very nature of actual experience.

Bernstein, then, is mistaken in believing this first part of the position to be internally inconsistent. It is not. Moreover, he is further mistaken in believing that the second part of the position he discusses is Dewey's view. Surely it is not. Bernstein mistakenly believes that it is Dewey's view because he does not recognize the *radical* nature of Dewey's *activity* metaphysics: Things *are* what they are experienced to be, and this experience is transactive, including and intrinsically uniting both organism and environment. Dewey neither believes in nor discusses the qualitative character of existences that supposedly do not enter into experience-transactions. Given his radically empirical view of experience, there is no such qualitative character and there

---

30. Ibid., p. 13.
31. In addition, of course, a thing may *be* immediate at a given *present* and *have been* mediated and funded during a given *past*. This is suggested in a different context, in terms of a "process of qualification" by Victor Kestenbaum, *The Phenomenological Sense of John Dewey: Habit and Meaning* (Atlantic Highlands, N.J.: Humanities Press, 1977), and in terms of the "precognitive and necessary conditions for the cognitive" by Rodman Webb, *The Presence of the Past: John Dewey and Alfred Schutz on the Genesis and Organization of Experience* (Gainesville, Fla.: University Presses of Florida, 1976).

are no such existences. All quality is experienced quality, and so to claim that natural existences have immediate quality and "is-ness" is to claim that they are features of *an* experience, a situation. Quasimodo *is*, for example, frightening to the children; this actual, immediate quality pervades the experience.[32] "Something" supposedly wholly independent of experience, of involvement and interaction with experiencing organisms, is *not anything,* qualitative or otherwise—at least according to Dewey.

In "Dewey's Struggle with the Ineffable," Roland Garrett makes a related criticism. Garrett suggests that there are four parallel ambiguities in Dewey's theory of quality, ambiguities that reflect an underlying problem. The four "surface" ambiguities or contradictions are the following: quality, in Dewey's theory according to Garrett, is: (1) both outside and within the causal order; (2) both relationless and a member of a relational whole; (3) both unique and recurring; and, (4) both unknowable and an object of knowledge and communication. It is odd that Garrett takes these to be inconsistencies, since *he* offers an appropriate explanation for these so-called inconsistencies. This explanation distinguishes quality as it occurs and just is what it is from quality as it is referred beyond itself and becomes a sign of something else. Given this distinction, Garrett realizes, Dewey's views are not inconsistent:

> The quality proper is immediate, unrelated, and unknowable, but in connection with certain extraneous factors it is treated as if it has relations and is intelligible. This distinction sheds light on other commitments which Dewey makes, such as his notion that qualities possess "structure" not in their immediacy but in their "external" connections with organism and environment and his claim that the subject-matter of science includes the "occurrence" of qualities . . . but not their intrinsic nature.[33]

So, in subsequent inquiry or intellectual consideration, reference is made not to the quality itself, but to relations that substitute for and represent it. Thus Garrett writes that "overt inconsistency would be avoided by attributing one of the two competing groups of traits to qualities as such and the other to the epistemic replacements of qualities,"[34]—which, I wish to stress, are not qualities at all.

---

32. See Gail Kennedy, "Comments on Professor Bernstein's Paper," *Journal of Philosophy* 58.1 (1961): 15.ff. Note that in this example, Quasimodo *is* frightening and, moreover, *would be* frightening. Thus Dewey writes in "Peirce's Theory of Quality" that "When such quality is reflected upon in relation to existence, it is seen to be a potentiality and to be general" (p. 90).
33. Roland Garrett, "Dewey's Struggle with the Ineffable," *Transactions of the Charles S. Peirce Society* 9.2 (1973): 105.
34. Ibid., p. 106.

What then is the difficulty with Dewey's theory? The underlying, "monumental flaw," according to Garrett, is the introduction into metaphysics—the description of the pervasive features of existence—of entities that are unique, unrelated, unknowable, and outside causal sequences. Garrett simply wonders how Dewey can talk about any such entities at all. Here, however, Garrett wholly misses Dewey's point. We can talk *about* quality as long as we do not identify the *existent quality* with the *subject of our discourse* itself, the immediate activity with the sign-value of that occurrence. Reflection about an experience is not that experience; and experience as reflected about is not that experience as had.

Dewey recognizes and fully accepts this: discourse can only intimate connections that, if followed out, may lead one to *have* an experience. Examples are important, then, in pointing to this feature of experience, in *enabling* one to *have* this experience. They need to be drawn from a wide range of experience:

> A painting is said to have a quality, or a particular painting to have a Titian or Rembrandt quality. The word thus used most certainly does not refer to any particular line, color, or part of the painting. It is something that affects and modifies all the constituents of the picture and all of their relations.[35]

> We follow with apparently complete understanding a tale in which a certain quality or character is ascribed to a certain man. But something said causes us to interject, "Oh, you are speaking of Thomas Jones, I supposed you meant John Jones." Every detail related, every distinction set forth remains just what it was before. Yet the significance, the color and weight, of every detail is altered. For the quality that runs through them all, that gives meaning to each and binds them together, is transformed.[36]

It is important to stress that a quality "runs through" and "binds" the features of a situation. The quality is active and regulative—that is, intrinsically inclusive of its future transformation or negation. So, the pervasive quality of indeterminateness—a situation's being perplexed, unsettled—is one of the *conditions* of inquiry, as well as its *controlling* or directing feature. It is the pervasive presence which unifies and guides the various proposals, experiments, the complications and failures, and the resolution which transforms that quality itself into one of order and determinateness. Similarly, in artistic creation, the pervasive quality of a given creative process or activity guides the transformation (in, and through, a medium of that experience) into something final, settled, and complete. Dewey writes that "the underlying

---

35. Dewey, *Logic: The Theory of Inquiry*, p. 75.
36. Dewey, "Qualitative Thought," p. 245.

quality that defines the work, that circumscribes it externally and integrates it internally controls the thinking of the artist; his logic is the logic of what I have called qualitative thinking."[37]

Dewey's account of temporal quality, then is neither confused nor unintelligible. It is, rather, an important part of a comprehensive and sensitive description of experience as temporally qualitative and time as irreducibly experiential. When rightly understood, it is also a starting point for creating social experience of positive moral, aesthetic, and religious quality.

A Pragmatic Politics of Time

So what? Does any of this matter? What are the practical bearings of a pragmatic account of time?

I want to consider two sorts of practical consequences of a temporal account of experience and an experiential account of time. These consequences concern (1) individuality and (2) community (and their interrelationship in, and through, action).

First, to take time pragmatically is to grasp the intrinsically and irreducibly temporal character of individuality. As Dewey writes: "The unescapable conclusion is that . . . human individuality can be understood only in terms of time as fundamental reality."[38] Any adequate account of individuality must be historicist. As Charles Sherover puts it, because individuality reflects the particular cultural conditions that fostered it, it is historical and thus irreducibly temporal: "As social beings, any individual thinking thus necessarily incorporates particularized time predicates, as particular differentiating descriptions of the historically developed social milieu out of which whatever individuality we each manifest has arisen."[39] This means that individuality is precarious and never static or secure. Individuality is fragile and delicate. When fortunate conditions and appropriate actions support its emergence and operation, individuality arises as an achievement—and not as something "ready-made," given, provided once and for all at birth, secured by mere physical separation and difference from all others.

---

37. Ibid., p. 251. Inquiry and artistic creation are similar in that both are characterized by a controlling pervasive temporal quality. The controlling, however, has different purposes—explanation vs. expression—and different natures—the sign of the quality vs. the quality itself.
38. Dewey, "Time and Individuality," p. 107. See also the discussion of human finitude and death in chapter 15.
39. Charles Sherover, "*Res Cogitans*: The Time of Mind" in *Time and Mind: Interdisciplinary Issues, The Study of Time*, vol. 6, ed. J. T. Fraser (Madison, Conn.: International Universities Press, 1989), p. 284. Dewey, unlike Sherover, differentiates between the self and the individual as a self who achieves individuality.

Like most political philosophers and theorists, we often take individuality for granted and fail to see that not only do human beings "go out of existence,"[40] but that while they exist they can and in fact often do fail to be genuine individuals. This is not because individuals somehow at times fail to *be* themselves, as though individuality were a matter of permanently embodying an original personal essence. Instead, it is because individuals often fail to *become* themselves, because individuality is a matter of continuity and the ongoing development and realization of possibilities and capacities that are not self-identical or unchanging over time.[41]

The identity of the individual, long sought after by philosophers in theory, exists in life only in time. Put this way, it should be clear that an individual does not *have* a history; rather, an individual *is* a history. As Dewey points out, time does not merely surround an individual externally:

> The human individual is himself a history, a career, and for this reason his biography can be related only as a temporal event. That which comes later explains the earlier quite as truly as the earlier explains the later. . . . Temporal seriality is the very essence, then, of the human individual.[42]

The continuing development of an individual's possibilities and capacities, then, can take place only if there exist in time the social conditions necessary to support this development.

When this development is thought to be the natural unfolding of some innate, natural end that controls development toward it, then the sociopolitical agenda is largely defined and constituted by a negative task. This task is that of removing restrictions on, and getting out of the way of, the individual. It is the task of making sure that society, and especially big government, does not impede the natural development of the individual.

This once liberal (but now reactionary) position rightly prizes the individual, but lacks historical and temporal sense. As a result, this view fails to identify the necessary conditions of the individual's development. When it is recognized that the capacities and potentials of individuals are themselves intrinsically temporal matters, then a different, less traditional, and more radical political agenda arises. This agenda is more positive than negative in character; it is not a matter of simply getting out of the way of the individual's supposedly natural development or teleology, but of creating and re-creating the conditions needed for the development and realization of individual po-

---

40. See J. T. Fraser, "The Study of Time, " in *The Voices of Time*, p. 589.
41. See the discussion of organism, self, and individuality in chapter 12.
42. Dewey, "Time and Individuality," p. 102.

tentials. Moreover, this agenda is more fully social than merely political in scope; it is not simply a matter of sustaining a democratic form of politics or government, but of fostering a thoroughly democratic way of community or social life. Dewey correctly draws "the only reasonable conclusion":

> "[P]otentialities are not fixed and intrinsic, but are a matter of an indefinite range of interactions in which an individual may engage. . . . There are at a given time unactualized potentialities in an individual because and in so far as there are in existence other things with which it has not as yet interacted.[43]

These "other things" are the social environment of every individual, and this social environment (for better or worse) is the indispensable condition of the formation and realization of the individual. The pragmatic point, then, is not simply that the individual inhabits a social environment (and is related to that environment as a part to a whole). Rather, the point is that the individual, internally and intrinsically, is social (such that individual and environment mutually constitute each other).

This means that individuality, understood temporally, requires freedom—where freedom is understood not simply as the absence of restriction but as the presence of those resources necessary for the temporal development of the self.[44] It also means that individuality requires intelligence in the direction of this freedom—where intelligence is understood as the temporal (and thus fallible) application of methods of critical, experimental inquiry to human life. But above all, it means that individuality requires social arrangements such that the intelligent free action of one person contributes to the development of the individuality of others. This is the requirement of community. In short, a pragmatic theory of time makes possible a temporal account of individuality that in turn requires a social theory committed to the free and intelligent development of genuine communities.

This pragmatic social theory that defines individuality in terms of community stands in a reciprocal relation to a pragmatic theory of time that defines temporality as sociotemporality. That is, a pragmatic social theory and a pragmatic theory of time mutually imply one another. From the standpoint of this social theory, then, and against all reductionist, abstractionist, and dualistic views of time, it is clear that *all* temporality is sociotemporality, qualitative differences among experiences notwithstanding. Put more simply, to the extent that human societies fail to be genuine communities, human

---

43. Ibid., p. 109.
44. See the discussion of the economic prerequisites of individuality and community in chapter 14.

beings fail to be genuine individuals. The realization in life of individuality and the realization of community are one. On this issue, as well as others, the differences between pragmatists (such as Dewey) and some of the influential twentieth-century existential phenomenologists (such as Martin Heidegger) could not be greater or more obvious. Heidegger fails to grasp this intrinsic connection between individuality and community, and so identifies authentic individuality with the very social conditions that Dewey thinks constitute the loss of individuality and the absence of a democratic way of life. As Hubert Dreyfus has aptly put it, individuality emerges for Heidegger only when one member of society "experiences an anxiety attack."[45]

By contrast, this notion of community lies at the heart of the pragmatic link between individuality and democracy—wherein democracy is understood primarily and most fully as a way of life rather than only a form of government. As Dewey argued, democratic government is only a part of a democratic way of life.[46] It is a means for realizing democratic ends in individual lives and social relationships. And while it is the best and most effective means yet devised to achieve these ends, still it is only a means. Thus, Dewey warned that we must not treat temporal means—that is, institutions and practices of democratic government such as majority rule, broad suffrage, and periodic elections—as ends, final or complete in themselves. These practices, the political dimension of democracy, are "external and very largely mechanical symbols and expressions of a fully democratic way of life."[47]

Because democratic structures and institutions of government have a value that is temporal rather than eternal, they must be dynamic rather than static if they are to continue to nurture a democratic way of life under changing conditions and through changing times. This means that democracy itself must be understood temporally: It is not something fixed, "a kind of lump sum that we could live off and upon," something finished and final that simply can be "handed on from one person or generation to another," or something so natural that it simply forever maintains itself once established.[48]

---

45. Hubert Dreyfus, "Human Temporality," in *The Study of Time*, vol. 2, p. 158.
46. I draw here on my "Democracy as a Way of Life," *Philosophy and the Reconstruction of Culture: Pragmatic Essays After Dewey,* ed. John J. Stuhr (Albany: State University of New York Press, 1993), pp. 37–58.
47. John Dewey, "Democracy and Educational Administration," *John Dewey: The Later Works, 1925–1953*, vol. 11 (Carbondale, Ill.: Southern Illinois University Press, 1987 [1937]), p. 218. See also John Dewey, "Democracy and Education in the World of Today," *John Dewey: The Later Works, 1925–1953,* vol. 13 (Carbondale, Ill.: Southern Illinois University Press, 1988 [1938]).
48. Dewey, "Democracy and Education in the World of Today," pp. 298–99; John Dewey, "The Democratic Faith and Education," *John Dewey: The Later Works, 1925–1953,* vol. 15 (Carbondale, Ill.: Southern Illinois University Press, 1989 [1944]), p. 259.

Accordingly, we can't afford passively to idolize practice and institutions that proved instrumental in the past. We constantly must appraise and be ready to revise them with respect to their present and projected future contributions to a democratic way of life.

The basis of this democratic way of life is the conviction that no person or group of persons is sufficiently wise and good to govern others without their consent, "without some expression on their own part of their own needs, their own desires and their own conception of how social affairs should go on and social problems should be handled."[49] This conviction, in turn, requires both equality (such that social decisions are cooperative expressions) and opportunity (such that all people have both a right and a duty to participate in this decision-making process). This means that all persons involved in, and affected by, social practices should participate in their formation and direction. Dewey viewed this as the generic meaning of democracy and termed it the "key-note of democracy as a way of life . . . necessary from the standpoint of both the general social welfare and the full development of human beings as individuals."[50] As Dewey said succinctly and compellingly:

> From the standpoint of the individual, it [the idea of democracy] consists in having a responsible share according to capacity in forming and directing the activities of the groups to which one belongs and in participating according to need in the values which the groups sustain. From the standpoint of the groups, it demands a liberation of the potentialities of members of a group in harmony with the interests and goods which are common. . . . Regarded as an idea, democracy is not an alternative to other principles of associated life. It is the idea of community life itself. . . . Wherever there is conjoint activity whose consequences are appreciated as good by all singular persons who take part in it, and where the realization of the good is such as to effect an energetic desire and effort to sustain it in being just because it is a good shared by all, there is in so far a community. The clear consciousness of a communal life, in all its implications, constitutes the idea of democracy.[51]

Both this idea of democracy as temporal community and the consequences of attempting to implement this idea are revolutionary and radical: "*The fundamental principle of democracy is that the ends of freedom and*

---

49. Dewey, "Democracy and Education in the World of Today," p. 295.
50. Dewey, "Democracy and Educational Administration," pp. 217–18.
51. John Dewey, *The Public and Its Problems, John Dewey: The Later Works, 1925–1953*, vol. 2 (Carbondale, Ill.: Southern Illinois University Press, 1984 [1927]), pp. 327–28.

individuality for all can be attained only by means that accord with those ends."[52] Thus, to the extent to which a given person does not participate consistently and fully in the consideration, formation, and implementation of social values, decisions, and policies, democracy as an individual's self-determining and self-realizing way of life simply does not exist—in actual life. And, to the extent that given social practices, groups, and institutions do not foster shared interests, harmonious differences, and individual growth, democracy as a free community's way of life does not really exist—again, in life.

Just as an experiential account of time and a temporal account of experience—a pragmatic metaphysics—leads directly to an understanding of individuality and community as irreducibly temporal—a pragmatic social theory—so too this pragmatic social theory leads directly to a commitment to social action. To take time seriously—in life and not just in theory—is to be committed to social action that strives to secure the changing conditions necessary for the realization of genuine individuality and community.

This social *action*, in turn, requires or presupposes a democratic *faith*. It requires that we make democracy as a way of life an *ideal*. Now, to say that a democratic way of life is an ideal is not to say that it is something unreal. As real ideals, individuality and community would be deep commitments, grasped by our imagination, that unify our lives, make meaningful our efforts, and direct our actions. As ideals, they are generated through imagination, but are not "made out of imaginary stuff." Instead, anything but "unreal" or "imaginary," ideals are "made out of the hard stuff of the world of physical and social experience—the material and energies and capacities that are the conditions for its existence."[53]

To describe individuality and community as ideals, however, is not so much to state a present fact as it is to recommend a future course of action—

---

52. John Dewey, "Democracy is Radical," *John Dewey: The Later Works, 1925–1953*, vol. 11 (Carbondale, Ill.: Southern Illinois University Press, 1987 [1937]), pp. 298–99. It is this radical insistence on understanding democracy in terms of temporal, *participatory community* that separates Dewey's social philosophy from more conservative, "republican" political theories (usually grounded not in pragmatic accounts of experience but in idealist and phenomenological accounts of the subject). Charles Sherover's excellent work articulates this "republican" position, rejected (rightly, I think) by Dewey. See *Time, Freedom, and the Common Good: An Essay in Public Philosophy* (Albany: State University of New York Press, 1989) and "The Process of Polity" in *The Study of Time*, vol. 7, ed. J. T. Fraser (Madison, Conn.: International Universities, 1993), pp. 243–61. See also the discussion of this point in the context of pragmatism's meliorism and will to intimacy in chapter 5.

53. John Dewey, *A Common Faith, John Dewey: The Later Works, 1925–1953*, vol. 9 (Carbondale, Ill.: Southern Illinois University Press, 1986 [1934]), pp. 33–34; John Dewey, "Democracy and America," *John Dewey: The Later Works, 1925–1953*, vol. 13 (Carbondale, Ill.: Southern Illinois University Press, 1988 [1939]), p. 174.

an admittedly radical course of action. To quietly favor, idly wish and hope for, or routinely assent to such a democratic course of action, however, is not thereby to make it an ideal. Today, we still must make individuality and community real ideals. We have not done so yet. Thus, idealizing individuality and community is the first step in the task of realizing individuality and community. When, and if, our idealizing imagination does seize upon individuality and community, personal life may begin to express this ideal in action. In Dewey's terms, individuality, freedom, intelligence, communication, cooperation, and community may become loyalties or values-in-action, instead of mere values-in-name only.[54] As ideals, individuality and community require this committed expression and action from each of us.

It is neither possible nor desirable to detail in advance or in the abstract just what form this action should take in the future. As Ralph Waldo Emerson noted, each age must write its own books; as Dewey echoed this sentiment, each age knows its own ills. Still, it is possible to indicate the general outline and spirit of this action and, at the same time, to indicate briefly the special social value at this time of a pragmatic politics of time.

First, pragmatism constitutes a middle path between, and an alternative to, both the pervasive pessimism and the rampant self-righteous optimism of our day. In the face of complex, interdependent, and massive contemporary social problems—injustice, poverty, disease, violence, conflict, destruction, and death—many people readily feel overwhelmed and powerless. Our sense of impotence makes for pessimism—things are bad and they will continue to be bad because we can't do anything about them. This, in turn, often leads to: self-confirming apathy—since we can't do anything about it, why bother; self-defeating withdrawal from the community—the best we can do is look out for ourselves and keep the barbarians at the gate; and, self-destructive nihilism—it doesn't matter what we do, nothing is better than anything else, at least we won't be fooled again. By contrast, many other people embrace absolutism in their response to these same large social problems. They are convinced that they have the Truth, that they have seen Reality, that their cause is Just, that God has chosen them. Supremely confident, they are optimists, convinced that time is on their side. Pragmatism provides a political alternative to both pessimism and optimism.

The alternative is pluralistic meliorism. Meliorism is the spirit of the politics of time: it rejects the belief that things will be bad (pessimism) and the belief that things will be good (optimism). Instead, it asserts that how ever

---

54. I take this pragmatic point about individuality and ethics to parallel Nathaniel Lawrence's remark about time and metaphysics: "Time is as time does." "My Time is Your Time," *The Study of Time*, vol. 4, p. 11.

bad or good things now may be, intelligent action may make them better. As a political theory, pragmatism offers no guarantees about the future. It provides only the demand to act in the present—on behalf of the future and in light of the past. The need for this intelligent social inquiry and action has never been greater.

Second, pragmatism also constitutes a middle path between, and an alternative to, short-term thinking and the view from eternity. For many people and groups today, the only way of thinking is short-term thinking. Unfortunately, in most cases, short-term thinking is not effective thinking at all. We seem to have concluded that we can avoid unwanted consequences simply by refusing to think about them. Unfortunately, this is not so—as an examination of our "policies" on the environment, education, the economy, families, health, and foreign affairs makes clear. In order not to be short term leaders, our thinkers typically must think in the short term. We want to know what they have done for us today. We demand instant communication, power, and gratification. We spend next week's paycheck this week, buy and bury disposable diapers, record the ways in which we amuse ourselves with disposable cameras, and enter and exit as we see fit today from disposable relationships.

It is impossible to overestimate the extent to which pragmatism, just as it provides a middle path between political pessimism and optimism, also provides a way around both the short-term thinking that cripples our ability to plan for our future, and the thinking from eternity that justifies looking past current suffering and injustice to a supposedly real and supposedly better afterlife. By contrast, pragmatism provides a genuinely temporal political stance—a politics in the service of fragile communities of memory and fleeting communities of hope.[55] Whether or not President Clinton is correct in saying that all (and not just some) Americans live in an "Age of Possibility" (as he claimed in his 1996 State of the Union Address) remains to be seen. There can be no question, however, that pragmatism is a philosophy of possibility— a philosophy of hope and intimacy, and a stimulus to action on behalf of those possibilities.

Of course, this philosophy, as pragmatists stress and skeptical neighbors feel—cannot be justified by anything written in any book. Its justification, if any at all, is a function of the results of the actions it may call forth. Today, this philosophy remains largely untested. *But today, like any other day, there is no time like the present.*[56]

---

55. See the discussion of identity, difference, and community in chapter 13.

56. An earlier version of portions of this chapter appeared in "Pragmatism, Life, and the Politics of Time," *Dimensions of Time and Life: The Study of Time VIII*, ed. J. T. Fraser and M. P. Soulsby (Madison, Conn.: International Universities Press, 1996), pp. 267–83. These revised passages appear here with the kind permission of the editors and the publisher.

III

Community

11

Theory, Practice, and Community in Peirce's Normative Science

> I should be the very first to insist that logic can never be learned from logic-books or logic lectures.

> —Charles Sanders Peirce

According to Charles Sanders Peirce, it is "the primary rule of the ethics of rhetoric that every prose composition should begin by informing the reader what its aim is, with sufficient precision to enable him [or her] to decide whether to read it or not" (*N* 2.277).[1] So, at the outset, I should make clear that my aim in this chapter is not simply to praise Peirce, to restate or summarize his philosophy, or to confirm readers' "preconceived opinions" and estimates of that philosophy (*CP* 1.2). Instead, I seek to identify, critically assess, and develop some of the practical implications of Peirce's account of normative science. More specifically, after briefly noting several crucial (though questionable) presuppositions about theory and practice that underlie Peirce's analysis of logic, ethics, and aesthetics, I will focus on consequences for individual and social action of Peirce's view that the ideal of conduct involves "rendering the world more reasonable" (*CP* 1.615).

Writers owe their readers not simply a clear statement of their intentions but also, Peirce claimed, an account of how their opinions were formed. In place of an autobiography (that might cure many cases of insomnia), let me

---

1. References to the writings of Peirce are included in the body of this chapter, and follow standard citation and abbreviation practices. References to *The Collected Papers of Charles Sanders Peirce*, ed. Charles Hartshorne, Paul Weiss, and Arthur Burks, 8 vols. (Cambridge, Mass.: Harvard University Press, 1931, 1933, 1934–35, and 1958) are abbreviated *CP*, followed by the volume and paragraph numbers. For example, *CP* 7.69 refers to volume 7, paragraph 69 of *The Collected Papers*. References to *Charles Sanders Peirce: Contributions to the Nation*, ed. Kenneth Laine Ketner and James Edward Cook, 3 vols. (Lubbock, Tex.: Texas Tech Press, 1975, 1978, and 1979) are abbreviate *N*, followed, again, by the volume and paragraph numbers. References to unpublished manuscripts, abbreviated MS, follow the numbering system employed in Richard Robin, *Annotated Catalogue of the Papers of Charles S. Peirce* (Amherst: University of Massachusetts Press, 1967).

indicate briefly my approach to Peirce. While my perspective is pragmatic and thus sympathetic, it is a perspective closer to that of James and, especially, Dewey than that of Peirce. Peirce's view of his relation to James, expressed in a letter to James, effectively captures my own perspective on Peirce: "Your mind and mine are as little adapted to understanding one another as two minds could be, and therefore I always feel that I have more to learn from you than from anybody. At the same time, it gives great weight in my mind to our numerous agreements of opinion" (*CP* 8. 296). Central among my many agreements of opinion with Peirce is a shared commitment to scientific inquiry as he characterized it:

> Science and philosophy seem to have been changed in their cradles. For it is not knowing, but the love of learning, that characterizes the scientific man; while the "philosopher" is a man with a system which he thinks embodies all that is best worth knowing. If a man burns to learn and sets himself to comparing his ideas with experimental results in order that he may correct those ideas, every scientific man will recognize him as a brother, no matter how small his knowledge may be. (*CP* 1.44)

It is this burning desire to learn and the thoroughgoing dissatisfaction with one's present thinking, of course, that led Peirce to issue his famous command: "Do not block the way of inquiry" (*CP* 1.135).

The Nature of Normative Science

For Peirce, logic is a science. In contrast to many contemporary thinkers, Peirce held that logic, like ethics and aesthetics, is a normative science. What is *normative* science?[2]

---

2. Detailed and very helpful accounts of Peirce's account of normative science are provided by Beverly Kent, *Charles S. Peirce: Logic and the Classification of the Sciences* (Montreal: McGill-Queen's University Press, 1987) and Vincent J. Potter. *Charles S. Peirce: On Norms & Ideals* (Amherst: University of Massachusetts Press, 1967). Peirce's optimism is explicated revealingly through contrast to Santayana's pessimism by John Lachs, *Mind and Philosophers* (Nashville, Tenn.: Vanderbilt University Press, 1987) and through comparison to the meliorism of James and Dewey by John J. McDermott, *Streams of Experience: Reflections on the History and Philosophy of American Culture* (Amherst: University of Massachusetts Press, 1986) and *The Culture of Experience: Philosophical Essays in the American Grain* (Prospect Heights, Ill.: Waveland Press, 1987). It is further illuminated, indirectly, by the insightful contrast of Peirce's and Dewey's logics and conceptions of philosophy in Ralph Sleeper, *The Necessity of Pragmatism: John Dewey's Conception of Philosophy* (New Haven, Conn.: Yale University Press, 1986). Discussion of both theory and practice and individual and community in Peirce's philosophy may be found in several sympathetic sources: Justus Buchler, *Charles Peirce's Empiricism* (New York:

First, normative science, the second of Peirce's three well-known basic subdivisions of philosophy, "treats of the laws of the relation of phenomena to ends; that is, it treats of Phenomena in their Secondness" (*CP* 5.123). As such, the normative sciences presuppose and utilize the categories of phenomenology (*CP* 5.37), just as the normative sciences in turn are presupposed and utilized by metaphysics. In this light, Peirce defined normative science as the study of "what ought to be" (*CP* 1.281) but need not be (*CP* 2.156). Normative science in turn is subdivided into logic, ethics, and aesthetics. Logic concerns what ought to be in relation to thought; ethics concerns what ought to be in relation to action; and, aesthetics concerns what ought to be in relation to feeling (*CP* 1.574). Peirce understood these relations in a broad, non-Cartesian sense: "A subtle and almost ineradicable narrowness in the conception of Normative Science runs through almost all modern philosophy in making it relate exclusively to the human mind. The beautiful is conceived to be relative to human taste, right and wrong concern human conduct alone, logic deals with human reasoning" (*CP* 5.128). Peirce sometimes put a little differently this characterization of the subject-matter of aesthetics, ethics, and logic: "For Normative Science in general being the science of the laws of conformity of things to ends, esthetics considers those things whose ends are to embody qualities of feeling, ethics those things whose ends lie in action, and logic those things whose end is to represent something" (*CP* 5.129). Or, stated somewhat more differently still: "the three normative sciences are logic, ethics, and esthetics, being the three doctrines that distinguish good and bad; *Logic* in regard to representations of truth, *Ethics* in regard to efforts of will, and *Esthetics* in objects considered simply in their presentation" (*CP* 5.36). Or, once more, emphasizing the dualisms involved in the normative sciences,

---

Octagon Books, 1980); Vincent Colapietro, *Peirce's Approach to the Self* (Albany: State University of New York Press, 1989); and Peter Skagestadt, *The Road of Inquiry: Charles Peirce's Pragmatic Realism* (New York: Columbia University Press, 1981). Valuable, more critical sources include: Richard J. Bernstein, "Action, Conduct, and Self-Control," in *Perspectives on Peirce*, ed. John E. Smith (New Haven, Conn.: Yale University Press, 1965); Thomas L. Haskell, *The Authority of Experts: Studies in History and Theory* (Bloomington, Ind.: Indiana University Press, 1984); Christopher Hookway, *Peirce* (London: Routledge & Kegan Paul, 1985); John E. Smith, "Community and Reality," *Perspectives on Peirce*; and R. Jackson Wilson, *In Quest of Community: Social Philosophy in the United States, 1860–1920* (New York: John Wiley, 1968). In *Charles S. Peirce: From Pragmatism to Pragmaticism* (Amherst: University of Massachusetts Press, 1981), Karl Otto Appel briefly connects Peirce's views of community to those of Royce and Dewey, as well as some contemporary philosophers and sociologists. Other very useful studies include: Douglas R. Anderson, *Strands of System: The Philosophy of Charles Peirce* (West Lafayette, Ind.: Purdue University Press, 1995); Carl R. Hausman, *Charles S. Peirce's Evolutionary Philosophy* (Cambridge: Cambridge University Press, 1993); and, Sandra B. Rosenthal, *Charles S. Peirce's Pragmatic Pluralism* (Albany: State University of New York Press, 1994).

Peirce called logic the science of "the conditions of truth and falsity," ethics the science of "wise and foolish conduct," and aesthetics the science of "attractive and repulsive ideas" (*CP* 5.551). And, finally, he wrote: "These three normative sciences correspond to my three categories, which in their psychological aspect, appear as Feeling, Reaction, Thought" (*CP* 8.256).

Second, the three normative sciences are hierarchically interrelated and arranged. For Peirce, logic presupposes and requires the conclusions of ethics, and ethics in turn presupposes and requires the conclusions of aesthetics. Peirce made this clear in a discussion of right reasoning and the ideals of conduct. He wrote:

> What does right reasoning consist in? It consists in such reasoning as shall be conducive to our ultimate aim. What, then, is our ultimate aim? . . . It would seem to be the business of the moralist to find this out, and that the logician has to accept the teaching of ethics in this regard. But the moralist, as far as I can make it out, merely tells us that we have a power of self-control, that no narrow or selfish aim can ever prove satisfactory, that the only satisfactory aim is the broadest, highest, and most general possible aim; and for any more definite information, as I conceive the matter, he has to refer us to the esthetician, whose business it is to say what is the state of things which is most admirable in itself regardless of any ulterior reason. (*CP* 1.612)

Thus, as Peirce stated succinctly, logic is preceded by ethics and aesthetics (*CP* 2.197): "the morally good will be the esthetically good specially determined by a peculiar superadded element; and the logically good will be the morally good specially determined by a special superadded element" (*CP* 5.131). Peirce acknowledged that for a long time he was hesitant to categorize ethics and aesthetics as normative sciences at all, and so was slow to recognize the hierarchical relations among the normative sciences. Like most logicians, he said, he long thought logic and aesthetics seemed to belong to different universes: "It is only very recently that I have become persuaded that that seeming is illusory, and that, on the contrary, logic needs the help of esthetics" (*CP* 2.197) and ethics (*CP* 5.111). He continued:

> Ethics is another subject which for many years seemed to to me to be completely foreign to logic. . . . Now logic is a study of the means of attaining the end of thought. It cannot solve that problem until it clearly knows what that end is. Life can have but one end. It is Ethics which defines that end. It is therefore, impossible to be thoroughly and rationally logical except upon an ethical basis. . . .
>
> What I have found to be true of Ethics I am beginning to see is true of Esthetics likewise. . . . Ethics asks to what end all effort shall be directed.

That question obviously depends upon the question what it would be that, independently of the effort, we should like to experience. . . . Upon this question ethics must depend, just as logic must depend upon ethics. Esthetics, therefore, although I have terribly neglected it, appears to be possibly the first indispensable propedeutic to logic. (*CP* 2.198–99)

Third, although Peirce used familiar terms—ethics and aesthetics—in labeling and subdividing normative science, he assigns unfamiliar, special meanings to these terms. In fact, his early reluctance to categorize ethics and aesthetics as normative sciences is evidence of the uncommon meanings he finally assigns to these common terms. Although, for example, aesthetics "is evidently the basic normative science upon which as a foundation, the doctrine of ethics must be reared to be surmounted in its turn by the doctrine of logic" (*CP* 5.36), aesthetics does not determine what is beautiful or ugly, and ethics does not determine what is right or wrong. For Peirce, aesthetics and ethics (and logic) do not directly evaluate phenomena. Instead, they are theories or logics of such evaluation. They establish ideal norms in terms of which particular evaluations are meaningful and possible (*CP* 1.600). Thus, aesthetics determines what makes beautiful qualities beautiful or ugly qualities ugly. Ethics determines what makes right actions right or wrong actions wrong. Similarly, logic does not judge directly truth or falsity. Instead, it determines what makes true propositions true or false ones false.

So, fourth, the normative sciences are not practical. Instead, they are distinct and separate from practical sciences—from the arts of reasoning, the conduct of life, and the production and appreciation of fine art (*CP* 1.281). For Peirce, the normative sciences seek to understand or analyze or define ideals and norms. The normative sciences are constituted by propositions, provisional and risk-free, rather than beliefs or rules of action (*CP* 1.635). Unlike the practical sciences or arts—as well as the moral conservatism that blocks inquiry (*CP* 1.666; 1.573; 2.198)—the normative sciences do not seek primarily or directly actually to attain or sustain ideals (*CP* 1.575; 1.618; 7.185). As a result, Peirce claimed emphatically that it is impossible to serve both "the two masters, *theory* and *practice*" (*CP* 1.642) since "pure science has nothing at all to do with *action*" (*CP* 1.635). Rather, the normative sciences are "entirely distinct from the business of shaping one's own conduct" though Peirce does confess that "the study is more or less favorable to right living" (*CP* 1.600).

The Three Goods of the Normative Sciences

So, what are the "ultimate goods" of the normative sciences (*CP* 1.581)? What is aesthetic goodness? What is ethical goodness? And, what is logical goodness?

Before turning to Peirce's answers to these questions, it is instructive to note that Peirce thought there are three general schools of thought on issues of ultimate goods or ends: "there have been those who have made the end purely subjective, a feeling of pleasure; there have been those who have made the end purely objective and material, the multiplication of the race; and finally there have been those who have attributed to the end the same kind of being that a law of nature has, making it lie in the rationalization of the universe" (*CP* 1.590). Peirce, not surprisingly, held the third view. He asserted that both merely subjective and merely objective ends could not "content us as the sole ultimate good independently of any ulterior result" and so are not in themselves goods at all (*CP* 1.581). Peirce offered several rhetorical questions, examples, and intuitions (*CP* 1.584) but little sustained argument to support this view about what could or could not content us. Perhaps recognizing this, he referred to his view as an "opinion" and admitted that on this issue there is room for conflicting opinions (*CP* 1.601)—though not any or all opinions, such as those of egoists and hedonists whom he compared to hogs, poultry, dogs, and idiots (*CP* 5.130; 1.584).

Whatever one's opinion on this issue, Pierce stressed that the good or end in question must be ultimate in its structure. Right action is deliberate, self-controlled action in conformity with this end—"The only moral evil is not to have an ultimate aim" (*CP* 5.133)—and right reasoning is deliberate, self-controlled thought in conformity with this end. Such an ultimate end is aesthetic and "reasonably recommends itself in itself aside from any ulterior consideration" (*CP* 5.130). Thus Peirce claimed that "an object, to be esthetically good, must have a multitude of parts so related to one another as to impart a positive simple immediate quality to their totality; and whatever does this is, in so far, esthetically good, no matter what the particular quality of the total may be" (*CP* 5.132) This quality is single, and constitutes a unified ideal (*CP* 1.613).

But, once again, what is the nature of this ideal, this "ultimate aim, capable of being pursued in an indefinitely prolonged course of action" (*CP* 5.135). "The deduction is somewhat intricate," Peirce wrote; "I cannot go into details" (*CP* 5.136). He continued:

> In order that the aim should be immutable under all circumstances, without which it will not be an ultimate aim, it is requisite that it should accord with a free development of the agent's own esthetic quality. At the same time it is requisite that it should not ultimately tend to be disturbed by the reactions upon the agent of that outward world which is supposed in the very idea of action. It is plain that these two conditions can be fulfilled at once only if it happens that the esthetic quality toward which the agent's free development tends and that of the ultimate action of experience upon him are parts of one esthetic total. Whether or not this is really so, is a metaphysical

question which it does not fall within the scope of Normative Science to answer. . . . Meantime, it is comforting to know that all experience is favorable to that assumption. (*CP* 5.136)

Does this mean that men and women are compelled to make their lives more pleasurable? This view deserves consideration, Peirce admitted, but it is incorrect (*CP* 1.614). Pleasure, Peirce asserted (but did not argue), is too fixed and static to be admirable in itself.

Instead, with optimism that now may seem both dated and unwarranted, Peirce observed:

Only, in these days of evolutionary ideas . . . against attempts to bind down human reason to any prescriptions fixed in advance— in these days, I say, when these ideas of progress and growth have themselves grown up so as to occupy our minds as they do now, how can we be expected to allow the assumption to pass that the admirable in itself is any stationary result? The explanation of the circumstance that the only result that is satisfied with itself is a quality of feeling is that reason always looks forward to an endless future and expects endlessly to improve its results. (*CP* 1.614)

This means that man (and presumably woman) is *compelled to make life more reasonable* (*CP* 1.602) because "the essence of Reason is such that its being never can have been completely perfected" (*CP* 1.615). Peirce concluded clearly:

I do not see how one can have a more satisfying ideal of the admirable than the development of Reason so understood. The one thing whose admirableness is not due to an ulterior reason is Reason itself comprehended in all its fullness, so far as we can comprehend it. Under this conception, the ideal of conduct will be to execute our little function in the operation of the creation by giving a hand toward rendering the world more reasonable whenever, as the slang is, it is "up to us" to do so. In logic, it will be observed that knowledge is reasonableness; and the ideal of reasoning will be to follow such methods as must develope [sic] knowledge the most speedily. (*CP* 1.615)

Theoretical Presuppositions about Theory and Practice

From this perspective, I want to explore the practical implications of Peirce's view of the normative sciences. While apparently admirably pragmatic (and perhaps even "vitally important"), this whole undertaking may seem thoroughly confused and wrong-headed from the outset. After all, Peirce repeatedly emphasized that there is a sharp separation between science

(including normative science) and action. Science, Peirce said straightfor-
wardly, "has nothing directly to say concerning practical matters, and nothing
even applicable at all to vital crises" (*CP* 1.637).

This separation of science from action is only one element of a broad,
widespread, and fundamental dualism of theory and practice in much of
Peirce's philosophy. (His well-known "pragmatic" account of belief and doubt
is a notable exception.) Despite his considerable emphasis elsewhere on
continuity, this dualism is a basic theoretical presupposition of Peirce's phenomenology and metaphysics as well as his normative science. In addition to
the separation of science from action (the separation of propositions and
knowledge from beliefs and experience), Peirce's theory/practice dualism
includes: the separation of ends from means; the separation of facts from
values; and the separation of logical theory from actual practices of inquiry.

The separation of ends from means is most evident in Peirce's aesthetics
and its central notion of an end-in-itself, a general process that is its own end
and thus admirable simply for its own sake (*CP* 5.433; MS 329.20; MS
283.105). Dewey's account of context and selective interests, and his analysis
of supposed "ends-in-themselves" as "ends-in-view" within a "means-ends
continuum" provides a sharp contrast to Peirce's dualistic position.

The separation of facts and values is evident in Peirce's description of
phenomenology as "a science that does not draw any distinction of good and
bad in any sense whatever, but just contemplates phenomena as they are,
simply opens its eyes and describes what it sees" (*CP* 5.37), as though neither
"open-eyed describing" nor phenomena involve ideals. This separation is
evident, moreover, in Peirce's view that phenomena may be "prescinded"
(*CP* 1.549) from ideals but not vice versa.

Finally, Peirce's separation of logic from actual inquiry is evident in his
efforts to derive metaphysics from logic, instead of logic from metaphysics.
This separation is built into Peirce's account and ordering of the branches of
philosophy. Moreover, it pervades his revealing criticisms of Dewey's logic
of experience, pattern of inquiry, and pragmatic account of necessity.

Although I am interested here primarily in examining the practical implications of Peirce's account of normative science, this theory/practice dualism, as a theoretical presupposition of that account, merits attention and
appraisal. Peirce did not argue effectively for any of the elements of this
dualism. As a result, both theoretical and practical difficulties arise.

The basic theoretical difficulty results from Peirce's well-intentioned
efforts to ensure—though theoretically rather than practically—obedience to
his command not to block the way of inquiry. Peirce rightly recognized, of
course, that many different practices and practical interests historically have
blocked, and today continue to block, the way of inquiry. Peirce's response
to this situation was to define inquiry in terms of science and to understand

science in terms of pure theory unpolluted by practical interests. However, contrary to Peirce, to engage in science—that is, scientific inquiry—is to engage in a practice. Theorizing, like experimenting, is a practice, an action, something we do. And, like other practices, science is pervaded by, rather than free from, practical interests. As John Dewey noted, to strive to be objective is not to be thoroughly disinterested; it is to have a certain selective, practical interest operative. Love of learning, expansion of knowledge, and pursuit of truth are practical interests—the interests of certain practices. These interests are served best, if Peirce was correct, by leaving open the way of inquiry—though Peirce seemed not to realize that every leaving open is at the same time a closing off other interests.

Peirce's presupposition of a theory/practice dualism results in practical difficulties as well. Separated by Peirce from theory, practice not only begins but also largely must end under the direction of sentiment, instinct, the heart, and so-called common sense. For Peirce, this is an unavoidable fact of human life. It is evident, he thought, to all but those who vainly overrate their own reasoning (*CP* 1.627; 1.631), unsuccessfully attempt to substitute speculation for experience, and fail to observe that "the heart is more than the head, and is in fact everything in our highest concerns" (MS 435). Peirce did allow that instinct slowly can develop and grow along lines parallel to those of reasoning: "The eternal forms" that the "sciences make us acquainted with, will by slow percolation gradually reach the very core of one's being; and will come to influence our lives; and this they will do, not because they involve truths of merely vital importance, but because they are ideal and eternal verities" (*CP* 1.648). But, contrary to Peirce, reason does not dictate the supremacy of sentiment—sentiment uninformed and unreconstructed by reason—in human affairs (*CP* 1.634). In fact, reason reveals that sentiment is no more "practically infallible" (*CP* 1.633), as Peirce wrongly claimed, than it is theoretically infallible.

This is particularly so in matters of conduct and morals. "Common sense" in today's world is anything but common or shared. The failure to reconstruct collectively sentiments, values, traditions, and ways of life in light of the results of inquiry contributes to ignorance, prejudice, absolutism, isolation, frustration, and conflict. Peirce was correct to note the force of sentiment in practice. This, however, is a historical fact that rests on contingent practices and situations rather than any theoretically necessary separation of theory and practice. As such, the considerable control of practice by sentiment constitutes a practical agenda item. It is an issue that demands action, rather than a necessary presupposition that demands acceptance. Peirce's theory/practice dualism provides no incentive to undertake this needed action. (Unlike James and Dewey, Peirce seems to be an optimist rather than a meliorist.) It is not enough to deny, with Peirce, that practice or "*sentiment* is never to be influenced by reason" (*CP* 1.633). Instead, reason must regularly and richly reconstruct practice.

Practical Implications of the Normative Sciences

There is no reason, then, to suppose that the normative sciences have no practical implications. Indeed, as Peirce sometimes admitted, the task of the theoretical normative sciences by definition includes practice. That task is to find out "how Feeling, Conduct, and Thought, ought to be controlled supposing them to be subject in a measure, and only in a measure, to self-control, exercised by means of self-criticism, and the purposive formation of habit, as common sense tells us they are in a measure controllable" (MS 655). Similarly, the task of practical self-control by definition includes theory. This self-control consists "first in comparing one's past deeds with standards, second, in rational deliberation concerning how one will act in the future, in itself a highly complicated operation, third, in the formation of a resolve, fourth, in the creation on the basis of the resolve, of a strong determination, or modification of habit" (*CP* 8.320).

We must form habits, Peirce claimed, that help us render the world more reasonable (*CP* 1.615) and self-controlled (*CP* 5.418). In logic, this means that we must develop those methods of thought that most speedily lead to knowledge. What methods of conduct or habits of action must we develop? What are the practical consequences of this demand to make the world more reasonable? Ought we to aid the hungry and homeless? If so, how? Should we "just say no" to drugs? Or disposable diapers? Should we register AIDS patients? Or register for the military? Ought we to spend more time with our families? Should we exercise more, and exercise more self-control in the presence of chocolate-chip cookies? Would it be more reasonable not to fly to conferences on small planes? Would a world with no abortions and more capital punishment be not only "a kinder and gentler" one but also a more reasonable one? These obviously are important questions. Reasonable action in these cases depends upon specific results and contexts of particular inquiries. Peirce's account of the normative sciences implies no specific course of action in such cases.

It does, however, have more general implications for conduct and its self-control. Most broadly, rendering the world more reasonable involves acting so as to create and sustain community. As a consequence of Peirce's principle of continuity, complete individuality or particularity is impossible. Accordingly, like reason, knowledge, truth, and reality, rendering the world more reasonable is a public rather than private matter, a social rather than solitary affair (*CP* 1.673; 2.693; 5.311; 5.407; 5.421; 6.264; 6.6100). Here several points must be emphasized.

In the first place, in actively aiming to nurture community, we must distinguish between community and society. Although explicit in the writings of other American philosophers such as Royce and Dewey, this distinction is only implicit, if present at all, in Peirce's work. The distinction is important because very few societies or social groups are communities. A society is a genuine community only when its members imaginatively share inclusive ideals and concern for the self-realization of one another, and actively participate in the direction of those social forces that shape their lives. These forces include the production and use of knowledges[3] as well as the production and use of political, economic, and other forms of power.

As such, in the second place, the existence of community is not a fixed fact about nature, evolution, or reality. Instead, the existence of community is precarious, fragile, local, and rare. Like the lives of many others, Peirce's own life, if not his philosophy, provided clear evidence of this. Community has no transcendental foundation (in, for instance, God, Being, language, or communicative competence) or metaphysical necessity or universality; instead, its realization—if and when it is realized—depends upon ongoing inquiry and action. This action, moreover, must include not simply the reconstruction of human knowledge but also the reconstruction of human ideals and human institutions. Indeed, without the ongoing reconstruction of institutions, the conditions necessary for reconstruction of knowledge may be absent.

This means, in the third place, that the community in question must not be simply a community of scientists, theorists, or knowers. Since experience includes more than knowing and knowledge, a community's members must be full, whole, live creatures who act and undergo, rejoice and suffer, endure and perish. The ultimate value of such a community does not consist in its products—whether new knowledge, increasing proximity to truth, or a higher GNP—but in its process or living itself. Peirce's notion of a community of inquirers is insufficiently inclusive. It seems to depend upon philosophers' common but unwarranted and unpragmatic identifications of reality with objects of knowledge, and experience with knowing. Moreover, in the hands of institutionalized academics who rightly reject this assumption but wrongly cling to its worst consequences, a community of inquirers may become little more than an association of professionals whose motto becomes: "Do not block the way of conversation."

In the fourth place, as Peirce recognized, the live creature is a creature of habit, and so rendering the world more reasonable requires nurturing individual habits (of action as well as thought) consonant with the ideals of community and reason themselves. This amounts to the full development of individuals—both as individuals and as members of communities. Community and individuality reciprocally depend upon one another: a society becomes a community only as its members are genuine individuals, and separate selves become individuals only as they jointly constitute a community. The realization of community does not require the subordination or negation of

---

3. See the discussion of this point in chapters 1 and 3.

individuality, as Peirce claimed (*CP* 1.673; 5.317). The self need not necessarily be only a manifestation of insignificance, limitation, and error. It may and should be the self-controlled pursuit of concrete reasonableness. Thus self-control is the development of the self, not its elimination.

The consequences of this are far-reaching. In the fifth place, then, it means that, despite the naturally conservative force of habits, individuals must continuously reshape their beliefs and values in a manner consistent with the methods and results of ongoing experimental inquiry. More importantly, it means that individuals must hold their beliefs and values in a manner consistent with the fallibilist, anti-absolutist spirit of experimental inquiry. And, decisively, it means that individuals must embody in their daily lives these beliefs and values consistent with inquiry and its spirit. To do otherwise is to pretend to believe in philosophy what we do not believe in our hearts.

Finally, to accomplish this, a reconstruction of education is required. Peirce recognized this: "This is the age of methods; and the university which is to be the exponent of the living condition of the human mind, must be the university of methods. . . . And a liberal education—so far as its relation to the understanding goes—means logic. That is indispensable to it, and no other thing is" (*CP* 7.62; 7.64). Thus, the import of results of inquiries— including philosophic inquiries—must be widely disseminated. Methods of inquiry must be made familiar. And the spirit of science must be made contagious (without resulting in scientism). These are distant objectives today. In the face of increasing intellectual specialization, professionalization, and isolation, a genuine community of inquirers readily may become an impossibility for society and only an abstraction within colleges and universities. Worse yet, other cultural institutions and arrangements effectively educate—that is, forge habits of thought and action—contrary to the ideals of concrete reasonableness community, individuality, and the value of education itself. The educational message in our society today largely is one of: force rather than inquiry; manipulation rather than reason; material wealth rather than knowledge; self-certainty rather than fallibility; and, selfishness rather than love. In this situation, it is to be expected that Peirce's theory is discussed by small groups of scholars. The practical importance of his message, however, deserves a wider audience, and that audience needs his message. To a large extent, we scholars have failed to deliver it. Though unsettling, the practical implications of this should be clear even to theorists: As Peirce said, "every one knows that . . . mere *thinking* will accomplish nothing" (*CP* 7.59).[4]

---

4. An earlier version of portions of this essay appeared in "Rendering the World More Reasonable: The Practical Significance of Peirce's Normative Science," *Peirce and Value Theory: On Peircean Ethics and Aesthetics*, ed. Herman Parret (Amsterdam and Philadelphia: John Benjamins, 1994), pp. 3–15. These revised passages appear here with the kind permission of the editor and the publisher.

12

Bodies, Selves, and Individuals: Personalism and Pragmatism

How To Write Scholarly Essays on Personalism and Pragmatism

It is surprising that at present there is no careful, thorough, full-length comparative analysis of personalism and pragmatism.[1] It is surprising in part simply because academics desperate to publish before they perish have produced comparisons of almost all permutations of philosophies: Marxism and deconstruction, Platonism and postmodernism, process thought and Buddhism, feminism and phenomenology, and act-utilitarianism and existentialism. Many of these studies embody a formula embraced warmly by most academic presses, learned journals, and tenure review committees: they assert that two philosophies usually thought to be similar really are different in significant ways, or else claim that two philosophies usually thought to be importantly different really have much in common.

---

1. Let me indicate at the outset my understanding of both personalism and pragmatism. First, I take pragmatism to be the philosophy set forth by Charles Peirce, William James, John Dewey, George Herbert Mead, C. I. Lewis, and others, and developed more recently in the work of writers such as John J. McDermott, John E. Smith, John Lachs, Sandra Rosenthal, and many others (most of whom are associated with the Society for the Advancement of American Philosophy). The resurgence of interest in pragmatism thus understood is summarized neatly by John J. McDermott in "The Renascence of Classical American Philosophy" in his *Streams of Experience: Reflections on the History and Philosophy of American Culture* (Amherst: University of Massachusetts Press, 1986). This broad body of work, in my view, does not include the antitheory views often termed "pragmatism" by some contemporary literary theorists. Nor does it include the so-called neopragmatism of philosophers such as Richard Rorty. Second, I take personalism to be the philosophy set forth by George Holmes Howison, Borden Parker Bowne, Ralph Tyler Flewelling, Albert C. Knudson, Edgar Sheffield Brightman, and others, and developed more recently by Walter G. Muelder, Warren Steinkraus, John Lavely, Peter A. Bertocci, and many others (most of whom are associated with the Personalist Discussion Group). This is, I think, the philosophy that John Lavely has termed "personal idealism" in his *Encyclopedia of Philosophy* entry on "Personalism." To a large extent it also is the tradition chronicled by Paul Deats and Carol Robb in their collection, *The Boston Personalist Tradition in Philosophy, Social Ethics, and Theology* (Macon, Ga.: Mercer University Press, 1986).

This formula certainly could be applied to personalism and pragmatism. On the surface, at least, these two philosophies seem intellectually and culturally close in many important ways and, at the same time, significantly different in other respects. This makes possible (and perhaps desirable) an immense (and perhaps not wholly artificial) scholarly research program for the near future. The following questions, for instance, invite extended examination: To what extent are there parallels between personalist and pragmatist efforts to make compatible science and religion? Is the naturalist strain in pragmatism at odds in the end with a supernaturalist strain in personalism? Is personalism more "tender-minded" than pragmatism? Just how similar is the personalist social gospel and the pragmatist focus on community and social action? In what ways do both personalism and pragmatism utilize shared methods and conceptions of truth, inquiry, and communication? To what extent do personalism and pragmatism incorporate, exemplify, or overcome idealism? In what ways does personalism share pragmatism's rejection of modern philosophy's central dualisms of mind and body, individual and society, subject and object, and fact and value? To what degree is personalism, like pragmatism, committed to radical empiricism, meliorism, and pluralism? How similar is the account of mind, body, and nature in personalism and pragmatism? Do personalists accept the pragmatic characterization of metaphysics as criticism of criticism? Is the personalist position philosophically close to pragmatism on issues in, for instance, aesthetics, logic, philosophy of science, ecology, or education? To what extent and in what ways are both personalism and pragmatism the products of a distinctively American situation? How similar are personalist and pragmatist historical relations to writers as diverse as Descartes, Leibniz, Hegel, and Walt Whitman? To what extent might personalism and pragmatism provide similar rich resources or redirection either to analytic philosophy or its postmodern critics?

These and other issues may be pursued profitably by experts of both pragmatism and personalism. While the number of such scholars may be very small, the value of these undertakings in fact may be very large at present. The time may be especially ripe for personalists and pragmatists to discover and learn from each other. Certainly, the recent fragmentation and ongoing expansion of once dominant strains and constraints in professional philosophy in America both contribute to, and draw on, the present resurgence of interest in pragmatism and the persistence of attention to personalism.

A Basic Orientation Shared

Despite their promise, I will not explore the above issues in this chapter. I do this in part out of necessity. I do not write as a personalist; instead, I write as a pragmatist—with the acknowledged selective emphases of a pragmatist. More importantly, however, I forego consideration of what, if anything, personalism and pragmatism have to offer one another largely because this sort of academic issue itself is not central to the agendas of either personalists or pragmatists. It should not be (but too often is) central to professional professors who are personalists or pragmatists. For both personalism and pragmatism, the subject-matter, the method, and the value of a philosophy must be found in the actual lives and social arrangements of individuals. Accordingly, the fundamental issue is not whether personalism and pragmatism can do something valuable for one another in theory. Instead, the issue ultimately is whether personalism and pragmatism, alone or jointly, now can do something valuable for persons in practice.

This stance is deeply ingrained in both personalist and pragmatist temperaments, and, in American thought far earlier and more broadly. It runs throughout the development of pragmatism, including: Charles Peirce's rejection of the incapacities of Cartesianism and his classification of logic as a normative science; William James's biological psychology, theory of truth, and meliorism; John Dewey's theory of inquiry, his demand for a recovery of philosophy, and his distinction between the "problems of philosophers" and the "problems of men"; and, George Herbert Mead's social behaviorism and philosophy of the act.

This same orientation also is evident throughout personalism, as evidenced by: Howison's "eternal republic"; Bowne's rejection of abstract ethics and his meliorism; Brightman's theory of coherence and his account of individuals as centers of value; and Martin Luther King's use of this philosophy in the service of nonviolent resistance to the oppression of persons. In fact, this philosophic orientation to the practice of persons, basic to and shared by pragmatism and personalism, is reflected succinctly by the credo or mission statement of the *Personalist Forum*, a journal "devoted to publishing scholarly work that addresses issues of being persons in the world," with "a common conviction that philosophy must take personal categories seriously; speak to issues that confront persons and do so in a language that strives for maximal comprehensibility." Powerful institutional structures and dominant professional practices within philosophy, higher education, and society more generally make this a difficult goal today.[2] Still, as poet Robert Browning noted, one's reach should exceed one's grasp, and this surely is a reach or commitment that both personalism and pragmatism make deeply and pervasively.

---

2. See the discussions of the humanities and higher education in chapter 1 and the appendix to chapter 3.

A Central Issue Disputed

In this light, personalists' and pragmatists' extensive mutual disinterest is perhaps even more surprising than the absence of comparisons of the two philosophies by scholars. What has separated these two philosophies that share a general practical, personal stance—as well as, to a large extent, a common time, place, and language? This is a complex issue, at once historical and philosophical. Is the mutual disinterest between personalists and pragmatists rooted in conflicting supernaturalist and naturalist religious views and accounts of God? Is it the result of competing subjective and holistic perspectives on the nature of nature? Is it a function of incompatible theories of final and instrumental values and ends? Is it, no more and no less, largely a matter of individual temperament and personality? (Perhaps this last suggestion is appropriately personalistic.)

These questions all suggest factors important in the mutual inattention and disregard of personalists and pragmatists. However, another factor appears more central. I want to suggest that, at least from the perspective of many pragmatists, a major source of the disinterest and gap between personalists and pragmatists is the very core of personalism itself.

What is this core of personalism? Surely, it is the personalist account of the nature of persons. What is this account? Admittedly, there is no single, definitive personalist account of the nature of persons. Different personalists have defined personality as, for example: an individual rational substance; a supernatural, spiritual being; a self-active unity of consciousness operating with memory, freedom, purpose, and reason; a self-directing, uncreated intelligent creator; and, a self-identifying complex unity of activity-potentials. However, throughout these different accounts of the nature of persons—differences that I do not wish to minimize although I skim over them here—personalists do seem to agree on the metaphysical and ethical status of persons. Most broadly and generally, personalists assert that persons are ontologically or morally ultimate. Personalists typically thus hold that the notion of personality and the category of persons provide philosophy with its basic principle of explanation. This commitment, it seems, is a minimal, necessary condition that any philosophy must meet if it is to be classified meaningfully as a form or type of personalism.

Pragmatism does not meet this minimum condition. For better or worse—though clearly I think for better—it does not fulfill this requirement. How so? Pragmatism fails to cross the threshold into personalism in an interesting way. It does not reject as philosophically false personalism's central commitments and positions so much as it rejects as culturally outmoded and artificial many of the very questions and issues that personalism seeks to address and resolve. Put simply, personalism and pragmatism largely have failed to engage one another not because they end in different answers but because they begin with different problems. John Dewey made this clear when he argued that pragmatism does not seek principally to criticize the positions of other philosophers, but rather seeks to recover philosophy from traditional philosophical problems and attachments that changing cultural conditions now have rendered obsolete and no longer genuine.

As a result, pragmatists tend not to enter into discussion or argument with personalists on issues central to personalists' views of persons. For instance, pragmatists do not counter personalists' idealism with some form of materialism or realism. Instead, pragmatists reject both idealism and materialism, and the assumptions that give rise to the particular problems to which these positions are responses. Similarly, pragmatists do not counter personalists' commitment to the primacy of persons with an opposing commitment to the primacy of nonpersons in some form. Instead, pragmatists reject the primacy of persons and the primacy of nonpersons, as well as the metaphysical and moral presuppositions that underlie and call forth these views.

Pragmatism, then, executes an extended end-run on personalism—and many other philosophies as well. But philosophy is a contact sport, and, as suggested above, there are points of contact in pragmatism's effort to turn the corner on personalism. In some sense, pragmatists might be able to accept the personalist insistence on the moral primacy or ultimacy of persons. For pragmatists, however, this primacy does not denote a metaphysical fact or a moral reality secure and fixed antecedent to human action. Instead, it signifies a moral ideal, and thus leads straight to a practical agenda for social action and societal reconstruction. Similarly, in some sense, pragmatists might be able to accept the personalist insistence on the ontological primacy of personal life or experience. For pragmatists, though, this primacy is intelligible only in light of radical empiricist accounts of experience as transactional and selves as intrinsically social—accounts in which both experiencing social subject and experienced natural object are reciprocal aspects of an irreducible primary unity.

Viewed from this perspective, pragmatism may provide an expansion of personalism—rather than its critical rejection or indifferent dismissal. That is, pragmatism may make possible an expanded understanding of the metaphysical nature, social development, and moral value of persons. The success of such a pragmatist expansion of a philosophy of persons depends upon an articulation of persons as: (1) natural organisms; (2) social selves; and (3) communal individuals. I will develop briefly each of these three pragmatist notions.

Persons as Bodily Organisms

For pragmatists, there is a basic continuity between persons and monkeys, kangaroos, lizards, frogs, spiders, trout, maples, mushrooms, plankton, and viruses: All are living organisms that strive and suffer, satisfy and need, grow and decay, and act, and are acted upon, in a particular environment.

Dewey emphasizes this point by asserting that organisms do not live *in* their environment but *through* and *by* their environment. Activity is as much the act of an environment as it is the act of an organism. The relation of an organism to its environment is not a simple *interaction*—a mixing of two entities that otherwise exist independently from one another. It is a *transaction*—a primary, unified whole in which parts or aspects distinguished by reflection exist only in mutual relation to one another.

For pragmatists, there also is a basic difference (though not a discontinuity) between persons and other forms of life: The lives of persons are marked by the development and activity of mind—that is, by the presence of meaning or significance. This is a key point and it easily is misunderstood: For pragmatists, mind is not something that a person has—somewhere, such as the pineal gland, heart, or brain; mind is not something separate from, alien to, or independent of body or nature; and, mind is not innate, eternal, mystic, or in principle private.

What, then, is mind? Though it may seem otherwise at first, to ask this question, with the pragmatists, is not to raise the traditional mind/body problem. Instead, it is to reject this problem in its entirety: There simply is no general philosophical mind/body problem. For pragmatists, mind and body are not separate original sorts of being. Accordingly, there is no special philosophical task of putting them together again, and there also is no special philosophical problem about how supposedly separate kinds of things interact or how interacting kinds of things remain supposedly separate.

Instead, there is a need for factual inquiry into the development, function, consequences, and conditions of the organization of various modes of life. This inquiry may identify the emergence and presence of mind or personality at a particular point in the development of these kinds of organization. Because this point is basic to the pragmatist view of persons, I quote at length Dewey's summary of the development of mind in "Nature, Life and Body-Mind," the seventh chapter of *Experience and Nature*:

> If we identify, as common speech does, the physical as such with the inanimate we need another word to denote the activity of organisms as such. Psycho-physical is an appropriate term. Thus employed, "psycho-physical" denotes the conjunctive presence in activity of need-demand-satisfaction. . . . Psycho-physical does not denote an abrogation of the physico-chemical; nor a peculiar mixture of something physical and something psychical (as a centaur is half man and half horse); it denotes the possession of certain qualities and efficacies not displayed by the inanimate. . . . With the multiplication of sensitive discriminatory reactions to different energies of the environment . . . and with the increase in scope and delicacy of movements . . . feelings vary more and more in quality and intensity. Complex and active animals *have*, therefore feelings which vary abundantly. . . . They *have* them, but they do not know they have them. Activity is psycho-physical, but not

"mental," that is not aware of meanings. . . . "[M]ind" is an added property assumed by a feeling creature, when it reaches that organized interaction with other living creatures which is language, communication. Then the qualities of feeling become significant of objective differences in external things and of episodes past and to come. This state of things in which qualitatively different feelings are not just had but are significant of objective differences, is mind. Feelings are no longer just felt. They have and they make *sense*; record and prophesy.[3]

This view of the emergence and nature of mind has both presuppositions and implications. As a theory of the links intrinsic to body and mind, it presupposes, and is part of, a larger pragmatic theory that joins nature and experience. This theory is set forth most fully by James in *Principles of Psychology* and *Essays in Radical Empiricism*, and by Dewey in *Experience and Nature*. I do not want here to explicate at length this theory, but I do want to call attention to one of its revolutionary implications. Because pragmatists insist that experience is an irreducible unified exchange or transaction between organism and environment, the categories of traditional metaphysics become simply the more or less useful products of reflection. That is, categories such as subject and object, mind and body, thoughts and things, experience and nature, self and others, and fact and value are reflective distinctions rather than existential dichotomies. These categories have functional status in thought; they do not have metaphysical status in reality. In reality, an experiencing subject and an experienced object are unified in an as-yet-unanalyzed totality.

It is in this sense that James and Dewey term experience (or "culture") "double-barreled"—it includes both subject and object as features of an irreducible whole. By contrast, to the extent that personalism asserts the metaphysical primacy of persons, subjects, experiences, or thoughts over nonpersons, objects, nature, or things, it is "single-barreled" and stands in opposition to pragmatism. Just as pragmatists have argued on this issue that honest empiricists must become *radical* empiricists, so too at this point I think experience compels honest personalists to become *radical* personalists, "double-barreled" personalists, pragmatists.

The major immediate implication of this view is straightforward. Because the development of mind requires language and communication, the development of communication and the production of meanings are one with the development of mind. Any adequate philosophy of persons must capture this transformation effected by, and through, communication. It also must recognize that the pragmatic account of persons as natural organisms with minds points to the irreducibly and centrally social character of persons. In

---

3. John Dewey, *Experience and Nature, John Dewey: The Later Works, 1925–1953*, vol. 1 (Carbondale, Ill.: Southern Illinois University Press, 1981 [1925]), pp. 195–96, 198.

pragmatist terms, the self, always a body-self, is fundamentally and thoroughly a social self. As such, it is a precarious product of social arrangements rather than a secure, given fact about individual nature or reality at large.

Persons as Social Selves

For pragmatists, the emergence of mind marks the transformation or reorganization of an organism into a self. This transformation is a social process and the resulting self is an intrinsically social being.

This point is more startling and far-reaching than at first it may seem. Pragmatists agree, of course, with Aristotle's observation that human beings are social creatures. We are born, grow up, live, and die in the presence of others. But pragmatists also assert something different and deeper. The point here is not simply that persons live in society (any more than organisms live in their environment). Instead, it is that persons live through, and by, social relations and arrangements that thus enter into, and are inseparable from, their very being. The relation of person to society is not one of detachable part to composite whole. A person is not like a separable marble incidentally surrounded by other marbles in a child's bucket. A person is not even like a spark plug in an automobile engine, able to function only in connection with many other parts. Rather, a person's relation to society is organic, historical, and mutually constitutive and transformative.

There simply is no self stripped of complex social relations. George Herbert Mead makes this point effectively by sharply distinguishing a person as a self from a person as a body, and by contrasting the social with the physiological. In a well-known passage in *Mind, Self, and Society*, he argues that the defining characteristic of the self, unlike the body, is that it is an object to itself. As such, the self experiences itself as a self only indirectly, only from the standpoints of other individual selves or the generalized standpoint of a social group or society as a whole. Mead writes that the self (presumably female as well as male!)

> enters his own experience as a self or individual, only in so far as he first becomes an object to himself just as other individuals are objects to him or his experience; and he becomes an object to himself only by taking the attitudes of other individuals toward himself. . . . Such a self is not . . . primarily a physiological organism. . . . The self, as that which can be an object to itself, is essentially a social structure, and it arises in social experiences.[4]

---

4. George Herbert Mead, *Mind, Self, and Society: From the Standpoint of a Social Behaviorist*, ed. Charles W. Morris (Chicago: University of Chicago Press, 1934), pp. 139–40.

The formation of selves, then, depends upon organized social practices, effective institutions, and shared meanings—what Mead terms the "Generalized Other." There is nothing automatic about this; there is no guarantee that societies always, everywhere, and fully will manifest these prerequisite conditions of self development. When these conditions in fact are not satisfied, their satisfaction constitutes a pressing educational and political agenda for pragmatists.

From the standpoint of education, this agenda reaches far beyond the schools. Social institutions such as the government, the economy, the legal system, religious traditions, the family, the hospital, the prison, sports, the military, and the workplace all have educational consequences. Frequently, these results are much broader and longer lasting than those of schools, even though it is only in the schools that particular educational results are the most immediate and directly intended institutional goals. These institutions have far-reaching educational consequences in that they transmit a culture's concerns, knowledge, skills, and way of life to its immature members.

Without this educative transmission and communication, social life could not continue. It is in this context that Dewey virtually identifies the development of selves with communication and education. Thus, in *Democracy and Education*, he asserts that "men live in a community in virtue of the things which they have in common; and communication is the way in which they come to possess things in common. Not only is social life identical with communication, but all communication (and hence all genuine social life) is educative."[5]

These institutions, accordingly, can be evaluated in terms of the meanings, habits, and character that they produce and transmit. In this light, pragmatists measure the worth of any social institution by its effects—by its role in developing or stunting selves, enlarging or narrowing experience, and deepening or impoverishing meaning. Dewey employs precisely this strategy throughout his later work: from his efforts in *Liberalism and Social Action* to reconstruct traditional liberalism to his criticism in *Freedom and Culture* of markets that serve private interests under the guise of freedom; from his analysis in *Individualism: Old and New* of the "lost" individual and his sketch of a new individualism to his efforts in *A Common Faith* to expand religious experience and detach it from supernaturalist doctrines; and, from his attempts in *Art as Experience* to free aesthetic experience from the confines of museums to his focus in *The Public and Its Problems* on democracy as a way

---

5. John Dewey, *Democracy and Education*, *John Dewey: The Middle Works, 1899–1924*, vol. 9 (Carbondale, Ill.: Southern Illinois University Press, 1980 [1916]), pp. 7–8. See also the discussion of community, identity, and difference in chapter 13.

of life rather than merely a way of government. For pragmatists, then, growth is not simply the aim of education. It also is the moral basis for cultural criticism and cultural reconstruction.

In this way, attention to the social production and growth of persons as genuine selves underlies the pragmatist fusing of education and democracy. Education as the development of genuine selves is possible only in a thoroughly democratic society—what Dewey calls a "great community" in contrast to a "great society." Democracy in turn can flourish only if its members are educated, grow, and become selves. Only education, understood as the ongoing growth of persons as selves, continually creates free activities and shared meanings; such shared activities and meanings are the very core of a democratic way of life.

Thus, for pragmatists, the growth of persons as selves is the basic *method* of social progress, as well as both the goal of education and the moral basis of social action. In the absence of an understanding of persons as social selves, this method cannot be adopted and utilized. Many philosophers have failed to recognize this, and as a result they mistakenly have regarded an ideal for action as a fact for belief. Here it makes no pragmatic difference whether this supposed fact is metaphysically "grounded"—as it appears, I think, for many idealists and personalists—or "ungrounded"—as it is for neopragmatists who hold to a sharp public/private dualism and like to pretend that the development of a person as a self is a matter of one's own private invention. When this happens, concern for persons in theory ironically hinders the social development of persons in practice. In such a situation, it is crucial that personalists, like pragmatists, preach practice.

Persons as Communal Individuals

For pragmatists, it is a fact that the development of persons as selves is a social process. Now, the existence of this process is distinct from the value of its products. There is a gap, that is, between the social formation of a self—the self's mere social existence—and the social fulfillment of that self—its social self-realization.

This notion of an actualized self is, for pragmatists, the notion of a person as a genuine individual. Recognizing that individuality is a social product, two central questions arise: What is it—just what product of social forces is it? And, how is it produced—what social arrangements facilitate or impede its development?

Pragmatists often begin to address these issues by disputing popular misconceptions and arguing about what individuality is not. So, in the first place, for example, individuality is not an innate characteristic or possession. For pragmatists, individuals are made (if and when they exist), not born. This may provide hope, but it offers no assurance. In the second place, individuality is not a matter of personal self-sufficiency. It is not something learned at survivalist camps, taught in New Age self-help books, or observed in old movies of the American West and new television commercials for cigarettes and Japanese automobiles. These images aside, everyone is involved in innumerable primary social interdependencies, as crop failures, distant wars, global pollution, sick relatives, power outages, teachers' strikes, and international markets, for instance, make painfully clear. This may be a depressing message to the rich, the smart, and the hard-working. It means that no one person—no matter how wealthy, intelligent, or persistent—can become fully an individual on his or her own in the absence of appropriate, sustaining social conditions. A Walkman, home security system, and more hours in the library, office, or gym aren't enough. In the third place, genuine individuality is not a matter of simply acting, looking, or being different from everyone else. Attempting to be unlike others for its own sake is no less mindless conformity than attempting to be like others for its own sake. In each case, whether doing or avoiding something, a person's actions are uncritical, unstable, and directed by others. This, of course, runs against the grain of carefully marketed messages of both our culture and countercultures. Finally, uniqueness, no more than mere difference from others, is no guarantee of individuality. This is not to deny that each of us is unique in various ways. However, the mere uniqueness of a person is quite distinct from that person's ongoing self-realization. So, it simply is to deny that uniqueness of any sort, and by itself, is a sufficient condition of individuality.

Instead, individuality is a matter of associated activities, harmonious values, shared meanings, and developed character. It is the social realization of the social self. This social realization is possible only to the extent that a society is or becomes a community. That is, the self is social, and when the self's society is a genuine community, then the self may be fully an individual. Put in the language of an SAT analogy exam: society:community; self:individual.

To grasp this point, it is essential to recall the very special, technical, different meanings that pragmatists give to the very ordinary terms "society" and "community. For Dewey (much like Royce), a community is a special kind of society. It is a society that embodies a democratic way of life (and not simply a democratic form of government), a society in which all persons affected by institutions and practices participate in their direction, and a society in which social groups serve their individual members in ways that promote the harmony and common goods of those different and differing individuals.[6] When these conditions are not fulfilled, society fails to be a

---

6. See John Dewey, *The Public and Its Problems, John Dewey: The Later Works, 1925–1953*, vol. 2 (Carbondale, Ill.: Southern Illinois University Press, 1984 [1927]), pp. 327–28.

community, and persons fail to be individuals. For Dewey, this is the reality with which, and in which, we now live. Changing this unsatisfactory situation will require new inquiry, communication, and a radical reconstruction of almost all our institutions and practices: "The highest and most difficult kind of inquiry and a subtle, delicate, vivid and responsive art of communication must take possession of the physical machinery of transmission and circulation and breathe life into it."[7]

Rather than explore here pragmatist strategies for such changes, I want to return to the meaning of this situation for a pragmatic account of persons as communal individuals. For pragmatists, the actual lives of persons today fail to exhibit the loyalties, hopes, and meanings characteristic of fully communal individuals. Accordingly, at worst this category of persons as individuals is a mere fiction, an unreality. At best, it is an ideal. It is an ideal, however, only to the extent that it involves a deep imaginative commitment, in action as well as belief, that unifies our lives and directs our efforts.

Dewey terms this commitment "faith." It is not a faith in God or Being or Spirit or nature or history. Instead, it is a human faith, a democratic faith, a faith in the possibilities of collective human imagination, intelligence, and will. This faith, Dewey claims, has emerged only recently and incompletely in human history. Even in democratic governments today, beliefs and values include strong preferences developed much earlier for authority instead of participation, inquiry, and communication. Anything but rare in traditional philosophy, these preferences for authority—including the authority of business and the business mind—today powerfully stall and threaten the development of persons and community. More immediately, they even greatly undermine action on behalf of faith in these ideals.

In this context, the relation of personalism to pragmatism is both uncertain and malleable. Pragmatists may worry that personalists effectively and principally are committed only to an *idealism of persons*. At the same time, pragmatists may hope that personalists, with pragmatists, instead are committed centrally in theory and practice to an *ideal of persons*. From a pragmatic standpoint, this is a difference that makes a difference—both to philosophers and to the persons about whom they philosophize.[8]

---

7. Ibid., p. 350.

8. An earlier version of portions of this essay appeared in "Personalist Persons and Pragmatist Persons," *The Personalist Forum* 6.2 (1990): 143–61. These revised passages appear here with the kind permission of the editor and the publisher.

13

Education and the Cultural Frontier:
Community, Identity, and Difference

I'm addressing you.
Are you going to let your emotional life be run by Time Magazine?
I'm obsessed by Time Magazine.
I read it every week.
Its cover stares at me every time I slink past the corner candystore.
I read it in the basement of the Berkeley Public Library.
It's always telling me about responsibility. Business men are serious.
Movie producers are serious. Everybody's serious but me.
It occurs to me that I am America.
I am talking to myself again.

—Allen Ginsberg, "America"

I have prayed for America
I was made for America
Her shining dream plays in my mind
By the rockets red glare
A generation's blank stare
We better wake her up this time . . .
I can't let go till she comes around
Until the land of the free
Is awake and can see
And until her conscience has been found

—Jackson Browne, "For America"

Community as Cultural Frontier

Like life, this chapter has no introduction. We find ourselves always in transition, unsure but surely underway. Any explanation, criticism, change of course, reconstruction, or new direction must be made on the move, piecemeal, and imperfectly.

Accordingly, this chapter, again like life, provides no certainty, complete or lasting generality, guarantee, final conclusion, or proof. With Ralph Waldo

Emerson, I say that "I hope it is somewhat better than whim at last, but we cannot spend the day in explanation."[1] This fact, of course, marks a parameter, rather than an incapacity, of our thought, as Charles Peirce made clear.[2] Accordingly, it is not cause for regret. Wallace Stevens captured this fallibilistic spirit in "The Poems of Our Climate":

> The imperfect is our paradise.
> Note that, in this bitterness, delight,
> Since the imperfect is so hot in us,
> Lies in flawed words and stubborn sounds.[3]

Though undeniably situated and socially conditioned, my words and sounds are also irreducibly personal in origin, form, and aim. Thus, as Walt Whitman announced: "Behold, I do not give lectures or a little charity. When I give I give myself."[4] And, as William James showed, thought is owned,[5] and all philosophy, even professional philosophy, and even professional philosophy that denies its own irreducibly personal connection, is inescapably biographical. At its best, it is personal vision: "vision is the great fact . . . A philosophy is the expression of a man's intimate character, and all the definitions of the universe are but the deliberately adopted reactions of human characters upon it."[6] As a consequence of James's work, as George Santayana explained in his critical discussion of the "genteel tradition" in American thought, we now "need not be afraid of being less profound, for being direct and sincere."[7] The intellectual world, perhaps in spite of some scholarly work in the humanities today, must be and legitimately may be traversed personally and directly, in many ways and in many directions.

To attempt to do this, I suspect, is to transgress present intellectual, professional, and institutional boundaries. It is to take up residence in marginal

---

1. Ralph Waldo Emerson, *The Complete Works of Ralph Waldo Emerson*, vol. 2, ed. Edward Waldo Emerson (Boston and New York: Scribner's, 1903 [1838]), p. 52.
2. Charles S. Peirce, "Some Consequences of Four Incapacities," *The Journal of Speculative Philosophy* 2 (1868): 140–41.
3. Wallace Stevens, *Parts of a World* (New York: Knopf, 1942), p. 18. For a discussion of Stevens's poetry in the context of American legal philosophy and pragmatism, see Thomas Grey, "Hear the Other Side: Wallace Stevens and Pragmatist Legal Theory," *Southern California Law Review* 63.2 (1990): 1569–95.
4. Walt Whitman, *Leaves of Grass*, 10th ed. (New York, 1855), p. 40.
5. William James, *The Principles of Psychology*, vol. 1, *The Works of William James* (Cambridge, Mass.: Harvard University Press, 1981 [1890]), p. 220.
6. William James, *A Pluralistic Universe*, *The Works of William James* (Cambridge, Mass.: Harvard University Press, 1977 [1909]), p. 14.
7. George Santayana, *Winds of Doctrine* and *Platonism and the Spiritual Life* (Gloucester, Mass.: Peter Smith, 1971 [1913]), p. 211.

territories and new lands. The exploratory purpose may require unfamiliar, even camouflaged form, a style that may be risky, nonconformist, and, as William Carlos Williams put it, unsanctioned: "This is plainly not scholarship, neither is it a man. It is writing about knowledge which must seize a sanction before it can seriously proceed, valid in the eyes of scholarship itself."[8]

To think in a new direction, to think at the frontier, to think in a manner consonant with the transitions evident everywhere in our lives: This is a difficult requirement for American philosophers. The difficulty is due not simply to the fact that we have become habituated to philosophical inquiry done in the safety of established intellectual settlements guarded by professional garrisons of scholars. The difficulty of thinking in new philosophical directions is due also and mainly to the fact that this very thinking anew is itself a settled and long-established form of thought and goal for characteristically American philosophers.

Of course, we too may set out for intellectual rebirth, the philosophical frontier, or a cultural horizon. We may pack with us Emerson, James, and Dewey, for instance. We may gain inspiration from them, utilize their categories and methods, quote their brilliant insights, and cite their work. These activities do seem familiar, I trust! But in proceeding this way, we may display knowledge, but fail to embody it. In proceeding this way, we may announce a new direction, but fail to take it. As a result, we easily may come to resemble not genuine explorers or original thinkers, but heavily laden campers in shiny, plush motor homes, rising, as Emerson put it, for another day of dependence and long apprenticeship—reciting quotations from "The American Scholar" but failing to capture its moving spirit in our lives.[9]

Moreover, we may do this despite the clear warnings of the American philosophical tradition itself. What the philosophers of earlier periods did, Dewey told us, is no longer called for, and so we now must direct its logic of experience to our own needs: "Emphasis must vary with the stress and special impact of the troubles which perplex men. Each age know its own ills, and seeks it own remedies."[10] If philosophy fails to do this, the result is a dreary, shopworn overtechnicality—a philosophy buried in the past and a philosophy that is anything but pragmatic.[11] In contrast, the pragmatic issue

---

8. William Carlos Williams, *The Embodiment of Knowledge* (New York: New Directions, 1974 [1928–30]), p. 60.

9. Ralph Waldo Emerson, "The American Scholar," *Selected Writings of Ralph Waldo Emerson*, ed. William H. Gilman (New York: New American Library, 1965 [1837]), p. 224.

10. John Dewey, "The Need for a Recovery of Philosophy," *John Dewey: The Middle Works, 1899–1924*, vol. 10 (Carbondale, Ill.: Southern Illinois University Press, 1980 [1917]), p. 46.

11. James, *Pluralistic Universe*, p. 13.

is this: What changes in our intellectual inheritance are now required by, and for, life today? In response, Dewey warned:

> Imaginative recovery of the bygone is indispensable to successful invasion of the future, but its status is that of an instrument. To ignore its import is the sign of an undisciplined agent; but to isolate the past, dwelling upon it for its own sake and giving it the eulogistic name of knowledge, is to substitute the reminiscence of old-age for effective intelligence.[12]

At the frontier of this effective intelligence, American philosophy must pack few quotations and footnotes. Accordingly, in large part I will travel lightly here, relying confidently on past study and collective understanding—not simply of Emerson, Thoreau, Peirce, James, Royce, Santayana, Dewey, Mead, Lewis, and Whitehead, but also earlier and later American philosophical writers. And when, perhaps bound by academic habits, I do not journey without citing these thinkers, I will recall them in the spirit of Whitman:

> Do I contradict myself?
> Very well then I contradict myself
> (I am large, I contain multitudes).[13]

In any case, such thought cannot and will not be so much brand new as remade, reconstructed, reappropriated. Emerson, the self-proclaimed enemy of quotations, understood this too, of course. He noted: "In fact, it is as difficult to appropriate the thoughts of others as it is to invent."[14]

The future of American philosophy, then, lies not simply in the (admittedly valuable) scholarly recalling, repeating, rehearsing, fine-tuning, or defending characteristically American thought. Instead, this future must be charted by using, widening, extending, and reappropriating classical American philosophy so as to transform intelligently our own lives in response to changing cultural conditions. This alone points American philosophy in genuinely new directions. This alone keeps American philosophy always in transition, always at the frontier.

However, it is not enough now simply to say all this, particularly in the abstract, perhaps with a devotional tone, and to sympathetic, well-meaning philosophers and other humanists. It may make for good conversation, but this conversational strategy, favored and employed by right-wing pragmatists

---

12. Dewey, "The Need for a Recovery of Philosophy," pp. 4, 10.
13. Whitman, *Leaves of Grass*, p. 51.
14. Ralph Waldo Emerson, *Letters and Social Aims* (New York: 1876), p. 28.

like Richard Rorty—if there can be left-wing Hegelians then surely there can be right-wing pragmatists—evades the demand for ongoing, critical cultural reconstruction.[15] In the work of right-wing pragmatists, the characteristically pragmatic emphasis on experience, inquiry, and criticism is simply missing in action, having been transformed and allowed to deteriorate into escapist postcard messages mailed from motor homes broken down near intellectual and cultural wilderness areas.

What else, then, does thinking in transition, appropriating the thought of others, entail? In his account of Daniel Boone in his moving book *In the American Grain*, William Carlos Williams articulated both this task and its moral and aesthetic difficulties:

> Boone had run past the difficulties encountered by his fellows in making the New World their own. . . . To Boone, the Indian was his greatest master. Not for himself surely to be an Indian, though they eagerly sought to adopt him into their tribes, but the reverse: to be himself in a new world, *Indianlike*.[16]

Forty years later, Gary Snyder raised this issue in similar terms:

> I would like,
> with a sense of helpful order,
> with respect for laws
> of nature,
> to help my land
> with a burn, a hot clean
> burn.
> And then
> it would be more
> like,
> when it belonged to the Indians.
> Before.[17]

Is this simply nostalgia, a different kind of tame, romantic postcard message, perhaps like that sent from Alaska by Richard Brautigan's character, Trout Fishing in America, in the novel of the same name?[18] It has been a long time since America "belonged" to the Indians, a time before the European

---

15. See especially Rorty's *Philosophy and the Mirror of Nature* (Princeton, N.J.: Princeton University Press, 1979) and *Contingency, Irony, and Solidarity* (Cambridge: Cambridge University Press, 1989). See also discussions of Rorty in chapters 1 and 6.
16. William Carlos Williams, *In the American Grain* (New York: New Directions, 1956), p. 137.
17. Gary Snyder, *Turtle Island* (New York: New Directions, 1974), p. 19.
18. Richard Brautigan, *Trout Fishing in America* (New York: Dell, 1967), p. 77.

invasion of the Americas. Then, of course, America often (though not always) was described and understood by European explorers as a frontier paradise and opportunity for wealth. In 1492, Columbus described the beauty, diversity, and richness of the New World:

> There are mountains of very great size and beauty, vast plains, groves, and very fruitful fields, admirably adapted for tillage, pasture, and habitation. The convenience and excellence of the harbours in this island, and the abundance of the rivers, so indispensable to the health of man, surpass anything that would be believed by one who had not seen it.[19]

Eleven years later, Amerigo Vespucci offered a similar account of this "terrestrial paradise":

> The land is very fertile, abounding in many hills and valleys, and in large rivers, and is irrigated by very refreshing springs. It is covered with extensive and dense forests . . . and full of every kind of wild beast. . . . [A]nd there are innumerable different kinds of fruits and herbs. . . . If they were our property, I do not doubt but that they would be useful to man.[20]

Three hundred sixty-five years later, at the 1968 Democratic Presidential Convention in Chicago, poet Allen Ginsberg succinctly questioned this line of thinking, asking: Who wants to own paradise, "Who wants to be President of the Garden of Eden?"[21]

Vespucci was right that America would be useful—to some people, at least. We must remember that the historical physical American frontier was experienced quite differently by enslaved Africans transported to America, by women journeying west, and by native peoples viewing a new kind of wilderness with an advancing rather than receding frontier.[22] Recall the words of Chief Seattle, necessarily but reluctantly signing a treaty in the Northwest in 1854:

> It matters little where we pass the remnant of our days. They will not be many. A few more moons; a few more winters. . . . But why should I mourn

---

19. Christopher Columbus, "Letter of Lord Raphael Sanchez, Treasurer to Ferdinand and Isabella, King and Queen of Spain, on his First Voyage," *New World Metaphysics*, ed. Giles Gunn (New York: Oxford University Press, 1981), p. 7.

20. Amerigo Vespucci, *Mundus Novus, New World Metaphysics*, pp. 11–12.

21. Allen Ginsberg, *The Fall of America: Poems of These States, 1965–1971* (New York: New Directions, 1972), p. 101.

22. See, for example, Lillian Schlissel, *Women's Diaries of the Westward Journey* (New York: Schocken Books, 1982), and Howard Zinn, *A People's History of the United States* (New York: Harper & Row, 1980).

at the untimely fate of my people? Tribe follows tribe, and nation follows nation, like the waves of the sea. It is the order of nature, and regret is useless. Your time of decay may be distant, but it will surely come, for even the White Man whose God walked and talked with him as friend with friend, cannot be exempt from the common destiny. We may be brothers after all.[23]

Surely *this* is not nostalgia. But, still the fact is that the much celebrated and analyzed American frontier,[24] the physical frontier and its particular kinds of opportunities for action, the open land and life to the west, is now long gone. Toxic chemicals routinely spill, flow, and seep into the great rivers, lakes, and ground water of the middle west. Massive incinerators burn poisoned soil in Pennsylvania, home of the Three Mile Island Nuclear Reactor and the country's first oil wells. Black clouds of pollution hang over Denver, capital city of the plains. The greater Los Angeles area and its ever-increasing millions of people continue a concrete sprawl across the desert, valleys, and coast. The Colorado, Snake, and Columbia are dammed. The Oregon Trail is an interstate freeway, and the once pristine eastern Oregon deserts are covered with litter and torn up by off-road vehicles. New housing developments, malls, office buildings, and militia compounds replace farms, forests, and wetlands. Even Alaska is crisscrossed more and more by people, pipelines, and planes. In short, the city on the hill, the United States of America, has sprawled from coast to coast, and there is no physical frontier and precious little nature left in "nature's nation." Don Henley and Glenn Frey wrote and sang the clear, sad truth in "The Last Resort:"

> They call it paradise, I don't know why.
> You call someplace paradise, kiss it goodbye.[25]

Is there a new American frontier? Was Alaska, as some claim, the last American frontier? Or is Jacques Cousteau right—is the new frontier undersea?

---

23. Chief Seattle, Oratory, *New World Metaphysics*, p. 284. Surprisingly similar and equally striking points about the flourishing and decay of schools or cultures of thought are made by William Carlos Williams in "The Pluralism of Experience," in *The Embodiment of Knowledge*, and by Sigurd Olson in "Frontiers," *Reflections from the North Country* (New York: Knopf, 1976).

24. See, for example, the following: Arthur A. Ekirch Jr., *The Idea of Progress in America, 1815–1860* (New York: Columbia University Press, 1944); Henry Nash Smith, *Virgin Land: The American West as Symbol and Myth* (Cambridge, Mass.: Harvard University Press, 1950); George R. Taylor, ed., *The Turner Thesis* (Boston: Heath, 1956); Frederick Jackson Turner, *The Frontier in American History* (New York: Holt, Rinehart & Winston, 1962).

25. Don Henley and Glenn Frey, "The Last Resort," words and music. © 1976, 1978 Cass County Music/Red Cloud Music. All Rights Reserved. Used by Permission.

Or was Star Trek on target—is space the final frontier? Or, finally, is some inner (rather than outer) space the last frontier, beckoning "Inward Bound" enthusiasts and pioneers to new drugs, new religions, new genetic and cybernetic possibilities, and new computer-linked "virtual communities" full of promises for our terminal lives?

Surely remaining pockets of wilderness, the sea, space, and the human mind itself all are ripe for inquiry and exploration. In this sense, they unquestionably are new frontiers.

However, there is, in addition, another American frontier, another zone that continues to mark the limit of our expansion, development, and civilization. Pervasive, pressing, significant, and experienced with overwhelming immediacy, it is a cultural rather than a physical frontier. There is no more open land or new frontier. Instead, we must forge our lives and communities where we are; we must make it here. Said differently, collectively "making it here" is the new frontier, and it must become our new destination. In short, this cultural frontier constitutes the boundary or gap between the actually existing American *society*, on the one hand, and realization of a genuinely American (and global) *community*, on the other.

Community, Identity, and Difference

This notion of community, and the contrast of community with the notion of society, are brilliantly articulated and deeply developed in classical American philosophy. In this tradition, this distinction between society and community has profound theoretical and practical importance. As set forth by American philosophers, an association is a genuine community only to the extent that its members consciously share numerous, varied interests and interact fully and freely with other associations. A society is a community only when its members imaginatively share inclusive ideals and concern for the self-realization of one another, and actively participate in the direction of those social forces that shape their lives. As such, any future development of community is identical with, rather than opposed to, the future development of genuine individuals—both as individuals and as members of communities. Community and individuality are two sides of the same coin.

In "The Body and the Members," Josiah Royce outlined such a community in terms of selves who seek meaning and ideally enlarge their own lives so as to share an ideal common past and future. Such a community, Royce explained, requires: selves capable of ideally and imaginatively extending themselves into the past and future; self-directing and cooperating selves capable of, and engaged consciously in, communication and appreciative coordination with one another; and selves who share goals and at least some common ideal experience. Concluding that a highly organized society is by no means identical with a community in this more precise sense, Royce added that "There is a strong mutual opposition between the social tendencies which secure cooperation on a vast scale, and the very conditions which so interest the individual in the common life of his community that it forms part of his own ideally extended life."[26]

Because the self is irreducibly and intrinsically social (as Mead,[27] like Dewey, Royce, and, to some extent, Peirce, set forth), this has fundamental personal as well as social significance. But although the attitudes and behaviors of an organized social group are fundamental in the process of self-formation, when the social group fails to be a genuine community, then the selves it helps form fail to be genuine individuals. At times Mead obscures this point by failing to distinguish, as Dewey and Royce do, the notion of society from that of community in this more precise sense. Mead observes, for instance, that "the organized community or social group" gives to the individual unity of self.[28] But, in the absence of real community, these selves are incomplete and undeveloped, deprived and unfulfilled, isolated and, as Dewey described so well, lost.[29] The self, that is, arises in society, but individuals—selves with individuality—require (and, in turn, sustain) communities. For individuality to flourish, social groups and associations must become communities.

This need was thoroughly grasped by John Dewey in his writings on freedom, individualism, liberalism, and the public. Writing about American education, he observed that we stand at the frontier of culture, a culture still to be created and achieved: "To transmute a society built on an industry which is not yet humanized into a society which wields its knowledge and its industrial power in behalf of a democratic culture requires the courage of an inspired imagination."[30]

Although this observation may provide a beginning for "a culture stripped of egoistic illusions," it is only the barest of beginnings. Sadly, we have not yet substantially developed such a culture—what Royce termed "a

---

26. Josiah Royce, *The Problem of Christianity* (Chicago: University of Chicago Press, 1968 [1913]), p. 262. Further references are abbreviated "*PC*" in this chapter.

27. George Herbert Mead, *Mind, Self, and Society: From the Standpoint of a Social Behaviorist* (Chicago: University of Chicago Press, 1934), p. 331.

28. Ibid., p. 154.

29. John Dewey, *Individualism: Old and New, John Dewey: The Later Works, 1925–1953*, vol. 5 (Carbondale, Ill.: Southern Illinois University Press, 1984 [1930]), pp. 66–76. See also David L. Norton's "Community as the Sociality of True Individuals," *Democracy and Moral Development* (Berkeley: University of California Press, 1991).

30. John Dewey, "American Education and Culture," *John Dewey: The Middle Works, 1899–1924*, vol. 10 (Carbondale, Ill.: Southern Illinois University Press, 1980 [1916]), p. 198.

humanized society" or what Dewey labeled "the great community." In fact, in many respects it seems that we have made little if any recent progress. Perhaps since Dewey's death we have even lost ground to a spreading cultural wilderness. We are, after all, a society marked by: growing pollution, illiteracy, crime, drug abuse, terrorism, and institutional, personal, physical, and psychic violence; increasing polarization of wealth, cultural disenfranchisement, personal isolation, and often merely formal democracy; and leaders who govern more with image and power than with imagination and principle. In this context, Dewey's meliorism—not infrequently mistaken for simple optimism—feels out of tune to many. Paul Simon's "American Tune" about the shattered dreams of battered souls who have "lived so well so long" conveys a mood both more like that of Chief Seattle but also more contemporary:

> We come on a ship they call the Mayflower
> We come on the ship that sailed the moon
> We come in the age's most uncertain hour
> and sing an American tune
> But it's all right, it's all right
> You can't be forever blessed
> Still, tomorrow's going to be another working day
> And I'm trying to get some rest
> That's all I'm trying to get some rest.[31]

Classical American philosophy has provided us with a rich vision of fuller lives. Now, how can we appropriate and act to realize this vision? How, in Dewey's words, can we today convert the Great Society into the Great Community?[32] What should be our new direction?

These questions must be understood against the background of Emerson's and Dewey's calls for each generation or age to address its own problems with its own stress and slant. I agree, and so seek to reappropriate this view. In doing this, I wholeheartedly accept and recommend Williams's advice to those seeking education in America: "Let scholarship learn me—Knowledge must be proven to us, not we to it."[33]

---

31. Paul Simon, "America," *There Goes Rhymin' Simon* (Warner Bros., 1973), track 6. Words and music c. (1973) Paul Simon.
32. John Dewey, *The Public and Its Problems, John Dewey: The Later Works, 1925–1953*, vol. 2 (Carbondale, Ill.: Southern Illinois University Press, 1984 [1927]). Hereafter abbreviated "*P&IP*; *LW* 2" in this chapter. For an interesting discussion of different notions of community in more recent American thought, see Robert Booth Fowler, *The Dance with Community: The Contemporary Debate in American Political Thought* (Lawrence, Kan.: University Press of Kansas, 1991).
33. Williams, *The Embodiment of Knowledge*, pp. 44, 60.

There is no easy answer or sure strategy, of course, but for Royce and Dewey (and for many other great American thinkers), communication is a crucial prerequisite for community. Imagination, interpretation and inquiry are important, even necessary (though not sufficient), conditions for the creation of community. This view, insightfully set forth and compellingly developed, is, I think, deeply instructive and valuable for practice. For example, Royce's first requirement or prerequisite condition for the possibility of community is the existence of "the power of an individual self to extend his life, in ideal fashion, so as to regard it as including past and future events which lie far away in time, and which he does not now personally remember." Royce's selves thus say of distant past and distant future events " 'I view that event as a part of my own life' " (*PC*:252).

Is this possible? Royce told us that "we all know" that this power exists, even if, apparently, it is not always exercised. This power of ideal extension of the self, Royce claimed (drawing on Peirce's triadic account of interpretation), rests on the principle that the self is "no mere datum." Instead, the self "is in its essence a life which is interpreted, and which interprets itself, and which, apart from some sort of ideal interpretation, is a mere flight of ideas, or a meaningless flow of feelings, or a vision that sees nothing, or else a barren abstract conception" (*PC*:253).

Is Royce's view correct? The key issue is not Royce's recognition of the irreducible centrality of interpretation, but rather his insistence on the identity of different selves, the erasure of differences (and, in Peircean terms, the overcoming of Secondness). Though I agree, as I've said above, that the self is not a "mere datum" and that a self may, or, perhaps, must search for meaning that extends beyond his or her own life, I have to admit that I find nothing in my experience to support a belief in a self's power of ideal extension—as Royce understood it. In interpreting past and future, and in narratings of my own life, in myriad ways I am linked, bound, connected, and related— even constituted—in, through, and to the lives of other selves. But I do not and cannot *identify* these different lives with myself, *identify* these different events as events of *my own* life. Instead, it is precisely because these related events and related selves and lives are *other* events and *other* selves and *other* lives that I may develop as my self, this particular self, this different self. This process, importantly, involves as much contestation, opposition, destruction, and suffering as it does consensus, harmony, determination, and satisfaction.

Despite his claims that his view does not slight the actual variety and differences among real selves, or preclude their individuality, Royce's discussion of the ideally extended identity of a self—plural selves—in fact, and in practice, does involve loss of the self through its submergence, through submergence of its difference. This type of understanding of identity and difference suffers from an insufficiently robust conception of difference—a conception that mistakes the practical solidarity of agents for the theoretical identity of selves.[34]

As a result, Royce's first prerequisite condition for the creation of community—the requirement that selves possess the power to ideally extend their lives in the past and future so as to identify their lives with the lives of others—is problematic. But, does my objection perhaps simply mark a limit or deficiency of my own imagination, or some bias against the big, the general, or the whole? *I* doubt it, of course, but even if I could ideally extend myself in this way, I would not want to and, more importantly, I would not see it as a necessary precondition for the possibility of community. In fact, in many cases I think the possibility of community may depend on the inability or the refusal to ideally extend one's self or "identify" with other selves and affirm their actions. The differences and resistances that community presupposes do not all need to be transcended through, or in, idealization. Community, that is, requires difference no less than identity. So, the possible creation of community, I think, does not require that you identify as *your* actions, for instance, the actions of Christopher Columbus, Cotton Mather, William Penn, Carrie Nation, Geronimo, W. E. B. DuBois, Emily Dickinson, Theodore Roosevelt, Al Capone, Stan Laurel, Louis Armstrong, Rachel Carson, Bill Gates, Randy Shilts, Tonya Harding, Pat Buchanan, Janet Reno, or the current Executive Director of the American Philosophical Association. It does not require that you ideally incorporate into *your* life—constitute as your life—the lives of others. There may be a reason to say that these other selves are connected to you. However, in order to understand or evaluate or live with these other selves—in order to strive with or against or apart from them—there is no necessity to identify one's self with these other selves— to hold that they *are* you.

Communities of memory and communities of hope do not require this. They do not have to be communities of identity, communities of a single identity. Indeed, they must not be this. What now is needed in order to transform society into genuine community—into a community of communities—is not so much the *ideal* extension of selves, but the *actual* extension of social practices and institutions so as to create and sustain participation by, and benefit of, all members of the society. Royce, I think, was too worried, mistakenly worried, about exclusionary *conceptions* of the self—conceptions

---

34. For a strong defense of Royce, see Frank M. Oppenheim's "A Roycean Response to the Challenge of Individualism" *Beyond Individualism: Toward a Retrieval of Moral Discourse in America*, ed. Donald L. Gelphi, S.J. (Notre Dame, Ind.: University of Notre Dame Press, 1989), pp. 87–119. Oppenheim assumes that self-affirmation must be at odds with community-affirmation, and seems to think that shared communal action is possible only if there is shared psychic identity.

of the self that prevent one's ideal identification with others. He was not sufficiently worried about exclusionary *practices* of society—practices of a society that prevent some from actually living in harmony (but not identity) with others. In the context of his social philosophy, this constitutes his idealism—and the difference between idealism and thoroughgoing pragmatism.

Is it necessary here to interrupt in order to issue a warning? To ears unaccustomed to the American philosophical tradition, this language of community, inquiry, and reconstruction may sound overly optimistic, insufficiently dark, too little oriented to loss. Consider Foucault's advice: "The farthest I would go is to say that perhaps one must not be for consensuality, but one must be against nonconsensuality."[35] In this context, the American pragmatic tradition may seem too ready to assume and embrace the complete desirability of consensuality. However, be forewarned. This is not the case. Despite James's subtitle to his *Pragmatism*, pragmatism really is an old name for a *new* way of thinking. As Nietzsche remarked, we do not hear new music well. Accordingly, let me stress that this pragmatism is *not* a philosophy of universalism, optimism, identity and consensuality. I say this despite the fact—indeed, in face of the fact—that today professional philosophy is experiencing a kudzu-like growth of so-called "neopragmatist," "communitarian," and "liberal" attempts to demonstrate that pluralism can harmonize all differences, do away with all exclusions (or at least all important ones), and put an end to suffering and tragedy.[36] This is not so. American philosophy does not speak the language of simple optimism because it recognizes that efforts to establish community irreducibly and intrinsically produce and involve oppositions, coercions, subjugations, and exclusions that cannot be overcome. Moreover (and more darkly still), this recognition itself is made in a fully self-reflexive manner: For pragmatists, this recognition itself is understood as just as exclusionary and "pathogenic" as the community it recognizes or the "system of values that it questions." Further, this self-reflexivity means that to see darkly

---

35. Michel Foucault, quoted in J. Donald Moon, *Constructing Community* (Princeton, N.J.: Princeton University Press, 1993), p. 176. See the discussion of pragmatism and postmodernism in chapter 5.

36. From among many, see for example the following. J. Donald Moon, *Constructing Community*; Gene Outka and John P. Reeder Jr., eds., *Prospects for a Common Morality* (Princeton, N.J.: Princeton University Press, 1993); Marion Smiley, *Moral Responsibility and the Boundaries of Community: Power and Accountability from a Pragmatic Point of View* (Chicago: University of Chicago Press, 1992); David Held, "Contesting Democracy: Theoretical Disputes," *Prospects for Democracy* (Stanford, Calif.: Stanford University Press, 1993); Anne Phillips, *Democracy and Difference* (University Park, Penn.: Pennsylvania State University Press, 1993); James Fishkin, *The Dialogue of Justice: Toward a Self-Reflective Society* (New Haven, Conn.: Yale University Press, 1992).

the desperation by which we have sought to see in the dark is still to see desperately and still to see in darkness.[37]

This is not the language of simple optimism. It is the language of questioning and coping, the optimism made possible by genealogy and critical reconstruction, the reflection of a philosophy at once masked and disrobed. In Foucault's work, for example, this is the language of "The Masked Philosopher," an "optimism" "that so many things can be changed, fragile as they are, bound up more with circumstance than necessities, more arbitrary than self-evident, more a matter of complex but temporary, historical circumstance, than with inevitable constants."[38] In Dewey's philosophy, this is the language of localism and meliorism, a language of intellectual recovery and social action, the language that I have interrupted and now resume.

By concentrating on the establishment of an ideal self, rather than the transformation of actual social conditions, as fundamental for the possibility of community, Royce offered us a political as well as a philosophical idealism. He wrote that it is *not* "the fleeting individual of to-day" but "the ideally extended self that is worthy to belong to a significant community" (*PC*:256). In contrast, I believe that "the fleeting individual"—and there simply is no other sort of individual—*is* worthy of significant community, and that any idealized unity or harmony of selves is actually possible only if and when real, fleeting social conditions allow and sustain harmonious, inclusive interests and ways of life. Without this, those who have been denied full membership in a society will not likely identify with those who exclude them. Rather, at best, they will identify with, and demand, social change in the service of more fully communal values. They will say to themselves, as Langston Hughes observed in *The Black Man Speaks*, that genuine democracy cannot mean "everybody but me."[39]

Roadblocks to Community: Economics and Communication

As long as actual social conditions produce and reproduce selves with economic, political, religious, ethnic, racial, familial, environmental, technological, and sexual interests and powers that are in fundamental conflict with one another, neither actual community nor ideal self extension is possible

---

37. Charles E. Scott, *The Question of Ethics* (Bloomington, Ind.: Indiana University Press, 1990), pp. 1, 212.
38. Michel Foucault, "The Masked Philosopher," *Politics, Philosophy, Culture: Interviews and Other Writings, 1977–1984* (New York: Routledge, 1990 [1980]), pp. 323–30.
39. Langston Hughes, *The Black Man Speaks* (Boston: Heath, 1952), p. 23.

(except perhaps for small, sheltered groups). It is now the task of education in the broadest sense[40] to identify, to radically resist, and to begin to alter these continuing conditions that block community and intimacy and foster domination and opposition. Philosophers, if they are to be philosophers of community, must accept this task. Their inquiry must be countermemory and criticism, and must issue in public communication that itself effectively resists containment (*D&E: MW* 9).[41]

The consequences of this position are far-reaching for individuals. Despite the naturally conservative force of habits, individuals must continuously reshape and question their beliefs and values. Moreover, individuals must hold beliefs and values in a manner consistent with the fallibilist, anti-absolutist, self-questioning spirit of experience and inquiry. Finally, decisively, individuals must embody in their daily lives these beliefs and values.

This requires changes in communication and education, and, in this sense, the consequences of the above view extend far beyond individual life. Like Royce, Dewey saw a life of communion and communication—selves engaged in communication as Royce puts it—as a necessary condition for the existence of community. Unlike Royce, who simply briefly mentioned actual communication as a condition for the possibility of community and seemed to take for granted that this condition is satisfied, Dewey discussed the practical, educational need to create and develop the "highest and most difficult kind of inquiry and a subtle, delicate, vivid and responsive art of communication" (*P&IP; LW* 2:350).

In "The Search for the Great Community" in *The Public and Its Problems*, Dewey discussed the need to overcome deeply rooted emotional and intellectual habits that now limit free communication so as to apply an experimental method of inquiry to and in human concerns. In turn, he argued, the results of this inquiry must be disseminated so as to produce genuinely public judgment and opinion. Furthermore, both the inquiry and the dissemination of its results must be freed from manipulation and distortion by pecuniary interests, and must be presented so as to reach men's and women's *lives*. This process of effective presentation, Dewey said, is art: "Artists have always been the real purveyors of news" and thus, for Dewey, Walt Whitman

---

40. John Dewey, *Democracy and Education, John Dewey: The Middle Works, 1899–1924*, vol. 9 (Carbondale, Ill.: Southern Illinois University Press, 1980 [1916]), p. 9. Hereafter abbreviated "*D&E; MW* 9" in this chapter.

41. While both Dewey and Foucault characterize philosophy as criticism, and although there surely are parallels and overlaps between these views, Richard Rorty just as surely is wrong to claim that Foucault has traveled the very same road that Dewey took years earlier. Richard Rorty, "Social Method, Social Hope," *Consequences of Pragmatism* (Minneapolis: University of Minnesota Press, 1982), p. 207.

is the seer of democracy that achieves community (*P&IP*; *LW* 2:350). It is interesting to note that there are important parallels here between Dewey and William Carlos Williams. However, these parallels apparently were not evident to Williams, who complained that Dewey looked for solutions to educational problems in psychology and sociology when he should have sought solutions in poetry: "Philosophy could not be better occupied than in translating [the poetic forms of an age] to its idioms."[42]

To arrive at a solution to this problem of education, whether through philosophy or through poetry, is no easy task. It cannot be reached by armchair philosophizing or speculative theorizing. Dewey put this nicely: "Not all who say Ideals, Ideals, shall enter the kingdom of the ideal, but those who know and who respect the roads that conduct to the kingdom."[43] The roads to the kingdom of community are education, communication, and economic equity; they are prerequisites of democracy as a way of life, prerequisites of what Dewey called the formation of the Public and the transition from a Great Society to a Great Community. It is hard to satisfy these prerequisites.[44] The roadblocks to education, communication, and economic equity are many: exclusion from participation and denial of access; control of publicity and the dissemination of knowledge; manipulation of opinion and thought for selfish economic ends; interference with experimentation and dishonest research; ignorance and inarticulateness; distance, time, and cultural difference; conservative habits of belief and emotion; fear, greed, and selfishness; specialization and mediation; and, illusions of intellectual freedom in the absence of known external oppression.

These are immense obstacles, and the weight of history is on the side of those who are cynical about the prospects of overcoming them. Pragmatism, a faith in intelligence, carries no overarching or advance guarantees. It provides no specific assurances about the future existence or expansion of democratic life. Indeed, it provides no general warrant for any complacent expectation of progress. It finds nothing in human history, human nature, or the world situation today to support a rosy or comfortable vision of the future. Such mistaken visions merely treat present hopes as future realities. This faith in community, then, supports neither utopian thinking nor even optimism in the abstract.

---

42. Williams, *The Embodiment of Knowledge*, p. 7.

43. John Dewey, "The Pragmatic Acquiescence," *John Dewey: The Later Works, 1925–1953*, vol. 3 (Carbondale, Ill.: Southern Illinois University Press, 1984 [1927], p. 151.

44. Here I draw on "Democratic Challenges and Democratic Methods," included in my "Democracy as a Way of Life," *Philosophy and the Reconstruction of Culture: Pragmatic Essays after Dewey*, ed. John J. Stuhr (Albany: State University of New York Press, 1993), pp. 51–54.

This faith also stands in opposition to all pessimism, cynicism, and fatalism. It opposes every uncomfortable, but still in consequence complacent, dystopian future vision. Such mistaken visions merely treat present contingencies—for instance, social relations of power and personal traits of stupidity, selfishness, impatience, and laziness—as necessities. There is every reason to recognize soberly the serious problems that these realities pose for democracy, but there is no reason to treat them as fixed and impossible to change.

At the same time it is important to understand that the roadblocks to community now include existing educational, communication, and economic systems—"public" education, "free" communication, and "free" markets. These potential means to, and instruments of, community now function as key components of a cultural network at odds with a more fully democratic way of life. Criticizing the extensive, happy faith of our "democratic progenitors" in America, Dewey warned darkly:

> They certainly were not wrong in emphasizing the need of a free press and of common public schools to provide conditions favorable to democracy. But to them the enemy of freedom of the press was official governmental censorship and control; they did not foresee the non-political causes that might restrict its freedom, nor the economic factors that would put a heavy premium on centralization. And they failed to see how education in literacy could become a weapon in the hands of an oppressive government. . . . [W]hile free institutions over a wide territory are not possible without a mechanism, like the press, for quick and extensive communication of ideas and information, and without general literacy to take advantage of the mechanism, yet these very factors create a problem for a democracy instead of providing a final solution.[45]

In this light, how can we today produce more fully a genuinely communal social life, a democratic way of life? While "the struggle for democracy has to be maintained on as many fronts as culture has aspects" (*F&C; LW* 13:186), three problems stand out. The first is economic, and concerns what Dewey called the scandal of private appropriation of socially produced values, the emergence of the "business mind" and corporate mentality, and the narrow use of intelligence for selfish ends and class interests—all "economic

---

45. John Dewey, *Freedom and Culture, John Dewey: The Later Works, 1925–1953*, vol. 13 (Carbondale, Ill.: Southern Illinois University Press, 1988 [1939]), pp. 91–92. Hereafter abbreviated "*F&C; LW* 13" in this chapter. Many commentators have failed to note the fact that Dewey recognized and grappled with this problem. As an example, see John Patrick Diggins, *The Promise of Pragmatism: Modernism and the Crisis of Knowledge and Authority* (Chicago: University of Chicago Press, 1994), pp. 303–4.

developments which could not possibly have been anticipated when our political forms took shape" (*F&C*; *LW* 13:107). Today outdated ideas of economic "liberty" and "free" markets—the same ideas that Dewey debunked repeatedly in *Individualism: Old and New*, *Liberalism and Social Action*, and *Freedom and Culture*—still grip our minds and conduct.[46] But these ideas correspond less and less with actual social life. Instead, the gaps between wealthy and poor, idle and meaningfully active, and powerful and powerless, have never been greater, in this country and abroad. The poverty and insecurity of much of the economic underclass has never seemed more permanent or hopeless. Our institutionalized disregard, intolerance, and waste of the welfare of the sick, the weak, the hungry, and the homeless have never been more far-reaching. And, the cynical equation of maximum material consumption (including "readymade intellectual goods"), private prosperity, and pecuniary profit with the good life has never been more commonplace. Like Dewey, we must admit that "as liberty has been practiced in industry and trade, the economic inequalities produced have reacted against the existence of equality of opportunity" (*F&C*; *LW* 13:110).[47] Unlike Dewey, however, today we must "admit that our outer civilization is attaining an inner culture which corresponds to it, however much we might disesteem the quality of that culture."[48] Still, this situation is pathetic and outrageous, and it must be intolerable to anyone really committed to democracy. In short, we must invent ways to make our economy democratic and our rhetoric of equality of opportunity a reality.

There is a second problem that seems to threaten and undermine democratic life much more now than when Dewey confronted it. It cuts

---

46. Of course, outdated notions of community and democracy as a way of life also grip our minds and conduct. This is evident in many contemporary discussions of the relations between democracy and economics, especially socialism. These discussions, typically fixated on social contract liberalism and communitarianism, ignore pragmatic notions of democracy, community, and socialism. See, for example, Richard J. Arneson, "Socialism as the Extension of Democracy" and Joshua Cohen and Joel Rogers, "Associations and Democracy," in *Liberalism and the Economic Order*, ed. Ellen Frankel Paul, Fred D. Miller Jr., and Jeffrey Paul (Cambridge: Cambridge University Press, 1993). For a contrasting view, see Frank Cunningham, *The Real World of Democracy Revisited* (Atlantic Highlands, N.J.: Humanities Press, 1994). For an illuminating, successful contrast, see William E. Connolly, "Democracy, Equality, Normality," *The Ethos of Pluralization* (Minneapolis: University of Minnesota, 1995), pp. 75–104.

47. See Judith Shklar's discussion of "earning" and the right to work as an essential component of democratic citizenship. *American Citizenship: The Quest for Inclusion* (Cambridge, Mass.: Harvard University Press, 1991).

48. Dewey, *Individualism: Old and New*, p. 69. See the discussion of the "business mind" in chapter 1.

across our culture and concerns what Dewey called propaganda, cheap amusement, and the control of opinion.[49] Today naive beliefs about "freedom" of thought and "free" expression, "public" opinion, and "self-determination"—the same beliefs that Dewey thoroughly criticized in *Freedom and Culture* and *The Public and Its Problems* and many subsequent essays—still shape our images of ourselves and our society. Decades later, Dewey's criticism of the media and its social consequences reads as though it were written yesterday:

> Unless there are methods for detecting the energies which are at work and tracing them through an intricate network of interactions to their consequences, what passes as public opinion will be "opinion" in its derogatory sense rather than truly public, no matter how widespread the opinion is. . . . Opinion casually formed and formed under the direction of those who have something at stake in having a lie believed can be *public* opinion only in name. . . . The smoothest road to control of political conduct is by control of opinion. As long as interests of pecuniary profit are powerful, and a public has not located and identified itself, those who have this interest will have an unresisted motive for tampering with the springs of political action in all that affects them. (*P&IP*; *LW* 2:346, 348)

> Aside from the fact that the press may distract with trivialities or be an agent of a faction, or be an instrument of inculcating ideas in support of the hidden interest of a group or class (all in the name of public interest), the wide-world present scene is such that individuals are overwhelmed and emotionally confused by publicized reverberation of isolated events. . . . Before we engage in too much pity for the inhabitants of our rural regions before the days of invention of modern devices for circulation of information, we should recall that they knew more about the things that affected their own lives than the city dweller of today is likely to know about the causes of his affairs. They did not possess nearly as many separate items of information, but they were compelled to know, in the sense of understanding, the conditions that bore upon the conduct of their own affairs. Today the influences that affect the actions performed by individuals are so remote as to be unknown. We are at the mercy of events acting upon us in unexpected, abrupt, and violent ways. (*F&C*; *LW* 13:92, 94)

---

49. Dewey, "The New Paternalism," *John Dewey: The Middle Works, 1899-1924*, vol. 11 (Carbondale, Ill.: Southern Illinois University Press, 1982 [1918]), p. 118; *The Public and Its Problems*, pp. 321, 348; "A Critique of American Civilization," *John Dewey: The Later Works, 1925–1953*, vol. 3, p. 141; *Ethics, John Dewey: The Later Works, 1925–1953*, vol. 7 (Carbondale, Ill.: Southern Illinois University Press, 1985 [1932]), p. 361; and *Freedom and Culture*, p. 168.

Dewey's analysis is echoed—usually unconsciously—by more recent critical studies of communications and the media.[50] For example, asserting that "the communications environment as a whole produces an ambience for the promotion of consumer capitalism" and the special interests of commercial enterprise, Douglas Kellner argues that "the conflicts between commerce and communication are built into the system of commercial broadcasting developed in the United States." He concludes that "a severe imbalance between capitalism and democracy, between commerce and journalism, has occurred, such that capital and commerce dominate democracy and journalism. . . . Unless the media become responsible, investigative, and critical of the powers that be, there is no hope that a functioning, viable, and genuine democracy might someday exist in the United States."[51]

For the first time in human history, as Dewey noted decades ago, it is now possible for totalitarian governments to claim legitimacy based on the active consent of those governed. To a large extent, this consent, as much as the claim to legitimacy, is a media creation. In this spirit, John Fiske observes: "To make sense of the world is to exert power over it, and to circulate that sense socially is to exert power over those who use that sense as a way of coping with their daily lives."[52] However, our systems of communication

---

50. See, for example, the following: Douglas Kellner, *Media Culture: Cultural Studies, Identity and Politics Between the Modern and the Postmodern* (New York: Routledge, 1995) and *Television and the Crisis of Democracy* (Boulder, Colo.: Westview Press, 1990); John Fiske, *Media Matters: Everyday Culture and Political Change* (Minneapolis: University of Minnesota, 1994); Stanley Aronowitz, Barbara Martinsons and Michael Menser, eds., *Technoscience and Cyberculture* (New York: Routledge, 1996); David Morley and Kevin Robins, *Spaces of Identity: Global Media, Electronic Landscapes and Cultural Boundaries* (New York: Routledge, 1995); James Carey, *Communication as Culture* (Boston: Unwin Hyman, 1989); Mike Featherstone, *Consumer Culture and Postmodernism* (London: Sage Publishers, 1991); E. Ann Kaplan, *Rocking Around the Clock: Music Television, Postmodernism, and Consumer Culture* (New York: Methuen, 1987); Neil Postman, *Amusing Ourselves to Death* (New York: Viking, 1985); Michael Schudson, *Advertising: The Uneasy Persuasion* (New York: Basic Books, 1984); David Sholle and Stan Denski, *Media Education and the (Re)Production of Culture* (Westport, Conn.: Bergin and Garvey, 1994). See also Lenore Langsdorf and Andrew R. Smith, eds., *Recovering Pragmatism's Voice: The Classical Tradition, Rorty, and the Philosophy of Communication* (Albany: State University of New York Press, 1995); James B. Twitchell, *Adcult USA: The Triumph of Advertising in American Culture* (New York: Columbia University Press, 1995).

51. Kellner, *Television and the Crisis of Democracy*, pp. 90–91, 95, 173. Kellner concludes with a few suggestions "toward a democratic communication and information." These suggestions, all rooted in the possibilities of new information and communication technologies, may appear hopes rather than strategies to the extent that they are separated from larger economic and educational issues. Thus, Arthur Kroker emphasizes how these technologies may produce "virtual capitalism" and a "new virtual class war" instead of democracy. "Virtual Capitalism," *Technoscience and Cyberculture*, p. 175.

52. Fiske, *Media Matters*, p. 3.

rarely produce any such genuine, informed, critical consent. Instead, we are the unwitting, usually unconscious, targets of powerful public relations techniques and subtle marketing campaigns that promote everything from automobiles to philosophies, luxury cruises to news magazines, and domestic wines to foreign wars. We are inundated by influential sound bites and carefully controlled images that wash over us but do not wash us clean. We have become habituated to institutionalized restrictions and private economic influences on the gathering and dissemination of information. And we are happy consumers of entertainment, constantly craving and everywhere institutionalizing it (rather than criticism)—even in our schools. Unlike Dewey, we almost have given up concern for the eclipse of a community or public and effective publicity. Still, we must realize that this state of affairs is incompatible with a democratic way of life: In short, philosophers who take community seriously must find ways to transform mass communications and mass media—the whole "media system,"[53] an even wider information production system, or, most broadly, an entire media culture—into *public* communications and *public* media—communications and media of, by, and for a public. While there is good reason to think this is possible, there is at least as good reason to think it is only barely possible. First, the capacity of the media to contain its potential critics—to turn its would-be critics into its programming, its audience, or both—is remarkably high. Second, the capacity of the media to marginalize its critics, usually intellectuals, is also extremely high. When an intellectual becomes a celebrity or is recognized by the media as an expert, this frequently only "signifies she or he is qualified to contribute to the ideology that television, print, and radio news is factual. In this instance, professional credentials are mechanisms of the media's as much as the individual's legitimacy."[54] Finally, the capacity of the media to co-opt its celebrity "critics" is equally great. Mark C. Taylor's and Esa Saarinen's *Imagologies: Media Philosophy* constitutes a wonderful case-study of this phenomenon. The book or "antibook"—its unnumbered pages are filled with bold diagrams, drawings, references to gossip columns about one of the authors

---

53. Leo Bogart, *Commercial Culture: The Media System and the Public Interest* (New York: Oxford University Press, 1995). Although Bogart makes no mention of Dewey or pragmatism, his analysis of the media and its relation to an advertising-driven "culture of consumption" closely parallels and develops in greater detail Dewey's general concerns and his more specific observations, including his discussion of the transformation in America of the duty to be thrifty into a social duty to spend and consume. Bogart calls for "media criticism" and a new "national media policy"—a set of government policies to correct flaws that he argues cannot be corrected in the marketplace.

54. Stanley Aronowitz and William DiFazio, *The Jobless Future: Sci-Tech and the Dogma of Work* (Minneapolis: University of Minnesota Press, 1995), p. 182.

and his wife, unusual margins and type fonts, photographs, diary entries, e-mail reproductions, class notes beamed across an ocean by satellite, and a fashionable color photograph of the authors—breathlessly promotes imagologies as replacements for philosophy. Observing that philosophy today is unmarketable and that Enlightenment and critical thought no longer automatically sell, the authors write that "the challenge is to create a vision that sells":

> To sell your product, you must get down to business and take advertising and marketing seriously. . . . One would have thought that someone would have done superbly in the United States what I've done in Finland—broken out of the academy into the media—radio, TV, newspapers, gossip columns—to assume a celebrity status that makes it possible to serve as a critical commentator on manners, morals and politics, in the language of our age. In this way, the very title, "philosopher" takes its place in the public's awareness next to titles like "businessman," "artist," "rockstar," and "politician." The Andy Warhol of philosophy, the Madonna of philosophy: that's what is needed. Media philosophy in the USA and for the USA.[55]

Despite this hype, there is a difference between a philosophy's marketplace price and its pragmatic "cash value," a difference between taking communication and marketing *seriously* and taking communication and marketing *critically*. When a philosophy seeks to erase this difference, then no matter how much it sells, it contains nothing of value for community and a democratic way of life.

Roadblocks to Community: Education

The third problem concerns education and the ways in which the creation of community constitutes a challenge to education. In its broadest sense, education is the creation of habits of mind and character, and in this context all social institutions and arrangements—not just the schools—"are educational in the sense that they operate to form attitudes, dispositions, abilities and disabilities that constitute a concrete personality."[56] In this light, community and democracy simply stand for a particular sort of education; community provides a basis for a particular educational principle, measure, and policy. The principle is this: The social aim of education is the production of

---

55. Mark C. Taylor and Esa Saarinen, *Imagologies: Media Philosophy* (New York: Routledge, 1994). See the discussion of the Humanities, Inc. in chapter 1.
56. John Dewey, "Democracy and Educational Administration," *John Dewey: The Later Works, 1925–1953*, vol. 11 (Carbondale, Ill.: Southern Illinois University Press, 1987 [1937]), p. 221.

democratic attitudes, dispositions, and abilities—the free interaction and participation of individuals and their mutual interpenetration of interests in, and through, shared community life. This communal or democratic educational principle receives little more than lip-service from the most powerful educational institutions in America today—the economic system, the government, the military, the media, the family and neighborhood, and the school. To this extent, remarkably, America today is committed neither to democratic education nor to community and democracy. Any democratic reconstruction of American society is one with the democratic reconstruction of these institutions. And this, in turn, involves nothing less than the thoroughgoing change and adoption on all cultural fronts of democratic educational principles and their democratic social aims.

Dewey's philosophy of education constitutes an extended argument for this change—social change that employs democratic means to serve the democratic, community ends. How can social life best renew itself? This is the inescapable, central problem for social inquiry concerned with community. It is, Dewey said, an educational problem, and his response to this problem, particularly in *Democracy and Education*, merits a close reading. Social life exists only in and through a communicative process of transmission of "habits of doing, thinking, and feeling from the older to the younger":

> The primary ineluctable facts of the birth and death of each one of the constituent members in a social group determine the necessity of education. On the one hand, there is the contrast between the immaturity of the newborn members of the group—its future sole representatives—and the maturity of the adult members who possess the knowledge and the customs of the group. On the other hand, there is the necessity that these immature members be not merely physically preserved in adequate numbers, but that they be initiated into the interests, purposes, information, skill, and practices of the mature members; otherwise the group will cease its characteristic life. (*D&E*; *MW* 9:5)

As an educational problem, this task includes, but is broader than, problems of schooling and formal education. Schooling is simply a subset of education—one relatively superficial and weak means of the transmission of social life that must be understood in the context of other "more fundamental and persistent modes of tuition" (*D&E*; *MW* 9:7). Unlike schooling, education in this broad sense is one with the full range of social processes of communication through which the commonalities of aims, meanings, emotions, beliefs, and practices required for community may be established.

Stated negatively, this means that a genuine society exists only when its members share more than physical proximity. And it means that relations among individuals are not fully social relations unless they include communication and its results. When communication and meaningful association are absent, as is frequently the case today, the relations among individuals are merely mechanical and external. In these situations, individuals only manipulate one another, like machines, paying no attention to the quality of experience of others.

Now, this view of education as the meaningful renewal of social life through communication constitutes a far-reaching political theory, social criticism, and philosophy of community. Major social institutions such as the government, the economy, the family, the workplace, the legal system, community organizations, and religious traditions have broader and deeper educational consequences than the schools—even though these consequences are not their immediate institutional objectives. Accordingly, they can be evaluated, criticized, and reconstructed in terms of their educational failures and successes—in terms of community. In this vein, Dewey argued that because the chief business of all social institutions and arrangements is to enable the young to share and enrich a common life, we must consider critically whether or not all of our social institutions and arrangements actually serve this goal. He summarized: "If humanity has made some headway in realizing that the ultimate value of every institution is its distinctively human effect—its effect upon conscious experience—we may well believe that the lesson has been learned largely through dealings with the young" (*D&E*; *MW* 9:9–10).

Though the educational effects of schooling are small, few, and temporary in comparison with the effects of these broader social institutions, the social need for schooling or a more formal education is undeniable. In fact, Dewey argued, it has never been greater. The increasing complexity of our society and our explosive gains in knowledge immensely widen the gap between the capacities of the young to learn and the learning possible through day-to-day involvement with adults whose activities are increasingly "remote in space and in meaning" and so less and less open for playful imitation:

> Ability to share effectively in adult activities thus depends upon a prior training given with this end in view. Intentional agencies—schools—and explicit material—studies—are devised. The task of teaching certain things is delegated to a special group of persons. Without such formal education, it is not possible to transmit all the resources and achievements of a complex society. (*D&E*; *MW* 9:11)

While the promise of schooling or formal education is large, the dangers from this "pillar of democracy" also are large. One major danger is that the schools may reproduce, and thus strengthen, those aspects of individual character and social life that oppose and undermine the creation of community. When this happens, an important possible means to the realization of community becomes an effective mechanism in the prevention of community.

Just as a totalitarian government may employ the rhetoric of democracy, a totalitarian school system may employ the rhetoric of education. In this case, schools function as peculiarly effective prisons.

Schools, like the media, may also become trivial pursuits. This is another danger—the possibility that the activities and subject-matter of the schools may become remote from actual social practice, abstract, artificial, and trivial. This danger that the subjects formally taught in schools may become isolated from actual experience and life is a constant danger. When this happens theory and practice, thought and action, are separated—a separation noted by all students who find a gap between their schools and the so-called real world. This danger is especially high for critical philosophy.

In light of this central distinction between education and schooling, several major questions may be addressed: What is the end or goal of education? How might this goal be realized most effectively? What are the implications of meeting this goal for the formal institution of the school? What are the consequences of this for society more broadly?

The goal of education, Dewey wrote, is growth. In response to the anticipated question, "Growth toward what?," Dewey replied that the goal of growth is nothing but further growth. In order to understand this, it is important to grasp the conditions necessary for growth. The most important of these conditions is immaturity—not simply the absence of maturity, but rather the capacity or power or potential or ability to develop. While it may sound odd to treat immaturity as a positive capacity, the alternative, odder still, would be to regard maturity as the absence of any capacity for further development. As Dewey noted, every adult resents the imputation that he or she has no further possibilities for growth. The possibility for further development constitutes a kind of plasticity, an ability to learn from experience and retain that learning for coping with later difficulties. This capacity to learn from experience and utilize that learning in future experience signifies the capacity to acquire habits. Habits are skills, efficiencies, abilities to use means to ends. As such, they are primarily active rather than passive:

> Education is not infrequently defined as consisting in the acquisition of those habits that effect an adjustment of an individual and his environment. The definition expresses an essential phase of growth. But it is essential that adjustment be understood in its active sense of control of means for achieving ends. If we think of a habit simply as a change wrought in the organism, ignoring the fact that this change consists in ability to effect subsequent changes in the environment, we shall be led to think of "adjustment" as a conformity to environment as wax conforms to he seal which impresses it. But . . . habits transform the environment. . . . [and] mean formation of intellectual and emotional disposition as well as an increase in ease, economy, and efficiency of action. (D&E; MW 9:51–53)

Fixed habits are so well established as to be resources always available when needed. But habits, once fixed, in time may become merely routine habits—bad habits, unthinking habits, habits that are enslaving and divorced from intelligence. To the extent that this happens, the capacity to develop new habits (including new habits of thought) is stunted. The result is "habits that possess us instead of our possessing them." And so the capacity for further development, growth, education is lost. An environment in which intelligence habitually forms habits, a community of growth (and not only hope or memory), is necessary to counteract this tendency.

Education, then, is the social actualization of the capacity to develop new habits and the continuing renewal of this capacity itself. In the context of social life, this ongoing actualization constitutes the life of a real community. In the context of individuals and their education, Dewey called this "growth," and argued that just as the transactions that are experience constitute reality and just as inquiry supplies its own advance, growth is an end in itself and is one with life itself: "Translated into its educational equivalents, this means (i) that the educational process has no end beyond itself; it is its own end; and that (ii) the educational process is one of continual reorganizing, reconstructing, transforming" (*D&E*; *MW* 9:54).

So understood, growth is a criterion for evaluating and remaking our schools. The criterion of the value of formal schooling is the extent to which it creates and sustains desire for continuing growth and supplies the means necessary for realizing this desire in fact. Growth, moreover, is a criterion for evaluating and reconstructing all our social institutions, not just our schools. In this way, education—both the formal education of the young and the continuing education of adults—supplies a basis for an engaged, genealogical cultural criticism: "Democracy has many meanings, but if it has a moral meaning, it is found in resolving that the supreme test of all political institutions and industrial arrangements shall be the contribution they make to the all-around growth of every member of society."[57]

This makes evident the close connections that Dewey recognized between the notions of philosophy as criticism, education as growth, and community as a democratic way of life. For Dewey, philosophy is one with education, and education is possible only in a genuinely democratic society. And, democracy, in turn, requires the processes of education or growth for its operation and continuing existence. It is only active education understood as growth that creates and re-creates shared activities, shared meanings, and the freedom needed to realize shared ideals. A genuine community seeks and

---

57. John Dewey, *Reconstruction in Philosophy, John Dewey: The Middle Works, 1899–1924*, vol. 12 (Carbondale, Ill.: Southern Illinois University Press, 1982 [1920]), p. 186.

requires these freely shared lives and values. As a result, Dewey's views of experience, education, inquiry, and community mutually imply one another and constitute a unified perspective. The end of education is growth, but it is also, at once, community. This sheds light on Dewey's claims that philosophy may be defined as the general theory of education and that *Democracy and Education* is the fullest statement of his own philosophy:

> The reconstruction of philosophy, of education, and of social ideals and methods thus go hand in hand. If there is especial need of educational reconstruction at the present time, if this need makes urgent a reconsideration of the basic ideas of traditional philosophic systems, it is because of the thoroughgoing change in social life accompanying the advance of science, the industrial revolution, and development of democracy. Such practical changes cannot take place without demanding an educational re-formation to meet them, and without leading men to ask what ideas and ideals are implicit in these social changes, and what revisions they require of the ideas and ideals which are inherited from older and unlike cultures. (*D&E*; *MW* 9:341)

Accordingly, Dewey asserted that education is the fundamental and most effective method of social progress toward community. This fact creates a social duty for each of us:

> I believe that the community's duty to education is, therefore, its paramount moral duty. By law and punishment, by social agitation and discussion, society can regulate and form itself in a more or less haphazard and chance way. But through education society can formulate its own purposes, can organize its own means and resources, and thus shape itself with definiteness and economy in the direction in which it wishes to move. I believe that when society once recognizes the possibilities in this direction, and the obligations which these possibilities impose, it is impossible to conceive of the resources of time, attention, and money which will be put at the disposal of the educator.[58]

This view of education, if put into practice (almost inconceivable today), would require vast changes in our schools, as well as almost all our other major social institutions, including our economy and our communications media. Within the schools, these overhauls involve overcoming the splits and dualisms that pervade formal education—the separation of school

---

58. John Dewey, "My Pedagogic Creed," *John Dewey: The Early Works, 1882–1898*, vol. 5 (Carbondale, Ill.: Southern Illinois University Press, 1975 [1897]), p. 94.

and society, of child and curriculum, of the liberal arts and the vocations, of the mental and the physical, and of those who are schooled and those who are not. It is not an overstatement to say that Dewey's response to almost every educational issue—and so to almost every philosophic issue—is to deny the dualisms assumed by existing theories. Thus, to ask whether the organization of the school should be driven by the interests of the child or the content of the curriculum is to raise an artificial, dead question. To ask whether formal education should be liberal or vocational is to operate with assumptions unfounded in experience. Such dichotomies are the tedious fictions of philosophers who fail to inquire into the nature of schooling as it actually occurs.

Accordingly, effective education requires close ties between school and society. If the school does not seek its subject-matter in society's real activities—if the school does not extend into society—and if society does not utilize the new habits and dispositions acquired in school—if society does not reach into the school—then genuine education does not take place. Instead, Dewey argued, we merely produce bookishness, motor activity without meaning, specialized and compartmentalized knowledge without the intelligence to direct it. Moreover, by failing to produce the social sense that results from shared activity of shared meaning and shared value, efforts at isolated intellectual learning contradict their own aims and diminish the possibilities and prerequisites of community. The social sense that comes from shared activities and meanings is the social sense that defines the life of a community. Its development requires the experience of freedom and participation that lie at the heart of the meanings of democracy and education:

> If we train our children to take orders, to do things simply because they are told so, and fail to give them confidence to act and think for themselves, we are putting an almost insurmountable obstacle in the way of overcoming the present defects of our system and of establishing the truth of democratic ideals. Our State is founded on freedom, but when we train the State of tomorrow, we allow it just as little freedom as possible. Children in school must be allowed freedom so that they will know what its use means when they become the controlling body.[59]

This educational issue is bound up with the economic and communication problems noted above.[60] The means necessary for free educational development must be provided to all members of our society. This core value is

---

59. John Dewey, *Schools of To-Morrow, John Dewey: The Middle Works, 1899–1924*, vol. 8 (Carbondale, Ill.: Southern Illinois University Press, 1979 [1915]), p. 398.
60. Elizabeth A. Kelly provides an excellent, extended discussion of this issue—a discussion that updates many of Dewey's concerns, and a discussion that is more fully Deweyan than she realizes because of her insufficient attention to Dewey's extensive, systematic criticism of many aspects of capitalism. *Education, Democracy and Public Knowledge* (Boulder, Colo.: Westview Press, 1995).

intrinsic to the notion of community; it is central to the very meaning of a democratic way of life. Without this shared opportunity, common experience, and communication, there can be no government of, by, and for the people. Thus Dewey noted that because the formation of separate, fixed classes is fatal for democracy, there must not be separate, fixed systems of education that produce and reproduce class difference. Dewey wrote sternly: "There must not be one system for the children of parents who have more leisure and another for the children of those who are wage-earners. . . . The democracy which proclaims equality of opportunity as its ideal require an education in which learning and social application, ideas and practice, work and recognition of the meaning of what is done, are united from the beginning and for all."[61]

We do not provide this kind of education at present. We do not even come close. The pragmatic notion of community developed above provides an intellectual basis for doing so and a moral basis for social change. Without such change, philosophers in effect fail to be public educators, and their philosophies fail to be public philosophies. This does not mean that philosophy must simply translate poetic forms into its own idioms, as Williams advised Dewey. Instead, philosophy must translate its own forms into effective, moving artistic idioms—in Dewey's sense in which the communication of the results of critical inquiry is an art. Again, this does not mean that philosophers must imitate artists or entertainers. Williams got this right: At the frontier, in the New World, Daniel Boone did not become an Indian. Instead, he became *Indianlike*. Similarly, philosophers must become *artistlike* in order to reconstruct communities and critically engage their different individual members. All American philosophers who seek to travel in a new direction, who strive to think at the frontier, really have no other acceptable choice. In this new world, they must act so as to forge, and critically participate in, communities of individuals—communities, but communities of difference rather than identity. Of course, as in the past, there remain many subtle forms of retreat from this frontier—"some of which are erected into systems of philosophy."[62]

In *Democracy in America*, de Tocqueville remarked that in America that which is not yet done is only that which has not yet been attempted.[63] Pragmatic philosophers of community must be less upbeat and optimistic. They may proclaim only that that which has not yet been attempted surely is that which is not yet done—and will not be done, if ever done, *without the attempt*. This attempt constitutes the frontier for American philosophy.[64]

---

61. Dewey, *Schools of To-Morrow*, pp. 403–4. See the discussion of this point in chapter 14.
62. Dewey, *Individualism: Old and New*, p. 122.
63. Alexis de Tocqueville, *Democracy in America* (New York: Scribner's, 1905 [1848]), p. 265.
64. An earlier version of portions of this essay appeared in "Community and the Cultural Frontier," *Frontiers in American Philosophy*, vol. 2, ed. Robert Burch and Herman J. Saatkamp Jr. (College Station, Tex.: Texas A & M University Press, 1996). The revised passages appear here with the kind permission of the editors and the publisher.

14

Community, Economic Growth, and Family Income:
It's the Community, Stupid!

John Dewey defined philosophy as criticism. To the small extent that professional philosophers in America today do attempt to engage in criticism, they surely occupy the margins of their culture. They sit on the sidelines of America's big games—politics and law, economics and industry, religion and entertainment, science and technology, and even education (in the sense in which Dewey distinguished education from the narrower notion of formal schooling). Professional philosophers may get into these big games once in a while, and we may cheer for them when they do—like sports fans cheering the twelfth player on a basketball team that clears its bench and rests its starters. They even may score a point or two, but the game is really over before they get in. Our culture and its political agendas and individual hopes move around professional philosophers, not through them. Professional philosophers—even those with high salaries—simply have little "cash-value" in contemporary American culture. They may claim (with self-conscious irony, I trust) to be pragmatic in theory, but, for the overwhelming part, they are marginal and not very pragmatic in practice.

American philosophers are marginal in a second respect as well. They occupy not simply the margins of American culture but, ever increasingly and largely through their own actions alone, the margins of American philosophy itself—the small spaces at the edges of pages written by others. Recalling and explicating over and over, citing and quoting ever more, they—we—I—speak, write, and think in the margins of earlier philosophers and their work (even as this earlier work itself clearly articulates the difference between the problems of philosophers and the problems of men and women, the difference between the study of philosophical problems and the philosophical study of human problems, the difference between a derivative and an original relation to the universe). Of course, it is important that American philosophers—like professionals in any other field—periodically share with one another in a specialized language the results of specialized research. However, it is just as important that this not be the only way in which they think, speak, and listen, and that this not be the only group with whom they think, speak, and listen.

Now, in reflecting from the margins on some contemporary political realities, it is tempting to focus on current affairs, today's headlines, and immediate partisan matters: the most recent elections; the resurgence of the Republican Party and its "Contract for America"—or is it "Contract *on* America"; various pending proposals, both Republican and Democrat, to balance the budget, slash taxes, increase defense spending, close military bases, execute more criminals and build more prisons, reform (or repeal?) welfare "as we know it," terminate Affirmative Action, eliminate pesky environmental protection regulations, cut or eliminate funding for the National Endowment for the Humanities and the National Endowment for the Arts, reduce scholarships and aid for education, end unfunded mandates from the federal government to the States, and so on.

I confess that I almost gave in to this temptation, tentatively titling this chapter "Individualism: Old and Newt," and embarking on a footnote-filled scholarly comparison of John Dewey and Newt Gingrich on the nature of individualism and the proper scope of government. However, I have resisted this temptation in order to pursue a less partisan approach and to focus on a problem more politically fundamental and less directly linked to the present platform or announced agenda of either major political party.

Nonetheless, Newt Gingrich, Bob Dole, Steve Forbes, Pat Buchanan, and their fellow Republicans do provide a useful point of entry. They have claimed frequently that their "philosophy" or goal is to take back money, power, and decision-making from the federal government and return it to States and local *communities*. Gingrich and his supporters typically advance this goal by arguing that local *communities* have a right (moral and/or constitutional) to make most (if not all) of their own decisions. In addition, they argue that local *communities* as a practical matter almost always can make these decisions more effectively and successfully than the federal government.

The political consequences of the full implementation of this agenda would be striking and far-reaching. These consequences would include: more systematic social injustice, greater cultural disenfranchisement, and increased hopelessness and isolation. But the rhetoric of this agenda is equally striking. It is an agenda pursued in moralistic, patriotic, and unobjectionable terms: community, individuality and initiative, accountability and responsibility, and self-reliance and self-help.

In a relatively short period of time, the rhetoric of the Republican Party, conservatives, reactionaries, and much of the radical right in America has become a rhetoric of *community*. Increasingly, conservatives portray themselves as the champions of states and cities, counties and townships, precincts and neighborhoods, friends and families, you and me. Declaring that they want to recover the language and concerns of community, they increasingly talk about regional differences, local self-determinism, small-scale politics, and government with a human face. In doing so (to the irritation of liberals and many Democrats, I'm sure), these conservatives sometimes invoke and endorse what they take to be Jeffersonian democracy. And in doing so (to the irritation of most pragmatists, I suspect), they seem loudly to echo—sometimes and somehow—both Josiah Royce's discussion of a "new and wiser provincialism" and John Dewey's emphasis on face-to-face democratic associations and communities.

Now, this conservative, Republican Party rhetoric is partly rooted in, and partly arises from, an assumption that America is a patchwork or mosaic of local *communities* (ready and willing to take back, and take on, their own governance). However, this crucial assumption—that local *communities* now exist—is simply false. Indeed, in America this assumption perhaps has never been more false or more unsupported by the facts of actual social life. Rhetoric aside, this is a point that sharply separates contemporary conservatives from Jefferson, Royce, and Dewey. For example, in a discussion of Jefferson and community in *Freedom and Culture*, Dewey observes that while Jefferson warned against excessive federal power, he attached chief importance to local self-governance "on something like the New England town-meeting plan":

> His project for general political organization on the basis of small units, small enough so that all its members could have direct communication with one another and take care of all community affairs was never acted upon. . . . There is a difference between a society, in the sense of an association, and a community. . . . [A] community adds the function of communication in which emotions and ideas are shared as well as joint undertakings engaged in. Economic forces have immensely widened the scope of associational activities. But it has done so largely at the expense of the intimacy and directness of communal group interests and activities.[1]

This special sense of "community"—and the resulting distinction between community and any or all other associations or social groups)—is developed and set forth most fully by both Royce (in, for example, *The Problem of Christianity*) and Dewey (in, for example, *The Public and Its Problems*). Their shared point is straightforward: Not every society, association, or collection of individuals is a community. For Royce, a community is a collection of selves who actively share an ideal (or "ideally extended") common past and future. For Dewey, a community is defined by conjoint activity whose consequences are appreciated as good by all who take part in

---

1. John Dewey, *Freedom and Culture, John Dewey: The Later Writings, 1925–1953*, vol. 13 (Carbondale, Ill: Southern Illinois University Press, 1988 [1939]), pp. 176–76. Hereafter abbreviated *F&C; LW13* in this chapter.

the activity and who, as a result of this appreciation, desire and actively strive to sustain this activity just because it is a good shared by all.

For my present purposes, I want to stress that there is significant overlap between these accounts of community. I recognize, of course, that there also are significant differences between Royce and Dewey here, and I have argued in various margins that Dewey's account is superior on both more theoretical and more practical grounds.[2] I suspect that more tender-minded temperaments may be drawn to Royce, and more tough-minded ones to Dewey. But whatever one's temperament and whichever account of community one may prefer, one thing is clear: In the context of contemporary America, this idea of community in classical American philosophy is a *fantastic* idea—an utterly fantastic idea. Question: What do the Form of Forms, the Unmoved Mover, monads, the state of nature, things-in-themselves, absolute spirit, the problem of other minds, and in principle private languages have in common with the Great Community, as defined by Royce and Dewey? Answer: None of them exists. Even philosophers who think long and hard about a community than which there is none greater cannot thereby bring about or establish the existence of the Great Community. As a matter of simple fact, America is not, and never has been, a genuine community. As another matter of fact—a fact understood well by Royce and Dewey—America is not a collection of communities.

Of course, it is true that Republicans, conservatives, or reactionaries—or anyone else, for that matter—may have good reasons for seeking to reduce the size and scope of the federal government, and for trying to transfer some of its powers and functions to local associations, even though these associations are not now genuine communities. Perhaps some of these actions will ameliorate some of our pressing social problems. Certainly, we must make changes if we are to make improvements, and it is tempting at present to think that almost any change is bound to be a change for the better. Here, a genuinely experimental and fallibilistic orientation would forsake reliance on sweeping theories for careful genealogies of specific practices by specific persons at specific times and places. Moreover, to do this is by no means to abandon liberalism—unless one confuses liberalism's *central* values—what Ronald Dworkin in *A Matter of Principle* has called its "constitutive political positions"—with *particular* liberal policies and programs in particular times and places (e.g., Locke's England, Jefferson's early America, Roosevelt's New Deal, or Johnson's Great Society)—what Dworkin calls "derivative positions that are valued as strategies, as means of achieving the constitutive positions."[3] To join Gingrich, Rush Limbaugh, Pat Robertson, and others in this sort of confusion about liberal-

---

2. See the discussion of Royce and Dewey in chapter 13.
3. Ronald Dworkin, "Liberalism," *A Matter of Principle* (Cambridge, Mass.: Harvard University Press, 1985), p. 184.

ism—former President George Bush's dreaded "L-word"—is to engage in just the sort of ahistorical political theory that Dewey criticized so effectively in *Liberalism and Social Action* and other works.

Of course, liberals and conservatives can all agree that today we face social problems so serious and so numerous that it is not possible in a short space even to chronicle them—much less adequately analyze or respond to them. Accordingly, I want to narrow the focus by highlighting just one problem—actually, one cluster of problems—that I take to be critically important today. In selecting this particular focus, I am guided by familiar and penetrating philosophical advice from the so-called real world, advice articulated in its classic, briefest form in the 1992 campaign for the presidency of the United States. This was the advice: "It's the economy stupid!"

Yes, it is. However, there is a deeper point, best expressed this way: It's the community, stupid!

In order to understand this point, it is important to recognize that the existence—the creation and sustenance—of communities is difficult and fragile. Not all social groups and associations are communities. A community comes into existence only when certain social factors and conditions are present. These conditions, as Dewey stated in *The Public and Its Problems*, ensure individuals a responsible share according to capacity in forming and directing the activities of the groups to which they belong and to participating according to need in the values which the groups sustain. And they enable these groups to liberate the potentialities of their members in harmony with the goods common to the groups themselves.

Some of these community-enabling factors are economic, and, as Dewey recognized, it is pointless to ignore them because they "do not cease to operate because we refuse to note them, or because we smear them over with sentimental idealizations":

> What actually happens in consequence of industrial forces is dependent upon the presence or absence of perception and communication of consequences, upon foresight and its effect upon desire and endeavor. Economic agencies produce one result when they are left to work themselves out on the merely physical level, or on that level modified only as the knowledge, skill and technique which the community has accumulated are transmitted to its members unequally and by chance. They have a different outcome in the degree in which knowledge of consequences is equitably distributed, and action is animated by an informed and lively sense of shared interest.[4]

---

4. John Dewey, *The Public and Its Problems, John Dewey: The Later Works, 1925–1953*, vol. 2 (Carbondale, Ill.: Southern Illinois University Press, 1984 [1927]), pp. 332–33.

The issue here does not concern simply the distribution, or redistribution, of wealth. It is not simply an economic issue. Instead, the issue concerns the broad range of cultural meanings, values, beliefs, actions, and associations—the entire range of of cultural realities that produce, and are produced by, economic relations.

As a result, Dewey's point is more radical and complex than it may seem to those who are concerned simply to redistribute income or extend economic initiatives and opportunities to those who are poorest. For Dewey, this is insufficient: We must form a new psychological and moral type of individual; we must forge a new individualism, a new human nature. At the same time, Dewey fully recognized that part of this task is economic and that it may be impossible to create a blueprint for this new individualism until and unless more progress is made on the conditions of its production. Again discussing Jefferson, Dewey clearly made this point:

> Although it later became the fashion to blur the connection which exists between economics and politics, and even to reprove those who called attention to it, Madison as well as Jefferson was quite aware of the connection and of its bearing upon democracy. Knowledge that the connection demanded a general distribution of property and the prevention of rise of the extremely poor and the extremely rich, was however different from explicit recognition of a relation between culture and nature so intimate that the former may shape the patterns of thought and action. (*F&C; LW* 13:69)

At times, Dewey refers to this economic "shaping" of culture as "economic determinism," and he calls this determinism a fact at present, and not just a theory. Still, as he recognizes, the nature of this determinism is not independent of our choices and actions: "there is a difference and a choice between a blind, chaotic and unplanned determinism, issuing from business conducted for pecuniary profit, and the determinism of a socially planned and ordered development."[5] Similarly, there is a difference between formal equality under the law and real equality in social life. Discussing the failures of earlier liberalism (that has much in common with contemporary conservatism), Dewey observed that the idea that all persons are equal and equally free if only the same legal arrangements apply to all—"irrespective of differences in education, in command of capital, and the control of the social environment which is furnished by the institution of property—is a pure absurdity, as facts have demonstrated. . . . The only possible conclusion, both intellectually and prac-

---

5. John Dewey, *Individualism: Old and New, John Dewey: The Later Works, 1925–1953*, vol. 5 (Carbondale, Ill.: Southern Illinois University Press, 1984 [1930]), p. 98. Hereafter abbreviated *I:O&N; LW5* in this chapter.

tically, is that the attainment of freedom conceived as power to act in accord with choice depends upon positive and constructive changes in social arrangements."[6]

At present, our economy is not in the least guided by an ordered development, an equitable distribution of knowledge of its consequences, or by widely shared interest. Indeed, since 1979—since the beginning of the so-called Reagan Revolution and continuing through its 1994 aftershocks—we have been destroying—more extensively and rapidly than ever before—the economic conditions upon which the existence of community depends. This is a sad, terrible fact, but one that now must be stressed over and over.

This may appear ironic because, since the 1992 election of President Clinton, the overall economy in America has been enjoying an extraordinary boom: huge job growth—more than six million new jobs in the first three years after this election; an unemployment rate at a four-year low for most of this period; low inflation; and sharply increased productivity. However,

The Top-Heavy Concentration of Income Growth: 1979–1992
Shares of Average Household Income Growth

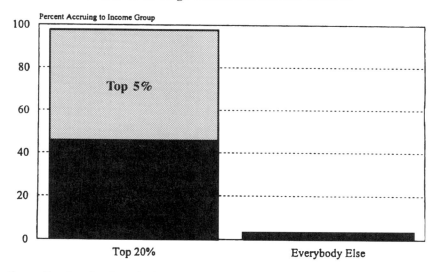

Source: Based on data from the Census Bureau, Current Population Survey. Household income is in constant 1992 dollars, and adjusted by CPI-U-X1, and population is normalized to a constant level.

---

6. John Dewey, "Philosophies of Freedom," *John Dewey: The Later Works, 1925–1953*, vol. 3 (Carbondale, Ill.: Southern Illinois University Press, 1984 [1928]), p. 101.

even though overall productivity and profits have risen dramatically, during the fifteen years from 1979 to 1994, the wages of most Americans have actually fallen (when adjustments for inflation are considered). As chart 1 makes clear, since 1979, household incomes have ballooned by $826 billion (in 1993 dollars). But almost 98 percent of this increase has gone only to those citizens in the top fifth of income. During this time, all others—more than four out of five American households, including the vast majority of households constituted by members of ethnic and racial minorities—have shared just 2 percent of these overall income gains. As a result, most American families are living on less, adjusted for inflation, than they did fifteen years ago.

This increasing disparity between the richest and the poorest continued—even accelerated—under the Democratic Clinton administration. As outlined in a 1996 U. S. Census Bureau Report, "A Brief Look at Postwar U. S. Income," in 1994, the average income for the top 20% of households was $105,945, a 44% increase (adjusted for inflation) since 1968; in contrast, the bottom 20% of households had annual incomes of $7,762, only a 7% increase (adjusted for inflation) since 1968. This means that the top 20% of households had annual incomes 13 times higher than the bottom 20%, and that the overall average household income was four times higher than this bottom 20%. As Bruce Bartlett, a senior fellow at the conservative National Center for Policy Analysis, put it, this reflects a development that is "beyond politics": "we cut taxes in the 1980s and the rich got richer. Here we've increased taxes in the 1990s, and they still got richer."[7] This makes the United States one of the countries in the world in which economic stratification is most pronounced. However, this is an international, and not just an American trend. As the United Nations Development Program 1996 *Human Development Report* makes clear, a global economic elite has emerged and has amassed great wealth and power while excluding most of humanity.[8] More than 3 billion people—more than half of the world's people—have incomes of less than $2 a day. As James Speth, administrator of the Development Program, notes: "For poor people in this two-class world, it is a breeding ground for hopelessness, for anger."[9]

It has not always been this way in America. As revealed in chart 2, during the three decades after World War II, nearly everyone's income grew as the overall American economy grew. However, as former U. S. Secretary of Labor Robert Reich has repeatedly remarked, today we are no longer

---

7. *New York Times*, June 20, 1996, p. A18.
8. United Nations Development Program, *Human Development Report* (New York: Oxford University Press, 1996).
9. *New York Times*, July 12, 1996, p. A10.

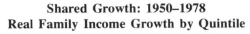

Shared Growth: 1950–1978
Real Family Income Growth by Quintile

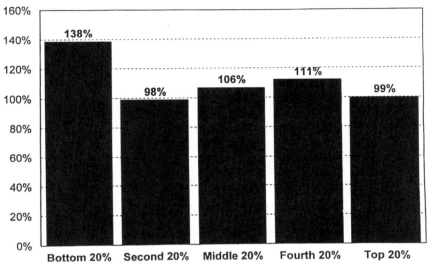

Source: Census Bureau, DOL calculations. All data converted to 1993 dollars.

growing together; rather we are growing apart—and at a quickening pace. This economic "growing apart" is nothing less than the destruction of economic conditions that are necessary for the existence of community and a fully democratic way of life.

From 1979 to 1994, as starkly illustrated by chart 3, the old saying has proved true in America: The rich—especially the very rich—have gotten much, much richer and the poor have gotten much, much poorer. This is most evident in the real lives of America's children. For an increasing number and percentage of these children, life is becoming measurably worse year after year, as assessed by basic standards of poverty rates, health, and education.

Consider some of the findings of the Children's Defense Fund's 1996 *State of America's Children Report* and the National Low Income Housing Coalition's 1996 study, *Housing America's Future: Children at Risk:*

- Poverty: The child poverty rate in the United States is 21.5%, much higher than the rates across Western Europe (from 2.7% in Sweden to 9.9% in Britain). In addition, in the United States, nearly 44% of all African American children, and more than 41% of Latino children live in poverty.

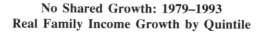

No Shared Growth: 1979–1993
Real Family Income Growth by Quintile

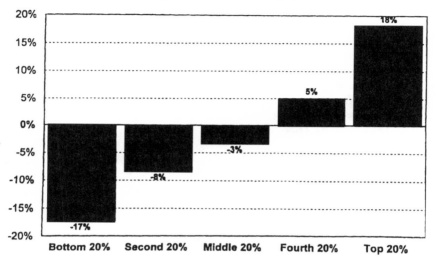

Source: Census Bureau, DOL calculations. All data converted to 1993 dollars.

- Health: The U. S. infant mortality rate is 8.5 per 1,000 live births—higher than any other industrialized nation in the world; in addition, 16.8% of all live-birth African American babies die before their first birthday; moreover, more than 10 million American children are at risk because they have no health insurance.

- Education: While 7.4% of all American children fail to finish high school, 24% of children who live in poverty at least one year fail to finish high school; and the percentages are even higher for poor children in single-parent families and families with parents who did not finish high school.

In this context, it is difficult to take seriously the claim that America is committed to equality of opportunity:

> Only those who have a special cause to plead will hold that even in the most democratic countries, under the most favorable conditions, have children of the poor the same chances as those of the well-to-do, even in a thing like schooling which is supported at public expense. And it is no consoling offset that the children of the rich often suffer because of the one-sided conditions under which they grow up. (*F&C*; *LW* 13:110)

Statistics from these and other reports on housing and homelessness, nutrition, and child abuse provide further evidence for this judgment. Moreover, recent welfare reform supported by most all Republicans and Democrats, the Personal Responsibility and Work Opportunity Act of 1996, will cut $56 billion in services to America's poorest families (including more than eight million children) and will put an estimated 2.6 million persons (including more than one million children) below the poverty level.

Finally, while it is impossible to fully or finally predict the future, there is substantial evidence that supports the belief that these trends will continue. Why will this economic polarization continue? One important reason, as the above studies suggest, involves formal education, its benefits, and its costs. The cost of formal education in America has never been greater and, at the same time, the correlation between education and income has never been higher. As indicated by chart 4, during the past fifteen years, the sharpest drop in income has been suffered by the 75% of American workers without college degrees. Fifteen years ago, a male college graduate typically earned 49% more than a man with only a high school diploma. By 1993, however, the average male college graduate was earning 83% more than his counterpart high school graduate. This difference is so great and is

The Economic Impact of Education: 1979–1995
Average Annual Earnings of Men by Educational Attainment

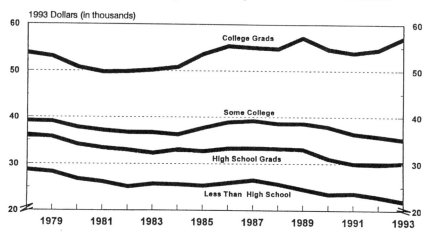

Note: Workers twenty-five years of age and older, working year round, full-time. Data on educational attainment for 1991 through 1993 are not directly comparable to those from prior years. Numbers for 1993 used 1990 population weights, whereas data for other years used 1980 population weights.

Source: Bureau of the Census, Current Population Survey.

growing so rapidly that the two groups share increasingly little common economic ground. Women increasingly are divided along similar lines, although not yet as sharply.

This is not fertile ground for community. We walk past homeless, hungry, sick people. We ignore the depressed bodies and empty minds of so many American workers. We close our eyes to the absence of opportunity that exists for so many members of our nation. We complain about their lack of initiative, but do little to understand its causes or make a change. We look for salvation not in community, as Royce and Dewey recommended, but in neighborhood patrols and big new prisons, proven financial planners and tax advisers, and the latest technology. We surely do not engage in the ideal extension of our self, detailed by Royce; we do not say that the sufferings, deprivations, and exclusions of other selves are parts of our own lives, parts of our extended lives, parts of the social body. It's the community, stupid!

This is not even fertile ground for philosophies of community. We have philosophers who wonder: What is it like to be a bat? Instead, we ought to wonder: What is it like to be a philosopher who asks what is it like to be a bat? We don't wonder: What is it like *for me—my community, myself, ideally extended*—to be homeless, hungry, sick, poor, without a stake, without hope? Of course, we frequently do contemplate a different issue: How can I make sure that I'm not one of the homeless, the sick, the hungry, the poor, the disenfranchised, the hopeless? As we think about this frightening issue, we only rarely think about public education in the largest sense—the impact on our characters and habits (including our habits of initiative, self-reliance, and responsibility) on our social associations, institutions, and practices. Occupied with self-interest as we conceive it, we ignore community interest and genuinely public education. Although our individual desires may implicate social, mutually understood meanings, as Dewey claimed, we do not act on these desires to forge new ties, build "a community of interest and endeavor," or establish a Great Community as articulated by the classical American philosophers. Today, we ignore the challenge to rewrite *Democracy and Education* for our own time, and ignore the challenge to enact it. Instead, if we can, we put our children in private schools. Democracy and education? To this question, more and more often, we reply: Are you kidding? Can I have a voucher? It's the community, stupid.

This notion of community, as pragmatism shows us, is a fantastic idea. It is nothing real, and its utter lack of reality is a large part of our contemporary political reality in America. Of course, the pragmatists never thought community was real. They viewed it as an ideal. As an ideal, community supplies a basis for cultural criticism and reconstruction. As an ideal, it instructs us to approach contemporary political realities and our own lives and choices in moral terms. It instructs us to consider the consequences for community of specific political platforms, policies, legislation, and social agendas. It instructs us to consider the consequences for community of our own lives and lifestyles. In turn, this would lead us to develop, in as shared and equitable ways possible, *community impact studies*—much as we now prepare environmental and economic impact reports.

Consider, for example, a recent Republican proposal, summarized in chart 5, for a large capital gains tax cut. Will this tax proposal advance Dewey's Great Community or Royce's new and wiser provincialism? Is there reason to think that it will promote or further undermine the realization of the ideal of a community of diverse individuals—at once the ideal of genuine community and genuine individuality? Will this proposed tax break provide a break for community? While issues such as tax proposals may be economic, the criteria by which we evaluate them cannot be merely economic. Our long-standing concern with the gross national product needs to be supplemented by, and in this sense replaced by, concern with the gross national absence of community.

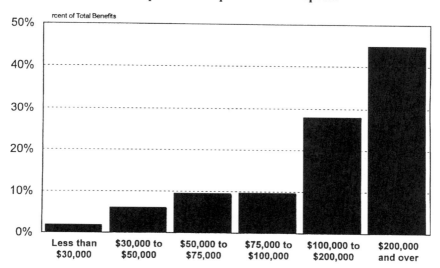

Capital Gains and Community Gains: Distribution of Benefits in 1999 from the 1995 Republican Capital Gains Proposal

Source: Joint Committee on Taxation, Publication D-94-25, "Distribution of the Change in Federal Tax Liability Resulting from a 50 Percent Exclusion and Indexation of Cost Basis," October 6, 1994.

Of course, to note that America is not a community, that community is not real, is not thereby to establish community as an ideal. In America today, community is not real. Even worse, in American today, community is not even an ideal. To be an ideal, this rich notion of community would have to imaginatively unify our beliefs, values, and possibilities, and would have to motivate our action on behalf of those possibilities. We exhibit in our actions virtually no such union of the possibilities of community with actual conditions and political realities. I am afraid that community, never a reality, is less and less—perhaps no longer at all—an ideality. We may still talk the talk of community, at least in certain philosophy courses and books, but less and less we walk its walk in American politics and life. Even in colleges and universities, the notion of a community of scholars increasingly is little more than old-fashioned rhetoric.

Since Dewey's time, as I have argued elsewhere in various margins,[10] the complex phenomenon that he identified as the business mind has expanded and become wholly unified or almost wholly unified. There is precious little place in the business culture for genuine community, and there is equally little place in this business mind for the ideal of community. Professional philosophers who write critical marginal notes for one another may tell themselves that they have escaped the reach of the business mind, but I do not believe that this often is so. As Dewey observed in this context in *Individualism: Old and New*:

> Intellectual and literary folks who conceive themselves devoted to pursuit of pure truth and uncontaminated beauty too readily overlook the fact that a similar narrowing and hardening takes place in them. Their goods are more refined, but they are also engaged in acquisition; unless they are concerned with use, with expansive interactions, they too become monopolists of capital. And the monopolization of spiritual capital may in the end be more harmful than that of material capital. (*I:O&N; LW* 5:117)

Contemporary political realities provide American philosophers with a telling choice today: Be monopolists of the spirit or be idealists of community. The latter option is uncomfortable and demanding, strains even the most melioristic and strenuous of spirits, and must involve social action as well as thought. To become a virtuous person, Aristotle wrote, you must act virtuously. Similarly, to become a pragmatist, you must act pragmatically. This action, depending on particular issues and specific alternatives, may or may not be undertaken in association with, or on behalf of, Republicans, Demo-

---

10. See the discussion of education and the business mind in chapter 1.

crats, or other political parties. However, it always must be undertaken on behalf of community—on behalf of developing community in reality and on behalf of nurturing community in ideality—on behalf of a community *culture* in all its aspects. In the largest sense, this is both a radical and an educational task. It is also a critical task, a task for pragmatism or any philosophy that understands itself as criticism. As Dewey recognized, we can only grasp the meaning of what now exists by forecasting the future consequences that it entails. Observation thus has a critical and a prophetic aspect:

> As one perceives different tendencies and different possible consequences, preference inevitably goes out to one or the other. Because acknowledgment in thought brings with it intelligent discrimination and choice, it is the first step out of confusion, the first step in forming those objects of significant allegiance out of which stable and efficacious individuality may grow. It might even perform the miracle of rendering conservativism relevant and thoughtful. It certainly is the prerequisite of an anchored liberalism. (*I:O&N; LW* 5:117)

Today, this is reality for American politics and economics. For many years now, we have pursued social policies that massively have eroded the *economic* conditions necessary for the development of a democratic way of life—conditions necessary (though not sufficient) for real community and real individualism. As it is for politics and economics, this is also reality for American philosophy. As we have eroded the economic prerequisites of community, we also have destroyed significantly the *intellectual* conditions necessary for the realization of community as an ideal. Moreover, at the same time we largely have submerged the *moral* will required for action on this ideal. Philosophers who fail to recognize this fact need to recognize their role in helping to make it a fact. If a reminder is needed to jump-start this realization and subsequent action, pragmatic social thought stands ready with a clear message: It really *is* the community.

15

Persons, Pluralism, and Death: Toward a Disillusioned Pragmatism

> I give back to the earth what the earth gave,
> All to the furrow, nothing to the grave.
> The candle's out, the spirit's vigil spent;
> Sight may not follow where the vision went.
>
> —George Santayana, "The Poet's Testament"

A Personal Question

My father died April 18, 1994. He was 76 years old. (I want to say: *only* 76 years old). For almost ten years, he had been suffering terribly from a little-understood degenerative illness similar to Parkinson's disease. Choking, moaning, unable to breathe, his autonomic nervous system finally failing, he died in his bed at his home on April 18, 1994.[1] He died: a few hours after I last saw him; after I left with other thoughts for the airport to fly to interview for the university position I now hold; a few hours after I squeezed his hand for the last time and wondered if he had any idea at all who I was or who he was; long after his days and nights had become occupied by my mother (always) and health-care professionals (later) who monitored him, moved him, fed him, and waited; and long after the brilliant, energetic, accomplished man who had been my father no longer existed. He died: a couple of days before I emptied his heavy ashes into a small hole at the base of a tree in a community church garden; a couple of days before I sat in his study, seeing, smelling, and touching his books, photographs, awards and medals, files and piles of paper, and an old typewriter; a couple of days before his friends and family gathered at his house; and days before we began to try to go on differently.

---

1. See Albert Camus's opening description of Meursault's notification of his mother's death in *The Stranger* [*L'Etranger*], trans. S. Gilbert (New York, Knopf, 1946 [1942]), p. 1.

I report all this not to grab your attention, not to gain your sympathy, and not to worry you that this chapter will be unprofessional, uncomfortable, or too personal. Philosophers, after all, are very rarely too personal: We've nearly perfected profoundly impersonal forms of thought and language. These impersonal professional forms, I realize, have become too much my own. Function sometimes follows form, and so I recall my father's death to signal a more personal function for thought, to endorse a more personal point of departure for criticism, and to pursue a more genuinely personal philosophy. This must not be an abstract philosophy undertaken in the name of persons in general, undertaken in the name of everybody but nobody in particular. Instead, it must be a concrete philosophy—a phase of concrete philosophies—undertaken in the names of actual individuals, undertaken in my name, your name, or somebody else's name, undertaken in the name of my father.

The most important questions for such a philosophy, like the most important questions in life, are moral questions. These questions concern not simply the nature of reality or truth or mind or body or language, but rather how one should live and what one should do. Philosophy constantly confronts each of us at each moment of our lives with this basic, critical question: *What sort of person should I strive to become?*

This is a *practical* question: It concerns what you and I do in practice, and not just what we contemplate in theory or entertain without commitment in a classroom.

It is also an *inescapable* question: You may not philosophize about it or explicitly address it or ever give it a thought, but all your decisions and choices and actions, no matter how unthinking, determine and constitute a response to it. You may answer the question badly or inconsistently or unreflectively, but you cannot fail to answer it, in some way or another to embody in your life a reply to this question.

It is, moreover, a *temporal, finite* question: Whatever answer you give, you answer only briefly; whatever choices you make, you choose for just a little while; whatever person you become, you are a person who will die. In 1900, preaching what he called "the doctrine of the strenuous life," Theodore Roosevelt observed "Death is always and under all circumstances a tragedy, for if it is not, then it means that life itself has become one."[2] This should chill even the strongest, most strenuous bull moose: Tragedy awaits each of us. Your life, you and I can be sure, will lead to the tragedy of death; if you are less fortunate, it leads first to the tragedy of life followed by the tragedy of death.

---

2. Theodore Roosevelt, "Letter to Cecil Spring-Rice," March 12, 1900. *The Works of Theodore Roosevelt*, vol. 2, ed. H. Hagedorn (New York: Charles Scribner's Sons, 1926), p. 102. See also *The Strenuous Life* (New York: The Review of Reviews Co., 1904).

Of course, these tragedies are not general—death in the abstract. They are inescapably particular—my death, your death, somebody else's death, my father's death. Awaiting personal tragedy, we each face a personal issue: *What sort of person should I strive to become?* This is, lastly, a *personal* question: It confronts equally all of us, but it demands (and must receive) an answer—a different answer, an individual answer, one's own answer—from each one of us.

Can Personalism Help Answer This Question?

So, what sort of person should *you* strive to become? This is a big and difficult question. There is, perhaps, no more difficult question. From any source, any genuine guidance should be welcomed.

Does the philosophy, or cluster of philosophies, known as personalism[3] provide us any help? Does this philosophy answer, or begin to answer, in a satisfactory manner this question about how we should live and what we should do? Of course, just the name—*person*alism—suggests that it is, or intends to be, a philosophy relevant to, and important for, key questions that face individual persons. Moreover, beyond its name, personalism proclaims the *primacy of persons* and declares that it *takes personal categories seriously.* In this context, to ask what sort of person one should strive to become is to ask about the moral implications of taking personal categories seriously. If we do take personal categories seriously, as personalism instructs us, just exactly what sort(s) of persons should we strive to become?

In order to address this question, it may appear necessary, and it may be tempting, briefly to address two related, apparently prior or preliminary questions. First, what does personalism mean by the *personal*? Just what—or who—is a *person*? What exactly are *personal* categories? We can't take them

---

3. I include here the work of Boston Personalists such as Borden Parker Bowne, Edgar S. Brightman, Albert C. Knudson, Francis J. McConnell, and later generations of this school of thought. For an overview, see *The Boston Personalist Tradition in Philosophy, Social Ethics, and Theology,* ed. Paul Deats and Carol Robb (Macon, Ga.: Mercer University Press, 1986). I also include the work of other sorts of personalists such as George H. Howison, Etienne Gilson, Emmanuel Mounier, and, less fully or centrally, Royce, Hocking, Whitehead, Hartshorne, and others, some of whom have attempted to distance personalism from idealism. For an overview, see John Lavely, "Personalism," *The Encyclopedia of Philosophy,* vol. 5 (New York: Macmillan, 1967), pp. 107–10. These philosophers, Erazim Kohak has written, cut through traditional debates in ethics "with a very different question": "Who ought we to be?" "Speaking of Persons," *The Personalist Forum* 7.2 (Fall 1991): 48.

seriously if we don't know what they are.[4] It is tempting to demand: What
are the necessary and sufficient conditions of something's being a person? Or:
To what, and why, do personal categories apply or fail to apply? For example,
do personal categories apply to human beings alone, thus distinguishing humans
from everything else? Are only humans persons? Or, for example, do bacte-
ria, moss, tomato plants, ants, dogs, dolphins, or entire ecosystems exhibit
personal categories? Instead, perhaps personal categories distinguish some
human beings from other human beings? Do you, human fetuses, very young
infants, sleeping humans, women, slaves, humans who do not own property,
seemingly amoral or irrational humans, brain-damaged humans, or brain-
dead humans exhibit personal categories? In a different light, do personal
categories include any important notice of race, gender, age, sexual preference, religion, nationality, language, wealth, educational level, time, or place?
Is personhood a matter of imagination or narrative? Which of a person's
many features—one's personal characteristics—are irrelevant to a person's
status as a person—one's personal categories? Finally, does the whole world
or the universe or all of reality possess or display or reflect personal categories? If so, aren't personal categories too abstract to have any practical ethical
implications at all? Is personalism, at least when understood as a worldview
or metaphysics *under*determined ethically and practically? Or does an account of reality in terms of personal categories include, at once and at no
extra cost, an account of the moral life and helpful, practical moral guidance?
Is such an account at once description and prescription, at once statement of
fact and statement of value?

Second, what does it means to take personal categories *seriously*? Even
assuming that we desperately want to take personal categories seriously, we
can't do it—either in theory or practice—if we do not understand what this
involves and what it means and how it is possible. Just how does taking
personal categories seriously differ, for example, from ignoring personal
categories, or taking personal categories humorously, haphazardly, casually,
too seriously, psychologically, religiously, anthropomorphically, phenomeno-
logically, naturalistically, temporally, or reductively?

These are important questions. If a personalist philosophy is to have any
moral implications or offer any practical guidance about how each of us

---

4. It may seem odd to ask what personalism means by the personal, but, as Thomas O. Buford
has pointed out, "no one in the tradition has adequately explained the concept of person."
"Introduction" to "Personalism: New Directions," *The Personalist Forum* 5.1 (Spring 1989): 1.
In the same context (and same journal issue), Harold H. Oliver wrote: "The greatest difficulty
plaguing Personalism has been its failure satisfactorily to define the meaning of 'personal being.'" "Relational Personalism," p. 27.

should lead our lives and what sorts of person we should strive to become, then it may appear that these questions must be addressed first.

The Eclipse of Personalism and Missing Persons

However, something now is beginning to go wrong here, just as it does at this point in most traditional, impersonal philosophies. To turn away from the moral question with which we began—What sort of person should I strive to become?—to these supposedly more basic metaphysical and methodological questions—What are personal categories and what is their proper place in philosophy?—is to replace a pressing, practical question about values with abstract, arcane, questions about reality, and knowledge of reality, supposedly independent of those values and the persons who hold them. Philosophers engage in just this substitution—a sort of "bait and switch" for unwary theory consumers—whenever they (mistakenly) treat moral questions as less central, less fundamental, or less primary than metaphysical and methodological/epistemological questions. They do this whenever they (mistakenly) claim or suggest that moral theory must be derived somehow from metaphysics or epistemology or philosophy of language.

This is a mistake because it is a failure to recognize that any effort to justify some worldview or metaphysical theory (or its superiority to other theories) necessarily presupposes a prior commitment to certain values and interests to which we appeal in our attempts to justify our worldview. When we say that one worldview or metaphysical theory is "better" than another, we highlight the irreducibly critical function of philosophy and the basic role in thought of values, even if we disguise these values as "theoretical commitments" or "systems criteria" or "standards of rationality." We affirm a particular metaphysical theory because we believe it best addresses certain values. Moral theory, not metaphysics, is first philosophy. Pragmatists recognize this point when they claim that philosophy is criticism.

When personalist philosophers fail to recognize this point and make this common mistake, they risk submerging morals in metaphysics and, thus, losing touch with the *life* of persons—my life, your life, my father's life— in pursuit of a *theory* of persons—personalism. At the very best, this is awfully ironic; at worst, it is deeply depressing.[5] In this context, when we

---

5. Contrasting persons with theories about persons, much as William James contrasted life with knowledge about life, John Lavely noted "If persons are of primary importance, then personalisms are also important, but secondary. "What is Personalism?," *The Personalist Forum* 7.2 (Fall 1991): 31.

define a person in one way rather than another, we affirm certain values and advance certain interests. These values and interests must be acknowledged and, in turn, critically evaluated. Accordingly, the task for a genuinely personal philosophy today is not to mysteriously or miraculously derive the moral implications of the metaphysical primacy of persons and personal categories. Instead, it is to acknowledge and critically examine the moral presuppositions and consequences of the centrality of persons and personal categories. Personalism needs to take a genealogical turn.

Of course, this strategy is not likely to be of much interest today. For better or worse, the simple fact is that personalism and its concerns with the nature and centrality of persons simply do not interest many people. Personalism's accounts of the personal are virtually unknown and stand as a living option for virtually no one today. Its concerns and issues readily seem tedious, interminable, and dusty. Personalism simply does not matter to the great majority of persons today.

Indeed, personalism appears doubly unimportant. In the first place, as a system of philosophy, it appears unimportant in a culture in which all philosophy, especially professional philosophy, has no centrality or vitality, existing only as a kind of antiquarian curiosity or cultural epiphenomenon for people busy buying, for example, *The Seven Habits of Highly Effective People*, *Why Bad Things Happen To Good People*, *The One-Minute Manager*, and *The Seven Spiritual Laws of Success*.

In the second place, even within philosophy and among philosophers, personalism now is largely ignored and viewed as unimportant. It is taught to few students, and familiarity with it is required of few professors. It is mentioned in few accounts of the discipline and its history, and many works and accounts of personalist philosophy now are out of print. It lives on primarily in the memories and minds of a few specialists, and in their tiny journals and infrequent gatherings. John Dewey observed that progress in philosophy typically takes place not as old problems are solved, but rather as they are abandoned. Whether or not this is progress, personalism and its problems largely have been abandoned. Of course, it wasn't always—or even recently—like this, but, for better or worse, it is now.

This double unimportance of personalism parallels a larger, farther-reaching double unimportance of persons themselves today. In the first place, our lives now are occupied not so much with persons as with actors—agents who play certain roles in our lives. Everywhere there are actors; everywhere persons are missing. These actors stand in a merely instrumental relation to us: They fix our cars and fly our planes, serve our meals and prescribe our medicine, build our houses and care for our children, own the house next door and work in the office across the hall, sit in the classes we teach and deliver papers at the conferences we attend, fill the obituaries we skip over and suffer without our knowledge tragedies we hope to escape. We experience almost all of them almost wholly in terms of the functions or roles they play in our lives. (There are exceptions, of course: Recall Santayana's observation that it is only our friends with whom we can be fully human, fully persons.) And if these roles are reassigned to other people, to animals, to corporations, or to machines, we rarely experience change or loss—as long as the role, or a better one, continues to be played for us. Today, we take actors, not persons, seriously. We are concerned with personae, not with persons.

In the second place, the myriad actors with whom we interact (for we too live largely as actors) do not even play the parts or roles of persons. (Remember the headache remedy commercial in which the distinguished man announces "I'm not a doctor but I play one on TV?" Today, offering no remedies, we in effect announce "I'm not a person and I don't play one.") As a result, we don't act like persons; we act like actors.[6] We regard others not so much as persons grappling with how to live and having large responsibility for being the persons they are.[7] Instead, as they regard themselves, we regard them as: patients in need of treatment; victims who deserve restitution; bureaucrats just doing their jobs; and aliens too different to judge. Moral discourse—ultimately a discourse of, by, and for persons—largely has been abandoned. Now a nearly lost language spoken principally by fundamentalists, tyrants, and absolutists more concerned with unthinking obedience than thoughtful self-actualization and the realization of full personhood, moral discourse has been replaced by: the therapeutic discourse of the hospital—a discourse of patients, providers, disability, illness, and treatment; the juridical discourse of the legal system—a discourse of victims, violators, lawsuits, helplessness, and co-dependence; the corporate discourse of large organizations and mass society—a bureaucratic discourse of directors, managers, employees ("just doing their jobs"), efficiency, and a-responsibility; and the nonjudgmental discourse of public schools—a sociological discourse of toleration of diversity and differences, all worthy of recognition and respect (at

---

6. See Friedrich Nietzsche, *The Twilight of the Idols* (New York: Penguin Books, 1990 [1889]): "Are you genuine? or only an actor? A representative? or that itself which is represented?— Finally you are no more than an imitation of an actor." (p. 37).

7. John Lachs has pointed out that one can take responsibility for an action only if the action can be appropriated or identified as one's own. However, "the magnitude of the social act and the sensed fragmentation of its elements make it difficult for us to see it as an action at all. At any rate, it does not look and feel like anyone's act.... But without such appropriation we cannot take responsibility for it or its consequences. Our psychologically accurate but morally empty disclaimer is that we did not mean it and did not do it and perhaps did not even intend for it to come about." "Persons and Technology," *The Personalist Forum*, 1.1 (Spring 1985): 17–18.

least to the extent that these differences are not so different as to exclude recognition and respect for differences).

Philosophical Stories: From Personalism to Pragmatism

Even if abandoned or viewed as unimportant, the original question remains: What sort of person should I strive to become? In a culture overpopulated by the morally challenged and the merely morally different, is it now possible to recover or reconstruct a living philosophy of persons? If possible, would it be desirable to do so?

To affirm the primacy of persons, of course, may be something quite distinct from embracing personalism. Personalism, after all, is not the only philosophy that claims to take personal categories seriously. How does personalism stand in relation to other philosophies that make this same claim? What are its strengths and weaknesses, its advantages and disadvantages?

The answer to these questions requires a story about philosophy and the different views of persons set forth in different philosophies. The success of personalism in addressing these questions depends upon which story is told and upon who tells the story. Let me briefly contrast three such stories. At the outset, I should note that many of these stories suggest that there are two kinds of philosophers: those who believe there are two kinds of philosophers and those who do not. Let me acknowledge at the outset that I tell these stories as a philosopher of the second kind!

The first story is one familiar to students of standard textbooks of modern philosophy. According to this story, philosophers who rejected the dualisms of much early modern philosophy—for example, mind and body, subject and object, person and nature, self and others, reason and experience, value and fact—pursued one of two nondualistic alternatives. These alternatives are idealism and materialism (or naturalism). From the standpoint of persons, according to this standard story about modern philosophy, idealism avoids dualism by personalizing nature; idealists take personhood to be ontologically primary and view nature as dependent on, created by, or a function of persons or mind. Idealists believe they take personal categories seriously by maintaining that the world is ultimately personal in character. Materialism, in contrast, avoids dualism not by personalizing nature but by naturalizing persons; materialists take nature to be ontologically primary, and view persons as dependent parts, emergent properties, or pieces or events within nature or matter. Materialists believe they take personal categories seriously by maintaining that persons arise within, and are continuous with, the world.

Not surprisingly, personalism tells a different story. Personalists classify philosophies not as idealistic or as materialistic, but rather as impersonal or personal.[8] On this view, both traditional idealism and traditional materialism are varieties of impersonalism. Naturalistic or materialistic impersonalism treats the things or objects of experience in abstraction from the experience of persons in which these things are given. Idealistic impersonalism postulates abstract first principles or realities from which the concrete experience of persons somehow is derived by some inference. On this view, both materialism and idealism commit the impersonalist fallacy of abstraction, whether by deriving abstract objects from personal experience, or by presupposing abstract first principles that ground personal experience. The only alternative, according to personalists, is personalism, the view that self-conscious existence—the existence of persons—is the ultimately real fact. In much the same way, then, that Santayana locates the transcendence of materialism and idealism in materialism itself, personalists locate this transcendence in idealism—in an idealism of persons (whether this idealism is labeled idealism, "transcendental empiricism," or something else).

Pragmatists tell yet a different story.[9] According to William James, there are more than two kinds of philosophies. There are many, many philosophies. Their differences and similarities shade into and away from one another, and constitute a wide spectrum. We usefully may approach this spectrum not in terms of doctrine—the claims made by a philosophy—but in terms of temperament—the attitudes that give rise to a philosophy. James thus classifies philosophies at one end of this spectrum as "tender-minded"—rationalistic, intellectualistic, idealistic, optimistic, religious, voluntaristic, monistic, dogmatic—and those at the other extreme as "tough-minded"—empiricist, sensationalistic, materialistic, pessimistic, irreligious, fatalistic, pluralistic, skeptical. In these terms, personalism certainly is tender-minded. Pragmatism, at least as James conceives it, stands in sharp contrast to personalism—not because pragmatism is tough-minded, but because it is equally tender-minded and tough-minded—empiricistic and optimistic, pluralistic and religious. It is a sort of compromise or synthesis, a solution to the dilemma that philosophy presents when it forces us to choose between either a tender-minded or a tough-minded perspective. Pragmatism thus promises escape from philosophies that occupy and classify themselves with the dualisms of modern philosophy.

---

8. For the best example, see Borden Parker Bowne, "The Failure of Impersonalism," *Personalism* (Boston and New York: Houghton Mifflin, 1908). In their *The Development of American Philosophy*, Walter Muelder and Laurence Sears judged that in the "curve of metaphysical speculation since Kant there is no more powerful and convincing chapter in metaphysical writing." (Boston: Houghton Mifflin, 1940), p. 222.

9. See the discussion of personalist and pragmatist accounts of persons in chapter 12.

John Dewey tells this same pragmatist story in a slightly tougher-minded form. Idealism and materialism are simply two different ways of committing the "fallacy of selective emphasis," the fallacy of treating distinctions made in thought as dualisms that exist antecedent to, and independent of, thought. Having destroyed at the outset the integrated unity of experiencing subject and experienced object, these philosophies try to get together what they have taken apart: "One thinker turns metaphysical materialist and denies reality to the mental; another turns psychological idealist, and holds that matter and force are merely disguised psychical events. Solutions are given up as a hopeless task, or else different schools pile one intellectual complication on another only to arrive by a long and tortuous course at that which naive experience already has in its own possession."[10] Pragmatism, as set forth by Dewey, avoids these dualisms. Do personal categories provide clues to the nature of reality? Or, do natural categories provide clues to the nature of persons? Pragmatism avoids these either/or formulations. Sticking to the actual experiences of actual persons, it avoids the tortuous course of personalism.

Pluralism and Moral Theory

Our experience of persons is experience of irreducible plurality. In order to take personal categories seriously, we must take pluralism seriously. Pragmatism, more a philosophy of plural experience*s* than a philosophy of block experience, does just this by insisting on the primacy of the partial, the particular, and the plural. "We are invincibly parts," William James wrote in *A Pluralistic Universe*, such that "there may ultimately never be an all-form at all, that the substance of reality may never get totally collected, that some of it may remain outside of the largest combination of it ever made, and that a distributive form of reality, the *each*-form, is logically as acceptable and empirically as probable as the all-form commonly acquiesced in as so obviously the self-evident thing."[11] This means that no philosophy, if it takes seriously real persons, can pretend to speak the single truth, the final truth, the whole truth, or the absolute truth.

What are the moral implications, if any, of pragmatism's commitment to the primacy of plural persons? Given pluralism, what sorts of persons should

---

10. John Dewey, *Experience and Nature, John Dewey: The Later Works, 1925–1953*, vol. 1 (Carbondale, Ill.: Southern Illinois University Press, 1981 [1925]), p. 20.
11. William James, "The Types of Philosophic Thinking," *A Pluralistic Universe* (Cambridge, Mass.: Harvard University Press, 1977 [1909]), pp. 23, 20. See the discussion of James's pluralism in chapter 4.

we strive to become? Of course, pragmatism offers no single, final, or absolute answer to this question; to do so would contradict its very commitment to pluralism.[12] James does, however, provide a very illuminating three-part response to this question. First, to ask what sort of persons we should strive to become is, in one sense, to ask what we should do given the options for action actually available now. James's response is radically empiricist, pluralist, and anti-Socratic.[13] Because *"the essence of good is simply to satisfy demand"* and because "there is always a pinch between the ideal and the actual which can only be got through by leaving part of the ideal behind," James claims that we should strive "to satisfy at all times *as many demands as we can,*" to perform the act that "makes for the *best whole,* and to act on those ideals that will *"prevail at the least cost"* ("MP&ML":153, 155). Pointing out that there are no *a priori* or "closet solutions" for real problems, and stressing that the success of our choices and actions can be judged only after the fact and after our action, James tells us that we should strive to become persons who respect and advance the ideals of other, different persons. To take persons seriously is to take seriously their ideals

Second, to ask what sorts of persons we should strive to become is, in another sense, to ask what we should do to expand or improve the options for action available to us in the future. Faced with interests that collide and conflicts that we cannot avoid, we should respond in a manner that least sacrifices ideals. However, we have a more important, overarching obligation to act in a manner that progressively brings interests into harmony and progressively lessens the conditions that cause conflict. Here James tells us to pursue "the more and more inclusive order": *"Invent some manner* of realizing your ideals which will also satisfy the alien demands" ("MP&ML":155). This is not a recipe for conformity or New-Age harmonic convergence; instead, it is a call for productive reciprocity between self-realization and social well-being—what I call *harmonic divergence.* In its largest sense, this is an educational and social task, and, as developed more fully by Dewey than James, it amounts to nothing less than the piecemeal creation of democracy as a way of life (and not simply as a form of government). James tells us, then, that we should strive to become persons who act so as to bring our ideals into harmony (though not identity) with one another and with the ideals of others. To take persons seriously is to take seriously their communities.

---

12. Arguing that the moral philosopher must wait on facts, that every situation or dilemma is unique and beyond the scope of any abstract moral rules, and that all moral theory must be tentative and suggestive, James develops this point forcefully in the fourth section of "The Moral Philosopher and the Moral Life," *The Will to Believe and Other Essays in Popular Philosophy* (Cambridge, Mass.: Harvard University Press, 1979 [1897]), pp. 157–59. Hereafter abbreviated "MP&ML" in this chapter.

13. See the discussion of James's radically empiricist ethics in chapter 8.

Third, to ask what sorts of persons we should strive to become is, in another sense, to ask how we should live (and not simply what we should do). This is not a question about what action to undertake; it is a question about with what attitude or outlook or temperament we should act. Moral theorists, typically concerned with prescriptions and prohibitions, focus more on action than temperament, more on intention than mood, more on the "what" than the "how" of life. James, however, reversed this emphasis: "The deepest difference, practically, in the moral life of man is the difference between the easy-going and the strenuous mood. When in the easy-going mood, the shrinking from present ill is our ruling consideration. The strenuous mood, on the contrary, makes us quite indifferent to present ill, if only the greater ideal be attained" ("MP&ML":159–60). Surely it is easy—all too easy—to shrink from moral involvement in the clash of ideals in the present and from opportunities to lessen that clash in the future. It is more agreeable, in contrast, to live with, and for, the comforts of the day, the comforts at hand. It is more pleasant to loaf than work, more pleasant to be than to work to become. Why work? Win the lottery and sit in the sun at the beach! Accept yourself as you are! Don't worry, be happy; sing the theme from "The Lion King." In a thousand years, it won't matter anyway. As James presents it, then, the presence of the strenuous mood is a precondition for the possibility of moral action, a precondition for the possibility of genuine personhood. To ask what sort of person I should strive to become is an empty exercise unless, following reflection, I engage in the striving. Unless I am able and willing to strive to become one sort of person rather than another, there is no point to reflection about this question. Here James tells us that we should strive to become persons who pursue distant ideals in the face of present ills. To take persons seriously is to grasp persons in terms of becoming rather than in terms of being. It is to take seriously (and, thus, strenuously) not only persons' ideals and communities, but also their futures.

The Strenuous Mood, Death, and Temperament

For a genuinely personal philosophy, the pragmatic, question is clear: *How is it possible to call forth the strenuous mood?* James observed that "the capacity for the strenuous mood probably lies slumbering in every man, but it has more difficulty in some than in others in waking up" ("MP&ML":160). Can pragmatism deliver a personal wake-up call? Pragmatism may seem ill-suited to this work of waking up the slumbering strenuous mood. Why? The strenuous mood commands us to look past the difficult present in the name of the future, but, unlike absolutist philosophies, pragmatism provides us no promises or guarantees for that future. As a result, pragmatism may appear to require us to adopt the strenuous mood, but leave us unable or unwilling to do so.[14]

First, this may seem to be the case because pragmatism's pluralism offers us an open, uncertain future. It instructs us that any action inspired by the strenuous mood will bring at best partial and temporary success. Pluralism, James noted, is a philosophy of "maybes." It requires us to live without assurances and without the consolation and motivation to adopt the strenuous mood that absolutism can provide to "sick souls."[15] For pluralistic pragmatists, then, the life of the strenuous mood is indeed strenuous: We bear full-force today's real and sure costs in an effort to enjoy incompletely tomorrow's possible, uncertain, and fleeting benefits. Is this, on James's own terms, an idea upon which we can ride? Does it satisfy? Does it work? Is it really pragmatic in the end?[16] Of course, it is not the message preached by most motivational speakers—from ministers and military leaders to marketing consultants and football coaches. Are they the real, really effective, pragmatists?

Second, pragmatism may seem unable to awaken and call forth the strenuous mood for another reason. In the face of the uncertainties, incompleteness, and impermanence of its pluralistic universe, pragmatism does offer us one certainty: human finitude, the death of all persons, my death and your death and the death of my father. The strenuous mood (like pragmatism itself) points persons toward the future, but this future is a future of personal death. Experience ends. Each person dies. For pragmatists, Roosevelt's "tragedy of death" is at once ineffable and undeniable. Ineffable: Although Dewey's writings on experience, communication, and inquiry constitute a thoroughgoing philosophy of finitude and temporality, the *Index* to the thirty-seven large volumes of his collected works contains only three references to death—all three about early rituals and attitudes rather than death itself or its philosophical importance.[17] Undeniable: Contrary to popular self-help books, counseling programs, coping strategies, and professional bereavement associations,

---

14. In the same vein but in a different context, John J. McDermott asks: "Still, how can human life, collectively understood, sustain such a vision, such a lonely vigilance on behalf of human values, stripped of their guarantee and lighted only by their human quality. . . . Can vision and concern as to man's immediate destiny, when trimmed of its pretense and overarching claims beyond the call of experience, liberate sufficient energy and commitment to the human struggle, necessary to the structuring of a noble and creative life?" "The Community of Experience and Religious Metaphors," *The Culture of Experience: Philosophical Essays in the American Grain* (New York: New York University Press, 1976), pp. 64, 75.
15. William James, "The Absolute and the Strenuous Life," *The Meaning of Truth*, p. 124.
16. See William James, *Pragmatism: A New Name for Some Old Ways of Thinking* (Cambridge, Mass.: Harvard University Press, 1975 [1907]), p. 34.
17. John Dewey, *Index, John Dewey: The Collected Works, 1882–1953*, ed. A. S. Sharpe (Carbondale, Ill: Southern Illinois University Press, 1991), p. 181.

death is not a stage of growth or passage to salvation. It is the end of the possibility of growth. It is also the end of the possibility of salvation. There is no salvation outside experience, independent of persons, or after death; any salvation available to you or me—there is none at all now, or ever again, available to my father—must be made within experience by each of us (individually and communally).[18] This is no philosophy for the tender-minded.[19] It is once more a strenuous, tough-minded message, even when expressed courageously (and properly, I think) in the language of celebration. Pragmatism's unblinking recognition of "the inevitability of our death," John J. McDermott writes eloquently, is a "celebration of time as a prelude to disaster."[20]

Of course, this message will strike few persons as cause for celebration. Suffering from fear of time—what I have termed "chronophobia"—they will run for cover, celebrating instead a metaphysics of permanence, an epistemology of certainty, and an ethics of order. Hasn't history shown us—as James himself admitted—that these more traditional philosophies are more effective in awakening the strenuous mood—indeed, the reckless, frenzied, and fanatical moods?

Given pragmatism's tough-minded commitments to pluralism and death, can it adequately awaken the strenuous mood? If James is correct that as a rule people *"habitually use only a small part of the powers which they actually possess and which they might use under appropriate conditions,"*[21] does pragmatism supply the conditions necessary to call forth greater, deeper powers? Can it help sustain you or me day after day until death in the effort to become the persons you or I should become?

James was not always sure, did not always talk tough, and wavered in his pragmatism. In the final section of "The Moral Philosopher and the Moral Life," he directly addressed this question. Because his response is both important and disturbing, I quote it at length:

---

18. William James, *Pragmatism,* p. 125.

19. See Ralph Barton Perry, "The Philosophy of William James," *Present Philosophical Tendencies* (Westport, Conn.: Greenwood Press, 1972 [1912]), p. 374.

20. John J. McDermott, "The Inevitability of Our Own Death: The Celebration of Time as a Prelude to Disaster," *Streams of Experience: Reflections on the History and Philosophy of American Culture* (Amherst: The University of Massachusetts Press, 1986), pp. 157–68.

21. William James, "The Powers of Men," *Essays in Religion and Morality, The Works of William James* (Cambridge, Mass.: Harvard University Press, 1982 [1906]), p. 150. James adds, perhaps too optimistically: "A new position of responsibility will usually show a man to be a far stronger creature than was supposed" (p. 153). As a philosophy, pragmatism is a new position of responsibility. Later, in a more measured tone, James observes: "But when the normal tasks and stimulations of life don't put a man's deeper levels of energy on tap, and he requires distinctly deleterious excitements, his constitution verges on the abnormal" (p. 155). As a philosophy, pragmatism offers us only the normal tasks and stimulations of life.

[1 In] a merely human world without a God, the appeal to our moral energy falls short of its maximal stimulating power. [2] Life, to be sure, is even in such a world a genuinely ethical symphony; but it is played in the compass of a couple of poor octaves, and the infinite scale of values fails to open up. [3] Many of us . . . would openly laugh at the very idea of the strenuous mood being awakened in us by those claims of remote posterity which constitute the last appeal of the religion of humanity. . . . [4] This is all too finite, we say; we see too well the vacuum beyond. . . . [5] When, however, we believe that a God is there, and that he is one of the claimants, the infinite perspective opens out. The scale of the symphony is incalculably prolonged. [6] The more imperative ideals now begin to speak with an altogether new objectivity and significance, and to utter the penetrating, shattering, tragically challenging note of appeal. . . . [7] All through history, in the periodical conflicts of puritanism with the don't-care temper, we see the antagonism of the strenuous and genial moods, and the contrast between the ethics of infinite and mysterious obligation from on high, and those of prudence and the satisfaction of merely finite need. . . . [8] Every sort of energy and endurance, of courage and capacity for handling life's evils, is set free in those who have religious faith. [9] For this reason the strenuous type of character will on the battlefield of human history always outwear the easy-going type, and [10] religion will drive irreligion to the wall. ("MP&ML":160–61; numbering added)

This passage merits close analysis.[22] What sorts of points has James made? First, are his claims primarily *autobiographical*? Although neither confessional in tone nor written in the first-person, many if not all of James's above remarks plausibly may be interpreted in this way. If James really is simply and honestly reporting his own desires, motivations, and faith, then there may be no reason for anyone to disagree with him—and equally no reason for anyone else to adopt his views or believe that those views have any relevance or reasonableness for anyone else.

---

22. James sounds this same theme in many, many other essays, including: "What Pragmatism Means," "The Sentiment of Rationality," and "The Will to Believe." Contrast the tone of these essays with the thoroughly tough-minded view set forth in "The Absolute and Strenuous Life." Ralph Barton Perry judged that this tough-mindedness "dominates James's philosophy of life," and distinguishes James's own tough-mindedness from James's "characteristic tenderness of mind where the interests of others were in question." *Present Philosophical Tendencies*, pp. 374–75. This appraisal stands in sharp contrast to the more recent view of John Patrick Diggins, who claims that James "sought in religion nothing less than cosmic certainty," reasoning (invalidly) that "I need the satisfaction of certainty, unity, and order; therefore, God exists!" *The Promise of Pragmatism: Modernism and the Crisis of Knowledge and Authority* (Chicago: University of Chicago Press, 1994), pp. 155–56. See also Harvey Gates Townsend's analysis of both James and Bowne as philosophers who widened the breach between knowledge and faith, making "the claims of faith a form of subjective irrationalism, and therefore incredible." *Philosophical Ideas in the United States* (New York: Octagon Books, 1968 [1934]), p. 156.

It does seem, however, that James intends his point to have broader scope and application. Is this passage, then, primarily a series of broad *socio-logical* and *historical* observations? Many of his claims—especially [3], [7], [9], and [10]—seem to be assertions about the desires, motivations, and faith of certain groups of people in certain places at certain times. On this inter-pretation, to determine the truth of James's claims, we would need to inves-tigate the actual beliefs and lives of these people. Still, in the absence of this specific, detailed information, James's point readily may seem relatively plau-sible: Many people who are not members of the "religion of humanity" do claim to have a faith in God or to desire and hold an "ethics of the infinite" that strongly and consistently motivates them to energetic, strenuous action.

It appears, however, that James believes his point to be more than an armchair public opinion poll or historical documentation. Is he, then, making a *psychological* claim about human nature? Many of his claims—especially [1], [2], [4], [5], and [8]—seem to support this interpretation. Without God, he seems to say at the beginning of the passage, *all* appeals to our moral energy *always* fall short and *all* life *always* fails to be a genuinely ethical symphony. *All* human history and *all* human battles, he seems to say at the close of the passage, demonstrate clearly that *all* moral energy and endurance belong to *all—and only to all*—who have religious faith. Interpreted in this manner, James is setting forth an immense theory, a sweeping tender-minded psychology. If he is asserting some universal principle of human behavior or unchanging law of human nature—for *all* who lack religious faith, *all* appeals to moral energy *always* fall short—then he must establish his view by evi-dence that results from inquiry into universal or permanent features of the human mind, personality, development, and motivation. At the very least, he has not here supplied that evidence.

Perhaps, however, James's ultimate concern is a more practical one. Is he, finally, making a *practical* claim? Many of his remarks—especially [7]–[10]—support this reading. If he is arguing that, simply as a practical matter, we should hold any belief whatever that maximally stimulates or appeals to our moral energies and capacities for heroic action, then (at least without some qualification and restriction) this claim seems little more than a highly problematic "license to believe." If, instead, he is arguing that adoption of the strenuous mood requires faith—faith in the real possibilities of strenu-ous, future-oriented personal action—then I suspect that our actions and endeavors support his view. This view, however, establishes the practical importance of faith. It does not establish that faith in God or the infinite or the mysterious has any special importance or priority or truth. It does not eliminate the possibility—indeed, the superiority—of a different sort of faith: a faith in the finite; a faith in persons, pluralism, and death; a thor-oughly tough-minded faith.

This tough-minded faith—the work ethic without the puritanism, the self's realization without its transcendence, the strenuous mood without the infinite—has been developed most fully by John Dewey. Distinguishing the properly religious dimension of life from the supernatural doctrines of religions, Dewey argued that tender-minded thinkers have (mis)treated ideals that demand our action as though they were realities antecedent to, and independent of, that action. They have pretended that what they want to exist already does exist: "Faith that something should be in existence as far as lies in our power is changed into the intellectual belief that it already is in existence. When physical existence does not bear out the assertion, the physical is subtly changed into the metaphysical."[23] This, Dewey observed, converts the strenuous mood into lazy self-assurance, and evinces a lack of moral faith.

However, the strenuous mood *is* irreducibly a matter of faith. This faith, though finite, may be religious. When the strenuous mood calls forth action on behalf of inclusive and general ideals, ideals that unify the self, it is religious. As Dewey wrote: "There is such a thing as faith in intelligence becoming religious in quality—a fact that perhaps explains the efforts of some religionists to disparage the possibilities of intelligence as a force. They properly feel such faith to be a dangerous rival. . . . Any activity pursued in behalf of an ideal end against obstacles and in spite of threats of personal loss because of conviction of its general and enduring value is religious in quality."[24] By insisting on the religious possibilities of the strenuous mood, Dewey was able to offer a natural, rather than supernatural, account of God—an account of God as an ideal rather than real being. He defined God in terms of ideal ends, unified through the imagination, that guide one's life.

Understood in this light, the strenuous mood is irreducibly a faith in the ideals of persons and pluralism. Dewey recognized this, and thus his characterization of God in *A Common Faith* is all one with his account of a new individualism in *Individualism: Old and New* and his articulation of democracy as a way of life in *The Public and Its Problems*. Dewey thus substituted: a social faith for James's superhuman faith; a faith in finite persons—a faith in you and me and my father—for James's faith in the infinite; a faith in pluralism—a faith in community and democracy as a way of life—for James's faith in God. He also substituted a faith in the strenuous mood itself for James's despair and gloomy pronouncements about the "religion of humanity." Before we infer the incompetency of finite, naturalistic ideals, Dewey wrote, "we should at least ask ourselves how much of the existing situation

---

23. John Dewey, *A Common Faith, John Dewey: The Later Works, 1925–1953*, vol. 9 (Carbondale, Ill.: Southern Illinois University Press, 1986 [1934]), p. 16.
24. Ibid., p. 19.

is due to the fact that the religious factors of experience have been drafted into supernatural channels and thereby loaded with irrelevant encumbrances."[25] Putting this same point more positively, Dewey noted:

> Faith in the power of intelligence to imagine a future which is the projection of the desirable in the present, and to invent the instrumentalities of its realization, is our salvation. And it is a faith which must be nurtured and made articulate.[26]

Here, as elsewhere in Dewey's writings, the strenuous mood emerges fully self-reliant, strong-willed, and self-assured. Of course, in a time marked by both fundamentalist absolutism and the death of the will, we may wonder how this is possible. We may suspect that this is just too cheerful. For thoroughgoing pragmatists, salvation is not a product—the final result of the strenuous exercise of intelligence, imagination, and will. Instead, it is a process—activity along the way, strenuous living itself. The strenuous mood can guarantee only itself, only the strenuous life. It can guarantee journey, but not destination. In this light, it should be clear that Dewey's faith in individual persons and pluralistic communities is not completely the pragmatic equivalent of James's faith in God. Instead, as a philosophy of death as well as a philosophy of persons and pluralism, it is no metaphysics of infinity and no ethics of "infinite and mysterious obligation from on high."

Calling us—you and me and, in the past, my father—to the work to be done, Dewey's philosophy is thoroughly melioristic. It highlights our future possibilities rather than our future deaths—"the vacuum beyond." But, to imagine a future, with Dewey, is not simply to imagine personal salvation along the way, but also to imagine and project personal death. A life filled with this imagination is not simply strenuous, but also disillusioned: Self-realization is self-depletion.

This point has been more fully recognized and more sensitively described by Santayana than by any other American philosopher. Though his account of the life of spirit must be detached from the excesses of his ontology and realms of being, it captures beautifully the self-aware strenuous life in which "laughter and tears pulse together:

> On the one hand, in its innocence, spirit is happy to live in the moment, taking no thought for the morrow; it can enjoy the least gift as gladly as the greatest; it is the fresh, the pure voice of nature, incapable of learned or moral snob-

---

25. Ibid.

26. John Dewey, "The Need for a Recovery of Philosophy," *John Dewey: The Middle Works, 1899–1924*, vol. 10 (Carbondale, Ill.: Southern Illinois University Press, 1980 [1917]), p. 48.

bery. It ignores its origin, so buoyant is it; its miraculous light seems to it a matter of course. Its career is everywhere conditioned and oppressed from without, yet it passes through the fire with a serene incredulity, an indomitable independence. On the other hand, the eye of spirit, in its virtual omniscience, sees the visible in its true setting of the invisible; it is fixed instinctively on the countless moments that are not this moment, on the joys that are not this sorrow and the sorrows that are not this joy, on the thousand opinions that are not this opinion and beauties that are not this beauty; understanding too much to be ever imprisoned, loving too much ever to be in love.[27]

Here are all the elements of a fully finite faith—a disillusioned pragmatism of persons, pluralism, and death. All too finite, all too human, this genealogical philosophy plays richly and hard in the compass of all the octaves available to persons.

For years and years, asking me to play him some music he would like— a transparent excuse for us to simply spend some time together—my father and I used to listen to this symphony. In one of his favorites, "For a Dancer," music written on the death of a friend, Jackson Browne sang:

> I don't know what happens when people die.
> Can't seem to grasp it as hard as I try.
> It's like a song I can hear playing right in my ear.
> But I can't sing it. I can't help listening. . . .
> Keep a fire for the human race, let your prayers go drifting into space
> You never know what will be coming down
> Perhaps a better world is drawing near, just as soon it could all disappear
> Along with whatever meaning you might have found
> Don't let the uncertainty turn you around
> —The world keeps turning around—
> Go and make a joyful sound
> And somewhere between the time you arrive and the time you go
> May lie a reason you were alive that you'll never know[28]

Looking ahead, the most pressing task for any philosophy—personalist, pragmatist, or other—is to help identify, illuminate, create and sustain those conditions—political, economic, technological, social—that allow the strenuous mood to awaken—bright, wide-eyed, and thoroughly disillusioned. Looking further ahead, the most pressing task for any person—you or me or anybody else— is to do this *soon*. In the name of my father, strive to become this sort of person.

---

27. George Santayana, *Platonism and the Spiritual Life* (Gloucester, Mass.: Peter Smith, 1971 [1913]), pp. 303–4.
28. Jackson Browne, "For a Dancer," *Late for the Sky* (Elektra/Asylum Records, 1974), track 6.

Index